HOW BUSH RULES

SIDNEY BLUMENTHAL

How Bush Rules
Chronicles
of a Radical Regime

PRINCETON UNIVERSITY PRESS

Princeton and Oxford

Requests for permission to reproduce material from this work should be sent to Permissions, Princeton University Press

Published by Princeton University Press, 41 William Street, Princeton, New Jersey 08540
All Rights Reserved

Library of Congress Cataloging-in-Publication Data

Blumenthal, Sidney, 1948–
   How Bush rules : chronicles of a radical regime / Sidney Blumenthal.
     p. cm.
   Includes index.
   ISBN-13: 978-0-691-12888-7 (hardcover : alk. paper)
   ISBN-10: 0-691-12888-X (hardcover : alk. paper)
   1. Bush, George W. (George Walker), 1946– —Political and social views. 2. Radicalism—United States.
3. Conservatism—United States. 4. Republican Party (U.S. : 1854–) 5. Executive power—United States.
6. United States—Politics and government—2001– 7. United States—Foreign relations—2001– 8. United
States—Politics and government—Philosophy. I. Title.
   E903.3.B55   2006
   973.931092—dc22

                 2006008221

This book has been composed in Minion with Congress display by Princeton Editorial Associates, Inc.,
Scottsdale, Arizona

Printed on acid-free paper. ∞

pup.princeton.edu
Printed in the United States of America

10 9 8 7 6 5 4 3 2 1

For Joseph C. Wilson IV

_____

Contents

PART THREE   **NEMESIS II**

"Heck of a Job": From the Landfall of Hurricane Katrina
to the Revolt of the Generals

Acknowledgments

I BEGAN WRITING ABOUT THE BUSH ADMINISTRATION in 2003, after the invasion of Iraq and on the eve of the 2004 presidential campaign, a brief interregnum when the initial euphoria of conquest had started to fade but arrogance was undimmed. Hubris, still rising, was creating its shadow; yet nemesis had not begun to exact its vengeance.

I was commissioned to write these pieces for the *Guardian* of London and *Salon,* the online magazine. I am grateful to Alan Rusbridger, editor of the *Guardian,* whose idea it was; Seumas Milne, editor of the Comment section; and Libby Brooks, also an editor for Comment. I am also grateful to the editors of *Salon,* especially Michal Keeley.

Peter Dougherty, the director of Princeton University Press, has overseen this book from conception to completion with calm intelligence and commitment. Working with him and the professional staff at Princeton University Press has been a pleasure. I am grateful to the production editor, Debbie Tegarden, and the designer, Leslie Flis, and for the copyediting and production efforts of Peter Strupp and the staff of Princeton Editorial Associates.

Sean Wilentz, professor of American history at Princeton University, is a champion of Princeton University Press. It was his idea to put us together, for which I am grateful. This book is one of the many reflections of our long friendship and endless conversation.

Once again, I could not have produced this book without the love and support of my wife, Jackie, and our sons, Max and Paul, who are at the beginning of brilliant careers.

I have chronicled the Bush presidency not only as a writer but also as a former presidential adviser. I spent years working in the White House. When I read or hear about the Oval Office my mind inevitably visualizes it. But I gained more than a tactile sense of the place. From my experience I came to know many of the career staff, especially those involved in national security. Their information about and insight into the radical transformation of the U.S. government under Bush have been central to my understanding. Many of them are or were Republicans. Their shock and anger has no partisan motivation but arises from their devotion to public service and the national interest. I am grateful for their assistance in helping, encouraging, and guiding my recent work.

This book is dedicated to one of them. Joseph C. Wilson IV, who served as director of the African Affairs desk of the National Security Council when I was assistant to President Clinton, is a former colleague, a friend, and a patriot. With his courage in this period, he has done more for the cause of truth and the restoration of integrity than anyone else I know.

The Radical President

No one predicted just how radical a president George W. Bush would be. Neither his opponents, nor the reporters covering him, nor his closest campaign aides suggested that he would be the most willfully radical president in American history.

In his 2000 campaign, Bush permitted himself few hints of radicalism. On the contrary, he made ready promises of moderation, judiciously offering himself as a "compassionate conservative," an identity carefully crafted to contrast with the discredited Republican radicals of the House of Representatives. After capturing the Congress in 1994 and proclaiming a "revolution," they had twice shut down the government over the budget and staged an impeachment trial that resulted in the acquittal of President Bill Clinton. Seeking to distance himself from the congressional Republicans, Bush declared that he was not hostile to government. He would, he said, "change the tone in Washington." He would be more reasonable than the House Republicans and more moral than Clinton. Governor Bush went out of his way to point to his record of bipartisan cooperation with Democrats in Texas, stressing that he would be "a uniter, not a divider."

Trying to remove the suspicion that falls on conservative Republicans, he pledged that he would protect the solvency of Social Security. On foreign policy, he said he would be "humble": "If we're an arrogant nation, they'll view us that way, but if we're a humble nation, they'll respect us." Here he was criticizing Clinton's peacemaking and nation-building efforts in the Balkans and suggesting he would be far more restrained. The sharpest criticism he made of Clinton's foreign policy was that he would be more mindful of the civil liberties of Arabs accused of terrorism: "Arab-Americans are racially profiled in what's called secret evidence. People are stopped, and we got to do something about that." This statement was not an off-the-cuff remark, but carefully crafted and presented in one of the debates with Vice President Al Gore. Bush's intent was to win an endorsement from the American Muslim Council, which was cued to back him after he delivered his debating point, and it was instrumental in his winning an overwhelming share of the Muslim vote, about ninety thousand of which votes were in Florida.

So Bush deliberately offered himself as an alternative to the divisive congressional Republicans, his father's son (at last) in political temperament, but also as an experienced executive who had learned the art of compromise with the other party, and differing from the incumbent Democratic president only in personality and degree. Bush wanted the press to report and discuss his resolve to reform and discipline his party, which had gone too far to the right. He encouraged commentary that he represented a "Fourth Way," a variation on the theme of Clinton's "Third Way."

In his second term, Clinton had the highest sustained popularity of any president since World War II, prosperity was in its longest recorded cycle, and the nation's international prestige was high. Bush's tack as a moderate was adroit, shrewd, and necessary. His political imperative was to create the public perception there were no major issues dividing the candidates and that the current halcyon days would continue under his aegis. Only through his positioning did Bush manage to come within just short of a half million votes of Gore nationwide and achieve an apparent tie in Florida, creating an Electoral College deadlock and forcing the election toward an extraordinary resolution.

Few political commentators at the time thought that the ruthless tactics used by the Bush camp in the Florida contest presaged those of his presidency. The battle there was seen as unique, a self-contained episode of high political drama. Tactics such as setting loose a mob, consisting mostly of Republican staff members from the House and Senate flown down from Washington to physically intimidate the Miami-Dade County Board of Supervisors from counting the votes there, and manipulating the Florida state government through the office of the governor, Jeb Bush, the candidate's brother, to forestall voting were justified as simply hardball politics.

The five-to-four Supreme Court decision in *Bush v. Gore* perversely sanctioned not counting thousands of votes (mostly African American) as somehow upholding the equal protection clause of the Fifteenth Amendment (enacted after the Civil War to guarantee the rights of newly enfranchised slaves, the ancestors of those disenfranchised by *Bush v. Gore*). In the majority opinion, Justice Antonin Scalia argued that counting votes would cast a shadow on the "legitimacy" of Bush's claim to the presidency. The court concluded that the ruling was to have applicability only this one time. By its very nature, it was declared to be unprecedented. Never before had the Supreme Court decided who would be president, much less by tortuous argument and by a one-vote margin that underlined and extended political polarization.

The constitutional system had ruptured, but it was widely believed by the political class in Washington, including most of the press corps, that Bush, who had benefited, would rush to repair the breach. The brutality that had enabled him to become president while losing the popular majority, and following a decade of partisan polarization, must spur him to make good on his campaign rhetoric of moderation, seek common ground, and enact centrist policies. Old family retainers, like James Baker (the former secretary of state who had been summoned to command the legal and political teams in Florida) and Brent Scowcroft (the elder Bush's national security adviser), were especially unprepared for what was to come, and they came to oppose Bush's radicalism, mounting a sub rosa opposition. In its brazen, cold-blooded, and single-minded partisanship, the Florida contest turned out in retrospect to be an augury, not an aberration. It was Bush's first opening, and, having charged through it to grab the presidency, he continued to widen the breach.

The precedents for a president who gained office without winning the popular vote were uniformly grim. John Quincy Adams, the first president elected without a plurality, never escaped the accusation of having made a "corrupt bargain" to secure the necessary Electoral College votes. After one term he was turned out of office with an overwhelming vote for his rival, Andrew Jackson. Rutherford B. Hayes and Benjamin Harrison, also having won the White House but not the popular vote, declined to run again. Like these three predecessors, Bush lacked a mandate, but unlike them he proceeded as though he had won by a landslide.

The Republicans had control of both houses of the Congress and the presidency for the first time since Dwight Eisenhower was elected. But Eisenhower had gained the White House with a resounding majority. He spent his early years in office trying to isolate his right wing in the Congress, quietly if belatedly encouraging efforts to censure Senator Joseph McCarthy. Eisenhower greeted the Democratic recovery of the Congress in 1954 with relief, and he governed smoothly for the rest of his tenure in tandem with the Senate majority leader, Lyndon Johnson. The outrageous behavior of the Republicans during the brief period in which they had held congressional power and unleashed McCarthy was a direct cause of their minority status for forty subsequent years. But the Republicans who gained control of the Congress in 1994 had not learned from their past.

The Republican radicals in charge of the House of Representatives remained unabashed by their smashing failures of the 1990s. They were willing to sacrifice two speakers of the House to scandals of their own in order to pursue an unconstitutional coup d'état to remove President Clinton. (It was unconstitutional, strictly speaking, because they had rejected any standards whatsoever for impeachment in the House Judiciary Committee, in contradistinction to the committee's exacting standards enacted in the impeachment proceedings of President Richard Nixon.) Now these Republicans welcomed the Bush ascension as deus ex machina, rescuing them from their exhaustion, disrepute, and dead end. They became Bush's indispensable partners.

Immediately on assuming office, Bush launched a series of initiatives that began to undo the bipartisan traditions of internationalism, environmentalism, fiscal discipline, and scientific progress. His first nine months in office were a quick march to the right. The reasons were manifold, ranging from Dick Cheney's and Donald Rumsfeld's extraordinary influence, Karl Rove's strategies, the neoconservatives' inordinate sway, and Bush's own Southern conservatism. These deeper patterns were initially obscured by the surprising rapidity of Bush's determined tack.

Bush withdrew from the diplomatic efforts to persuade North Korea to control its development and production of nuclear weapons. Secretary of State Colin Powell, after briefing the press that the diplomacy would continue, was sent out again to repudiate himself and announce the administration's reversal of almost a decade of negotiation. Powell did not realize that this humiliation would mark the first of many times his credibility would be abused. Swiftly, Bush rejected the Kyoto Protocol to reduce greenhouse gases and global warming and presented a "voluntary" alternative plan that was supported by no other nation. He also withdrew the United States from its historic role as negotiator among Israelis, Palestinians, and Arabs, a process to which his father had been particularly committed.

In short order, Bush also reversed his campaign promise to reduce carbon dioxide emissions from power plants and canceled the federal regulation reducing cancer-causing arsenic levels in water. He joked at a dinner: "As you know, we're studying safe levels for arsenic in drinking water. To base our decision on sound science, the scientists told us we needed to test the water glasses of about three thousand people. Thank you for participating." He appointed scores of former lobbyists and industry executives to oversee policies regulating the industries they previously represented.

As his top priority, Bush pushed for passage of a large tax cut that would redistribute income to the wealthy, drain the surplus that the Clinton administration had accumulated, and reverse the fiscal discipline embraced by both the Clinton and prior Bush administrations. The tax cut became Bush's chief instrument of social policy. By wiping out the surplus, he exerted budget pressure on domestic social programs. Under the Reagan administration, a tax cut had produced the largest deficit up to that time, bigger than the combined deficits accumulated by all previous presidents. But Reagan had stumbled onto this method of crushing social programs through the inadvertent though predictable failure of his fantasy of supply-side economics, in which slashing taxes would magically create increased federal revenues. Bush confronted alternatives in the recent Republican past: the Reagan example or his father's responsible counterexample of raising taxes to cut the deficit. Once again, he rejected his father's path. But unlike Reagan, he made his decision to foster a deficit deliberately and with full awareness of its consequences.

John DiIulio, a political scientist from the University of Pennsylvania, who had accepted his position as domestic policy adviser in the White House on the assumption that he would be working to give substance to the president's rhetoric of "compassionate conservatism," resigned in a state of shock. "There is no precedent in any modern White House for what is going on in this one: a complete lack of a policy apparatus," DiIulio told *Esquire* magazine. "What you've got is everything—and I mean everything —being run by the political arm. It's the reign of the Mayberry Machiavellis. . . . Besides the tax cut . . . the administration has not done much, either in absolute terms or in comparison to previous administrations at this stage, on domestic policy. There is a virtual absence as yet of any policy accomplishments that might, to a fair-minded non-partisan, count as the flesh on the bones of so-called compassionate conservatism."

After just four months into the Bush presidency, the Republicans lost control of the Senate. Senator Jim Jeffords of Vermont, who had served for twenty-six years as a moderate Republican in the House and the Senate, left his party in response to Bush's radicalism.

"In the past, without the presidency, the various wings of the Republican Party in Congress have had some freedom to argue and influence and ultimately to shape the party's agenda. The election of President Bush changed that dramatically," Jeffords said on May 24, 2001. Overnight, the majority in the upper chamber shifted to the Democrats.

Bush spent the entire month of August 2001 on vacation at his ranch in Crawford, Texas. His main public appearance was a speech imposing federal limits on scientific research involving stem cells that might lead to cures for many diseases. Bush's position was a sop to the religious right. On August 6, three days before his nationally televised address on stem cells, he was presented with a presidential daily brief from the CIA titled "Bin Laden Determined to Strike Inside U.S." The CIA director, George Tenet, later told the 9/11 Commission on Terrorist Attacks on the United States that "the system was blinking red." The commission reported: "The President told us the August 6 report was historical in nature. . . . We have found no indication of any further discussion before September 11 among the President and his top advisers of the possibility of a threat of an al Qaeda attack in the United States."

By September 10, Bush's job approval rating was the lowest of any president at that early point in his tenure. He appeared to be falling into the pattern of presidents who arrived without a popular mandate and lasted only one term. The deadliest foreign attack on American soil transformed his foundering presidency.

The events of September 11 lent Bush the aura of legitimacy that *Bush v. Gore* had not granted. Catastrophe infused him with the charisma of a "war president," as he proclaimed himself. Suddenly his radicalism had an unobstructed path.

Bush's political rhetoric reached Manichean and apocalyptic heights. He divided the world into good and evil. "You're either with the terrorists or with us," he said. He stood at the ramparts of Fortress America, defending it from evildoers without and within. His fervent messianism guided what he called his "crusade" in the Muslim realm. "Bring them on!" he exclaimed about Iraqi insurgents. Asked if he ever sought advice from his father, Bush replied, "There's a higher Father I appeal to."

After September 11, the American people were virtually united in sentiment. Support for the Afghanistan war was almost unanimous. "The nation is united and there is a resolve and a spirit that is just so fantastic to feel," said Bush. But two weeks after he made this statement, in January 2002, his chief political aide, whom he called "the Architect," Karl Rove, spoke before a meeting of the Republican National Committee, laying out the strategy for exploiting fear of terror for partisan advantage. "We can go to the country on this issue because they trust the Republican Party to do a better job of protecting and strengthening America's military might and thereby protecting America," said Rove. His strategy was premised on the idea that Republicans win elections by maximizing the turnout of their conservative base: his method was to polarize the electorate as much as possible. Rove planned to challenge the patriotism of Democrats by creating false issues of national security over which they could be demonized. September 11 gave his politics of polarization the urgency of national emergency.

Bush's politics sustained the remaking of the government that had been the agenda of his vice president from the start. Even before September 11, after which "wartime" was used to justify secrecy, Bush resisted transparency. He fought in the courts the disclosure of the names of the participants on Vice President Dick Cheney's energy panel. Kenneth Lay, Enron's chief executive officer, was among them. Enron was the biggest financial supporter of Bush's political career; before that Lay had been a partner in Bush's oil ventures and provided corporate jets to the Bush campaign for its Florida contest. Bush, who referred to Lay as "Kenny Boy," nevertheless claimed he didn't get to "know" Lay until after he became governor, and then hardly at all.

Vice President Cheney and Secretary of Defense Rumsfeld were the prime movers behind the concentration of power in the executive. Their experience, going back to the Nixon presidency, had imbued them with belief in absolute presidential power, disdain for the Congress ("a bunch of annoying gnats," Cheney called its members, of which he had once been one), and secrecy. Executive power was rationalized by a radical theory called the "unitary executive," asserting that the president had complete authority over independent federal agencies and was not bound by congressional oversight or even law in his role as commander in chief.

Bush constructed a hidden world of his "war on terror," consisting of "black sites"—secret CIA prisons holding thousands of detainees deprived of legal due process—and he abrogated U.S. adherence to the Geneva Conventions that prohibited torture. Cheney insisted it was necessary to go to "the dark side," as he called it.

Attorneys in the Office of Legal Counsel in the Department of Justice wrote numerous memos to justify the "unitary executive" and the president's unfettered right to engage in torture and domestic spying. The White House legal counsel, Alberto Gonzales (appointed attorney general in Bush's second term), derided the Geneva Conventions as "quaint," and Bush overruled strenuous objections from the military, Secretary of State Powell, and senior officials in the Department of Justice in disregarding them. Indeed, Bush signed a directive stipulating that as commander in chief he could establish any law he wished in dealing with those accused of terrorism.

At Gonzales's request, on August 1, 2002, the Office of Legal Counsel at the Justice Department sent him a memo on torture. It was signed by OLC's director, Jay Bybee (later appointed a federal judge), and written by an OLC deputy, John Yoo, who drafted at least a dozen crucial memos justifying absolute presidential power. In this memo, the president's right to authorize torture without any oversight and by rules he himself determined was asserted as fundamental to his power: "Any effort by the Congress to regulate the interrogation of battlefield combatants would violate the Constitution's sole vesting of the Commander in Chief authority in the President." The memo defined torture specifically and broadly: "Physical pain amounting to torture must be equivalent in intensity to the pain accompanying serious physical injury, such as organ failure, impairment of bodily function, or even death."

Revelations of torture at the Abu Ghraib prison in Iraq were the tip of the iceberg of the vast network of the detained and disappeared. The International Committee of the Red Cross was forbidden access. Those at the top of the chain of command were shielded from legal accountability, while a few soldiers and the female general in charge at Abu Ghraib were offered up as scapegoats. After FBI agents witnessed gruesome spectacles of torture at the detainee prison at Guantánamo Bay, the bureau issued orders that it would not participate in this netherworld.

At the same time, Bush ordered the National Security Agency to conduct domestic spying dragnets outside the legal confines of the Foreign Intelligence Surveillance Act and without seeking warrants from the FISA court. Conservative lawyers within the Justice Department wrote memos justifying the practice on the same grounds by which they had rationalized torture: the right of the commander in chief to do as he saw fit. Once again, the presidency was construed as a monarchy. Bush and Cheney argued publicly that operating outside the limits set by the FISA court might have prevented the terrorist attacks of September 11, though there were no legal barriers to the administration's getting warrants to eavesdrop on calls from the United States to al Qaeda before or afterward.

Foreign policy was captured by neoconservative ideologues, a small group of sectarians rooted in the hothouse environment of the capital's right-wing think tanks. Its principals had been fired from the Reagan administration after the Iran-contra scandal and banished from the elder Bush's administration, but Bush Junior rewarded them with positions at the strategic heights of national security. These cadres operated with a Leninist sensibility: following a party line, engaging in fierce polemics, using harsh invective, and showing equal contempt for traditional Republicans and liberal Democrats. Cheney acted as their sponsor, protector, and promoter. Under his aegis, they ran foreign policy from the White House and the Pentagon. Secretary of State Colin Powell was sidelined. The undersecretary of state for arms control, John Bolton, inserted by Cheney, blocked Powell's initiatives and spied on him and his team, reporting back to the Office of the Vice President. The national security adviser, Condoleezza Rice, made a separate peace and turned the National Security Council into an auxiliary force for Cheney and the neocons. Meanwhile, Republican realists, including the elder Bush's closest associates, such as Brent Scowcroft, were isolated or purged.

The sixty-year tradition of bipartisan internationalism was jettisoned. After the Afghanistan war against the Taliban, the administration elevated into a "Bush Doctrine" the policy of preemptive attack, previously alien to the principles of U.S. foreign policy and expressly rejected as dangerous to the nation's security by presidents Eisenhower and John F. Kennedy during the Cold War.

In the run-up to the Iraq war, an internal campaign was waged against professionals of the intelligence community and diplomatic corps who still upheld standards of objective analysis and the traditions of U.S. foreign policy. Intense political pressure was applied to them to distort or suppress their assessments if they contained caveats casting doubt on Saddam Hussein's possession of weapons for mass destruction, and to give credence to disinformation fabricated by Iraqi exiles favored by the neoconservatives. A special operation of neocons was set up at the Pentagon, the Office of Special Plans, to "stovepipe" information directly into the White House without passing it through the analytical filter of the CIA and other intelligence agencies. Cheney made several unprecedented personal visits to CIA headquarters to try to intimidate analysts into certifying the disinformation. The caveats and warnings of the State Department's Intelligence and Research Bureau, the Defense Intelligence Agency, the Department of Energy, and the intelligence services of Germany and France were all ignored.

In making its case for war, the administration stampeded public opinion with false and misleading information about Saddam Hussein's possession and development of weapons of mass destruction, particularly nuclear weapons. Later, Bush's national security adviser, Rice (promoted to secretary of state in the second term), admitted that the president had made a false statement in his 2003 State of the Union address about Iraq's seeking uranium to produce nuclear weapons. Yet Bush, Cheney, Rice, and other officials had constantly suggested that Hussein was linked to terrorism and to those behind the attacks on September 11. Secretary of State Powell's best-case presentation before the United Nations was later proved to contain twenty-six significant falsehoods. Not a single substantial claim he made turned out to be true. He explained he had been "deceived" and called the presentation the biggest "blot" on his record. His chief of staff, Colonel Lawrence Wilkerson, said it was the "lowest point of my life." It was certainly the lowest point of U.S. credibility.

After Wilkerson resigned in 2005, he revealed how a "Cheney-Rumsfeld cabal" controlled national security policy:

> Its insular and secret workings were efficient and swift—not unlike the decision-making one would associate more with a dictatorship than a democracy. This furtive process was camouflaged neatly by the dysfunction and inefficiency of the formal decision-making process, where decisions, if they were reached at all, had to wend their way through the bureaucracy, with its dissenters, obstructionists and "guardians of the turf." But the secret process was ultimately a failure. It produced a series of disastrous decisions and virtually ensured that the agencies charged with implementing them would not or could not execute them well.

Less than a year after September 11, the administration was beset by disclosures that it had refused to take terrorism seriously before the attacks and by stories about dysfunction at the FBI. An FBI agent at the Minneapolis bureau, Coleen Rowley, emerged with documentation of how the bureau had ignored warnings of the coming terrorist strike. On the day that she testified before the Senate, June 6, 2002, Bush suddenly announced a dramatic reversal of his position against the Democratic proposal for a Department of Homeland Security. Rowley's story was blotted out.

Bush now turned the issue of a new department against the Democrats in the midterm elections, following Rove's script. In Bush's proposal, the department would not recognize labor unions, and because the Democrats believed that employees should have the right to form unions, they were cast as weak on homeland security and terrorism. Against this backdrop, Rove helped direct attacks on the patriotism of Democrats in the 2002 midterm elections. In one Republican television commercial, the face of Senator Max Cleland of Georgia, a Vietnam veteran who had lost three limbs, was morphed into that of Osama bin Laden. Cleland lost his bid for reelection. The Republicans captured the Senate by one seat.

The tactics used against Democrats were also deployed to stifle contrary views within the administration and to taint the motives of those who had served and become critics. Loyalists, no matter how egregious their errors of judgment, were vaunted; heretics were burned. Bush's radical remaking of government demanded a relentless war against professionals who operated not according to ideological tenets but by objective standards of analysis.

In 2003, the disillusioned secretary of the treasury, Paul O'Neill, the former CEO of Alcoa and a traditional business-oriented Republican, published a memoir, *The Price of Loyalty*, recounting that the deficit was deliberately fostered as a political tool, contrary to sound economic judgment. He disclosed that the invasion of Iraq was discussed at a National Security Council meeting ten days after the inauguration. And he described the president among his advisers as being "like a blind man in a roomful of deaf people." The administration's response was to investigate O'Neill for supposedly unlawfully releasing classified materials. It was a patently false charge of which he was later exonerated, but it succeeded in changing the subject and silencing him.

When, in 2003, the retired Marine Corps general Anthony Zinni criticized the administration's Iraq policy and the neoconservatives' instrumental role in its formulation, the conservative media retaliated by labeling him anti-Semitic. The former U.S. commander of Central Command and Bush's envoy to the Middle East, who had endorsed Bush in 2000, had told the *Washington Post*, "The more I saw, the more I thought that this was the product of the neocons who didn't understand the region and were going to create havoc there. These were dilettantes from Washington think tanks who never had an idea that worked on the ground. . . . I don't know where the neocons came from—that wasn't the platform they ran on."

In July 2003, a former U.S. ambassador, Joseph Wilson, wrote an op-ed article in the *New York Times* detailing his mission at the behest of the CIA before the Iraq war to Niger. There he discovered that the administration claims that Saddam Hussein was trying to purchase enriched yellowcake uranium from Niger for building nuclear weapons were untrue. Despite his report and that of two others, the president insisted in his 2003 State of the Union address that Hussein was in fact seeking uranium for nuclear weaponry. The counterattack against Wilson was swift. A week after his piece appeared, the conservative columnist Robert Novak wrote that "two senior administration officials" had informed him that Wilson's wife, Valerie Plame, an undercover CIA operative, had been responsible for sending him on his mission. The intent was somehow to cast aspersions on Wilson's credibility. (For his service as the acting U.S. ambassador in Iraq during the Gulf War, the elder Bush had called Wilson "a hero.") The disclosure of Plame's identity was an apparent felony against national security, a violation of the Intelligence Identity Protection Act; soon a special prosecutor was appointed, and the president and the vice president were interviewed, along with much of the White House senior staff. Cheney's chief of staff and national security adviser, I. Lewis "Scooter" Libby, was indicted for perjury and obstruction of justice.

In March 2004, Richard Clarke, chief of counterterrorism on the National Security Council, testified before the 9/11 Commission and elaborated in a book, *Against All Enemies*, that the Bush administration had ignored terrorism before September 11. His credibility was attacked by the administration and his motivations questioned. By then, the smearing of whistleblower career professionals had become a familiar pattern.

Traditional Republicans numbered among Bush's most penetrating critics, from O'Neill to Wilkerson, from Zinni to Clarke. They were not hostile to Bush when he entered office; on the contrary, they were willing and eager to serve under him. They observed firsthand, more than opponents on the outside, the radical changes Bush was making within the government. As Republicans, they understood better than Democrats which of their own traditions were being traduced.

Bush's war on terror melded with his culture war at home. Never before had a president attempted so vigorously to batter down the wall of separation between church and state. In 2005, Bush proclaimed himself a votary of the "culture of life" as he signed unprecedented legislation seeking to reverse numerous state and federal court decisions allowing the husband of a woman named Terry Schiavo, in a persistent vegetative state for years, to end her life support. Political opportunism in the guise of theology trampled the constitution.

Bush's appointments to the federal judiciary were an attempt to reverse the direction of the law for at least seventy years. Nearly all of his nominees were members of the Federalist Society, a conservative group of lawyers who seek to propagate certain doctrines and advance each other's careers. One of these doctrines is "originalism," the belief that the intent of the Constitution's framers can be applied to all modern problems and lead to conservative legal solutions. Yet another is called the "Constitution in exile," a school of thought that argues that the true Constitution has been suppressed since President Franklin D. Roosevelt began naming justices to the Supreme Court and that its hidden law must be revived. One of Bush's judiciary appointments, Janice Rogers Brown, lecturing before a Federalist Society meeting, referred to the New Deal as the "Revolution of 1937" and denounced it as "the triumph of our socialist revolution." It was hardly a surprise that Bush's second nominee to the Supreme Court, the federal appellate court judge Samuel Alito, was a proponent of the theory of the "unitary executive" and a wholehearted supporter of executive power.

No other president has ever been hostile to science. Russell Train, the Environmental Protection Agency administrator under presidents Nixon and Ford, observed, "How radically we have moved away from regulation based on independent findings and professional analysis of scientific, health and economic data by the responsible agency to regulation controlled by the White House and driven primarily by political considerations."

Bush's opposition to stem cell research was just the beginning of his enmity toward science. The words *reproductive health* and *condoms* were banned from websites of agencies or organizations that received federal funds. At the Food and Drug Administration, staff scientists and two independent advisory panels were overruled in order to deny the public access to emergency contraception. On the website of the Centers for Disease Control, scientifically false information was posted to foster doubt about the effectiveness of condoms in preventing HIV/AIDS. On the President's Council on Bioethics, two scientists were fired for dissent based on scientific reasoning. At the National Cancer Institute, staff scientists were suppressed as the administration planted a story on its website falsely connecting breast cancer to abortion. The top climate scientist at NASA, James Hansen, the longtime director of the agency's Goddard Institute for Space Studies, was muzzled after he noted at a scientific conference the link between greenhouse gas emissions and climate change. The president also suggested that public schools should equally teach the theory of evolution, which is the basis of all biological science, and "intelligent design," a pseudoscientific version of creationism. "I think that part of education is to expose people to different schools of thought," Bush said.

Bush's antipathy to science had an overlapping political appeal to both the religious right and industrial special interests. Scientific research was distorted and suppressed at the U.S. Fish and Wildlife Service, the Department of Agriculture, and the Environmental Protection Agency. The administration censored and misrepresented scientific reports on climate change, air pollution, endangered species, soil conservation, mercury emissions, and forests. Scientists were dismissed or rejected from numerous science advisory committees, from the Lead Poisoning Prevention Panel to the Army Science Board.

In February 2004, sixty of the nation's leading scientists, university presidents, medical experts, and former federal agency directors from both Democratic and Republican administrations—a group that included twenty Nobel laureates—issued a statement titled "Restoring Scientific Integrity in Policymaking." It declared: "The distortion of scientific knowledge for partisan political ends must cease if the public is to be properly informed about issues central to its well being, and the nation is to benefit fully from its heavy investment in scientific research and education."

When Hurricane Katrina landed in September 2005, scientific reality and dysfunctional government collided. Bush had systematically distorted, suppressed, and ignored evidence of global warming, which scientists believed was responsible for intensifying hurricanes. The director of the National Hurricane Center had briefed Bush on the potentially devastating impact of Katrina on New Orleans and the Gulf Coast before it hit, but the president disregarded the warning. The Federal Emergency Management Agency, which under President Clinton had been one of the most efficient and effective federal agencies, had become a morass of incompetence and political cronyism. Amid its abject failure, Bush praised its director Michael Brown, whose previous experience was as the head of the International Arabian Horse Association, as doing "a heck of a job." New Orleans, an important and unique American city, was destroyed. In the immediate aftermath of the storm, Bush traveled six times to the city, promising to rebuild it to its former glory, but much of the city still lay in ruins almost a year later. In January 2006, Bush declared that he had received no rebuilding plan, apparently unaware that he had already rejected it.

During the 2004 campaign, Bush's essential appeal was that he alone could keep the country safe from terrorists. Before and after the Iraq war, he implied that Saddam Hussein was in league with those responsible for September 11. On May 1, 2002, in his speech on the U.S.S. *Abraham Lincoln*, behind a banner reading "Mission Accomplished," he declared, "The battle of Iraq is one victory in a war on terror that began on September the 11, 2001—and still goes on." This theme was at the core of his campaign message and stump speech. When, under questioning late in the campaign, he admitted Saddam Hussein had nothing to do with September 11, he still insisted that Saddam was involved with al Qaeda. Bush's last television commercial in his 2004 campaign showed a pack of wolves, symbolizing terrorists about to prey on the viewer. The voiceover intoned: "And weakness attracts those who are waiting to do America harm."

As his supporters saw him, his simplistic rhetoric was straight talk, his dogmatism fortitude, his swagger reassuring; his stubbornness made him seem like a bulwark against danger, and his rough edges were proof that he was a man of the people. His evangelical religion was central to his image as a man of conviction and purity of heart. This persona helped insulate Bush from accusations that he got things wrong, misled the public, and had ulterior motives.

Faith was as important in sustaining Bush's politics as fear. Evangelical ministers and conservative Catholic bishops turned their churches into political clubhouses. At the behest of Karl Rove, right-wingers put initiatives against gay marriage on the ballot in sixteen swing states. These initiatives were instrumental in maximizing the vote for Bush in the 2004 election.

The White House carefully tended an alternative universe of belief into which its supporters took a leap of faith. From the Schiavo case to intelligent design, from suppressing the morning-after pill to urging sexual abstinence, Bush sent signals of encouragement to the religious right. His antiscientific approach helped arouse public suspicion and detestation of "experts." Critics were tainted as "elitists." Contempt for contrary facts was cultivated as a psychological prop of the leader's authority.

In 2004, the University of Maryland Program on International Policy Attitudes issued a study titled *The Separate Realities of Bush and Kerry Supporters.* It reported that 72 percent of Bush supporters believed that Iraq had weapons of mass destruction even after the U.S. Iraq Survey Group had definitively concluded that it had none. Seventy-five percent of Bush supporters believed that Saddam Hussein had been providing help to al Qaeda; 55 percent believed that the 9/11 Commission had proved that point, though the commission's report had disproved it and Bush had been forced to deny it. The social scientists conducting the survey observed that respondents held these beliefs because they said the Bush administration and the conservative media had confirmed them.

Near the end of the campaign, a senior White House aide explained the "faith-based" school of political thought to the reporter Ron Suskind, who wrote in the *New York Times Magazine:* "The aide said that guys like me were 'in what we call the reality-based community,' which he defined as people who 'believe that solutions emerge from your judicious study of discernible reality.' I nodded and murmured something about enlightenment principles and empiricism. He cut me off. 'That's not the way the world really works anymore,' he continued. 'We're an empire now, and when we act, we create our own reality. And while you're studying that reality—judiciously, as you will—we'll act again, creating other new realities, which you can study too, and that's how things will sort out. We're history's actors . . . and you, all of you, will be left to just study what we do.' "

The method described by the Bush aide was an updated version of the insight of the philosopher Francis Bacon, who in 1625 wrote in his essay "Of Vaine-Glory": "For Lies are sufficient to breed Opinion, and Opinion brings on Substance."

The "separate realities" of Bush and Kerry supporters studied by the University of Maryland extended to the facts of the candidates' military records, controversies about which became decisive events in the campaign and case studies in the manipulation of information. Bush's record of service in the Texas Air National Guard during the Vietnam era contained several mysterious discrepancies, including an entire year during which he was apparently absent without leave. It is indisputable that he never actually completed his service. How he entered his unit through preferential treatment and under what circumstances he was discharged without having finished his requirements were the subjects of an investigation by CBS's *60 Minutes*. The program's use of documents that could not be authenticated (though various witnesses confirmed the underlying facts) aroused an intense attack from Republican activists and the White House, and the entire exposé was discredited because of the journalistic lapse.

The Bush White House had anticipated the potential scandal over his military background, particularly in contrast to the record of Senator John Kerry, who was a genuine war hero, awarded the Silver Star, Bronze Star, and three Purple Hearts. In order to undermine Kerry's strong point and defend Bush's weak one, a group called Swift Boat Veterans for Truth was created. It was funded and its public relations handled by Bush allies; it was led by one John O'Neill, who had been selected by the Nixon White House to hector Kerry during the Vietnam era. The group accused Kerry of having falsely earned his medals and subsequently lied about his war experiences. Though the U.S. Navy officially affirmed his right to his medals and those who served directly with him upheld his account, the Swift Boat Veterans were treated by the media as if their fabrications were a valid point of view that must be heard. On cable television especially, and on CNN in particular, a perverse form of assumed objectivity prevailed, in which the news organization abdicated establishing the facts and allowed defamation to be presented as though it were just one reasonable side of a debate.

The Bush White House, drawing cautionary lessons from the Nixon experience, considered the press a dangerous enemy to be treated with contempt—isolated, intimidated, and, if not made pliable, discredited. The administration favored Fox News and other conservative media, using them as quasi-official government propaganda organs. Joining the long project by the conservative movement, the administration sought to bring the press into disrepute and marginalize it. If journalists did not support the administration's talking points or operate from its premises, they were assailed as unfair and biased.

The conservative campaign against journalism as the "liberal media" was Leninist in its assumption that truth and fact were inherently sectarian and instrumental. Acting on this premise, it subjected the press to constant and elaborate campaigns of intimidation. The administration enjoyed unprecedented success. Not a single report in any major newspaper or on the broadcast news networks covered the campaign of intimidation as the press had once readily reported on Nixon's early effort, progenitor of the current strategy.

As giant corporate conglomerates with extensive holdings in industries subject to all manner of government regulation, media outlets were sensitive to pressure from the administration. The effort to make the mainstream media compliant was so dedicated that Cheney himself called corporate owners to complain about individual correspondents and stories. (In 2005, Time Warner, which owns CNN, hired the Republican House majority leader Tom DeLay's chief of staff, Timothy Berry, as its chief Washington lobbyist.)

After September 11 and in the rush to war in Iraq, a jingoist spirit infected elements of the press corps, and for a long time they largely abandoned holding the government accountable. The *New York Times'* news reports on weapons of mass destruction and the *Washington Post's* editorials were indispensable in lending credence to the disinformation on which the administration made its case for the Iraq war. (The *Times* later published a lengthy editor's note on the failures of its coverage, and its chief correspondent on weapons of mass destruction, Judith Miller, eventually resigned from the newspaper. The *Post* refused to acknowledge that it had been misled in its editorials before the war.) The long-term damage to the credibility of the prestige press is incalculable.

Reality was often too radical and threatening for many in the press to venture covering it. Those who dared were frequently thrust into fierce conflicts. Some were subject to legal investigations by the Justice Department (for example, the *New York Times* for reporting on Bush's warrantless domestic surveillance, and the *Washington Post* for reporting on secret prisons for detainees). Some were even subjected to innuendo and invasions of private life: for example, after broadcasting a story on army morale, an ABC News reporter was outed as gay by the right-wing gossip columnist Matt Drudge, who claimed he was given the information by a White House source.

A gay prostitute without journalistic background, carrying press credentials from a phony media operation financed by right-wing Texas Republicans, was granted access to the regular White House press briefings, and the press secretary employed the tactic of calling on him to break up the questioning of legitimate reporters. The White House also funneled federal funds to conservatives posing as legitimate journalists and commentators. The chair of the Public Broadcasting System, Kenneth Tomlinson, a Bush appointee, crusaded to drive the distinguished journalist Bill Moyers off the air for his heretical views and approved a show featuring the conservative writers of the *Wall Street Journal* editorial board. Tomlinson also commissioned an enemies list of "liberal media" on PBS in order to guide the purging of the network. (Tomlinson resigned in November 2005, after the inspector general of the Corporation for Public Broadcasting found he had violated PBS rules by meddling in programming and contracting.)

By containing and curbing the press, Bush attempted to remove another check on his power. When he made an extended joke at the 2004 Radio and Television Correspondents Dinner about his inability to find WMD in Iraq—"Not here," he said, narrating a film depicting him looking under his desk in the Oval Office—the 1,500 members of the assembled press corps burst into raucous laughter like pledges to his fraternity.

Bush's admirers have cast him in the mold of Shakespeare's Henry V, a wastrel royal son who, on rising to the purple, realizes his leadership in war. Some detractors offered an opposite portrait—that of the dry drunk. But these literary and psychological theories failed to assess Bush's radicalism in the historical and constitutional context of the American presidency.

Bush has sought to institute changes in the character of the presidency and American government that would permanently alter the constitutional system. He has used the "global war on terrorism" to impose a "unitary executive" of absolute power, disdainful of the Congress and brushing aside the judicial branch when he has felt it necessary (for example, regarding domestic surveillance without warrants from the FISA court). He issued many "signing statements" (a device originally designed by Samuel Alito when he served as an aide in the Reagan Justice Department) to express his own understanding of the meaning of enacted legislation and the way the executive branch will or will not enforce and abide by it. The Bush White House concept of the executive represents the full flowering of the imperial presidency as conceived by Richard Nixon.

Operationally, within the White House, the Office of the Vice President controls foreign policy—making the National Security Council its auxiliary —and the flow of information to the president. No vice president has ever been so powerful.

Bush has been unusually incurious and passive in seeking facts, never demanding worst-case scenarios and keeping his circle of advisers tightly restricted. Only a select few of the White House staff are permitted to see him, much less interact with him. He has made no effort to establish independent sources of information. He has never circulated to his staff articles that sparked a policy interest in him. As his popular support declines, he has soaked up the assurances of his aides that the people have only momentarily lapsed in their appreciation of his heroic strength and vision.

Accountability is treated as a threat to executive power, not as essential to democratic governance. No one at the top of the chain of command has been held responsible for the crimes of Abu Ghraib. No one who committed grievous errors of judgment in the Iraq war has been held to account. Instead they have been showered with honors, medals, and promotions.

Bush's radical White House has depended on one-party control of the Congress. The Republican Congress has supported the consolidation of executive power, even at the expense of congressional prerogatives. Oversight has been studiously neglected. On any matter that might cause irritation to the White House, hearings are quashed or simply not held. When the White House has failed to produce requested documents, for example in the inquiry into its conduct in response to Hurricane Katrina, there have been no repercussions from the Republican Congress. The intelligence committees and the House Armed Services Committee, among others, have covered up administration malfeasance. The Senate Intelligence Committee skewed and distorted its report on intelligence leading up to the Iraq war to acquit the administration of responsibility, and it refused to conduct a promised investigation into administration political pressures on the intelligence community.

The Republicans in Congress have enforced discipline by the creation of a pay-to-play system. Lobbyists, trade associations, and law firms have been told that unless they contributed to Republican campaign funds and hired Republicans, they would be treated with disfavor. The House majority leader, Tom DeLay, developed this political machine, called the K Street Project, into an entity with a high degree of control over Washington until he was forced to resign his post after his indictment for criminal campaign fund-raising practices. Jack Abramoff, a super-lobbyist, worked closely with DeLay, and when Abramoff pleaded guilty in January 2006 to fraud, tax evasion, and criminal conspiracy, he triggered the biggest congressional scandal in modern history. Abramoff was also plugged into the White House and linked to Rove; he even attended staff meetings.

Bush's presidency has been uniquely radical in its elevation of absolute executive power, dismissal of the other branches of government, contempt for the law, expansion of the power of the vice president, creation of networks of ideological cadres, rejection of accountability, stifling of internal debate, reliance on one-party rule, and overtly political use of war. Never before has a president shown such disdain for science and the constitutional separation between church and state. None of these actions seemed to be in the offing on Bush's inauguration in 2001; yet they were not sudden impulses, spontaneous reactions, or accidental gestures. They were based on a deliberate strategy to change the presidency and government fundamentally and forever. And these decisions have deep historical roots.

Bush is the first Southern conservative ever elected to the presidency. Southern politics has always contained varied and conflicting traditions. Through Bush, a reactionary Southern political tradition captured the center of the federal government, an unprecedented phenomenon. His brand of conservatism is the expression of a commodity-based oligarchy rooted in Texas, deeply hostile to the New Deal, actively dismissive of public services, and protective of class and racially based hierarchies. Using the rhetoric of limited government and states' rights, these Texas conservatives have claimed control over government in order to consolidate power and wealth. Both Bush and Cheney (the former CEO of Halliburton, a Texas-based company) come out of the oil patch. Bush's language about "compassionate conservatism" was a simple emollient applied to ease the way for his harsher political and policy imperatives.

In method, spirit, and goals, Bush's project is the opposite of the New Deal, which was a great improvisation in the spirit of American pragmatism, "bold, persistent experimentation," as Franklin D. Roosevelt put it. The New Deal, in the face of the greatest domestic crisis since the Civil War, mobilized the capacities of government for the general welfare. The New Frontier of John F. Kennedy and the Great Society of Lyndon Johnson extended the social inclusiveness of the New Deal, reforming immigration policy, reducing poverty among the elderly, and expanding education. Most significant, on racial justice, the frustrated legacy of Reconstruction and the great Civil War constitutional amendments was finally realized.

The three Southern presidents of the twentieth century were all progressive Democrats: Lyndon Johnson, Jimmy Carter, and Bill Clinton. If Woodrow Wilson were counted as a fourth (having been born in Virginia), he would also fit the profile of progressive (though definitely of the pre–civil rights era, given his support for segregation within the federal government). Harry Truman, from the border state of Missouri, must be categorized as one of the great liberals (on civil rights as well as other issues).

In the nineteenth century, the Southerners in the White House, from Thomas Jefferson through Andrew Jackson, represented expanded democracy. The only Southern conservative to hold the office before the Civil War was John Tyler, who acceded to the presidency after the sudden death of William Henry Harrison, the first Whig president. Tyler was a conservative Democrat from Virginia and a man without a party whose tenure was an accidental single term. Zachary Taylor from Louisiana, the last Whig, a national hero as the triumphant commander in the Mexican-American War, was setting himself against the proslavery forces from the South, including his son-in-law, Senator Jefferson Davis of Mississippi, at the time of his death. Andrew Johnson, another accident and anomaly, was both a vehement populist and a conservative who used the presidency to attempt to scuttle Reconstruction in the name of a white man's democracy. Lyndon Johnson, the first elected Southerner since the Civil War, of course, was the greatest president on civil rights since Ulysses Grant.

The two great epochal crises in American history after the revolution— the Civil War and the Great Depression—were accelerated and deepened by passive, accommodating, or stubbornly out-of-touch presidents— James Buchanan and Herbert Hoover. Political and economic forces they failed to control or understand overcame them. But neither sought conflict or courted turmoil, even though they accelerated it. By contrast, Bush purposefully polarized differences in the country for political advantage.

In foreign policy, Bush has freely appropriated the language of Woodrow Wilson about freedom and democracy. But whereas Wilson sought to bring the United States into a new international system of law, Bush's unilateralism has opposed the Wilsonian heritage at every turn, a stance exemplified by his appointment of John Bolton as ambassador to the United Nations.

Bush also claims to stand in the conservative tradition of Ronald Reagan. Indeed, Reagan sought to overturn longstanding policies of Democratic and Republican presidents alike in his pursuit of a radical and often fanciful conservatism. But when he found himself cornered by realities, Reagan the ideologue gave way to Reagan the old union negotiator, prepared for compromise. Facing reality, he gave up his rhetoric about privatizing Social Security to join with Democrats to fund its long-term solvency. After the Iran-contra scandal, he summarily dismissed his neoconservative aides and forged a détente with the Soviet leader Mikhail Gorbachev that helped to end the Cold War. That achievement, which required disenthralling his administration from the right wing, was his finest moment and the enduring basis of his presidential reputation. Had he not cast out the right, he would have remained covered with disgrace.

George H. W. Bush, George W. Bush's father and Reagan's vice president and successor, pointedly blackballed the neoconservatives from his administration. Yet the son George dusted off Reagan's discredited zealots and their doctrines to provide him with reasons for a war of choice in Iraq. His rejection of his father's realism in foreign policy was pointed, and that rejection signaled a larger radicalism.

Nothing like Bush's concerted radicalism has ever been seen in the White House. One would have to go back to the Civil War era to find politics as polarized. But not even the president of the Confederate States of America, Jefferson Davis, ran as extreme and insulated an administration. Davis, a former U.S. senator and secretary of war, appointed experienced politicians and diplomats to responsible positions within his government and kept the radical Fire-Eaters at bay. As soon as the Fire-Eaters' vision of an independent slave republic materialized through secession, they were consigned to the sidelines, where they remained as critics of the Confederate president for the duration of the Civil War.

Never before Bush has a president so singlehandedly and willfully precipitated national and international crises. The tragedy of September 11 cannot be offered as the sole justification for his actions. In his first inaugural address, Bush cited a biblical passage about an "angel in the whirlwind." His presidency has been a self-created whirlwind.

In 1900, Theodore Roosevelt wrote a sympathetic biography of Oliver Cromwell, the leader of the short-lived English republic of the seventeenth century. Although Roosevelt admired many of Cromwell's intentions to create representative government, he described how Cromwell's volatile temperament undermined his virtuous goals. But he added: "In criticizing Cromwell, however, we must remember that generally in such cases an even greater share of blame must attach to the nation than to the man." Roosevelt continued:

> Self-governing freemen must have the power to accept necessary com-
> promises, to make necessary concessions, each sacrificing somewhat of
> prejudice, and even of principle, and every group must show the necessary
> subordination of its particular interests to the interests of the community
> as a whole. When the people will not or cannot work together; when they
> permit groups of extremists to decline to accept anything that does not
> coincide with their own extreme views; or when they let power slip from
> their hands through sheer supine indifference; then they have themselves
> chiefly to blame if the power is grasped by stronger hands.

The tragedy that Theodore Roosevelt described is not restricted in its broad dimensions to Britain. Roosevelt wrote his history as a lesson for Americans, who had been spared the travesties of the English revolution. Instead of Cromwell, we had George Washington. Ultimately, a people is responsible for its leaders. Bush's legacy will precipitate a crisis over democracy that only the American people can resolve.

PART ONE

HUBRIS

"MISSION ACCOMPLISHED":
FROM THE VICTORY IN IRAQ
TO THE DEFEAT OF JOHN KERRY

The Intelligence Wars

NOVEMBER 1, 2003

In Baghdad, the Bush administration acts as though it is astonished by the postwar carnage. Its feigned shock is a consequence of Washington's intelligence wars. In fact, not only was it warned of the coming struggle and its nature—ignoring a $5 million State Department report titled *The Future of Iraq*—but Bush himself signed another document in which that predictive information is contained.

According to the congressional resolution authorizing the use of military force in Iraq, the administration is required to submit to the Congress reports of postwar planning every sixty days. This report, bearing Bush's signature and dated April 14, declares: "We are especially concerned that the remnants of the Saddam Hussein regime will continue to use Iraqi civilian populations as a shield for its regular and irregular combat forces or may attack the Iraqi population in an effort to undermine Coalition goals." The report goes on: "Coalition planners have prepared for these contingencies, and have designed the military campaign to minimize civilian casualties and damage to civilian infrastructure."

Yet, on August 25, as the violence in postwar Iraq flared, Secretary of Defense Donald Rumsfeld claimed that this possibility was not foreseen: "Now was—did we—was it possible to anticipate that the battles would take place south of Baghdad and that then there would be a collapse up north, and there would be very little killing and capturing of those folks, because they blended into the countryside and they're still fighting their war?"

"We read their reports," a Senate source told me. "Too bad they don't read their own reports."

In advance of the war, Bush (to be precise, Dick Cheney, the de facto prime minister to the distant monarch) viewed the CIA, the State Department, and other intelligence agencies not simply as uncooperative but even disloyal, as their analysts continued to sift through information to try to determine what exactly might be true. This process is the essence of their professionalism and mission. Yet their strict insistence on the empirical was a threat to the ideological, the facts an imminent danger to the doctrine. So those facts had to be suppressed, and the individuals creating contrary evidence had to be marginalized, intimidated, or discredited. Twice, in the run-up to the war, Vice President Cheney steered his motorcade to the George H. W. Bush Center for Intelligence in Langley, Virginia, where he personally tried to coerce CIA desk-level analysts to fit their work to specifications.

If the CIA would not serve, it would be trampled. At the Pentagon, Rumsfeld formed the Office of Special Plans, a parallel agency under the direction of the neoconservative deputy secretary of defense, Paul Wolfowitz, to "stovepipe" its own version of intelligence directly to the White House. Its reports were not to be mingled or shared with the CIA or State Department intelligence for fear of corruption by skepticism. Instead, the Pentagon's handpicked future leader of Iraq, Ahmed Chalabi of the Iraqi National Congress, replaced the CIA as the definitive source of information, little of which turned out to be true—though his deceit was consistent with his record. Chalabi was regarded at the CIA as a mountebank after he had lured the agency to support his "invasion" of Iraq in 1995—a tragicomic episode, but one that hardly discouraged his neoconservative sponsors.

Early last year, before Hans Blix, chief of the United Nations team to monitor Iraq's weapons of mass destruction, embarked on his mission, Wolfowitz ordered a report from the CIA to show that Blix had been soft on Iraq in the past and thus to undermine him before he even began his work. When the CIA reached an opposite conclusion, a former State Department official described Wolfowitz in the *Washington Post* as having "hit the ceiling." Then, according to James Rubin, former assistant secretary of state, in an article in *Foreign Affairs,* when Blix met with Cheney at the White House, the vice president told him what would happen if his efforts on WMDs did not support Bush policy: "We will not hesitate to discredit you." Blix's brush with Cheney was no different from the administration's treatment of the CIA.

Having already decided on its course in Iraq, the Bush administration demanded the fabrication of evidence to substantiate an imminent threat. Then, fulfilling the teleology of the Bush doctrine, preemptive action could be taken. Policy a priori dictated intelligence à la carte.

In Bush's Washington, politics is the continuation of war by other means. Rather than seeking to reform any abuse of intelligence, the Bush administration, through the Republican-dominated Senate Intelligence Committee, is producing a report that will accuse the CIA of giving faulty information.

While the CIA is being cast as a scapegoat, FBI agents are interviewing senior officials about a potential criminal conspiracy behind the public identification of a covert CIA operative—Valerie Plame, who, not coincidentally, happens to be the wife of a former U.S. ambassador, Joseph Wilson, the author of a report discrediting allegations that Saddam Hussein was seeking to purchase Niger yellowcake uranium (allegations which originated in Cheney's office). Wilson's irrefutable documentation was carefully shelved at the time in order to put sixteen false words about Saddam Hussein's nuclear threat in the mouth of George Bush in his 2003 State of the Union address.

When it comes to responsibility for the degradation of intelligence in developing rationales for the war, Bush is energetically trying not to get the bottom of anything. While he has asserted that the White House is cooperating with the investigation into the felony of outing Plame, his spokesman has assiduously drawn a fine line between the legal and the political. After all, though Karl Rove—the president's political strategist and senior adviser, indispensable to his reelection campaign—unquestionably called a journalist to suggest that Mrs. Wilson was "fair game," his summoning of the furies upon her apparently occurred after her name had already been made public by two unnamed "senior administration officials."

Rove is not considered to have committed a firing offense so long as he has merely behaved unethically. What Bush is not doing—not demanding that his staff sign affidavits swearing their innocence or asking his vice president point-blank what he knows—is glaringly obvious. Damaging national security must be secondary to political necessity.

"It's important to recognize," Joseph Wilson remarked to me, "that the person who decided to make a political point or that his political agenda was more important than a national security asset is still there in place. I'm appalled at the apparent nonchalance shown by the president."

Now, postwar, the intelligence wars, if anything, have grown more intense. Blame shifting by the administration is the order of the day. The Republican Senate Intelligence Committee report will point the finger at the CIA, but circumspectly will not review how Bush used intelligence. The Democrats, in the Senate minority, forced to act like a fringe group, held unofficial hearings this week with prominent former CIA agents: these are rock-ribbed Republicans who all voted for and even contributed money to

Bush but expressed their amazed anger at the assault being waged on the permanent national security apparatus by the Republican president whose father's name adorns the building where they worked. One of them compressed his disillusionment into the single most resonant word an intelligence agent can muster: "betrayal."

Bush and Blair:
Lessons in Leadership

NOVEMBER 14, 2003

TONY BLAIR, about to welcome George Bush to London with pomp and circumstance, has assumed the mantle of tutor to the un-learned president.

Bush originally came to Blair determined to go to war in Iraq, but without a strategy. Blair instructed him that the casus belli was Saddam Hussein's weapons of mass destruction, urged him to make the case before the United Nations, and—when the effort to obtain a U.N. resolution failed—convinced him to revive the Middle East peace process, which the president had abandoned. The road map for peace was the principal concession Blair wrested from him.

The prime minister argued that renewing the negotiations was essential to the long-term credibility of the coalition goals in Iraq and the whole region. But within the Bush administration, that initiative was systematically undermined. Now Blair welcomes a president who has taught him a lesson in statecraft that the prime minister refuses to acknowledge.

Flynt Leverett, a former CIA analyst, revealed to me that the substance of the road map was ready for public release before the end of 2002: "We had made commitments to key European and Arab allies. The White House lost its nerve. It took Blair to get Bush to put it out." This man knows what he's talking about. In addition to his CIA role, Leverett is a former senior director for Middle East affairs at the National Security Council, an author of the road map, and a fellow at the Saban Center for Middle East Policy at the Brookings Institution. "We needed to work this issue hard," he says, "but because we didn't want to make life difficult with [Israeli prime minister Ariel] Sharon, we undercut our credibility."

In the internal struggle over peace in the Middle East, the neoconservatives within the administration prevailed. Elliott Abrams, chief of Middle East affairs at the NSC, was their main man. During the Iran-contra scandal, Abrams had helped set up a rogue foreign-policy operation. His soliciting of $10 million from the Sultan of Brunei for the illegal enterprise turned farcical when he transposed numbers on a Swiss bank account and lost the money. He pleaded guilty to lying to Congress and then spent his purgatory as director of a neoconservative think tank, denouncing the Oslo Accords and arguing that "tomorrow's lobby for Israel has got to be conservative Christians, because there aren't going to be enough Jews to do it." Abrams was rehabilitated when George Bush appointed him to the NSC.

In his new position, Abrams set to work trying to gut the road map. He was suspicious of the Europeans and British, considering them to be anti-Israel, if not inherently anti-Semitic. But working in league with his allies in Cheney's office and at the Department of Defense, Abrams failed to prevent Blair from persuading Bush to issue the road map at last.

The key to the plan's success was U.S. support for the Palestinian prime minister, Abu Mazen, indispensable as a partner for peace but regarded as a threat by both Ariel Sharon and Yasir Arafat. At the June summit on the road map, Bush told Abu Mazen: "God told me to strike at al Qaeda and I struck them; then he instructed me to strike at Saddam, which I did; and now I am determined to solve the problem in the Middle East. If you help me I will act."

Abu Mazen was scheduled to come to Washington to meet Bush a month later. For his political survival, he desperately required the United States to press the Sharon government into making concessions on building settlements on the West Bank. Abu Mazen sent a secret emissary to the White House, Khalil Shikaki. I met Shikaki in Ramallah, where he gave his account of this urgent trip. He met Abrams and laid out what support was needed from Bush if Abu Mazen—and therefore the road map—was to survive. Abrams told him, he says, that Bush "could not agree to anything" because of domestic political considerations: Bush's reliance on the religious right, his refusal to offend the American Israel Public Affairs Committee, and the demands of the upcoming election. Shikaki pleaded that Abu Mazen presented "a window of opportunity" and could not go on without U.S. help. "He has to show he's capable of doing it himself," Abrams answered dismissively.

Inside the NSC, those in favor of the road map—the CIA analysts Flynt Leverett and Ben Miller, among others—were forced out. On September 6, Abu Mazen resigned, and the road map collapsed.

Blair provided Bush with a reason for the war in Iraq and led him to express his plan for peace for the Middle East, preventing Bush from appearing a reckless and isolated leader. In return, the teacher's seminar on the Middle East has been dropped.

Harold Macmillan remarked that after empire the British would act toward the Americans as the Greeks to the Romans. Though the Greeks were often tutors to the Romans, Macmillan neglected to mention that the Greeks were slaves.

How George Transformed Tony's World

NOVEMBER 27, 2003

NOVEMBER 22 MARKED THE FORTIETH ANNIVERSARY of John F. Kennedy's assassination. "For of those to whom much is given, much is required," he famously remarked in 1961. It was his idea not only of the citizen's relationship to the nation but of the United States' obligation to the world. However, George Bush has changed the maxim, at least with regard to Britain: "For to those of whom much is required, nothing is given."

In his speech of November 18 at the Banqueting Hall (avoiding an appearance before Parliament, where backbenchers might make rude noises), Bush freely displayed his erudition, citing the Earl of Shaftesbury and William Wilberforce, William Tyndale and John Wesley, to cast himself as a liberal idealist and internationalist in the tradition of Woodrow Wilson. "We're sometimes faulted for a naive faith that liberty can change the world," he said. "If that's an error, it began with reading too much John Locke and Adam Smith." One wonders how often Bush has perused *The Second Treatise of Civil Government*. Certainly his speech was a repudiation of his father's foreign policy realism: the Oedipal doctrine.

Putting his volume of Locke aside, Bush entered into negotiations with Blair to act out something more like Thomas Hobbes's *Leviathan*. Blair had been put into the position of having to appear before the president as petitioner. He asked for relief on U.S. steel tariffs; for the rendering of British prisoners at Guantánamo Bay to Britain; and for U.S. pressure on the Israel-Palestine peace process. But Blair was rebuffed.

Peter Riddell, in his book *Hug Them Close*, writes that, after his initial anxiety about representing British interests, Blair has grown to see Bush as something of a soulmate. Blair's rhetoric during the visit sounded trumpet notes as though it were still the call to the war in Iraq and the postwar realities had not intruded. Riddell reports that Blair in retrospect regards Bush's predecessor as "weird." That fact or factoid, true or not, may be interpreted as perhaps another gesture of ingratiation—demeaning Clinton is always deeply appreciated by Bush.

I recall being present at meetings between Blair and Clinton where, in ten minutes, apparently difficult problems, including trade, were resolved to Britain's advantage. How weird was that? Now Blair has equated the long-term interests aligning the United States and the United Kingdom with adamantine support for the short-term strategies of the Bush administration. Yet the tighter the embrace, the weaker the influence.

As Blair rightly insists, the United States is the world's most powerful democracy and sets an example for the rest of the West: the rise of the welfare state in Britain followed the New Deal; Labour's resurgence of the mid-1960s followed the New Frontier and the Great Society. Conversely, Margaret Thatcher followed the conservative reaction of Richard Nixon and became the partner for Ronald Reagan. Clinton was the trailblazer for Blair. Now Bush's America has taken a radical swerve toward authoritarian conservatism, creating an international undertow. Will Britain have a special exemption?

Wearing the laurels of his London triumph, Bush returned to Washington to roll back one of JFK's great social initiatives and challenge the patriotism of Democrats. Bush's draconian bill restricting Medicare is the most significant attack on the social compact since the New Deal. It will drop about one-quarter of seniors, six million people, from their coverage for prescription drugs, and another 3.8 million will have it reduced or eliminated.

The whole $400 billion program will be financed by regressive taxation, in contrast to the current untaxed entitlement; and $125 billion will flow into health-care and pharmaceutical companies, which are major Bush donors. Meanwhile, Karl Rove, Bush's senior political aide, announced that "reform" of Social Security, the foundation of the New Deal, is next.

While Republicans kept Democratic leaders out of the Senate conference committee, in violation of all precedent, to ram the bill through without any changes, the Republican National Committee began running an advertisement on TV. "Some are now attacking the president for attacking the terrorists," intoned the voiceover. But no Democrat was doing that. Bush himself appeared: "Some have said we must not act until the threat is imminent," he said. But it was Bush who ignored intelligence to make the case that "the threat is imminent" in Iraq. Then the voiceover: "Some call for us to retreat, putting our national security in the hands of others." But it was Bush who was planning troop reductions during the election year. Who are the "others"? The United Nations? He could not have been referring to Blair, who pays any price, bears any burden.

The Good Soldier

JANUARY 8, 2004

SHORTLY BEFORE THE HOLIDAYS, just before he underwent surgery for prostate cancer, Secretary of State Colin Powell gave a forlorn and illuminating interview to the *Washington Post*, of which only one brief excerpt was published. In it he explained that there was no matter of principle over which he would resign and depicted his tenure as a long mission of retreat and loss.

Powell's elegiac tone is in striking contrast to the reigning triumphalism of official Washington. Bush's popularity has spiked to one of its high points with Saddam Hussein's capture. His campaign operation is ginning up his national security doctrine of "preemptive self-defense" (as a Republican TV ad has put it) to pose against the supposedly soft Democrats. And, meanwhile, Powell presents himself as bereft, tragic, and noble.

In the full transcript of his interview, posted without fanfare on the State Department's website, Powell chooses to identify with two of his predecessors: Thomas Jefferson, the first secretary of state; and George C. Marshall, like Powell an army general. He observed that the "single trait that always comes to me when I think about these two guys is selfless service." When Marshall was passed over as commander of the D-Day invasion in favor of Dwight Eisenhower, Powell said that "whatever disappointment he felt over that, he simply ate it." When Marshall argued against President Harry Truman's recognition of the state of Israel, he took his loss in silence, and Powell quoted him: "No, gentlemen, you don't take a post of this sort, and then resign when the man who has the constitutional responsibility to make decisions makes one you don't like."

Powell said he raised these incidents because he wanted to illustrate his "personal code." Without prompting, he spoke about Jefferson: "He said something along the lines, 'I go now to the task that you have put before me, in the certain knowledge that I will come out of it diminished.'"

Powell's valedictory note suggests that the Bush administration's most prestigious and popular figure is almost certainly preparing for retirement. For many in Congress and among traditional allies, including Tony Blair, Powell has been seen as the voice of reason, the indispensable partner. Because his absence as a countervailing force in a second Bush term is hardly imaginable, his lame-duck status is certain to have consequences in a campaign centered on national security and in the conduct of foreign policy.

Powell's loyalty to those who have shepherded his career, from the Nixon administration to the present, has taken precedent over all else. He has won battles but lost the wars. His efforts, along with Blair's, to pursue the U.N. route on Iraq are now revealed by the former director of State Department policy planning, Richard Haass, to have been largely a matter of PR. Haass says the national security adviser, Condoleezza Rice, told him in June 2002: "Save your breath—the president has already decided what he's going to do on this."

Recently, Powell has made grand gestures and statements without anyone else in the administration lending him even face-saving rhetorical support. He is more isolated than ever. This week, for example, he praised a group of private citizens who traveled to North Korea and won apparent concessions from the regime that would open the way for successful negotiations on its nuclear weaponry and proliferation. But Powell's words on North Korea fall weightless.

The leader of that private delegation, Charles Pritchard, is not just some errant do-gooder. He is the former chief State Department negotiator for North Korea, and Powell's own man. He abruptly quit last August because he was stymied by one of Powell's many internal nemeses, the right-wing undersecretary of state, John Bolton (despised, incidentally, in the upper reaches of the British government). Powell may favor a policy on North Korea, but the United States has none.

Nothing with which Powell has disagreed has he apparently felt worth fighting to the end. He has given his best advice, husbanded his inherent power, and accepted policies—which he has privately told senators have been calamitous—on the diplomatic run-up to the Iraq war and the reconstruction, the Middle East peace process and North Korea. His presence has lent the appearance that there could have been another course, when on the important issues that has been proved an illusion.

In Errol Morris's documentary on Robert McNamara, *The Fog of War*, the former secretary of defense of the Vietnam War era justifies as selfless service to President Johnson his refusal to take a stand against a disastrous policy he believed could never succeed. Powell has now offered his case for failing to resign in the same terms, but making no argument for principle. His pathos raises the questions of whether he ever believed in anything greater than his sterling career, how complicit he has been in his own plight, and whether he has been the good soldier as enabler. Now the fate of the "diminished" Powell will inevitably be raised as a contentious issue in the harsh arena of campaign politics. In the final frame, Powell is about to lose all control.

An Unlikely Dissident

JANUARY 15, 2004

ONE OF THE BUSH ADMINISTRATION'S tacit operating assumptions is that the checks and balances have been checked. But that implacable wall has been cracked by an insider's surprising confessions. The former treasury secretary Paul O'Neill, fired and forgotten, mild-mannered and gray, appears an unlikely dissident. He was, after all, the CEO of Alcoa, a pillar of the Republican establishment.

More is involved for him than pride and pique. While O'Neill records slights and is dismissed by some as a dotty reject, he does more than tell a few tales in the book, *The Price of Loyalty*. The attack on him, consistent with Bush efforts to intimidate anyone who challenges the official version of events, underscores the inherent fragility of Bush's public persona, on which rests his popularity. Bush's greatest political asset is his image as a masterful commander in chief who happens to be a nice man. Alongside him, Dick Cheney is viewed as the sagacious Nestor.

O'Neill's persuasiveness and the long-term damage he does to these icons comes from his years in the Nixon and Ford administrations and his firsthand critique of a government radically unlike any before it, especially Republican ones. O'Neill's threat is to a president unusually dependent in an election campaign on fear and credibility to sustain a sense of power and inevitability. He sounds an alarm against an unfit president who lacks "credibility with his most senior officials," behind whom looms a dark "puppeteer," as O'Neill calls the vice president, and a closed cabal.

Invading Iraq was on the agenda of the first principals' meeting of the National Security Council, of which O'Neill was a member, months before September 11, and relentlessly pushed. Regressive tax cuts creating massive deficits were implemented without economic justification, as "the administration has managed to kill the whys at every turn."

When the political team distorts basic economic numbers on tax cuts and inserts them into the 2001 State of the Union address, O'Neill yells: "This is complete bullshit!" It is "something that knowledgeable people in the US government knew to be false." The business executive is shocked at the derogation of policy in favor of corporate interests—a "combination of confidentiality and influence by powerful interested parties." He learns that moderate Republicans like him—Christie Whitman, the director of the Environmental Protection Agency, who sees her efforts to affirm policy on global warming "slaughtered" by Cheney and the politicos, and Secretary of State Colin Powell—"may have been there, in large part, as cover."

Bush appears as a bully, using nicknames to demean people. He is querulous: when he waits impatiently for a cheeseburger, he summons his chief of staff. " 'You're the chief of staff. You think you're up to getting us some cheeseburgers?' . . . He all but raced out of the room." He is manipulated: " 'Stick to principle' is another phrase that has a tonic effect on Bush"—in this case, used by his senior adviser, Karl Rove, to push for additional tax cuts. He is incurious; and, above all, he is intently political. When Bush holds forth, it is often to show that he's not Clinton. He informs his NSC that on Middle East peace "Clinton overreached," but that he will take Ariel Sharon "at face value" and will not commit himself to the peace process: "I think it's time to pull out of that situation." Powell is "startled."

The "inscrutable" Cheney emerges as the power behind the throne, orchestrating leaks to undermine opposing views. He uses tariffs as "political bait" for the midterm elections. When O'Neill argues that out-of-control deficits will cause a "fiscal crisis," Cheney "cut him off. 'Reagan proved deficits don't matter,' he said. . . . 'This is our due.' " In the end, Cheney fires O'Neill, the first vice president to dismiss a cabinet member.

O'Neill's revelations cut deeper than mere polemics. They have been met not by any factual rebuttal but by anonymous character assassination from a "senior official": "Nobody listened to him when he was in office. Why should anybody now?"

Then the White House announced O'Neill was under investigation for abusing classified documents, though he asserts they were not classified, and the White House had shoveled carefully edited NSC documents at Bob Woodward for his shining portrait, *Bush at War*. Quietly, O'Neill and his publisher prepared an irrefutable response. Soon they will post each of the nineteen thousand documents underlying the book on the Internet. The story will not be calmed.

The Hunt for WMD

FEBRUARY 5, 2004

BEFORE HE DEPARTED on his quest for Saddam Hussein's fabled weapons of mass destruction last June, David Kay, chief of the Iraq Survey Group, told friends that he expected promptly to locate the cause of the preemptive war. On January 28, Kay appeared before the Senate to testify that there were no WMDs. "It turns out that we were all wrong," he said. President Bush, he added helpfully, was misinformed by the whole intelligence community, which, like Kay, made assumptions that turned out to be false.

Within days, Bush declared that he would, after all, appoint a commission to investigate; significantly, it would report its findings only after the presidential election.

Kay's testimony was the catalyst for this U-turn, but only one of his claims is correct: that he was wrong. The truth is that much of the intelligence community did not fail but presented correct assessments and warnings that were overridden and suppressed. On virtually every single important claim made by the Bush administration in its case for war, there was serious dissension. Discordant views—not from individual analysts but from several intelligence agencies as a whole—were kept from the public as momentum was built for a congressional vote on the war resolution.

Precisely because of the qualms the administration encountered, it created a rogue intelligence operation, the Office of Special Plans, located within the Pentagon and under the control of neoconservatives. The OSP roamed outside the ordinary interagency process, stamping its approval on stories from Iraqi exiles that the other agencies dismissed as lacking credibility and feeding them to the president.

At the same time, constant pressure was applied to the intelligence agencies to force their compliance. In one case, a senior intelligence officer who refused to knuckle under was removed.

Bruce Hardcastle was a senior officer for the Middle East for the Defense Intelligence Agency. When Bush insisted that Saddam was actively and urgently engaged in a nuclear weapons program and had renewed production of chemical weapons, the DIA reported otherwise. According to Patrick Lang, the former chief of counterterrorism and the Middle East at the DIA, Hardcastle "told [the Bush administration] that the way they were handling evidence was wrong." The response was not simply to remove Hardcastle from his post: "They did away with his job," Lang says. "They wanted only liaison officers . . . not a senior intelligence person who argued with them."

When the State Department's Bureau of Intelligence and Research (INR) submitted reports which did not support the administration's case—saying, for example, that the aluminum tubes Saddam possessed were for conventional rocketry, not nuclear weapons (a report corroborated by Department of Energy analysts), or that mobile laboratories found in Iraq were not for WMDs, or that the story about Saddam seeking uranium in Niger was bogus, or that there was no link between Saddam and al Qaeda (a report backed by the CIA)—its analyses were shunted aside. Greg Thielman, chief of the INR at the time, told me: "Everyone in the intelligence community knew that the White House couldn't care less about any information suggesting that there were no WMDs or that the U.N. inspectors were very effective."

When the CIA debunked the tales about Niger uranium and the Saddam–al Qaeda connection, its reports were ignored and direct pressure applied. In October 2002, the White House inserted mention of the uranium into a speech Bush was to deliver, but the CIA objected, and it was excised. Three months later, it reappeared in his State of the Union address. National Security Adviser Condoleezza Rice claimed never to have seen the original CIA memo, and her deputy, Stephen Hadley, said he had forgotten about it.

Never before had any senior White House official physically intruded into CIA's Langley headquarters to argue with midlevel managers and analysts about unfinished work. But twice Vice President Cheney and Lewis Libby, his chief of staff, came to offer their opinions. Patrick Lang told me: "They looked disapproving, questioned the reports, and left an impression of what you're supposed to do. They would say: 'you haven't looked at the evidence.' The answer would be, those reports [from Iraqi exiles] aren't valid. The analysts would be told, you should look at this again.' Finally, people gave up. You learn not to contradict them."

The CIA had other visitors, too, according to Ray McGovern, former CIA chief for the Middle East. Newt Gingrich came, and Condi Rice, and, as for Cheney, "he likes the soup in the CIA cafeteria," McGovern jokes.

Meanwhile, senior intelligence officers were kept in the dark about the OSP. "I didn't know about its existence," said Thielman. "They were cherry-picking intelligence and packaging it for Cheney and Donald Rumsfeld to take to the president. That's the kind of rogue operation that peer review is intended to prevent."

The CIA director, George Tenet, for his part, opted to become a political advocate for Bush's brief rather than a protector of the intelligence community. On the eve of the congressional debate, in the space of only three weeks, the agency wrote a ninety-page national intelligence estimate justifying the administration's position on WMDs and scrubbed of all dissent. Once the document was declassified after the invasion, it became known that it contained forty caveats—including fifteen uses of *probably*, all of which had been removed from the previously published version. Tenet further ingratiated himself by remaining silent about the OSP. "That's totally unacceptable for a CIA director," said Thielman.

On February 5, 2003, Colin Powell presented evidence of WMDs before the United Nations. Cheney and Libby had tried to inject material from Iraqi exiles and the OSP into his presentation, but Powell rejected most of it. Yet, for the most important speech of his career, he refused to allow the presence of any analysts from his own intelligence agency. "He didn't have anyone from INR near him," said Thielman. "Powell wanted to sell a rotten fish. He had decided there was no way to avoid war. His job was to go to war with as much legitimacy as we could scrape up."

Powell ignored INR analysts' comments on his speech. Almost every piece of evidence he unveiled turned out later to be false.

This week, when Bush announced he would appoint an investigative commission, Powell offered a limited mea culpa at a meeting at the *Washington Post*. He said that if only he had known the intelligence, he might not have supported an invasion. Thus he began to show carefully calibrated remorse, to distance himself from other members of the administration and especially Cheney. Powell also defended his U.N. speech, claiming "it reflected the best judgments of all of the intelligence agencies."

Powell is sensitive to the slightest political winds, especially if they might affect his reputation. If he is a bellwether, will it soon be that every man must save himself?

The Madrid Express:
3/11 Meets 9/11

MARCH 18, 2004

WHEN TERRORIST BOMBS EXPLODED at the Atocha train station in Madrid on March 11, a date that resonated like a European September 11, politics on both sides of the Atlantic were thrown into turmoil. Spain's ruling conservative Popular party and the Bush administration instantly staked the Spanish election on the presumed identity of the terrorists.

The Spanish government had supported Bush's war in Iraq against the overwhelming opposition of Spanish public opinion. March 11, therefore, must not be September 11. The culprits must be Eta, the Basque separatist organization, not al Qaeda. The prime minister, José María Aznar, repeatedly called Spanish newspapers to insist that Eta was responsible. Within hours of the attack, George Bush and his secretary of state, Colin Powell, helpfully pointed their fingers at Eta. A day before the election, however, alleged terrorists linked to al Qaeda were arrested. The credibility of the government was in tatters, and it suffered a shattering defeat.

José Luis Rodríguez Zapatera, the new Socialist prime minister, immediately pledged his commitment to the war on terror while calling the war in Iraq a "disaster" and, for good measure, announcing: "I want Kerry to win." John Kerry, for his part, called for Zapatera to reconsider his decision to withdraw Spanish troops from Iraq. Each statement reflected a complex reconfiguring of politics after March 11. The crisis in the Western alliance, a reaction to Bush, was a new peril for Kerry to navigate.

On the eve of the Spanish election, Bush's first wave of campaign spots on television—featuring a flag-draped coffin at Ground Zero—had failed. By more than a two-to-one majority, voters felt the ad was inappropriate, and it was hastily withdrawn. Bush replaced it with a more menacing commercial. The ad claimed, falsely, that Kerry had a plan to raise taxes by $900 million. Then came a triptych of rapid images: a U.S. soldier—was he patrolling in Iraq?—a young man looking over his shoulder as he ran down a city street at night—was he a mugger or escaping an attack?—and a close-up of the darting eyes of a swarthy man—was he a terrorist? The voiceover: Kerry would "weaken America."

The images were racial and subliminal, intended to play on irrational fear. A Bush spokesman explained that the generic olive-skinned figure was a hired actor and wasn't an Arab. Through this literal-mindedness the Bush campaign tried to deflect criticism as it sought to sow apprehension about Kerry.

Though Kerry is the presumptive Democratic presidential nominee and has served in the Senate for nineteen years, he is not well known. Yet he is even with or ahead of Bush in the polls. For Bush, the next sixty days may be decisive. The elder Bush, lagging in 1988, waited until after the Republican convention in late summer to paint his opponent as a soft liberal, somehow un-American. This President Bush cannot wait.

On every issue of domestic concern, Kerry defeats Bush. Only on foreign policy does Bush hold sway, so he must heighten and reinforce that difference. Kerry must be weak, Bush strong. Thus a new Bush ad: jets take off from an aircraft carrier, a female soldier hugs her family, and the voiceover: "Kerry . . . wrong on defense." The ad claims that Kerry voted against an $87 billion post-invasion defense appropriation, failing to note, of course, that he had proposed linking it to rescinding Bush's tax cut for the wealthy.

After the Spanish election, the White House that had insisted that Eta and not al Qaeda was responsible for the Madrid bombing pivoted its argument. The Spanish vote was not a triumph of democracy, a revulsion against the political manipulation of terror. Instead it was now being construed as a victory for al Qaeda, a blow in the "ideological war on terrorism," as Anne Applebaum, an neoconservative editorial writer of the *Washington Post,* put it.

The Bush doctrine has evaporated. Whether it was ever a doctrine rather than a rationale for an already-planned invasion of Iraq is questionable. Certainly, the war in Afghanistan was a response to an attack on the United States, not a preemptive strike. Rejected now by a member state of NATO through its democratic process, the doctrine per se has no practical future as an instrument of foreign policy, if it ever did.

But the consequences of Bush remain center stage. As the arrogance of power increasingly leads to the dissolution of power, the "ideological war" becomes more furious. For the neoconservatives, the political meaning of 3/11 must be forced into the Procrustean bed of Bush's 9/11. Bush's campaign, after all, turns on the preemptive strike.

The Counterterrorism Czar
Comes In from the Cold

MARCH 25, 2004

ONE OF THE FIRST OFFICIAL ACTS of the current Bush administration was to downgrade the office of national coordinator for counterterrorism on the National Security Council, a position held by Richard Clarke. Clarke had served in the Pentagon and State Department under presidents Reagan and the elder Bush, and was the first person to hold the counterterrorism job created by President Clinton. Under Clinton, he was elevated to cabinet rank, which gave him a seat at the principals' meeting, the highest decision-making group for national security.

By removing Clarke from the table, Bush put him in a box where he could speak only when spoken to. No longer would his memos go to the president; instead, they had to pass through a chain of command that included National Security Adviser Condoleezza Rice and her deputy, Stephen Hadley, who bounced each of them back.

Terrorism was a Clinton issue: "soft" and obscure, having something to do with "globalization" and other trends ridiculed by the Republican Party platform. "In January 2001 the new administration really thought Clinton's recommendation that eliminating al Qaeda be one of their highest priorities, well, rather odd, like so many of the Clinton administration's actions, from their perspective," Clarke writes in his new book, *Against All Enemies*. When Clarke first met Rice and immediately raised the question of dealing with al Qaeda, she "gave me the impression she had never heard the term before."

The controversy raging over Clarke's book, and his testimony before the 9/11 Commission that Bush ignored warnings about terrorism that might have prevented the attacks, revolves around his singularly unimpeachable credibility. In response, Bush has launched an offensive against him, impugning his personal motives, saying he is a disappointed job hunter, publicity-mad, a political partisan, ignorant, irrelevant—and a liar.

Clarke's reputation in the Clinton White House was that he could be brusque and passionate but also calm and singleminded. He was a complete professional who was a master of the bureaucracy. He didn't suffer fools gladly, stood up to superiors, and didn't care who he alienated. His flaw was his indispensable virtue: he was direct and candid in telling the unvarnished truth.

But his account need not stand on his reputation alone. Clarke was not the only national security professional who spanned both the Clinton and Bush administrations. General Donald Kerrick served as deputy national security adviser under Clinton and remained on the NSC in the early Bush administration. He wrote his replacement, Stephen Hadley, a two-page memo. "It was classified," Kerrick told me. "I said they needed to pay attention to al Qaeda and counterterrorism. I said we were going to be struck again. They never once asked me a question, nor did I see them having a serious discussion about it. . . . I agree with Dick [Clarke] that they saw those problems through an Iraqi prism. But the evidence, the intelligence, wasn't there."

Rice now claims about terrorism that "we were at battle stations." But Bush is quoted by Bob Woodward in *Bush at War* as saying that before September 11, "I was not on point . . . I didn't feel that sense of urgency." Cheney alleges that Clarke was "out of the loop." But if he was, then the administration was either running a rogue operation or doing nothing, as Clarke testifies.

Bush protests now: "And had my administration had any information that terrorists were going to attack New York City on September 11, we would have acted." But he had plenty of information. The former deputy attorney general, Jamie Gorelick, a member of the 9/11 Commission who read the president's daily briefs, revealed in the hearings that the documents "would set your hair on fire" and that the intelligence warnings of al Qaeda attacks "plateaued at a spike level for months" before September 11. Bush is fighting public release of these PDBs, which would show whether he had marked them up and demanded action.

The administration's furious response to Clarke only underscores his book. Rice is vague, forgetful, and dissembling. Cheney is belligerent, certain, and bluffing. In Clarke's account, as in the memoir of the former treasury secretary, Paul O'Neill, Bush is disengaged, incurious, manipulated by those in the circle around him; he adopts ill-conceived strategies that he has played little or no part in preparing. Bush is the wizard behind the curtain, but in the White House, unlike Oz, it is others who create the special effects. Especially on terrorism and September 11, his White House is at battle stations to prevent the curtain from being pulled open.

The White House Has the Last Laugh

APRIL 1, 2004

WITHIN HOURS OF THE TESTIMONY of Richard Clarke, the former counterterrorism chief, before the 9/11 Commission, where Clarke discussed how resources spent on the Iraq war undermined the war on terrorism, President Bush acknowledged that Saddam Hussein's weapons of mass destruction—the rationale for the war—remained absent. Bush's admission took the form of a comic monologue before about a thousand formally attired members of the Radio and TV Correspondents' Association, gathered for its annual dinner. The lights dimmed, and Bush presented a slide show of himself peering out of windows and looking under furniture in the Oval Office. "Those weapons of mass destruction have got to be somewhere . . . nope, no weapons over there . . . maybe under here?"

With each gag, the press corps roared. Bush was acting as the college fraternity-house president he once was and the journalists as pledges eager for acceptance by the Big Man on Campus. "I'm the commander—see, I don't need to explain—I do not need to explain why I say things," Bush told Bob Woodward in *Bush at War*. "That's the interesting thing about being president."

The press corps didn't grasp that the joke was on them. The problem is not that Bush's jest was inappropriate and tasteless: the widow of David Bloom, an NBC reporter who died in Iraq, had tearfully preceded Bush on the platform. It is not that much of the media, including elements of the quality press, had been complicit in the choreographed disinformation campaign in the rush to war. Rather, it is that the press is accepting of Bush's radical undermining of the long-established arrangements of Washington, including the demotion of the press's own role by breaking the off-the-record rule in order to have a weapon to use against Clarke. The implicit deal that the press thought it had with the Bush White House, as with previous White Houses, has been broken unilaterally, like other policies.

The new rules of the game are that there are no rules of the game. In the preface of his book *Against All Enemies*, Clarke wrote that he expected

48

an assault on his reputation from the "Bush White House leadership" that was "adept at revenge."

Clarke had observed the politics of intimidation become standard operating procedure. The former ambassador Joseph Wilson, who, at the administration's behest, looked into the claim that Saddam was seeking uranium in Niger and concluded it was bogus, was subjected to a sustained attack that included revealing the identity of his wife, a covert CIA operative. When Paul O'Neill, a former secretary of the treasury, revealed that an invasion of Iraq was being pushed from the earliest days of the administration, he instantly became the target for personal vituperation. Richard Foster, the chief actuary for the Centers for Medicare and Medicaid Services, was threatened that if he told Congress the actual cost of Bush's Medicare bill while it was being considered, he would be fired. So Clarke knew the new rules.

Throughout the long day that ended with the president's WMD joke, the White House directed strikes on Clarke's integrity. It declassified an off-the-record background briefing given by Clarke in 2002, when he had been ordered to put a "positive spin," as he put it, on Bush's pre–September 11 terrorism record in response to a critical report in *Time* magazine. The White House press secretary took portions of the briefing out of context and read them aloud. Condoleezza Rice, the national security adviser whose neglect of terrorism was among Clarke's revelations, summoned reporters to her office to point to the background briefing and call his story "scurrilous."

While she was putting a stiletto into Clarke, her press office shuffled the background briefing paper to Fox News to broadcast as Clarke testified. Republican members of the 9/11 Commission waved the paper at him, and much time was taken up by his explanation of how, as a staffer, he had been acting properly, like a lawyer representing a client, and why his briefing was not at odds with his information now.

This selective declassification signaled to professionals in government that anything they said to reporters could be held against them if they ever contradicted the Bush line. Yet not one news organization tried to uphold the old rule by threatening to reveal sources of off-the-record briefings unless the White House reverted to the accepted convention that makes informed journalism possible.

The Clarke episode is symptomatic of a systematic abuse of power. Reality is raw and dangerous to report—better to laugh along.

The Road Map to Nowhere

APRIL 8, 2004

CONDOLEEZZA RICE is to be questioned in public hearings only about the Bush administration's policy on terrorism before September 11. But her negligence and incompetence encompass the entirety of the Bush foreign policy.

The story of Rice's role in the destruction of the Middle East peace process has never been told. Yet the pattern of her conduct is all of a piece with the disregard of terrorism despite all warnings before 9/11. The national-al security adviser is the central organizer of foreign policy for the president, and Rice quickly became one of President Bush's most trusted aides.

In January 2002, Rice launched a serious effort to restart the Middle East peace process. She hired Flynt Leverett, a foreign service officer on the policy planning staff of the State Department, to direct it. Rice told him she understood that the absence of a peace process was hurting the war on terrorism and that Leverett should propose any measures he thought necessary, regardless of political controversy. He developed a plan dealing with security, Palestinian political reform, and Jerusalem. Its core was essentially the same as the last peace proposal put forward by President Clinton. Rice rejected it as politically untenable for Bush, who would have been forced to confront Israel's prime minister, Ariel Sharon, to enact it.

On April 4, Bush delivered a speech calling for a "two-state" solution, but without any details, and sent his secretary of state, Colin Powell, to the region. Leverett traveled with him. Powell gained agreement for the basic outline of the original plan. But, just as he was to announce his breakthrough, Rice intervened, instructing him that he could not discuss any political process and that the whole burden of accountability must be put on the Palestinians and none on the Israelis.

Rice had crumbled in the face of internal political opposition from the neoconservative armada. "The neocons in the Pentagon and the vice president's office, plus Karl Rove's political shop, prevailed," Leverett told me. Undeterred, Leverett turned to work on what became known as "the road map." On July 31, the Jordanian foreign minister, Marwan Muasher, met

Rice to urge support for it. "Condi says no. All you get is a speech, no plan," said Leverett. The next day King Abdullah of Jordan came to see the president, bringing his foreign minister with him. "Condi had told the president nothing of her conversation," said Leverett, who was present. Bush instantly said of Abdullah's proposal: "Good idea, let's see what we can do on that." Leverett said, "That was the origin of the road map."

By November, the road map was ready. But Sharon opposed its public release, claiming that it would interfere with the upcoming Israeli election. Leverett argued to Rice: "We had promised to put it out. If we pull it now, we reverse a commitment and would be intervening in Israeli politics in another way. That argument was not appreciated by Condi. So they didn't put out the road map." It was only under pressure from Tony Blair, as a condition of his alliance on the eve of the Iraq invasion, that Bush announced the road map on March 14, 2003.

In June, Bush attended two summits on the road map, in Aqaba and Sharm el-Sheik, where he expressed commitment. He turned the project over to Rice, who never presented him with a plan for how to achieve it. "He said that Condi would ride herd on this process. She never even saddled up," said Leverett. Six months earlier, Rice had appointed the neoconservative Elliott Abrams as her Middle East coordinator on the National Security Council, and he threw up obstacles to prevent the road map from going forward. Bush, for his part, never followed up on his own rhetoric and was utterly absent from the policymaking. So Leverett decided he must quit: "I didn't want to stick around for a charade."

On terrorism, Rice insists Bush wanted a strategy rather than to be "swatting flies." But the strategy that lay on her desk unimplemented on September 11 was virtually the same as the one presented to her by the NSC counterterrorism chief, Richard Clarke, on January 25, 2001. On that fateful September 11, Rice was to deliver a speech on the administration priorities that stressed missile defense and not terrorism. Now she will not release the full text of that speech.

The story of the Middle East debacle, like that of the pre-9/11 terrorism fiasco, reveals the inner workings of Bush's White House: the president aggressive and manipulated, ignorant of his own policies and their consequences, negligent; the secretary of state proud, instinctively subordinate, constantly in retreat; the vice president a Cardinal Richelieu, the conniving head of a neoconservative cabal, the power behind the throne; the national security adviser seemingly open, even vulnerable, posing as the honest broker, but deceitful and derelict, an underhanded lightweight.

The President Goes Blank

APRIL 15, 2004

ON APRIL 21, 1961, President Kennedy held a press conference to answer questions on the disastrous Bay of Pigs invasion by Cuban exiles that he had approved. "There's an old saying," he said, "that victory has a hundred fathers and defeat is an orphan. . . . I am the responsible officer of the government and that is quite obvious."

On Wednesday, President Bush held only his third press conference and was asked three times whether he accepted responsibility for failing to act on warning before September 11. "I'm sure something will pop into my head here in the midst of this press conference with all the pressure of trying to come up with an answer, but it hadn't [sic] yet," he said. "I just haven't—you just put me under the spot here and maybe I'm not quick—as quick on my feet as I should be in coming up with one."

Bush's press conference was the culmination of his recent efforts to stanch the political wounds of his bleeding polls since the 9/11 Commission began public hearings and violence spiraled in Iraq. Bush had tried to divert blame by declaring that the August 6 memo he was forced to declassify at the commission's insistence contained no "actionable intelligence," even though it specifically mentioned the World Trade Center and Washington as targets.

Bush, in fact, does not read his president's daily briefs but has them orally summarized every morning by the CIA director, George Tenet. President Clinton, by contrast, read them closely and alone, preventing any aides from interpreting what he wanted to know firsthand. He extensively marked up his PDBs, demanding action on this or that. This contrast is almost certainly the likely reason the Bush administration withheld his memoranda from the 9/11 Commission.

"I know he doesn't read," one former Bush National Security Council staffer told me. Several other former NSC staffers corroborated this. It seems highly unlikely that he read the national intelligence estimate on weapons of mass destruction before the Iraq war, which consigned contrary evidence and caveats that undermined the case to footnotes and fine print. Nor is there any evidence that he read the State Department's seventeen-volume report, *The Future of Iraq*, warning of nearly all the postwar pitfalls that the United States has encountered, which was shelved by the neocons in the Pentagon and Vice President Cheney's office.

Nor was Bush aware of similar warnings urgently being sounded by the military's top strategic analysts. One monograph, *Reconstructing Iraq*, by the U.S. Army War College's Strategic Studies Institute, predicted in detail "possible severe security difficulties" and conflicts among Iraqis that U.S. forces "can barely comprehend." I have learned that it was suppressed by the Pentagon neocons and only released to U.S. Central Command after Senator Joseph Biden, the ranking Democrat on the Foreign Relations Committee, directly intervened. A revolt within the military against Bush is brewing. Many in the military's strategic echelon share the same feelings of being ignored and ill-treated by the administration that senior intelligence officers voice in private. "The Pentagon began with fantasy assumptions on Iraq and worked back," a strategist at the U.S. Army War College remarked to me.

As the iconic image of the war president has tattered, another picture has emerged. Bush appears as a passive manager who enjoys sitting atop a hierarchical structure, unwilling and unable to do the hard work necessary to run the largest enterprise in the world. He does not seem to absorb data unless it is presented in simple, clear fashion by people whose judgment he trusts. He is receptive to information that agrees with his point of view rather than information that challenges it. This bestows enormous power on his trusted interlocutors, who know and bolster his predilections.

At his press conference, Bush was a confusion of absolute confidence and panic. He jumbled facts and conflated threats, redoubling the vehemence of his incoherence at every mildly skeptical question. He attempted to create a false political dichotomy between "retreat" and his own vague and evolving position on Iraq, which now appears to follow Senator John Kerry's, of granting more authority to the United Nations and bringing in NATO.

The ultimate revelation was Bush's vision of a divinely inspired apocalyptic struggle in which he is the leader of a crusade bringing the Lord's "gift." "I also have this belief, strong belief that freedom is not this country's gift to the world. Freedom is the Almighty's gift to every man and woman in this world. And as the greatest power on the face of the earth we have an obligation to help the spread of freedom." But religious war is not part of official U.S. military doctrine.

The Silence of Colin Powell

APRIL 22, 2004

"History? We won't know," George Bush tells Bob Woodward. "We'll all be dead." But in his book *Plan of Attack,* Woodward's facts move the past from the shadows, adding significant new documentation to the story of the rush to war in Iraq.

The serious constitutional issues and governmental abuses, the methods and even the continuity of some personnel that Woodward catalogues evoke memories of the Reagan Iran-contra scandal. That involved a network of aides outsourcing U.S. foreign policy to circumvent the separation of powers: selling missiles to Iran to fund the Nicaraguan contras. President Bush and his war cabinet conceived the Iraq war in an apparent effort to evade constitutional checks and balances. In Iran-contra, the National Security Council, CIA, and Pentagon were stealthily exploited from within; in Iraq, they were abused from the top.

When the Iran-contra scandal was revealed, the Reagan administration was placed into receivership by the old Republican establishment. Neoconservatives and adventurers, criminal or not, were purged, from Elliott Abrams to Richard Perle. Now they are at the center of power.

Woodward reports that in July 2002 Bush ordered the use of $700 million to prepare for the invasion of Iraq, funds that had not been specifically appropriated by Congress, which alone holds that constitutional authority. No adequate explanation has been offered for what, strictly speaking, might well be an impeachable offense.

Woodward also reports that the battle plan was unfurled for Prince Bandar bin Sultan, the Saudi ambassador to the United States. It was stamped "Top Secret: Noforn"—that is, "no foreign," not to be seen by anyone but Americans with the highest security clearance. Following Bush's instructions, Vice President Cheney and Secretary of Defense Rumsfeld briefed Bandar, who responded by promising to lower oil prices just before the election. As we can now see, prices have skyrocketed, giving oil producers windfall profits upfront and ultimately exaggerating the political effect of any subsequent drop in prices.

While Bandar was treated as an ex officio member of the war cabinet, the secretary of state, Colin Powell, was kept in the dark. "Mr. President," the national security adviser, Condoleezza Rice, gently suggested, according to Woodward, "if you're getting to a place that you really think this might happen, you need to call Colin in and talk to him." So after Bandar had been told of the battle plan, Bush decided to inform his secretary of state. As a frequent squash-playing partner of the Saudi prince, he was bound to learn anyway.

Powell had sought to warn Bush on Iraq: if you break it, you own it. "Time to put your war uniform on," says Bush. Powell snaps to attention.

Powell is obviously Woodward's source. Powell believed the government had been seized by a "Gestapo office" of neoconservatives directed by Cheney. "It was a separate little government that was out there," writes Woodward of Powell's view. The only precedent was Iran-contra.

Powell was appalled by the mangling of intelligence as Cheney and the neocons made their case to an eager Bush and manipulated public opinion. But Powell had put on his uniform for his commander in chief. In the White House, his capitulation was greeted with a combination of glee and scorn. Powell would make the case before the world at the United Nations. Cheney's chief of staff, I. Lewis "Scooter" Libby, gave him a sixty-page brief that Powell dismissed as filled with "murky" intelligence. Powell went to CIA headquarters himself, where he discovered that "he could no longer trace anything because it had been 'masticated over in the White House so that the exhibits didn't match the words.'" He hastily constructed his own case, which turned out to be replete with falsehood.

Powell played the good soldier, not revealing his qualms and knowledge to the Congress or the American people. The most popular man in the country, he never used his inherent veto power to promote his position. Rather than fight his battles in earnest when it counted, before his army was put in harm's way, he chose to settle scores by speaking to Woodward.

Bush tells Woodward that he is "frightened" by detailed questions. He admires Cheney for not needing to explain himself in public. Pointedly, Bush says, unlike Tony Blair, "I haven't suffered doubt." Asked if he seeks advice from his father, the former president, Bush says: "He is the wrong father to appeal to in terms of strength. There is a higher Father that I appeal to."

Bush gazes upward for guidance, or turns to Cheney. Judgment Day may not come before election day. Here on earth, the Republican establishment that rescued Reagan after Iran-contra has become superannuated and powerless. There is no one to intervene.

Pulp Fictions

APRIL 29, 2004

PERHAPS THE MOST IMPORTANT DIVIDE in the presidential campaign is between fact and fiction. There are, of course, other sharp distinctions based on region and religiosity, guns and gays, abstinence and abortion. But were the election to be decided on domestic concerns alone, George Bush would be near certain to join the ranks of one-term presidents—like his father after the aura of the Gulf war evaporated.

But one year after Bush's triumphant May Day landing on the deck of the USS *Abraham Lincoln* and his appearance under a "Mission Accomplished" banner, his splendid little war has entered a Stalingrad-like phase of urban siege and house-to-house combat. April has been the bloodiest month by far, with 122 U.S. soldiers killed, compared with 73 last April, in the supposed last month of the war. The unending war has inspired Bush's backers to rally round the flag, redoubling their belief.

They believe in the cause as articulated by the vice president, Dick Cheney, this week in his speech at Westminster College in Fulton, Missouri, where Winston Churchill delivered his "iron curtain" oration. "You and I are living in such a time," a time of the "gravest of threats," said Cheney. Once again he explained the motive for the Iraq war, implicitly conflating Saddam Hussein with al Qaeda and impervious to the failure to discover WMD.

"His regime cultivated ties to terror," he said, "and had built, possessed, and used weapons of mass destruction." And Saddam "would still be in power," he continued, coming to the point of his allegory, if John Kerry, cast as Neville Chamberlain to Bush's Churchill, had had his way.

These misperceptions are pillars of Bush's support, according to a study by the University of Maryland: 57 percent of those surveyed "believe that before the war Iraq was providing substantial support to al Qaeda," and 45 percent "believe that evidence that Iraq was supporting al Qaeda has been found." Moreover, 65 percent believe that "experts" have confirmed that Iraq had WMD.

Among those who perceived experts as saying that Iraq had WMD, 72 percent said they would vote for Bush and 23 percent for Kerry. Among those who perceived experts as saying that Iraq had supported al Qaeda, 62 percent said they would vote for Bush and 36 percent for Kerry. The reason given by respondents for their views was that they had heard these claims from the Bush administration.

These political pulp fictions are embraced out of faith and fear. This is a classic case study in "the will to believe," as the American philosopher William James called it. The greater insecurity would be not to believe Bush. It would mean the president had lied on issues of national security. And how could the Iraq war be seen as a pure, moral choice once its premises had been shown to be false? The idea of proof has shifted from fact to fervor.

Kerry is attacked as an opponent of national security and therefore un-American. When Kerry committed the gaffe of uttering the truth that many world leaders secretly hope for his victory, he provided the Bush campaign with an opening. The secretary of commerce, Donald Evans, has repeatedly said that Kerry "looks French." The Republican house majority leader, Tom DeLay, begins every speech: "As John Kerry would say, bonjour."

The European mission this month of Senator Joseph Biden, a Democrat on the Foreign Relations Committee, is a telling if overlooked footnote to the campaign xenophobia. After meetings with Jacques Chirac and Tony Blair, he learned firsthand of the Bush administration's almost complete lack of consultation. Chirac offered first steps toward French assistance in Iraq, and Biden wrote Bush a letter spelling them out. Bush referred him to the national security adviser, Condoleezza Rice, who in turn politely listened and never responded.

Meanwhile, the Republican chair of the Foreign Relations Committee, Senator Richard Lugar, who has been granted just one meeting in the past year with the president, remarked to negligible press notice: "The diplomacy is deficient. By that I simply mean not many people agree with us, or like us, or are prepared to work with us. That will really have to change." A senate source told me: "The only hope for real internationalization is in regime change in the United States."

The brazen smears about Kerry's wounds and medals, his voting record on military programs as a senator, and his loyalty have been communicated by the Bush-Cheney campaign through an estimated $50 million in TV and radio advertising in less than sixty days in seventeen swing states. This storm of unremitting negativity has bolstered the faith of his supporters, tested by recent events, and has managed to maintain the contest at a draw.

The attacks against Kerry are a bodyguard of lies to protect the original ones that are the praetorian guard of Bush's presidency.

The Secrets of Abu Ghraib

MAY 6, 2004

IT WAS "UNACCEPTABLE" and "un-American," but was it torture? "My impression is that what has been charged thus far is abuse, which I believe technically is different from torture," said Donald Rumsfeld, the secretary of defense, on Tuesday. "I don't know if it is correct to say what you just said, that torture has taken place, or that there's been a conviction for torture. And therefore I'm not going to address the torture word."

He confessed he had still not read the March 9 report by Major General Antonio Taguba on "abuse" at the Abu Ghraib prison. Some highlights: "Pouring cold water on naked detainees; beating detainees with a broom handle and a chair; threatening male detainees with rape . . . sodomizing a detainee with a chemical light and perhaps a broom stick."

The same day that Rumsfeld added his contribution to the history of Orwellian statements by high officials, the Senate Armed Services Committee was briefed behind closed doors for the first time not only about Abu Ghraib but also about military and CIA prisons in Afghanistan. It learned of the deaths of twenty-five prisoners and the murder of two others in Iraq; it learned that private contractors were at the center of these lethal incidents and that no one had been charged. The senators were given no details about the private contractors. They might as well have been fitted with hoods.

Many of them, Democratic and Republican, were infuriated that there was no accountability and no punishment, and demanded a special investigation, but the Republican leadership quashed the proposal. The senators want Rumsfeld to testify in a public hearing, but he is resisting, and the Republican leaders are blocking the idea.

The Bush administration was well aware of the Taguba report but more concerned about its exposure than its contents. General Richard Myers, the chair of the Joint Chiefs of Staff, was dispatched to tell CBS News to suppress its story and the horrifying pictures. For two weeks, CBS's

60 Minutes II show complied, until it became known that the *New Yorker* magazine planned to publish excerpts of the report. Myers was then sent on to the Sunday morning news programs to explain, but under questioning he acknowledged that he had still not read the report he had tried to keep from the public for weeks.

President Bush, Condoleezza Rice, and other officials, unable to contain the controversy any longer, engaged in profuse apologies and scheduled appearances on Arab television. Still nobody responsible was fired. One of the administration's chief talking points was that the "abuse" was an aberration. But Abu Ghraib was a predictable consequence of the Bush administration imperatives and policies.

Bush has created what is in effect a gulag. It stretches from prisons in Afghanistan to Iraq, from Guantánamo Bay to secret CIA prisons around the world. There are perhaps ten thousand people being held in Iraq, one thousand in Afghanistan, and almost seven hundred in Guantánamo Bay, but no one knows the exact numbers. The law as it applies to them is whatever the executive deems necessary. There has been nothing like this system since the fall of the Soviet Union. The U.S. military embraced the Geneva Conventions after the Second World War because applying them to prisoners of war protects American soldiers. But the Bush administration, in an internal fight, trumped this argument by designating those at Guantánamo "enemy combatants." Rumsfeld extended this system— "a legal black hole," according to Human Rights Watch—to Afghanistan and then Iraq, openly rejecting the conventions.

Private contractors, according to the Taguba report, ordered U.S. soldiers to torture prisoners. Their presence in Iraq is a result of the Bush military strategy of invading with a relatively light force. Private contractors, who are not subject to Iraqi law or the U.S. military code of justice, have filled the gap. Now, there are an estimated twenty thousand of them on the ground in Iraq, a larger force than the British army.

It is not surprising that the spread of the insurgency in Iraq centers on these contractors: the four killed in Fallujah, and Abu Ghraib's interrogators. The Bush legal doctrine creates a system beyond law to defend the rule of law against terrorism; it defends democracy by inhibiting democracy. Law is there to constrain "evildoers." Who doubts our love of freedom?

But the arrogance of virtuous certainty masks the egotism of power. It is the opposite of American pragmatism, which always understands that knowledge is contingent, tentative, and imperfect. This is a conflict in the American mind between two claims on democracy: one with a sense of paradox, limits, and debate, the other purporting to be omniscient, even messianic, requiring no checks because of its purity, and contemptuous of accountability.

"This is the only one where they took pictures," I was told by Tom Malinowski, Washington advocate of Human Rights Watch, and a former staff member of the National Security Council. "This was not considered a debatable topic until people had to stare at the pictures."

The American Military Coup of 2012

MAY 13, 2004

DONALD RUMSFELD told George Bush in February about torture at the Abu Ghraib military prison in Iraq. From the limited details Rumsfeld recalled of that meeting, it can be deduced that Bush gave no orders, insisted on no responsibility, did not ask to see the report the military had already commissioned from Major General Antonio Taguba. If there are exculpatory facts, Rumsfeld has failed to mention them.

For decades, Rumsfeld has had a reputation as a great white shark of the bureaucratic seas: sleek, fast-moving, and voracious. As counselor to Richard Nixon during the impeachment crisis, his deputy was the young Dick Cheney, and together they helped to right the ship of state under Gerald Ford.

Here they were given a misleading gloss as moderates; competence at handling power was confused with pragmatism. Cheney became the most hard-line of congressmen, and Rumsfeld informed acquaintances that he was always more conservative than they imagined. One lesson they seem to have learned from the Nixon debacle was ruthlessness. His collapse confirmed in them a belief in the imperial presidency based on executive secrecy. One gets the impression that, unlike Nixon, they would have burned the White House tapes.

Under Bush, the team of Cheney and Rumsfeld filled the top rungs of government, drawing staff from the neoconservative cabal and infusing their hard temperaments with ideological imperatives. The unvarnished will to power took on a veneer of ideas and idealism. Iraq was not a cause of vengeance or power, but the cause of democracy and human rights.

The fate of the neoconservative project depends on Rumsfeld. If he were to go, so would his deputy, the neoconservative Robespierre, Paul Wolfowitz. Also threatened would be the cadres who stovepiped the disinformation that the neoconservative darling Ahmed Chalabi produced to manipulate public opinion about Iraq before the war. In his Senate testimony last week, Rumsfeld explained that the government asking the press not to report Abu Ghraib "is not against our principles. It is not suppression of the news." War is peace.

Six National Guard soldiers from a Maryland unit who treated Abu Ghraib as a playpen of pornographic torture have been designated as scapegoats. Will the show trials of these working-class antiheroes put an end to any inquiries about the chain of command? In an extraordinary editorial, the *Army Times*, which had not previously ventured into such controversy, declared that "the folks in the Pentagon are talking about the wrong morons. . . . This was not just a failure of leadership at the local command level. This was a failure that ran straight to the top. Accountability here is essential—even if that means relieving leaders from duty in a time of war."

William Odom, a retired general and former member of the National Security Council who is now at the Hudson Institute, a conservative think tank, reflects a wide swath of opinion in the upper ranks of the military. "It was never in our interest to go into Iraq," he told me. It is a "diversion" from the war on terrorism; the rationale for the Iraq war (finding WMD) is "phony"; the U.S. Army is overstretched and being driven "into the ground"; and the prospect of building a democracy is "zero." In Iraqi politics, he says, "Legitimacy is going to be tied to expelling us. Wisdom in military affairs dictates withdrawal in this situation. We can't afford to fail, that's mindless. The issue is how we stop failing more. I am arguing a strategic decision."

One high-level military strategist told me that Rumsfeld is "detested," and that "if there's a sentiment in the army it is: Support our troops—impeach Rumsfeld."

The Council on Foreign Relations has been showing old movies with renewed relevance to its members. *The Battle of Algiers,* depicting the nature and costs of a struggle with terrorism, is the latest feature. The seething in the military against Bush and Rumsfeld might prompt a showing of *Seven Days in May,* about a coup staged by a right-wing general against a weak liberal president, an artifact of the conservative hatred directed at President Kennedy in the early sixties.

In 1992, General Colin Powell, chair of the Joint Chiefs of Staff, awarded the prize for his strategy essay competition at the National Defense University to Lieutenant Colonel Charles Dunlap for "The Origins of the American Military Coup of 2012." Dunlap's cautionary tale imagined an incapable civilian government creating a vacuum that draws a competent military into a coup that proves disastrous for democracy. The military, of course, is bound to uphold the Constitution. But Dunlap wrote: "The catastrophe that occurred on our watch took place because we failed to speak out against policies we knew were wrong. It's too late for me to do any more. But it's not for you."

"The Origins of the American Military Coup of 2012" is today circulating among top U.S. military strategists. Donald Rumsfeld has a new war on his hands—the U.S. officer corps has turned on the government.

The Holy Warrior

MAY 20, 2004

SAVING GENERAL BOYKIN seemed like a strange sideshow last October. After it was revealed that the deputy undersecretary of defense for intelligence had been regularly appearing at evangelical revivals preaching that the United States was in a holy war as a "Christian nation" battling "Satan," the furor was quickly calmed.

Donald Rumsfeld explained that Lieutenant General William G. "Jerry" Boykin was exercising his rights as a citizen: "We're a free people." President Bush declared that Boykin "doesn't reflect my point of view or the point of view of this administration." Bush's commission on public diplomacy had reported that in nine Muslim countries, just 12 percent of those polled believed that "Americans respect Arab/Islamic values." The Pentagon announced that its inspector general would investigate Boykin, though he has yet to report.

Boykin was not removed or transferred. At that moment, he was at the heart of a secret operation to "Gitmo-ize" the Abu Ghraib prison (Guantánamo Bay is known as Gitmo). He had flown to Guantánamo, where he met Major General Geoffrey Miller, in charge of Camp X-Ray. Boykin, acting on instructions from Rumsfeld, ordered Miller to fly to Iraq and extend X-Ray methods to the prison system there.

Boykin was recommended to his position by his record in the elite Delta forces: he was a commander in the failed effort to rescue U.S. hostages in Iran, tracked the drug lord Pablo Escobar in Colombia, advised the botched attack on barricaded cultists in Waco, Texas, and lost eighteen men in Somalia trying to capture a warlord in the notorious "Black Hawk Down" fiasco of 1993.

Boykin told an evangelical gathering last year how the Somalia incident fostered his spiritual crisis. "There is no God," he said. "If there was a God, he would have been here to protect my soldiers." But he was thunderstruck by the insight that his battle with the warlord was between good and evil, between the true God and the false one. "I knew that my God was bigger than his. I knew that my God was a real God and his was an idol."

Boykin was the action-hero sidekick of his boss, Stephen Cambone, a conservative defense intellectual appointed to the new post of undersecretary of intelligence. Cambone is universally despised by the officer corps for his arrogant, abrasive, and dictatorial style and regarded as the personal symbol of Rumsfeldism. A former senior Pentagon official told me of a conversation with a three-star general, who remarked: "If we were being overrun by the enemy and I had only one bullet left, I'd use it on Cambone."

Cambone set about cutting the CIA and the State Department out of the war on terror, but he had no knowledge of special operations. For these, the rarefied civilian relied on the gruff soldier Boykin—a melding of "ignorance and recklessness," as a military intelligence source told me.

Just before Boykin was put in charge of the hunt for Osama bin Laden and then inserted into Iraqi prison reform, he was a circuit rider for the religious right. He allied himself with a small group called the Faith Force Multiplier that advocates applying military principles to evangelism. Its manifesto, "Warrior Message," summons "warriors in this spiritual war for souls of this nation and the world."

Around the country Boykin staged a slide show that featured pictures of Osama bin Laden and Saddam Hussein. "Satan wants to destroy this nation, he wants to destroy us as a nation, and he wants to destroy us as a Christian army," he preached. They "will only be defeated if we come against them in the name of Jesus." It was the reporting of his remarks at a revival meeting in Oregon that made them briefly the subject of controversy.

There can be little doubt that he envisages the global war on terror as a crusade. With the Geneva Conventions deleted, biblical law supplants international law. Boykin is in God's chain of command. President Bush, he told an Oregon congregation last June, is "a man who prays in the Oval Office." And the president, too, is on a divine mission. "George Bush was not elected by a majority of the voters in the U.S. He was appointed by God."

Boykin is not alone in his belief that Bush is God's anointed warrior against evildoers. Before his 2000 campaign, Bush confided to a leader of the religious right: "I feel like God wants me to run for president. . . . I sense my country is going to need me. Something is going to happen."

Michael Gerson, Bush's chief speechwriter, tells colleagues that on September 20, 2001, after Bush delivered his speech to the Congress declaring a war on terror, he called Gerson to thank him for writing it. "God wants you here," Gerson says he told the president. And he says that Bush replied: "God wants us here."

But it's Bush who wants Rumsfeld, Cambone, and Boykin here.

Riding the Trojan Horse

MAY 27, 2004

AT A CONSERVATIVE THINK TANK in downtown Washington, and across the Potomac at the Pentagon, FBI agents have begun paying quiet calls on prominent neoconservatives in connection with an investigation of potential espionage, according to intelligence sources. Who gave Ahmed Chalabi classified information about the plans of the U.S. government and military?

The Iraqi neocon favorite, tipped to lead his liberated country after the invasion, has been identified by the CIA and Defense Intelligence Agency as an Iranian double agent, passing secrets to that citadel of the "axis of evil" for decades. All the while the neocons cosseted, promoted, and paid more than $30 million to the George Washington manqué of Iraq. In return, he fed them a steady diet of disinformation, and in the run-up to the war he sent various exiles to nine nations' intelligence agencies to spread falsehoods about weapons of mass destruction. If the administration had wanted other material to provide a rationale for invasion, no doubt that would have been fabricated to order. Either Chalabi perpetrated the greatest con since the Trojan horse, or he was the agent of influence for the most successful intelligence operation conducted by Iran, or both.

The CIA and other U.S. agencies had long ago decided that Chalabi was a charlatan, so their dismissive and correct analysis of his lies prompted their suppression by the Bush White House. In place of the normal channels of intelligence vetting, a jerry-rigged system was hastily constructed, running from the Office of the Vice President to the newly created Office of Special Plans inside the Pentagon, staffed by fervent neocons. The CIA director, George Tenet, possessed with the survival instinct of the career staffer, ceased protecting the sanctity of his agency and cast in his lot with them. The secretary of state, Colin Powell, resistant internally but overcome, decided to become the campaign's most ardent champion, unveiling a series of neatly manufactured lies before the United Nations.

Last week, Powell declared "it turned out that the sourcing was inaccurate and wrong and, in some cases, deliberately misleading. And for that I'm disappointed, and I regret it." But who had "deliberately" misled him? He did not say. Now the FBI is investigating espionage, fraud and, by implication, treason.

A former staff member of the Office of Special Plans and a currently serving Defense Department official, two of those said to be questioned by the FBI, are considered witnesses, at least for now. Higher figures are under suspicion. Were they witting or unwitting? If those who are being questioned turn out to be misleading the investigators, they could be charged with perjury and obstruction of justice. For them, the Watergate principle applies: it's not the crime, it's the cover-up.

The espionage investigation into the neocons' relationship with Chalabi is only one of the inquiries engulfing the Bush administration. In his speech to the Army War College on May 24, Bush blamed the Abu Ghraib torture scandal on "a few American troops." In other words, there was no chain of command. But the orders to use the abusive techniques came from the secretary of defense, Donald Rumsfeld.

The trials and investigations surrounding Abu Ghraib raise the question of whether it was an extension of the far-flung gulag operating outside the Geneva Conventions that has been built after September 11. The fallout from the Chalabi affair has also implicated the nation's newspaper of record, the *New York Times,* which yesterday published an apology for running numerous stories containing disinformation that emanated from Chalabi and those in the Bush administration who were funneling his fabrications. The *Washington Post,* which published editorials and several columnists trumpeting Chalabi's talking points, has yet to acknowledge the extent to which it was deceived.

Washington, just weeks ago in the grip of neoconservative orthodoxy, an absolute belief in Bush's inevitability and righteousness, is being ripped apart by investigations. Things fall apart: the military, loyal and lumbering, betrayed and embittered; the general in the field, General Ricardo Sanchez, disgraced; the intelligence agencies abused and angry, their retired operatives plying their craft with the press corps, leaking dangerous truths; the press, hesitating and wobbly, investigating its own falsehoods; the neocons, publicly redoubling defense of their hero and deceiver Chalabi, privately squabbling, anxiously awaiting the footsteps of FBI agents; Colin Powell, once the most acclaimed man in America, embarked on an endless quest to restore his reputation, damaged above all by his failure of nerve; everyone in the line of fire motioning toward the chain of command, spiraling upward and sideways, until the finger-pointing forms a phalanx directed at the hollow crown.

The Specter of Vietnam

JUNE 3, 2004

"SHOCK AND AWE" was more than the first phase of the invasion of Iraq. It was the premise of Bush's foreign policy. Fear of unrivaled power would prompt the dominoes to fall. The triumph of Iraqi democracy, a beacon to the Arab world, would refute argument and opposition.

On this gamble rested the entire edifice of Bush's policy. From the "cakewalk" would follow the collapse of Iranian influence, the rescue of Saudi Arabia from radical Islamist threat, Palestinian quiescence and instant solution of the Middle East crisis, the rapid spread of democracy across the former Ottoman Empire, the fervent gratitude of Iraqis as the United States withdrew its military forces (leaving the leader of "free Iraq," the former exile Ahmad Chalabi, in charge), and the reduction of the French to anxious waiters seeking only to please Bush with his order.

Now the FBI investigates neoconservatives in the Pentagon to discover who may have given secret U.S. intelligence to Chalabi that he allegedly passed to the Iranians. The Iraqi Governing Council, a U.S. creation, has shed Chalabi and transformed itself into the interim government, hoping that its new identity will lend it a mask of legitimacy. Al Qaeda has found fresh fields for its deadly work. The Saudis cannot protect Western businesspeople from terrorism. The Middle East peace process is in ruins. The U.S. casualty count reached and then exceeded eight hundred dead soldiers on Memorial Day. The French case that there was not a WMD threat, and that invading Iraq would lead to fragmentation of the country and trigger more terrorism, has been vindicated.

Bush's emissaries cannot decide whether Iraq can be a democracy or at best a warlord state like Afghanistan. They plead before the United Nations, a forum they once spurned, for symbolic justification. Meanwhile, Bush has launched a month of European travel, less diplomacy than a tableau vivant of international cooperation that, on his departure from the stage, will instantly dissolve into grim realpolitik. As polls show him at his low ebb, he hopes that the American public will accept the illusion as reality and reject the reality as illusion.

At the United Nations, the United States has proposed a resolution whose only substantive element is obviously meaningless. No nation that is not already in Iraq will contribute troops to a multinational force. The rest is window dressing. Having disdained the United Nations at the start and failed to protect the U.N. mission in Baghdad, which was blown up last August with seventeen killed, the Bush administration now desperately clings to U.N. involvement as a fig leaf of internationalism. Bush even claimed that the U.N. representative in Iraq, Lakhdar Brahimi, was the "quarterback" for choosing the new Iraqi prime minister and president, and that Bush played "zero" role.

In truth, according to U.N. sources, Iraqis on the Governing Council seeking to perpetuate their power outmaneuvered Brahimi. Paul Bremer, the head of the Coalition Provisional Authority, announced the new prime minister before Brahimi had been informed, an extension of the doctrine of preemption. Then Brahimi was sidelined again in the selection of the president. Presented with this fait accompli, the U.N. sources say, he had to accept it or else strip the proceedings of any remnant of legality they possessed. "Once it was done, it was done," a senior official at the U.N. told me. The United Nations plans for no central part in the new Iraq except a small mission performing humanitarian work that will be ringed by Gurkhas.

At home and abroad, Bush is investing his rhetoric about the "clash of ideologies" and "global war" with historical analogies. On his European visits, Bush will compare Iraq to rebuilding Germany and Japan after the Second World War. He will raise the specter of the communist threat faced down by the West in the Cold War. He will contrast Nazi atrocities to Islamist terrorism. He has even said that he will explain to Europeans that Iraq is like the United States before its Constitutional Convention: "I will remind them that the articles of confederation was a rather bumpy period for American democracy." But missing are analogous figures to George Washington, Benjamin Franklin, and James Madison.

Bush's principal analogy conflates al Qaeda and Saddam Hussein into a combined threat of "weapons of mass destruction" and a "totalitarian political ideology" that is "not an expression of religion," as he explained in his speech before the Army War College on May 24. This is a world war of "two visions" that first "clashed in Afghanistan" and "have now met in Iraq."

It was in this speech that he proposed tearing down and replacing the Abu Ghraib prison, despite having neglected to provide for the replacement in his budget. The grand gesture was widely reported, the grubby absence of funding little noticed. By means of a few words, Abu Ghraib was transformed at least for a moment into a gleaming Potemkin village.

Prophetically, on the eve of Bush's appearance at the Army War College, its Strategic Studies Institute released a report, *Vietnam and Iraq: Differences, Similarities and Insights,* observing the similarities as failures of strategy, maintaining public support, and nation building. It also noted: "Prospects for creating a stable, prosperous, and democratic Iraq are problematic, and observers and decision makers should not be misled by false analogies to American state-building success in Germany and Japan after World War II."

"They haven't known what they've been doing since the statue of Saddam came down," a military strategist at the Army War College told me. "Bush's speech was a vision speech with no connection to facts on the ground. That seems to be the limit of his understanding and ability. Even Vietnam doesn't look so bad in retrospect." But Bush will not make reference to "Vietnam and Iraq" in Europe.

The Reagan Legacy

JUNE 10, 2004

RONALD REAGAN'S PRESIDENCY collapsed at the precise moment on November 25, 1986, when he appeared without notice in the White House briefing room, introduced his attorney general, Edwin Meese, and instantly departed from the stage. Meese announced that funds raised by members of the National Security Council and others by selling arms to Iran had been used to aid the Nicaraguan contras. Antiterrorism laws and congressional resolutions had been willfully violated. Eventually eleven people were convicted of felonies. In less than a week, Reagan's approval rating plunged from 67 percent to 46 percent, the greatest and quickest decline ever for a president.

On December 17, 1986, William Casey, the director of the CIA, was scheduled to testify before the Senate Intelligence Committee. But he collapsed into a coma, suffering from brain cancer, never to recover. Lieutenant Colonel Oliver North, Casey's action officer on the NSC, explained to a select congressional investigation that Casey had been the mastermind in creating an "overseas entity . . . self-financing, independent," that would conduct "U.S. foreign policy" as a "stand-alone." Called the "Enterprise," it was the apotheosis of the Reagan doctrine, waging a global war against communism.

The hard-line secretary of defense, Caspar Weinberger, and his neoconservative underlings were summarily dismissed, the NSC purged. "Let Reagan be Reagan," had long been the cry of conservatives. Now they screamed that Reagan was either being held prisoner or had sold out.

In interviews with investigators, Reagan said he couldn't recall what had happened. But he retained the utopianism and idealism that had propelled him from left-wing liberal in Hollywood to right-wing man on horseback, switching his ideologies but never his temperament.

At his first meeting with Mikhail Gorbachev in 1985, Reagan had perplexed him by talking about how they might work together if there were an invasion of aliens from outer space. Reagan had got his idea from a 1951 science fiction movie in which an alien warns of earth's destruction if nuclear weapons are not abolished.

At the Reykjavik summit in October 1986, Reagan had agreed to eliminate all nuclear weapons (to the consternation of his advisers) until Gorbachev insisted that testing for the Star Wars missile defense shield be suspended. Two of Reagan's utopian dreams collided. But after the exposure of the Iran-contra scandal, Gorbachev dropped the objection to Star Wars. Instead, he crafted a practical arms reduction agreement, the Intermediate Nuclear Forces Treaty. And, despite opposition from conservatives, Reagan seized on it.

With script in hand, Reagan was Reagan again. In September 1987, he addressed the United Nations General Assembly: "I occasionally think how our differences worldwide would vanish if we were facing an alien threat from outside this world." That December, Gorbachev came to the White House to sign the treaty. Then, in June 1988, Reagan went to Moscow, where he declared that "of course" the Cold War was over and that his famous reference to the "evil empire" was from "another time."

Reagan did not bring about the downfall of the Soviet Union. But he lent support to the liberalizing reform that hastened the end. In reaching out to Gorbachev, Reagan blithely discarded the right-wing faith that totalitarian communism was unchangeable and that only rollback, not containment and negotiation, would lead to its demise.

Reagan was acutely self-conscious on the matter of his about-face, and on his trip to Moscow he explained it. "In the movie business actors often get what we call typecast," he said. "Well, politics is a little like that too. So I've had a lot of time and reason to think about my role."

Reagan's embrace of Gorbachev rescued his own political standing. The recovery of his approval rating to the midfifties was essential to his vice president's presidential ambitions, for the elder Bush was moon to Reagan's sun. Yet Bush distanced himself, adopting the "realist" view that Reagan suffered from "euphoria" and that nothing fundamental in the world was changing.

Now, George W. Bush eulogizes Reagan, who died on June 5, as his example. Bush has his own doctrine, a Manichean battle with evildoers, and an army of neoconservatives to lend complex rationalizations to his simplifications. Yet Reagan was saved by the wholesale firing of the neoconservatives, the rejection of conservative dogma, and a deliberate strategy to transcend his old typecasting. This transformation is why he rose above his ruin, and rides, even in death, into the sunset of a happy Hollywood ending.

Reagan's Funeral and Clinton's Portrait

JUNE 17, 2004

TIME STOOD STILL. It was a late gray morning in Washington, covered with a light mist, as Ronald Reagan's funeral cortege rode slowly up Embassy Row to the National Cathedral. For a full week, the business of government ceased, the political campaign was suspended, and the relentless momentum of negative stories undermining the Bush administration skidded to a halt.

Tributes to Reagan filled the airwaves. Actual history was relegated to the back pew. Nostalgia was always the aesthetic of Reaganism—morning again for small-town life, a dream of restoring an illusory, idealized past that would magically reappear if only we believed. Reagan's scenario of bucolic paradise was unlike his own small-town upbringing, where his Irish Catholic, alcoholic father was the town liberal and Democrat who did not echo the boosterism of the Republican Protestant Midwest of the 1920s, and whose chronic unemployment was resolved only by a government job with the advent of the New Deal. Nor was the small town Reagan imagined like the one of *Kings Row,* his greatest film, in which he is literally sliced apart in its vicious undercurrents of class and intolerance. Nor was it the Babylon of Hollywood, where he lived most of his adult life.

Spurning reality, President Bush sought to enter the warm haze of Reagan's evanescent and static world. Nostalgia for Reagan became Bush's motif. His campaign website turned itself entirely into a Reagan memorial.

Bush presented himself as the political son Reagan never had. His war on terrorism and in Iraq became the equivalent of Reagan's Cold War. Ken Mehlman, the president's campaign manager, told an Iowa Republican Party convention that Reagan had become a hovering angel. "Every time an American soldier, sailor, airman or marine risks his or her life to ensure our security and peace, Ronald Reagan will be there," he said.

Reagan, though he once told Prime Minister Yitzhak Shamir of Israel that he had personally liberated concentration camps, in fact served during the Second World War at the Hal Roach Studios (known as Fort

Wacky) in Culver City, California, making motivational movies such as *This Is the Army.* But Reagan's career had nevertheless come to exemplify the epigram of the classic John Ford Western, *The Man Who Shot Liberty Valance:* "When the legend becomes the fact, print the legend."

Then time started again. The campaign that had nestled in Reagan's shadow found itself in the shadow of another president. On Monday, June 14, Bill Clinton and Hillary Clinton, now a U.S. senator, returned to the White House for the unveiling of their official portraits. They, too, had been at the Reagan funeral in the cathedral, and afterward had lunch with Tony and Cherie Blair, the old friends meeting out of the limelight to discuss the future.

I joined a boisterous reunion of more than two hundred former cabinet members, advisers, staffers, friends, and Harvey Weinstein, the movie mogul of Miramax. Hardly any of us had set foot in the White House since Clinton departed. We felt completely at home, yet out of place. We had worked here every day for years and were now infidels in the temple.

The ceremony was like a Christmas truce in the trenches during the First World War. Bush, who had previously denigrated his predecessor, now graciously paid tribute, listing attributes that inevitably created comparison with himself but were different from Reagan's: "A deep and far-ranging knowledge of public policy, a great compassion for people in need, and the forward-looking spirit that Americans like in a president."

Once the life-size regal portraits were unveiled, Clinton spoke of his "mixed feelings" about his induction into the presidential portrait gallery. He recalled once meeting a little boy who had said, "Are you really president? But you're not dead yet." Obliquely, but pointedly, Clinton remarked that "politics is noble work" and that we need to "return to vigorous debate about who's right and wrong, not who's good and bad."

As we made our way along the receiving line from the East Room, I noticed that the Georgia O'Keefe painting that Hillary had hung, the first and only twentieth-century work of modern art in the White House, was gone. In its place was a nostalgic scene of the Old West.

President Bush did not stay to receive us. He left the task of shaking hands and posing for photographs with Bill and Hillary and their crowd to his wife, Laura. When the line ended, the former president and first lady met on the north portico with dozens of members of the permanent working White House staff. Bill was getting ready for his interviews about his memoir, which will be published next week; he was bottled up and eager for new campaigns. Hillary went back up to Capitol Hill to prepare, as a member of the Senate Armed Services Committee, for more hearings on torture at Abu Ghraib. And while the portraits were unveiled, Bush's press secretary, Scott McClellan, announced the rejection of Nancy Reagan's plea for the administration to reverse its policy inhibiting research on stem cell research, which might find a cure for the Alzheimer's disease that afflicted President Reagan. "The policy," McClellan said, "remains the same." Nostalgia is swept away; the clock ticks; the truce is over.

Cheney's Mask Slips

JULY 1, 2004

IN WASHINGTON, political identities cultivated over decades can crumble in a minute. Vice President Dick Cheney presides under the Constitution as president of the Senate and is addressed as "Mr. President," but the former Congressman Cheney is not a man of the Senate. (The Senate considers itself as distant from the House of Representatives as the Metropolitan Club is from the Bullfeathers saloon near the House side of Capitol Hill.)

Cheney earned his executive-branch credentials as President Gerald Ford's wunderkind chief of staff and the elder Bush's secretary of defense, but on the Hill he is remembered as the former House Republican whip during the Reagan period, his only previous elected position. In the House, the Republicans were then in the minority, and Cheney was the driver behind the scenes of the hard right, protector of obstreperous young reactionaries like Newt Gingrich, yet still presentable to the broader establishment as a respectable, saturnine figure. Those who watched him operate in the House saw through his veneer, but he elevated himself by advancing the persona of the statesman.

The self-control that had served him so long broke down in public on June 22, during a photo session on the floor of the Senate. As Cheney was posing with members, Senator Patrick Leahy ambled over. Leahy, the ranking Democrat on the Judiciary Committee, had recently been critical, along with other Democrats, of no-bid contracts for reconstruction in Iraq granted to Halliburton, the company Cheney had run and in which he still holds stock options and receives deferred compensation (despite his prior claims to the contrary). "Go fuck yourself," the vice president greeted him.

Cheney's spokesman appeared to deny that those words had been spoken: "That doesn't sound like language the vice president would use." But Cheney raced onto Fox News to congratulate himself on his bold emotional authenticity. "I expressed myself rather forcefully, felt better after I

79

had done it." Then he elaborated that his ejaculation was an administration policy: "I think that a lot of my colleagues felt that what I had said badly needed to be said, that it was long overdue." Leahy's seeming civility, he explained, was just a charade: "I didn't like the fact that . . . he wanted to act like, you know, everything's peaches and cream."

A main source of Cheney's effectiveness and image of competence has been his ability to avoid putting his cards on the table. But in a moment of pique, he dropped the entire deck. His game face vanished, and his malicious streak broke through. Cheney's usual blandness had suggested he was deliberate, experienced, and imperturbable. In the first Bush administration, victory in the Gulf war solidified that reputation. When the president was defeated, Cheney was not. He emerged from those ashes unscathed.

Just as the elder Bush picked someone who might have been one of his sons, the younger Bush chose a version of his father. Dan Quayle was light as a feather, another scion from a wealthy Republican family, the vice president as understudy. Cheney was appointed the mentor of the Bush family's Prince Hal and widely believed to represent the father's realism. In 2000, put in charge of selecting George W. Bush's running mate, he collected the dossiers of potential candidates and then chose himself. Asked who vetted Cheney's financial records, Karen Hughes, Bush's communications aide, replied: "Just as with other candidates, Secretary Cheney is the one who handled that."

Much of Bush's executive branch has been concentrated in Cheney. He has been as powerful as Quayle was irrelevant. It was Cheney who said to the U.N. weapons inspector Hans Blix as he embarked on his mission to Iraq: "We will not hesitate to discredit you"; Cheney who personally tried to force the CIA to give credence to Ahmed Chalabi's fabricated and false evidence on WMD; Cheney who, along with Secretary of Defense Donald Rumsfeld (to whom he was deputy in the Nixon White House), undermined Secretary of State Colin Powell at every turn. And it is Cheney who is the neoconservatives' godfather.

It is worth remembering that Cheney's link to the neocons largely developed after the last Bush administration and was arranged by his wife, Lynne Cheney, cultural warrior on the right, former chair of the National Endowment for the Humanities, and resident scholar at the American Enterprise Institute, the principal neocon think tank. Even before his outburst, Cheney had come to stand for special interests, secrecy, and political coercion. Under the stress of Bush's falling polls, he cracked.

Bush still strains to project optimism and cast the Democrats as demagogic pessimists. His campaign this week produced a commercial, "John Kerry's coalition of the wild-eyed," that featured snippets of Al Gore, Howard Dean, Michael Moore, and Kerry criticizing Bush. Interspersed among the Democrats was a frothing and saluting Adolf Hitler. Bush's apparent remake of the "Springtime for Hitler" number from Mel Brooks's *The Producers* is partly an attempt to counter the box-office success of Michael Moore's *Fahrenheit 9/11*. Running against Hitler is also an effort to transform the sober Kerry, not Cheney, into the "wild-eyed" threat.

Perhaps the grandest political gesture Bush could make would be to drop Cheney. When Cheney's mask drops, he reveals not only his own face but also Bush's. "The idea of dumping Cheney is nuts, makes no sense," one of Cheney's political advisers told me. "One of the reasons he's there is they don't have someone to anoint as a successor. Dumping Cheney would be seen as a sign of weakness. Cheney is very popular in the party." The Bush campaign's premise depends on turning out the maximum Republican vote. Bush can no more repudiate Cheney than he can repudiate himself. Cheney will never hear from Bush the words he hurled at Leahy.

The Senate's Da Vinci Code

JULY 15, 2004

THE SENATE INTELLIGENCE COMMITTEE report is the Da Vinci code of the Iraq war. Some of the clues are in plain sight, but unless one knows how to read them, they remain cryptic. Deletions, covering one-fifth of the report, and omissions, stretching endlessly, are as significant as what's included. The storyline is jumbled into incoherence, the main characters are often spectral, and it's all extremely dangerous.

By virtue of a deal struck before the committee investigated, the belligerent Republican majority persuaded timorous Democrats to separate the inquiry into halves, leaving the question of the Bush administration's culpability for a second report, which almost certainly will not be filed until after the election, if ever. This unholy arrangement enabled the report to put the burden of blame on the CIA. For months, Bush and his national security team escalated its rhetoric about Iraqi weapons of mass destruction. But there was no national intelligence estimate (NIE) until demands by Democratic senators on the Intelligence Committee forced its writing.

Most such assessments take months to assemble, but this one was slapped together in about three weeks. "Most of the major key judgments in the intelligence community's October 2002 NIE, *Iraq's Continuing Programs for Weapons of Mass Destruction,* were either overstated, or were not supported by the underlying intelligence reporting," the report states.

The freakish cognitive dissonance at the NIE's core should have been detected at the start. It broke down its judgments into levels of confidence, from high to moderate to low. Utter absence of proof, however, did not deter the conclusion from being stamped "high confidence."

What the report does not note is the name or background of the NIE's director: Robert Walpole, a former national intelligence officer on nuclear weapons and a factotum of the secretary of defense, Donald Rumsfeld. Walpole had demonstrated his bona fides in an incident that prefigures the WMD debacle: the writing of the alarmist report of the Rumsfeld

Commission in 1998, which asserted that the ballistic missile threat from "rogue states" was imminent. A similar commission rejected that claim, used to bolster the case for a Star Wars program, two years earlier.

The report also does not deal with the creation of an alternative intelligence operation inside the Pentagon, the Office of Special Plans, which bypassed regular channels to disseminate fabricated material, originating mostly in Ahmed Chalabi's disinformation factory.

But, buried in the appendix, Senator John D. Rockefeller, Democrat of West Virginia, included an account of an internal operation against the CIA conducted by the undersecretary of defense, Douglas Feith, an entrenched neoconservative.

While the CIA composed a report on the Iraq–al Qaeda connection, which the administration still trumpets but for which the intelligence community could never find proof, Feith held briefings trashing the CIA on its impending report. Then, without informing the CIA, Feith's version was presented to the deputy national security adviser and the vice president.

Colin Powell put himself in the hands of people he hoped would protect him. Predictably, he was betrayed. Before his February 5, 2002, speech to the United Nations, making the case for WMD, Powell spent days at the CIA. He was given disinformation about mobile biological weapons laboratories, which came from Iraqi exile sources that the CIA didn't trust. The day before Powell's speech, one CIA official wanted to warn him. Another said, "Let's keep in mind the fact that this war's going to happen regardless of what [the source] said or didn't say, and the Powers That Be probably aren't terribly interested in whether [the source] knows what he's talking about." Powell was sent before the world to speak the falsehoods, with the CIA director, George Tenet, sitting behind him. Never before has a secretary of state, the highest-ranking cabinet officer, been manipulated so contemptuously by his own administration.

The NIE was condensed into a one-page document and sent to the White House, which still refuses to release it to the Senate Intelligence Committee. The full, classified version contains dissenting caveats in its footnotes. But were those included in the one-page summary? And did Bush read the NIE in any form? On July 18, 2003, in an overlooked briefing to the White House press corps, "a senior administration official" explained: "I don't think he sat down over a long weekend and read every word of it. But he's familiar, intimately familiar, with the case."

In the bestselling thriller *The Da Vinci Code*, paintings and signs contain the keys to its ludicrous secret. The Senate report, despite missing crucial information, still helps crack the code about Bush and his apostles. Bush is revealed as having a blithe disregard for anything that might interfere with his articles of absolute belief: as a man of faith.

The Senate's report is very revealing about Bush and his apostles—but the secrets are buried deep.

Code Orange

AUGUST 5, 2004

THE FOG OF WAR has descended over the campaign. Within seventy-two hours of the end of the Democratic convention, the Department of Homeland Security declared a new terror alert, and the color-coded threat level was jacked up to orange, verging on red. The reason, the government reported, was that the computer of an al Qaeda operative captured in Pakistan contained precise information about threats to five financial institutions in New York and Washington.

Then additional information was revealed: the intelligence was mostly three years old, the al Qaeda surveillance of U.S. buildings had been mostly conducted through the Internet, the computer file had been opened again in January for uncertain reasons and with no new surveillance data added to it, and Pakistani officials said that the captured material indicated no new al Qaeda planning.

The effect of the alert has been to throw the campaign into turmoil and momentarily freeze it. John Kerry decided to accept the administration's explanations at face value. His critique of Bush's war on terrorism must be made with iron discipline, based on the facts, not suspicions. Other Democrats, however, claimed the administration was using the situation for political advantage, putting additional pressure on Kerry, who has to hold fast.

In part, the level of partisanship increased because of the clumsy performance of Tom Ridge, the secretary of homeland security, who turned the announcement into a political rally. "We must understand that the kind of information available to us today is the result of the president's leadership in the war against terror," he said. Whether planned or not, the alert exposed that for Bush, fear is the irreducible basis of his campaign. And while the news starkly elevated his profile as the "war president," it also revealed indirectly the vacuum of his second-term program. His hard-right issues are insufficient for a national majority, he is weak on the realities of homeland security, and he is desperate to smudge the history of inaction that led to 9/11 and his responsibility for the deterioration of the Iraq situation.

The widespread cynicism about alerts that may have no grounding is a product of Bush's intense politicization of national security and his record of misleading statements about almost every aspect of war.

The 9/11 Commission's report is a damning record of Bush's passivity on terrorism, beginning with his first act: the demotion of the counterterrorism chief, Richard Clarke. The report documents that the administration "was not ready to confront Islamabad" on Pakistani support for the Taliban or to "engage actively against al Qaeda," and that it "did not develop new diplomatic initiatives on al Qaeda with the Saudi government." Bush told the commission that the August 6, 2001, presidential daily brief headed "Bin Laden Determined To Strike In U.S." was "historical in nature," though it contained current information. The neoconservatives, such as the deputy secretary of defense, Paul Wolfowitz, are depicted as dismissive of such threats—Wolfowitz opposed retaliation for the al Qaeda attack on the USS *Cole* as "stale"—and obsessed about Iraq as the source of all terrorism.

Bush's campaign must try to blur memory of his history. When Kerry seized on the commission's recommendations, Bush reacted by endorsing one: the appointment of a new national intelligence chief. But he was prepared to give this new post no control over budget or personnel, no White House office, and no authority over intelligence operations. Once again, he appeared to be acting only on political motives.

Various bills for homeland security languish before the Congress as Bush neglects them. His paltry $46 million proposal for port security is more than a billion dollars short of what the U.S. Coast Guard says is required. On port security, ten Democratic amendments have already been defeated while Bush has slept. He prefers the money to be appropriated for tax cuts for the upper bracket.

Bush is haunted not only by the ghosts of his own past but the ghosts of presidents past. While he attempts to redeem his father's political fall by avoiding his father's mistakes, his effort at reversal is creating a similar estrangement from the voters. When the elder Bush won his war against Iraq and withdrew without toppling Saddam Hussein, his ratings were at their peak. But his obliviousness to economic circumstances undermined the heroic image. Lyndon Johnson had an ambitious domestic agenda backed by a landslide mandate. But he squandered it in the Vietnam quagmire and undermined his party's political credibility for a generation. Now, Bush's faltering credibility is tearing at trust in U.S. national security. Perversely, his campaign must exploit the fears that his failures have helped engender. For him, this is not a war of choice, but of necessity.

The Oath of True Believers

AUGUST 19, 2004

BEFORE ATTENDING a rally to hear Vice President Dick Cheney, citizens in New Mexico were required to sign a political loyalty oath approved by the Republican National Committee: "I, [full name] . . . do herby [*sic*] endorse George W. Bush for reelection of the United States [*sic*]." The form noted: "In signing the above endorsement you are consenting to use and release of your name by Bush-Cheney as an endorser of President Bush."

Bush is campaigning at events billed as "Ask President Bush." Only supporters are allowed in. Talking points are distributed to questioners. In Traverse City, Michigan, a fifty-five-year-old social studies teacher who wore a Kerry sticker had her ticket torn up at the door. "How can anyone in the U.S. deny someone entry?" she asked. "Isn't this a democracy?"

At every rally, Bush repeats the same speech, touting a "vibrant economy" and his leadership in a war in which "you cannot show weakness." He introduces local entrepreneurs who praise his tax cuts. (More than one million jobs have been lost in his term.) Then Bush calls on questioners. More than one-fifth of them profess their evangelical faith or denounce gay marriage. In Niceville, Florida, one said: "This is the very first time that I have felt that God was in the White House." "Thank you," replied Bush. Another: "Mr. President, as a child, how can I help you get votes?" In Albuquerque, he was told: "It's an honor every day when I get to pray for you as president." And this one: "Thank God we finally have a commander in chief." Others repeat attacks on John Kerry's military record, to which Bush responds with an oblique but encouraging "Thanks."

Bush's overriding strategy is to bolster his credentials as a decisive military figure and to impugn his opponent's manhood. In his latest TV commercial, he says: "We cannot hesitate, we cannot yield, we must do everything in our power to bring an enemy to justice before they hurt us again." But, according to the *Washington Post*, for the last two years he has uttered the elusive Osama bin Laden's name only ten times, and "on six of those occasions it was because he was asked a direct question. . . . Not once during that period has he talked about Bin Laden at any length, or said anything substantive." At "Ask President Bush" events, he mentions 9/11 only to raise the threat of Saddam Hussein.

Vice President Cheney sneered at Kerry for even using the word "sensitive" with respect to counterterrorism. Not one war was "won by being sensitive," mocked Cheney. Kerry, in fact, had called for fighting "a more effective, more thoughtful, more strategic, more proactive, more sensitive war on terror that reaches out to other nations and brings them to our side and lives up to American values in history." Cheney's distortion is calculated to portray Kerry as effeminate.

At the same time, a Republican front group of Vietnam veterans, financed by a major Bush contributor, is running an ad campaign claiming Kerry's account of his military record is false. But not one of these veterans served with him on his boat.

During the Vietnam War, Bush famously used his father's connections to get a posting as a pilot in the Texas Air National Guard, which was filled with the sons of privilege. After refusing to submit to a routine drug test, he was suspended and never flew again. He got himself transferred to the Alabama National Guard but didn't turn up for his tour of duty. Since then, he has withheld his full military records. Now he encourages allegations that a genuine war hero has lied about his service and is a coward. But this is more than a case of projection. The more profound issue is not who served in Vietnam and who dodged. It is whether the president is a sovereign.

Since the birth of the U.S. party system, presidential candidates have gone directly to the sovereign people to make their case. After the Democratic convention, Kerry traveled from New England to the Northwest doing just that. Because not one of the hundreds of thousands who attended his open-air rallies had to pledge allegiance to him, he encountered organized Bush hecklers. At his rallies, Bush is a pseudo-populist. But these controlled environments reflect his deeper view of the presidency as sovereign rule, preempting democracy.

Floundering in the polls, without a strategy for Iraq, unwilling to speak the name of Bin Laden, he is secure in the knowledge that the cheering multitudes have been selected. "Ask President Bush" has crystallized the underlying issue, framed succinctly by the greatest American poet of democracy, Walt Whitman: "The President is there in the White House for you, it is not you who are here for him."

The Rule of Chaos

AUGUST 26, 2004

THERE WAS NO "imminent threat" to the United States from Iraq. Then there was no strategy for building a new Iraq. "Hubris and ideology" ruled. Now, "Iraq is more dangerous to the U.S. potentially than it was at the moment we went to war."

These are the reluctant judgments of one of the key U.S. officials who participated in the highest levels of decision making of the Coalition Provisional Authority (CPA). Both interviewed by me and in a forthcoming article in the journal *Foreign Affairs,* Larry Diamond offers from the heart of the Green Zone an unvarnished, firsthand account of the unfolding strategic catastrophe.

Diamond, a scholar at the Hoover Institution, a conservative think tank located on the Stanford University campus, was personally recruited to serve as a senior adviser to the CPA by National Security Adviser Condoleezza Rice, once provost of Stanford.

When he arrived in Baghdad, Diamond observed "a highly centralized decision-making process. There were weighty Americans with decades of experience in the region who were not consulted or integrated into decision making, foreign service officers up to the level of ambassadors." The neoconservatives in the Pentagon were in charge, and the CPA head, Paul Bremer, "was the agent more of the Pentagon than the State Department." The Pentagon cut out State because the neocons viewed it as "not on board" ideologically.

The British were regarded as warily as was the State Department. The British ambassador to the United Nations, Jeremy Greenstock, was systematically shut out. "In terms of the final decision making on key issues, I never saw much evidence that [the British] had the opportunity to weigh in." When British officials in Basra urged conducting local elections there, "they were vetoed," Diamond told me. "It would have helped. If the British had been listened to, it might have been better. They had a history with this country."

The U.N. was considered useful only as a rubber stamp for the flawed decisions. After the August 19 bombing that killed twenty-two U.N. personnel, "the organization felt that they suffered this trauma, and for what? They were so ignored, they felt used. The combination of the risk and the trauma with the lack of impact and consultation left the organization feeling wounded." But when the U.N. representative Lakhdar Brahimi appeared in Iraq this February, he negotiated the standoff between the Shia leader Grand Ayatollah Sayyid Ali Husaini Sistani and the United States.

"The reasons there are six women in the [Iraqi] cabinet, corrupt members were jettisoned, why the ministers are regarded as able and serious, has a lot to do with the U.N. team," said Diamond. "It's indicative of what we could have accomplished.

"There are so many bungled elements. We haven't had a strategy for the beginning for dealing with Moqtada al-Sadr. We were flying blind from the start. The result was we didn't neutralize him early on."

In Fallujah, after the murder of four American contractors, the U.S. military pounded the city and withdrew. "We now have a terrorist base in Fallujah. The Bush administration looked at the political cost, at what would have been necessary to destroy this terrorist haven. A country not an imminent threat to the security of the U.S. is now in some areas a haven of the most murderous, dedicated enemies of the U.S., including al Qaeda."

In Iraq, the United States cannot escape from its own trap without even more ruinous consequences. "If we walk away, the place falls apart disastrously. Americans are not only a bulwark against civil war. They are a stimulus for nationalist and Islamic fundamentalist mobilization. We need to reduce that stimulus and provocation without robbing the new Iraqi state of the bulwark it needs.

"We have been dealt a bad hand by mistaken decisions, going to war, in prewar planning, and in the first few months after the war ended. A lot of negative things are difficult to alter because of mistakes that were not inevitable. There are really no good options."

Fallujah remains under terrorist control; insurgents run rampant even beyond the Sunni triangle; the number of U.S. soldiers killed spirals toward one thousand; the Iraqi army, disastrously disbanded by the CPA, is being reassembled and trained. The American campaign is consumed with false charges made by a Republican front group about the medals that John Kerry earned in a war more than thirty years ago. The arrogant and incompetent blunders of the Bush administration in Iraq are not debated. On the eve of the Republican convention, Bush burnishes his image as a prudent and reassuring leader. The lethal realities of his "hubris and ideology" are for the moment off the screen. Mission accomplished.

Shock and Awe

The Republican National Convention, Day One

SEPTEMBER 1, 2004

ON THE FIRST DAY of the Republican convention, not one speaker mentioned a domestic issue—not education, health care, or the economy. Delegates were summoned back to another time, a past that began on 9/11. That was a moment crystallizing enduring national unity, one that saw the emergence of a president whose strategy against terrorism required an invasion of Iraq. Anyone who believed other than the patriotic consensus wrought by the moral clarity of the president was being misled by the documentary filmmaker and prankster Michael Moore.

The remembrance of things past was evoked by the two most erratic partisan Republicans, now recasting themselves as the ultimate loyalists, perhaps because both still harbor wild and quixotic ambitions to become president themselves.

The former New York City mayor Rudy Giuliani and Senator John Mc-Cain are outriders from the entire Bush social agenda, but neither is representative of the evanescent moderate wing of the party—"a dying breed," as a retiring moderate Republican congressman lamented that day. In the afternoon, a radical conservative platform against stem cell research, abortion, and gay rights was approved by the convention without a murmur of dissent.

Once, the moderates of the Northeast repelled right-wing insurgencies, sending them back into their dark woods to nurse their resentments. In 1960, the New York governor Nelson Rockefeller compelled the nominee Richard Nixon to accept his provisions for the platform, an agreement called the Treaty of Fifth Avenue, long recalled with bitterness by conservatives as evidence of pragmatic betrayal. Under Bush, the moderates are a nonentity, and the appearance of Giuliani and McCain was testament to the decline of that historic wing of the party.

The moderate remnant that filled positions in the Bush administration—the former New Jersey governor Christine Todd Whitman as Environmental Protection Agency administrator, and the corporate executive

Paul O'Neill as secretary of the treasury—have left in disillusionment. Colin Powell has become the invisible man.

While the true powers of the party, such as the House majority leader Tom "the Hammer" DeLay, are like hidden imams in New York, Giuliani and McCain assume the stage.

Giuliani's political reputation was rescued by his steady public performance on 9/11 and an unexpected favor from Bush. In the jungle of New York politics, he had made a world of enemies. Beyond the Hudson, he was a pariah. When he dropped out of the U.S. Senate race in 2000 with operatic flourish, after jettisoning his second wife and parading his girlfriend before photographers, he was already doomed in the contest against Hillary Clinton. But when the planes struck the World Trade Center towers, he became a national beacon of reassurance, in large part because President Bush was not to be seen for days. Giuliani's fame in the crisis rested on Bush's absence.

Now he came to praise Bush's steadfastness. "Let us write our own history," said Giuliani. Bush was no less than the reincarnation of Winston Churchill, who "saw the dangers of Hitler while his opponents characterized him as a warmongering gadfly." The Bush who ignored his presidential daily brief from the CIA of August 6, 2001, titled "Bin Laden Determined to Strike Inside U.S."—a memo described by the National Security Adviser, Condoleezza Rice, as "speculative" and containing only "historic information"—went down the memory hole.

Bush was "clear, precise, and consistent"; Kerry, Giuliani told his audience eleven times, was not. Saddam Hussein was removed not just because of his weapons of mass destruction, but because, in the classic threat conflation of the Bush administration, he was "a pillar of support for global terrorism"—this despite the 9/11 Commission's conclusion that he was not. McCain—in truth intensely disliked and distrusted by many Republicans and Bush's internal nemesis—now embraced him, raising a storm of questions.

What does McCain want? "Emperor has always appealed to me," he said the day before the convention. One source close to him suggested that he nursed the idea that Bush might dump Dick Cheney for him. Others conjectured that this was a case of Stockholm syndrome.

McCain, too, evoked the spirit of the rewritten 9/11 past. "We were not two countries. We were Americans." The divisions that had split the country ever since—nearly half a million had marched against Bush the day before—went unmentioned. The Iraq war, McCain explained, "was between war and a graver threat. Don't let anyone tell you otherwise. Not our political opponents. And certainly not a disingenuous filmmaker."

"Now there are some who would like to rewrite history," Bush said on the subject of Iraq last year. "Revisionist historians is what I like to call them." In the past few days, however, his explanation has wandered. Now the turmoil in Iraq is a consequence of "catastrophic success." It is the speed of the military's victory that is at the root of the failures. "Shock and awe" was not the prelude to the Allied liberation of Paris in 1944. But at the convention, it is the revisionist history that is "on message."

Fear and Narcissism

The Republican National
Convention, Day Two

SEPTEMBER 2, 2004

DANGEROUS CONFUSION threatened the Republicans on the second day of their convention. In an interview aired on NBC's *Today Show,* President Bush was deferentially asked about the war on terrorism. "I don't think you can win it," he replied. For hours afterward, his campaign issued bulletins that he hadn't meant it. Finally, Bush appeared at a speech before the American Legion, a conservative veterans' group, in Nashville, Tennessee. "We will win," he declared. Vice President Cheney helpfully appeared on a right-wing radio talk show to explain: "The president certainly never intended to convey the notion that we can't win."

By breaking his own iron law—"I don't do nuance"—Bush had blurred his own image with the Republicans' negative image of John Kerry as a flip-flopper. Nuance leads to ambivalence, which can lead to inaction, and who then can be an action hero?

Bush's mistaken nuance set the stage for the larger-than-life persona of Conan the Barbarian, Predator, the Terminator, Commando, and, not least, Kindergarten Cop. "This is like winning an Oscar, as if I would know," said Arnold Schwarzenegger, governor of California, as the delegates cheered like fans.

Schwarzenegger is the only political figure in America who is married to a Kennedy and is an old Bush family retainer. His ability to operate in several dimensions at once has been intrinsic to his rise. In 1988, he campaigned for the elder Bush. "They call me the Terminator, but when it comes to America's future Michael Dukakis is the real Terminator," he said. For that contribution, he was rewarded with the chairmanship of the President's Council on Physical Fitness and Sports, and he appeared at the White House, where he directed General Colin Powell in a push-up drill on the South Lawn.

Schwarzenegger's policies as governor—pro-gay, pro-choice on abortion, pro-environment—have little in common with Bush's, and he has no chance of carrying California for Bush, who is anathema in the Golden

State. Billed as a principal speaker on "People of Compassion" night, he understood that his role as supporting actor was greater than merely backing any policy; it was to transfer his image to Bush and the party.

Schwarzenegger has an aesthetic sense that passes above the heads of the Republicans. To them, it seems he's appealing to simplicity, strength, and old-fashioned patriotism.

But he puts a strange emphasis on the body-politic Kultur. The puritanical delegates responded with an emotional intensity to themes they can't fully grasp. No matter how scripted Schwarzenegger may be, he remains pure in his underlying message. He makes the case for the narcissism of power through the power of narcissism.

No one is more narcissistic than a bodybuilder. He builds his reputation standing before mirrors and panels of other men, flexing his muscles to see who has the largest.

Schwarzenegger offered the Republican Convention totemic worship of virility, born out of fear of its fading. He has been perfecting this act for decades. In essence, he offered a sexual-identity panic speech.

The governor recounted his tale of being a "once-scrawny" little boy in postwar Austria, frightened of the bullying "Soviet boot. . . . I was not an action hero back then." But he would "daydream for hours" about becoming an American, inspired by watching movies starring John Wayne. Too bad he was not "transfixed," as he says, by Gary Cooper (or James Dean). At last, in 1968, Arnold came to America, in the midst of a presidential campaign. The Democratic candidate Hubert Humphrey was "saying things that sounded like socialism." Suddenly, another figure appeared before him. "Then I heard Nixon speak. . . . Listening to Nixon speak sounded more like a breath of fresh air.

"I said to my friend, I said, 'What party is he?' My friend said, 'He's a Republican.'

"I said, 'Then I am a Republican.' "

On one level, Schwarzenegger is the wild and crazy guy from Mitteleuropa who gets the cultural cues wrong, like seeing Nixon in 1968 as hip. Yet the incident reveals an unerring identification with, and will to, power.

In his convention speech, he offered the flattery of the immigrant to the native. His rhetoric of gratitude seems to be boilerplate: "Everything I have, my career, my success, my family, I owe to America." But this is the immigrant as Nordic god. What could be more flattering than to have Mr. Universe declaim his love for you and desire above all to be like you?

Having established his citizenship, Schwarzenegger felt entitled to articulate the Republican credo of power over weakness. "If you believe this country, not the United Nations, is the best hope for democracy, then you are a Republican." Thus the immigrant blasted internationalism. "If you believe that we must be fierce and relentless and terminate terrorism, then you are a Republican." Thus he declared the Democrats soft. "And to those critics who are so pessimistic about our economy, I say: Don't be economic girlie men."

So beyond unilateralism, jingoism, and social Darwinism lies sexual apprehension. Those who aren't with the program are queer. But the anxiety is even deeper than that of homosexuality. "Girlie man" is a peculiar accusation for being effeminate. It reveals fear of women and their complex values. The name-calling is a frantic effort to suppress nuance, which the action hero fears he may harbor within.

None Dare Call It Treason
The Republican National Convention, Day Three

SEPTEMBER 3, 2004

THE BELLIGERENCE of the Republican Convention's keynote speaker was so overpowering that it easily obscured the monochromatic performance of Dick Cheney. Senator Zell Miller of Georgia did not vary his grim, hooded expression or his style of delivery, shouting like a backwoods preacher casting out the devil. But his raw rhetoric framed the most profound questions about patriotism and democracy in wartime.

The previous speakers, from Rudy Giuliani to Arnold Schwarzenegger, had been chosen for their lack of partisan regularity in order to better carry the attack against John Kerry. Superficially, Miller was to be the crescendo of this tactical march to the podium, a Democrat regretting his party's fall from grace and singing the praises of the Republican president.

Miller had been a keynote speaker before, but at the Democratic convention of 1992 that nominated Bill Clinton. His politics then were a vibrant Southern populism against the special interests. In the Republican sweep two years later, however, Miller experienced a near-death experience, almost losing as governor because he had suggested removing the Confederate battle flag from its corner of the state flag, where it had been placed during the white resistance to civil rights laws. Afterward, Miller tacked sharply and steadily rightward. On leaving the governorship, he jettisoned his Democratic alliances and became a lobbyist for the Philip Morris tobacco conglomerate. Elected as a U.S. senator, Miller played as though he had been betrayed, aligning himself with the Republicans. In this he was following the tragic trajectory of Southern populists past who had transformed themselves into their opposites.

Miller's speech was a recasting of the paradox of post–Civil War Southern patriotism that clung to the myth that Southern soldiers were more valiant, and, having been estranged from the Union, asserted superior identification with the nation through the glorification of arms.

"Today," Miller said, "at the same time young Americans are dying in the sands of Iraq and the mountains of Afghanistan, our nation is being

98

torn apart and made weaker because of the Democrats' manic obsession to bring down our commander in chief." In one compact sentence, he advanced a new stab-in-the-back theory, effected the seamless unification of Iraq and Afghanistan, attributed political division to the Democrats (who had supported the war in Afghanistan and overwhelmingly backed the congressional war resolution on Iraq), and stripped the presidency down to its military function.

Next, he offered a peculiar history of the Constitution and the Bill of Rights that owed more to Caesar than to Washington, who had resolutely presented himself as Cincinnatus. "For it has been said so truthfully," said Miller, "that it is the soldier, not the reporter, who has given us the freedom of the press. It is the soldier, not the poet, who has given us freedom of speech. It is the soldier, not the agitator, who has given us the freedom to protest."

Miller proposed a higher patriotism for the opposition party that should "rather lose the election than make national security a partisan campaign issue. . . . Where are such statesmen today?" Kerry, by contrast, was plotting a betrayal to the United Nations and even worse: "Kerry would let Paris decide when America needs defending."

After Miller, Cheney seemed anticlimactic in his rote smear of Kerry's masculinity for using the word *sensitive*. Cheney's lack of emotional affect and energy lends him a strange gravity, as though he were begrudging in his attacks. But he remains an unpopular politician whose natural habitat is not the public stage. His effectiveness rests behind the curtain.

Miller's oration, extraordinary in its hostility and shrillness, was hardly pitched to win over undecided voters, mostly women. It reflected more a Republican base strategy calculated for maximum partisan motivation, but also an ingrained confidence that unforgiving disdain is a majority sentiment. Miller's skewed history of the United States was intended to taint political debate itself as subversive. But it was Woodrow Wilson who said: "We have been told that it is unpatriotic to criticize public action. Well, if it is, then there is a deep disgrace resting upon the origins of this nation." And it was Theodore Roosevelt who said: "To announce that there must be no criticism of the president, or that we are to stand by the president, right or wrong, is not only unpatriotic and servile, but is morally treasonable to the American public."

The burden of Bush's polarizing convention now strains his ability to revive his former theme as "a uniter, not a divider." But as Miller's and Cheney's speeches make plain, one of the tests of strength of the "war president" is not to look back, for that would be weak.

"A Certain Swagger"
The Republican National Convention, Day Four

SEPTEMBER 4, 2004

GEORGE W. BUSH EMERGED between two gigantic American flags and walked down a runway to the center of a stage emblazoned with the seal of the presidency. The proscenium behind him resembled a Roman temple, engraved in large gold letters with the words "The United States of America."

The overpowering evidence of his authority did not foster distance between him and the crowd; instead his elevation excited charismatic deference. Standing alone on the image of the American eagle, he was simultaneously both amid and above the rapturous delegates at the Republican convention. His solitary presence brought him closer to them in fulfilling their dream of leadership—the president as Lone Ranger.

Bush has always benefited from what he calls in another context "the soft bigotry of low expectations." The dismissals of him as stupid, crude, and impulsive allow the widest play for his well-planned and sophisticated shrewdness. The spoiled son of privilege, who gained admission to Yale as a favor of legacy to his family, sloughed off his military service, ignored the intricacies of international affairs that compelled the career of his father, and failed in business until salvaged by family friends, has in fact been a diligent student in one crucial area.

The field in which he is expert is politics. Assimilating by osmosis its lessons in a political family, he was apprenticed, beginning in his early twenties, to the most talented and slyest Southern political consultants, the innovators of the post–civil rights Southern strategy, and became their equal. Part of his cleverness lies in hiding this true identity.

Bush's acceptance speech was intended in part to present the gloss of a "vision" of domestic policy. Until this moment, he had avoided laying out any program beyond his adherence to the social agenda of the religious right on gay marriage, stem cell research, and abortion.

His tax cuts have fostered a wildly burgeoning deficit that he steadfastly refuses to address for fear of repeating the nightmare of his father's rescinding of his principal promise: "Read my lips—no new taxes." Bush's "Leave No Child Behind" education initiative, which was fashioned as the signature program of his "compassionate conservatism," is crushing the schools and desperately unpopular, even in the most conservative states, such as Utah. The policy demands adherence to certain standards of performance, but Bush has refused to provide the $27 billion in necessary funding. His Medicare program for prescription drugs for seniors, a partial privatization, has older voters up in arms.

In his speech, Bush seized on rhetorical shards of Clintonism about helping workers cope with the impact of globalization but offered only the bleached bones of old Republicanism—privatization schemes for Social Security and Medicare. He attached no price tag to these plans, which policy experts calculate will cost trillions of dollars and detonate further explosions in the deficit. But this portion of the speech was the way Bush had to fill his blank page on domestic accomplishment.

For him, 9/11 is the entire casus belli of his presidency. It is the beginning, middle, and end of the drama: the moment when the enemy enters and calls forth the hero. Fear and uncertainty demand his absolute conviction. The hero stands tall and defiant, doing whatever it takes.

"Nothing will hold us back," Bush said repeatedly. Every action is seen in the light of 9/11. "Do I forget the lessons of September 11 and take the word of a madman?" he asked the crowd, referring to Saddam Hussein. "No!" they cried. "Or do I take action to defend our country?"

But even this defense of his strategy of preemption was not the most revealing section of his speech. Now Bush described his "flaws": some people have to "correct my English," and sometimes "I come across as a little too blunt." Plain-speaking and honest, he is a natural man. "Some folks look at me," he said, "and see a certain swagger, which in Texas is called 'walking.'"

With this remark Bush cast himself as the born cowboy. Suddenly the war on terrorism was folded into the myth of the frontier and its stories of captivity and battles with savages. The hero is the rescuer and avenger, an isolate caught in a moral landscape between civilization and wilderness. In this primal struggle, the savages use cruel methods to terrorize the settlers, even taking hostages. Law and chaos rage in conflict.

In the nineteenth-century novels of James Fenimore Cooper, such as *The Last of the Mohicans*, Hawkeye, the frontier hero, knows the savages and their ways. Part of what makes him a hero is that he is an unassuming natural man, in touch with the primitive, beyond the rigid hierarchies of the town. Because of his intimate knowledge, he can use the methods of the savages against them.

In Western iconography, the lineage runs from Hawkeye to Buffalo Bill, from the Lone Ranger to George W. Bush. But the danger for the Lone Ranger is that without friends like Tonto he may become General Custer. Instead of achieving a bonanza, he may find himself through rash judgment surrounded at Little Big Horn, or in Mesopotamia. For now, though, with "a certain swagger," Bush gets his convention bump.

Staring at Defeat

SEPTEMBER 16, 2004

"BRING THEM ON!" President Bush challenged the early Iraqi insurgency in July of last year. Since then, 812 American soldiers have been killed and 6,290 wounded, according to the Pentagon. Almost every day, in campaign speeches, Bush speaks with bravado about how he is "winning" in Iraq. "Our strategy is succeeding," he boasted to the National Guard convention on Tuesday.

But, according to the U.S. military's leading strategists and prominent retired generals, Bush's war is already lost. Retired general William Odom, former head of the National Security Agency, told me: "Bush hasn't found the WMD. Al Qaeda, it's worse, he's lost on that front. That he's going to achieve a democracy there? That goal is lost, too. It's lost." He adds: "Right now, the course we're on, we're achieving Bin Laden's ends."

Retired general Joseph Hoar, the former Marine commander and head of U.S. Central Command, told me: "The idea that this is going to go the way these guys planned is ludicrous. There are no good options. We're conducting a campaign as though it were being conducted in Iowa, no sense of the realities on the ground. It's so unrealistic for anyone who knows that part of the world. The priorities are just all wrong."

Jeffrey Record, professor of strategy at the Air War College, said: "I see no ray of light on the horizon at all. The worst case has become true. There's no analogy whatsoever between the situation in Iraq and the advantages we had after the Second World War in Germany and Japan."

W. Andrew Terrill, professor at the Army War College's Strategic Studies Institute, and the top expert on Iraq there, said: "I don't think that you can kill the insurgency." According to Terrill, the anti-U.S. insurgency, centered in the Sunni triangle and holding several cities and towns—including Fallujah—is expanding and becoming more capable as a consequence of U.S. policy.

"We have a growing, maturing insurgency group," he told me. "We see larger and more coordinated military attacks. They are getting better, and they can self-regenerate. The idea there are x number of insurgents, and that when they're all dead we can get out, is wrong. The insurgency has shown an ability to regenerate itself because there are people willing to fill the ranks of those who are killed. The political culture is more hostile to the U.S. presence. The longer we stay, the more they are confirmed in that view."

After the killing of four U.S. contractors in Fallujah, the U.S. Marines besieged the city for three weeks in April—the watershed event for the insurgency. "I think the president ordered the attack on Fallujah," said General Hoar. "I asked a three-star Marine general who gave the order to go to Fallujah, and he wouldn't tell me. I came to the conclusion that the order came directly from the White House." Then, just as suddenly, the order was rescinded, and Islamist radicals gained control, using the city as a base.

"If you are a Muslim and the community is under occupation by a non-Islamic power, it becomes a religious requirement to resist that occupation," Terrill explained. "Most Iraqis consider us occupiers, not liberators." He describes the religious imagery common now in Fallujah and the Sunni triangle: "There's talk of angels and the Prophet Mohammed coming down from heaven to lead the fighting, talk of martyrs whose bodies are glowing and emanating wonderful scents."

"I see no exit," said Record. "We've been down that road before. It's called Vietnamization. The idea that we're going to have an Iraqi force trained to defeat an enemy we can't defeat stretches the imagination. They will be tainted by their very association with the foreign occupier. In fact, we had more time and money in state building in Vietnam than in Iraq."

General Odom said: "This is far graver than Vietnam. There wasn't as much at stake strategically, though in both cases we mindlessly went ahead with the war that was not constructive for U.S. aims. But now we're in a region far more volatile, and we're in much worse shape with our allies."

Terrill believes that any sustained U.S. military offensive against the no-go areas "could become so controversial that members of the Iraqi government would feel compelled to resign." Thus, an attempted military solution would destroy the slightest remaining political legitimacy. "If we leave and there's no civil war, that's a victory."

General Hoar believes from the information he has received that "a decision has been made" to attack Fallujah "after the first Tuesday in November. That's the cynical part of it—after the election. The signs are all there."

He compares any such planned attack to the late Syrian dictator Hafez al-Assad's razing of the rebel city of Hama in 1982. "You could flatten it," said Hoar. "U.S. military forces would prevail, casualties would be high, there would be inconclusive results with respect to the bad guys, their leadership would escape, and civilians would be caught in the middle. I hate that phrase *collateral damage.* And they talked about dancing in the street, a beacon for democracy."

General Odom remarked that the tension between the Bush administration and the senior military officers over Iraq was worse than any he has ever seen with any previous government, even during the Vietnam era. "I've never seen it so bad between the Office of the Secretary of Defense and the military. There's a significant majority believing this is a disaster. The two parties whose interests have been advanced have been the Iranians and al Qaeda. Bin Laden could argue with some cogency that our going into Iraq was the equivalent of the Germans in Stalingrad. They defeated themselves by pouring more in there. Tragic."

Falls the Shadow

SEPTEMBER 23, 2004

THE NEWS IS GRIM, but the president is "optimistic." The intelligence is sobering, but he tosses aside "pessimistic predictions." His opponent says he has "no credibility," but the president replies that it is his rival who is "twisting in the wind." The U.N. secretary general speaks of the "rule of law," but Bush talks before a mute General Assembly of "a new definition of security." Between the rhetoric and the reality falls the campaign.

In Iraq, U.S. commanders have plans for this week and the next, but there is "no overarching strategy," I was told by a reliable source who has just returned after assessing the facts on the ground for U.S. intelligence services. The *New York Times* reports that an offensive is in the works to capture the insurgent stronghold of Fallujah—after the election. In the meantime, Abu Musab al-Zarqawi and other terrorists linked to al Qaeda operate from there at will, as they have for more than a year. The president speaks of new Iraqi security forces, but not even half the U.S. personnel required to train them have been assigned to the headquarters of the Multinational Security Transition Command.

George Bush's vision of the liberation of Iraq has melted before harsh facts. But reality cannot be allowed to obscure the image. The liberation is "succeeding," he insists, and only pessimists can fail to see it.

In July, the CIA delivered to the president a new national intelligence estimate that detailed three gloomy scenarios for Iraq's future, the worst being all-out civil war. Perhaps it was his reading of the estimate that prompted Bush to remark in August that the war on terrorism could not be won, a judgment he swiftly reversed. And at the United Nations, Bush held a press conference at which he rebuffed the latest intelligence.

Bush explained that, for him, intelligence exists not to inform decision making but to be used or rejected to advance an ideological and political agenda. His dismissal is an affirmation of the politicization and corruption of intelligence that rationalized the war.

In his stump speech, which he repeats word for word across the country, Bush explains that he invaded Iraq because of "the lesson of September the 11th." WMD goes unmentioned; the only reason Bush offers is Saddam Hussein as an agent of terrorism. "He was a sworn enemy of the United States of America; he had ties to terrorist networks. Do you remember Abu Nidal? He's the guy that killed Leon Klinghoffer. Leon Klinghoffer was murdered because of his religion. Abu Nidal was in Baghdad, as was his organization."

The period of Leon Klinghoffer's murder in 1985 on the liner *Achille Lauro* (by Abu Abbas, in fact) coincided with the U.S. courtship of Saddam Hussein, which was marked by the celebrated visits of Ronald Reagan's Middle East envoy, Donald Rumsfeld. The U.S. collaborated in intelligence exchanges and materially supported Saddam in his war with Iran, authorizing the sale of biological agents for Saddam's laboratories.

The reason for this cooperation was not idealism but necessity: the threat of an expansive, Iran-controlled Shia fundamentalism across the entire Gulf.

The policy of courting Saddam continued until he invaded Kuwait. Realpolitik prevailed when U.S. forces held back from capturing Baghdad. The first Bush grasped that, in wars to come, the United States would need ad hoc coalitions to share the military burden and financial cost. Taking Baghdad would have violated the U.N. resolution that gave legitimacy to the first Gulf war and created a nightmare of "Lebanonization," as the Secretary of State, James Baker, called it. Realism prevailed; Saddam's power was subdued and drastically reduced. It was the greatest accomplishment of the first President Bush.

When he honored the U.N. resolution, the credibility of the United States in the region was enormously enhanced, enabling serious movement on the Middle East peace process. Now this President Bush has undone the foundation of his father's work, which was built on by President Clinton.

Bush's campaign depends on the containment of any contrary perception of reality. He must evade, deny, and suppress it. His true opponent is not his Democratic foe—called unpatriotic and the candidate of al Qaeda by the vice president—but events. Bush's latest vision is his shield against them. He invokes the power of positive thinking, as taught by Émile Coué, the guru of autosuggestion in the giddy 1920s, who urged mental improvement through constant self-affirmation: "Every day, in every way, I am getting better and better."

It was during this era of illusion that T. S. Eliot wrote "The Hollow Men": "Between the idea / And the reality / Between the motion / And the act / Falls the Shadow."

"The Right God"

NOVEMBER 4, 2004

"THIS COUNTRY IS GOING so far to the right you are not even going to recognize it," remarked John Mitchell, Richard Nixon's attorney general, in 1970. Mitchell's prophecy became the mission of Nixon's College Republicans president, Karl Rove, who implemented the strategy of authoritarian populism behind George Bush's victory.

In the aftermath, the Democrats will form their ritual circular firing squad of recriminations. But, in the end, the loss was not due to the candidate's personality, the flaws of this or that adviser, or the party's platform. The Democrats surprised themselves at their ability to raise tens of millions, inspire hundreds of thousands of activists, and present themselves as unified around a centrist position. Expectations were not dashed. Turnout was vastly increased among African Americans and Hispanics. More than 60 percent of the newly registered voters went for John Kerry. Those concerned about the economy voted overwhelmingly for him; so did those citing the war in Iraq as an issue. But the Democrats' surge was more than matched.

Using the White House as a machine of centripetal force, Rove spread fear and fused its elements. Fear of the besieging terrorist, appearing in Bush TV ads as the shifty eyes of a swarthy man or a pack of wolves, was joined with fear of the besieging queer. Bush's support for a constitutional amendment to ban gay marriage was underscored by referendums against it in eleven states—all of which won.

The evangelical churches became instruments of political organization. Ideology was enforced as theology, turning nonconformity into sin, and the faithful, following voter guides with biblical literalism, were shepherded to the polls as though to the rapture. White Protestants, especially in the South, especially married men, gave their souls and votes for flag and cross. The campaign was one long revival. Abortion and stem cell research became a lever for prying loose white Catholics. To help in Florida, a referendum was put on the ballot to deny young women the right to abortion without parental approval, and it galvanized evangelicals and conservative Catholics alike.

While Kerry ran on mainstream traditions of international cooperation and domestic investments, and transparency and rationality as essential to democratic government, Bush campaigned directly against these very ideas. At his rallies, Bush was introduced as standing for "the right God." During the closing weeks, Bush and Cheney ridiculed internationalism, falsifying Kerry's statement about a "global test." They disdained Kerry's internationalism as effeminate, unpatriotic, a character flaw, and elitist. "You can put lipstick on a pig, but it's still a pig," Cheney derided in every speech. They grafted imperial unilateralism on to provincial isolationism. Fear of the rest of the world was to be mastered with contempt for it.

This strategy was linked to what are euphemistically called "moral values"—that is, the incitement of social and sexual panic over the rights of women and gender roles. Only manly authority brought to bear against "girlie men," girls, and lurking terrorists can save the nation. Above all, the exit polls showed that "strong leader" was the primary reason people voted for Bush.

Voted in along with Bush is a gallery of grotesques in the Senate. More than one new senator advocates capital punishment for doctors performing abortions; another urges that all gay teachers be fired. The new majority is more theocratic than Republican, as Republican was previously understood; the defeat of the old, moderate Republican Party is as decisive as the loss by the Democrats. There are no checks and balances.

The terminal illness of Chief Justice William Rehnquist signals new appointments to the Supreme Court that will alter law for more than a generation. Conservative promises to dismantle constitutional law since the New Deal will be acted on.

Now without constraints, Bush can pursue the dreams he has campaigned for: the use of U.S. military might to bring God's gift of freedom to the world with no further need for global approval, and, at home, the enactment of the imperatives of "the right God." The international system of collective security forged in the Second World War and tempered in the Cold War is a thing of the past. The Democratic Party, despite its efforts, has failed to rein in the radicalism sweeping the country. The world is in an emergency, but also irrelevant. The New World, with all its power and might, stepping forth to the rescue and the liberation of the old? Goodbye to all that.

"The Lowest Grade of Ignorance"

NOVEMBER 11, 2004

THE 2004 ELECTION marks the rise of a quasi-clerical party for the first time in the United States. Ecclesiastical organization has become the sinew and muscle of the Republican Party, essential in George Bush's reelection. His narrow margins in the key states of Florida, Iowa, and Ohio, among others, he owed to the direct intervention of the churches. None of this occurred suddenly or by happenstance. For years, Bush has schooled himself in the machinations of the religious right.

Bush's clerisy is an unprecedented alliance of historically anti-Catholic, nativist evangelical Protestants with the most reactionary elements of the Catholic hierarchy. Preacher, priest, and politician have combined on the grounds that John Kennedy disputed in his famous speech before the Greater Houston Ministerial Association in September 1960. Kennedy's every principle is flouted and contradicted by Bush: "I believe in an America where the separation of church and state is absolute; where no Catholic prelate would tell the president—should he be Catholic—how to act, and no Protestant minister would tell his parishioners for whom to vote; where no church or church school is granted any public funds or political preference . . . where no religious body seeks to impose its will directly or indirectly upon the general populace or the public acts of its officials."

From the White House, during the campaign, Karl Rove held a weekly conference call with religious leaders. Evangelical churches handed over membership directories to the Bush campaign for voter-registration drives. A group associated with the Reverend Pat Robertson advised 45,000 churches how to work for Bush. One popular preacher alone sent letters to 136,000 pastors advising them on "non-negotiable" issues—gay marriage, stem cell research, abortion—to mobilize the faithful. Perhaps the most influential figure of all was the far-right Dr. James Dobson, whose program, broadcast daily on more than three thousand radio stations and eighty TV stations, and whose organization has affiliates in thirty-six states.

On June 4, Bush traveled to see the Pope. In another meeting that day, with the Vatican secretary of state, Cardinal Angelo Sodano, according to a Vatican official, Bush "complained that the U.S. bishops were not being vocal enough in supporting [Bush] on social issues like gay marriage and abortion," and urged that the Vatican "push the bishops."

The Vatican was astonished at the brazen pressure and did not accede. Nonetheless, more than forty conservative bishops worked with the Bush campaign against John Kerry—part of a crusade against their own declining moral authority.

The American Catholic Church is in crisis, as Catholic opinion on abortion and stem cell research is no different from that of the general public. And the exposure of rampant pedophilia among priests has undermined traditional belief in the church's sanctity. Electing a liberal Catholic as president would have been a severe blow. So conservative bishops denounced Kerry, spoke of denying him communion, and even talked of excommunication.

The Catholic Kerry received 6 percent less of the Catholic vote than the Southern Baptist Al Gore had done four years earlier. In the crucial state of Ohio, where an anti–gay marriage initiative was on the ballot, Bush won two-thirds of the "faithful" Catholic vote and 55 percent of the Catholic total. Combined with the votes of 79 percent of white evangelicals, this gave him his critical margin nationally and in the swing states.

The religious right is not a majority, but it was indispensable to Bush's victory. Across the country, it has become the most energetic, reliable, and productive part of the Republican organization. The worth of its values-based politics is power, just as worldly power sustained the medieval church, and the assertion of that power began within days after the election.

When the moderate Republican senator Arlen Specter of Pennsylvania, chair of the Judiciary Committee, said he would oppose any nominee to the Supreme Court who sought to outlaw abortion—and one might come soon, as Chief Justice William Rehnquist is dying—Dr. Dobson said of Specter: "He is a problem, and he must be derailed." Almost instantly, Specter clarified his position, announcing that he meant no such thing and that he had approved many judges who were against abortion.

"History," Thomas Jefferson wrote, "furnishes no example of a priest-ridden people maintaining a free civil government. This marks the lowest grade of ignorance of which their civil as well as religious leaders will always avail themselves for their own purposes." But we're not all Jeffersonians now.

Colin Powell's Final Days

NOVEMBER 18, 2004

COLIN POWELL'S FINAL SCENE was a poignant but harsh exposure of his self-delusion and humiliation. The former general cherished a self-image as sacrificing and disciplined. But the good soldier was dismissed at last by his commander in chief as a bad egg. Bush, Cheney, and Rumsfeld regarded him either as a useful idiot or a vain obstructionist. They deployed his reputation as the most popular man and the most credible face in the United States for their own ends, and when he contributed an independent view he was isolated and undermined.

As secretary of state Powell has been a peripheral figure, even a fig leaf, ever since the climactic moment before the U.N. Security Council on which he staked his credibility. There he presented the case that the existence of weapons of mass destruction in Iraq required war. His case rested on twenty-six falsehoods, about which he later claimed to have been deceived. When the statue of Saddam Hussein was toppled, he offered President Bush the seventeen volumes of his *Future of Iraq* report, but the offer was rejected. Predicting everything from the looting to the insurgency, and suggesting how it might be avoided, the project was politically incorrect.

Powell had wanted to stay on for the first six months of Bush's second term to help shepherd a new Middle East peace process, but the president insisted on his resignation. Condoleezza Rice was named in his place. She had failed at every important task as national security adviser, pointedly neglecting terrorism before September 11, enthusiastically parroting the false claim that Saddam had a nuclear weapons program while suppressing contrary intelligence, mismanaging her part of postwar policy so completely that she had to cede it to a deputy, and eviscerating the Middle East road map.

As incompetent as she was at her actual job, she was agile at bureaucratic positioning. Early on, she figured out how to align with the neoconservatives and how to damage Powell. Her usurpation is a lesson to him in blind ambition and loyalty.

Powell's sacking and Rice's promotion are more than examples of be-havior punished and rewarded. His fall and her rise may signal the purge of the CIA and the State Department, a neocon night of the long knives. Bush's attitude is that of the intimidating loyalty enforcer, the role he played in his father's political campaigns.

The CIA has not been forgiven for failing to support Cheney's phantas-magorical case linking Saddam to al Qaeda. And the release in September of the outline of the most recent national intelligence estimate, laying out dark scenarios for Iraq, was considered an act of insubordination intended to help oust Bush in the election. The new CIA director, Porter Goss, has installed partisan aides at the top, and senior officials have been fired. He has issued a party-line diktat that the CIA's mission is to "support the ad-ministration and its policies."

At the State Department, senior career officers, especially those who were close to Powell, fear they are next on the chopping block. Indeed, Bush has charged Rice with bringing the department under control. Its Bureau of Intelligence and Research, which has provided the most accu-rate analysis of Iraq, is a special target for purging. Cheney is heavily in-volved in the planning, and he intends to fill key slots with neocons and fellow travelers. "By the time she takes over, Rice will have been maneu-vered into a prestructured department staff," I was told by State Depart-ment source who has been close to Powell.

The dictation of a political line has conquered policymaking. Since the United States emerged as a world power, the executive, because of its im-mense responsibilities and powers, has relied on impartial information and analysis from its departments and agencies. But vindictiveness against the institutions of government based on expertise, evidence, and experience is clearing the way for the low intellectual standards and cooked conclusions of right-wing think tanks and those appointees who emerge from them.

A system of bureaucratic fear and one-party allegiance is being created in this strange soviet Washington. Only loyalists are rewarded. Rice stands as the model. One can never be too loyal. And the loyalists compete to outdo each other. Dissonant information is seen as motivated to injure the president, an act of disloyalty bordering on treason. Success is defined as support for the political line, failure as departure from the line. An atmos-phere of personal vendetta and an incentive system for suppressing realities prevails. This is not an administration; it does not administer. It is a regime.

On one of Powell's futile diplomatic trips, his informal conversation with reporters turned to a new book, *The Accidental American: Tony Blair and the Presidency,* by James Naughtie. In it, Powell is quoted as describing the neocons to the British foreign minister, Jack Straw, as "fucking crazies." That, the reporters suggested, might be an apt title for his next volume of memoirs. Powell laughed uncontrollably.

Dedication Day

NOVEMBER 25, 2004

AT THE DEDICATION of the William J. Clinton Library last week in Little Rock, Karl Rove and President Bush received separate tours of the dramatic building, a glistening silver, suspended boxcar filled with light and commanding a panoramic view of the Arkansas River. Spanning the river stands an old railroad bridge—and to Clinton watchers, bridges represent "the bridge to the twenty-first century," the former president's re-election slogan in 1996.

The opening ceremony was biblical in its spectacle, length, and rain. For more than four hours we huddled in thin ponchos under the downpour, awaiting four presidents. For the Democrats among us—former advisers and cabinet secretaries, celebrity supporters, and high-school friends of Bill—this was an unofficial convention, a kind of counterinaugural, with rueful discussions of the recent defeat.

John Kerry arrived to defiant cheering from the crowd. Then, when the presidents were announced, Bush tried to push his way past Clinton at the library door to be first in line, against the already accepted protocol for the event—as though the walk to the platform were a contest for alpha male. In his speech, Clinton sought to clarify the present by his broad analysis of globalization—"an age of interdependence with new possibilities and new dangers"—and the offer of conciliation: "America has two great dominant strands of political thought; we're represented up here on this stage: conservatism, which at its very best draws lines that should not be crossed; and progressivism, which at its very best breaks down barriers that are no longer needed or should never have been erected in the first place."

In his effort to transcend the division of America into two nations, red and blue, Clinton was attempting to demonstrate his tradition—the absence of dogma, the belief that good ideas can come from anywhere, and that solutions cannot be imposed but must be worked out in democratic politics, involving the arts of building coalitions, compromises, and experimentation—of which he was the leading practitioner and survivor.

Offstage, beforehand, Rove and Bush had had their library tours. According to two eyewitnesses, Rove showed keen interest in everything he saw, and asked questions, including about costs, obviously thinking about a future George W. Bush library and legacy. "You're not such a scary guy," joked his guide. "Yes, I am," Rove replied. Walking away, he muttered deliberately and loudly: "I change constitutions, I put churches in schools." Thus he identified himself as more than the ruthless campaign tactician: he was also the invisible hand of power, pervasive and expansive, designing to alter the fundamental American compact.

Bush appeared distracted and glanced repeatedly at his watch. When he stopped to gaze at the river, where secret service agents were stationed in boats, the guide said: "Usually, you might see some bass fishermen out there." Bush replied: "A submarine could take this place out."

Was the president warning of an al Qaeda submarine, sneaking undetected up the Mississippi, through the locks and dams of the Arkansas River, surfacing under the bridge to the twenty-first century to dispatch the Clinton Library? Is that where Osama bin Laden is hiding?

Or was this a wishful paranoid fantasy of ubiquitous terrorism destroying Clinton's legacy with one blow? Or a projection of menace and messianism, with only Bush grasping the true danger, standing between submerged threat and civilization? Perhaps it was simply his way of saying he wouldn't build his library near water.

Clinton concluded his remarks with a challenge to Bush couched in terms of his own failure: "Where we fell short . . . the biggest disappointment in the world to me . . . peace in the Middle East . . . I did all I could." He then faced Bush: "But when we had seven years of progress toward peace, there was one whole year when, for the first time in the history of the state of Israel, not one person died of a terrorist attack, when the Palestinians began to believe they could have a shared future. And so, Mr. President, again, I say: I hope you get to cross over into the promised land of Middle East peace. We have a good opportunity, and we are all praying for you."

At the private luncheon afterwards, in a heated tent pitched behind the library, Shimon Peres delivered a heartfelt toast to Clinton's perseverance in pursuing the Middle East peace process. On entering the tent, Bush, according to an eyewitness, told an aide: "One gulp and we're out of here." He had informed the Clintons he would stay through the lunch, but by the time Peres arose with wine glass in hand, the president was gone.

PART TWO

NEMESIS I

"CATASTROPHIC SUCCESS":
FROM THE DEATH OF TERRY SCHIAVO
TO THE VIGIL OF CINDY SHEEHAN

Mission Misconceived

DECEMBER 2, 2004

WHO WROTE THIS—a pop sociologist, obscure blogger, or anti-war playwright? "Muslims see Americans as strangely narcissistic—namely, that the war is all about us. As the Muslims see it, everything about the war is—for Americans—really no more than an extension of American domestic politics and its great game. This perception is . . . heightened by election-year atmospherics, but none the less sustains their impression that when Americans talk to Muslims, they are talking to themselves."

In fact, this is the conclusion of the report of the Defense Science Board task force on strategic communication—the product of a Pentagon advisory panel—delivered in September. Its 102 pages were not made public in the presidential campaign but, barely noticed by the U.S. press, silently slipped on to a Pentagon website on Thanksgiving eve.

The task force of military, diplomatic, academic, and business experts, assigned to develop a strategy for communications in the "global war on terrorism," had unfettered access, denied to journalists, to the inner workings of the national security apparatus. There was no intent to contribute to public debate, much less political controversy; the report was for internal consumption only.

The group discovered more than a government sector "in crisis," though it observed: "Missing are strong leadership, strategic direction, adequate coordination, sufficient resources, and a culture of measurement and evaluation." As it journeyed into the recesses of the Bush foreign policy, the task force documented the failure of fundamental premises. "America's negative image in world opinion and diminished ability to persuade are consequences of factors other than the failure to implement communications strategies," the report declares. What emerges is an indictment of an expanding and unmitigated disaster based on stubborn ignorance of the world and failed concepts that bear little relation to empirical reality, except insofar as they confirm and incite growing hatred among Muslims.

The Bush administration, according to the Defense Science Board, has misconceived a war on terrorism in the image of the Cold War. However, the struggle is not the West versus Islam; while we blindly call this a "war on terrorism," Muslims "in contrast see a history-shaking movement of Islamic restoration" against "apostate" Arab regimes allied with the United States and "western modernity—an agenda hidden within the official rubric of a 'war on terrorism.' "

In this conflict, "wholly unlike the cold war," the Bush administration's impulse has been to "imitate the routines and bureaucratic . . . mindset that so characterized that era." So the United States projects Iraqis and other Arabs as people to be liberated, like those "oppressed by Soviet rule." And the United States accepts authoritarian Arab regimes as allies against the "radical fighters." All this is nothing less than a gigantic "strategic mistake."

"There is no yearning-to-be-liberated-by-the-US groundswell among Muslim societies—except to be liberated perhaps from what they see as apostate tyrannies that the US so determinedly promotes and defends." Rhetoric about freedom is received as "no more than self-serving hypocrisy," highlighted daily by the U.S. occupation in Iraq. "Muslims do not 'hate our freedom,' but rather they hate our policies." The "dramatic narrative . . . of the war on terrorism," Bush's grand story line connecting all the dots from the World Trade Center to Baghdad, has "borne out the entire radical Islamist bill of particulars." As a result, jihadists have been able to transform themselves from marginal figures in the Muslim world into defenders against invasion, with a following of millions.

"Thus the critical problem in American public diplomacy directed toward the Muslim world is not one of 'dissemination of information,' or even one of crafting and delivering the 'right' message. Rather, it is a fundamental problem of credibility. Simply, there is none—the United States is without a working channel of communication to the world of Muslims. . . . Inevitably, therefore, whatever Americans do and say only serves the party that has both the message and the 'loud and clear' channel: the enemy."

Almost three months ago, the board delivered its report to the White House. But, a source told me, it has received no word back. Those to whom its recommendations are directed have ignored them.

For the Bush administration, expert analysis is extraneous, as it is making clear to national security professionals in its partisan scapegoating of the CIA. Experts can be expert only in telling the White House what it wants to hear. Expertise is valued not for the evidence it offers for correction, but for propaganda and validation. But no one, not in the White House, Congress, or the dwindling coalition of the willing, can claim the catastrophe has not been foretold by the best and most objective minds commissioned by the Pentagon—perhaps for the last time.

All Hail Caligula's Horse!

DECEMBER 9, 2004

IN THE LEGEND of the war on terrorism, Bernard Kerik, with his trademark shaven head, bristling mustache, and black belt in karate, occupies a special place as rough-and-ready hero. Having risen from military policeman to narcotics detective to New York City police commissioner, he finds himself on 9/11 shoulder to shoulder with Mayor Rudy Giuliani. As the towers crumble, the mayor confides in his buddy: "Bernie, thank God George Bush is president."

After the invasion of Iraq, Bush assigns Kerik to train the new Iraqi security forces. Mission accomplished, he returns to Giuliani Partners and becomes motivational speaker to captains of industry, his net worth skyrocketing. One of his most notable aphorisms: "Political criticism is our enemies' best friend." Kerik, the decorated detective, leads an investigation into the safety of cheaper Canadian prescription drugs and accompanies Giuliani before the Senate Subcommittee on Investigations, where he testifies to their danger. (Kerik and Giuliani are rewarded handsomely by their client, the U.S. pharmaceutical drug lobby.)

After John Kerry closes the gap in the presidential debates, Kerik rushes to the rescue, ominously warning of terrorist attacks: "If you put Senator Kerry in the White House, I think you are going to see that happen." Finally, Bush announces Bernard Kerik as the new secretary of homeland security.

The Department of Homeland Security is a bureaucratic Byzantium, consisting of twenty-two agencies with a budget exceeding $40 billion. Giuliani suggested Bernard Kerik's appointment to Bush. With this favor, Kerik's meteoric career has reached its zenith. The high school dropout Kerik fathered an illegitimate daughter in Korea, whom he refused to acknowledge and support. He became a bodyguard for Saudi royals and then a New York narcotics cop. In 1993, he was tapped as Giuliani's chauffeur and bodyguard.

Giuliani made Kerik deputy police commissioner and chief of the Corrections Department. One million dollars in taxpayers' money, earmarked to buy tobacco for inmates, disappeared into a private foundation run by Kerik without any accounting. In 2000, Giuliani leapfrogged Kerik over many more-qualified candidates to appoint him police commissioner.

Kerik spent much of his time after 9/11 writing a self-promoting autobiography, *The Lost Son*. The city's conflict-of-interest board eventually fined him $2,500 for using three police officers to conduct his research.

Dispatched to Iraq to whip the local security forces into shape, Kerik dubbed himself the "interim interior minister of Iraq." British police advisers called him the "Baghdad Terminator" and reported that his reckless bullying was alienating Iraqis. "I will be there at least six months," he said. He left after three.

In waging bureaucratic battles among complex organizations and players, Kerik has less experience in Washington than in Baghdad. He cannot be expected to change the funding formula determined by Bush's political calculations to favor interior Republican states. And, undoubtedly, many of those seeking the department's lucrative contracts will be signing up as clients of Giuliani Partners. The looting of Washington, unlike that of post-invasion Iraq, is legal.

In line with other second-term cabinet appointments—Alberto Gonzales as attorney general, Condoleezza Rice as secretary of state—Kerik will be an enforcer, a loyalist, and an incompetent. The resemblance is less to Inspector Clouseau or Chauncy Gardner than to Caligula's horse.

Medals of Failure

DECEMBER 16, 2004

THOUGH IT IS EARLY DAYS since Bush's reelection, the way he will handle the difficulties of imperial management which so vex him is already apparent.

No sooner was the election over than the administration began the finger-pointing at the U.N. secretary general, Kofi Annan, who had called the invasion of Iraq "illegal." News was leaked that Annan's son had been a consultant to a company involved with the U.N. oil-for-food program, though Annan said he knew nothing about it. The outgoing U.S. ambassador to the United Nations, John Danforth, was sent out to declare that Annan's resignation was a live issue.

The relevant facts about the oil-for-food program were pushed to one side. James Dobbins, the former U.S. ambassador to Afghanistan, wrote in the *Washington Post:* "First, no American funds were stolen. Second, no U.N. funds were stolen. Third, the oil-for-food program achieved its two objectives: providing food to the Iraqi people and preventing Saddam Hussein from rebuilding his military threat to the region."

Then the *Post* published a story that the United States was wiretapping Mohamed ElBaradei, director general of the U.N.'s International Atomic Energy Agency, in an attempt to demonstrate that he was secretly aiding Iran in hiding its nuclear weapons program. In fact, ElBaradei was working with the Europeans in negotiating a resolution with the Iranians. It was this diplomacy that neoconservatives were seeking to discredit. The neocons don't want Iran's compliance with international monitoring of its nuclear development; they want regime change, Iraq redux.

The techniques of the permanent campaign, especially negative attacks, recently applied in the reelection contest, are being transferred seamlessly and shamelessly to international relations.

In part, the slash-and-smear campaign against Annan and ElBaradei is the Bush administration's effort to subjugate international civil servants and organizations. But this episode also reflects the rolling coup of the neocons as they struggle for power, position, and policy in a second Bush term.

In the wake of "catastrophic success" in Iraq, as Bush called it, they are trying to foster a new conflict with Iran. Even Karl Rove, Bush's political strategist, plays in this arena, with his very own Iran adviser—Michael Ledeen, a sleazy operator on the fringes who was suspected even by Oliver North of skimming money during the Iran-contra scandal that Ledeen helped instigate.

At the least, the attacks on the United Nations serve as a political distraction from Iraq, where 178 U.S. soldiers have been killed since the election. But frontline troops have not been distracted from the reality of carnage. On December 8, they asked Secretary of Defense Donald Rumsfeld about the failure to provide sufficient armor.

Rumsfeld said: "You go to war with the army you have. They're not the army you might want or wish to have at a later time." He said the soldiers, who were jerry-rigging their armor, might be killed anyway. "It's interesting. . . . You can have all the armor in the world on a tank, and a tank can be blown up."

Never before has a defense secretary been rebuked by the troops; never has a defense secretary insulted them. Two Republican mavericks, senators John McCain and Chuck Hagel, called for his resignation, but they were whistling in the dark. Rumsfeld's disasters are Bush's. They are of such monumental dimensions that to lose him is to admit failure: he cannot be thrown overboard.

On Wednesday Bush gave honors for failure, with his bestowal of the Presidential Medal of Freedom on Tommy Franks, the former U.S. leader of Central Command, who allowed Osama bin Laden to escape at Tora Bora; George Tenet, the former CIA director, who jumped on the bandwagon for the Iraq war, informing Bush that the WMD claims were "a slam dunk"; and L. Paul Bremer, the former chief of the Coalition Provisional Authority, who disbanded the Iraqi army, among other blunders. Failure will be celebrated as success in the second term.

The farcical unraveling of the nomination of former New York City police commissioner Bernard Kerik as secretary of homeland security further illuminated the administration's methods. The fact that Kerik neglected to pay taxes on a nanny who was an illegal immigrant was a convenient alibi. Beyond his extramarital affairs, secret marriage, and love nests, he appears also to be married to the mob—on the take from the Gambino crime family. Yet Bush had been attracted to Kerik's Rambo-like aggression; the

White House vetting process seems to be as credulous as the Mickey Mouse Club, and the impulse to cover up instant.

The fall guy is the former New York mayor Rudy Giuliani, Kerik's patron. Inadvertently, Giuliani's tainting eliminates him as a moderate Republican pretender to the throne. If only Kerik's foibles had passed beneath the radar, Giuliani might have been honored for any calamity. Thus the risks and rewards in Bush's imperial capital.

Purging Poppy

DECEMBER 30, 2004

THE TRANSITION TO President Bush's second term, filled with backstage betrayals, plots, and pathologies, would make for an excellent chapter of *I, Claudius*. To begin with, Bush has unceremoniously and without public acknowledgement dumped Brent Scowcroft, his father's closest associate and friend, as chair of the Foreign Intelligence Advisory Board. The elder Bush's national security adviser was the last remnant of traditional Republican realism permitted to exist within the administration.

At the same time, the vice president, Dick Cheney, has imposed his authority over secretary of state designate Condoleezza Rice in order to blackball Arnold Kanter, former undersecretary of state to James Baker and partner in the Scowcroft group, as a candidate for deputy secretary of state.

"Words like *incoherent* come to mind," one top State Department official told me about Rice's effort to organize her office. She is unable to assert herself against Cheney, her wobbliness a sign that the State Department will mostly be sidelined as a power center for the next four years.

Rice may have wanted to appoint as a deputy her old friend Robert Blackwill, whom she had put in charge of Iraq at the National Security Council. But Blackwill, a mercurial personality, allegedly assaulted a female U.S. foreign-service officer in Kuwait and was forced to resign in November. Secretary of State Colin Powell and his deputy, Richard Armitage, presented the evidence against Blackwill to Rice. "Condi only dismissed him after Powell and Armitage threatened to go public," a State Department source said.

Meanwhile, key senior State Department professionals, such as Marc Grossman, assistant secretary of state for European affairs, have abruptly resigned. According to colleagues who have chosen to remain (at least for now), they foresee the damage that will be done as Rice is charged with whipping the State Department into line with the White House and Pentagon neocons. Rice has pleaded with Armitage to stay on, but "he colorfully said he would not," a State Department official told me. Rice's radio silence when her former mentor, Scowcroft, was defenestrated was taken by the State Department professionals as a sign of things to come.

Bush has long resented Scowcroft, his father's alter ego. Scowcroft privately rebuked him for his Iraq follies more than a year ago—an incident that has not previously been reported. Bush "did not receive it well," said a friend of Scowcroft.

In *A World Transformed,* the elder Bush's 1998 memoir, coauthored with Scowcroft, they explained why Baghdad was not seized in the first Gulf war: "Had we gone the invasion route, the U.S. could conceivably still be an occupying power in a bitterly hostile land." In the run-up to the Iraq war, Scowcroft again warned of the danger. Bush's conservative biographers Peter and Rachel Schweizer quoted the president as responding: "Scowcroft has become a pain in the ass in his old age." And they wrote: "Although he never went public with them, the president's own father shared many of Scowcroft's concerns."

The rejection of Kanter is a compound rejection of Scowcroft and James Baker—the tough, results-oriented operator who, as White House chief of staff, saved the Reagan presidency from its ideologues, managed the elder Bush's campaign in 1988, and was summoned in 2000 to rescue Junior in Florida. In his 1995 memoir, Baker observed that the administration's "overriding strategic concern in the [first] Gulf war was to avoid what we often referred to as the Lebanonization of Iraq, which we believed would create a geopolitical nightmare."

In private, Baker is scathing about the current occupant of the White House. Now the one indispensable creator of the Bush family political fortunes is repudiated.

Republican elders who warned of endless war are purged. Those who advised Bush that Saddam was building nuclear weapons, that with a light military force the operation would be a "cakewalk," and that capturing Baghdad was "mission accomplished," are rewarded.

The outgoing secretary of state, fighting his last battle, is leaking stories to the *Washington Post* about how his advice went unheeded. Secretary of Defense Donald Rumsfeld, whose heart beats with the compassion of a crocodile, clings to his job by staging Florence Nightingale–like tableaux of comforting the wounded while declaiming into the desert wind about "victory." Since the election, 203 U.S. soldiers have been killed and 1,674 wounded.

Metrics

JANUARY 14, 2005

"METRICS" IS ONE of Secretary of Defense Donald Rumsfeld's obsessions. In October 2003, he sent a memo to his deputies and the chair of the Joint Chiefs of Staff: "Today, we lack metrics to know if we are winning or losing the global war on terror." Rumsfeld demanded precise measurements of progress, including the "ideological." By the "war on terror" he meant operations in Iraq as well as Afghanistan. A study was commissioned by the JCS and conducted by the Institute for Defense Analyses, a military think tank. In utterly neutral terms, the IDA report detailed a grim picture at odds with the Bush administration's rosy scenarios. Not only has Rumsfeld suppressed the report, but the Pentagon has yet to acknowledge its existence.

In the invasion of Iraq, Rumsfeld applied his doctrine of using a light combat force, against the advice of the senior military. General Eric Shinseki, commander of the army, was cashiered and publicly ridiculed for suggesting that a larger force would be required. But Rumsfeld and the neocons assumed that there would be no long occupation because democracy would spontaneously flower.

In April 2004 the Strategic Studies Institute of the Army War College produced a report on the metrics of the Rumsfeld doctrine: *Toppling Saddam: Iraq and American Military Transformation*. It concluded that the swift victory over Saddam was achieved by overwhelming technological superiority and Iraqi weakness, and therefore using Operation Iraqi Freedom as "evidence" for Rumsfeld's "transformation proposals could be a mistake." The Pentagon has refused to release the study.

"Intellectual terrorism" prevails through the defense establishment, I was told by a leading military strategist at one of the war colleges, who deals in calm, measured expertise of a nonpartisan nature. Even the Rand Corporation, the respected defense research institute, is being "cut out of the loop," denied contracts for studies because the "metrics" are at odds with Rumsfeld's projections.

President Bush clings to good news and happy talk, such as the number of school openings in Iraq. Those with gloomy assessments are not permitted to appear before him. The president orders no meetings on options based on worst-case scenarios. Military strategists and officers are systematically ignored. Suppression of contrary "metrics" is done in his name and spirit. Bush makes his decisions from a self-constructed bunker, a situation room of the mind, where ideological fantasies substitute for reality.

"I think elections will be such a hopeful experience for the Iraqi people. . . . And I look at the elections as a . . . as a . . . you know, as a . . . as . . . as a historical marker for our Iraq policy," Bush said last week. His statement was prompted by the actions of Brent Scowcroft, his father's national security adviser and alter ego. Fired as chair of the Foreign Intelligence Advisory Board, Scowcroft aired his views at a lunch sponsored by a Washington think tank. The Iraq election, he said, has "deep potential for deepening the conflict," acting as an impetus to "civil war." He reflected sadly that being a "realist" has become a "pejorative." "A road map is helpful if you know where you are," he said.

Scowcroft was joined by Zbigniew Brzezinski, President Jimmy Carter's national security adviser, who spelled out the minimal metrics for winning the Iraq war—half a million troops, $500 billion, a military draft, and a wartime tax—and said that even then it would take at least ten years. Unwillingness to pay this price while continuing on the current path would be a sign of "decadence."

Bush speaks of the Iraqi election as though it is the climax of democracy. But by failing to provide for Sunni presence in the new government—proportional representation would easily have accomplished this—it is as ill-conceived a blunder as invading with a light force, disbanding the Iraqi army, attacking Fallujah, halting the attack, and finally destroying the city in order to save it, Vietnam style. The British had proposed local elections, beginning in southern Iraq, but Bush's Coalition Provisional Authority rejected this plan. According to the former CPA official Larry Diamond: "One British official lamented to me, 'The CPA [officials] didn't want anything to happen that they didn't control.' "

Bush, meanwhile, works on his second inaugural address, to be delivered next week, for which his speechwriters can be counted on to produce a bravura speech filled with high-flown patriotism and evangelical code words, a paean to can-do optimism. "They're not code words; they're our culture," his chief speechwriter, Michael Gerson, explained recently.

This rhetoric summons purity of heart ("written in the human heart"), divine blessing ("God is not neutral"), and the power of faith ("there's power, wonder-working power, in the goodness and idealism and faith of the American people").

As Bush draws the sword of righteousness against the forces of darkness, the enemy being evil itself ("evildoers," the "axis of evil"), he ascends on messianic imagery. "Do you not think an angel rides in the whirlwind and directs this storm?" he said in his first inaugural, quoting a letter written by a Virginian friend to Thomas Jefferson during the American Revolution. "This story goes on," said Bush. "And an angel still rides in the whirlwind and directs this storm."

That particular verse originates in the book of the prophet Nahum. It contains no "angel," but the Lord, "a jealous and avenging God . . . full of wrath . . . The Lord is long suffering, and great in power, and will by no means clear the guilty; The Lord, in the whirlwind and in the storm is His way, And the clouds are the dust of His feet . . . Woe to the bloody city! It is all full of lies and rapine . . . Thy crowned are as the locusts, And thy marshals as the swarms of grasshoppers."

These metrics continue for several more verses: "There is no assuaging of thy hurt, thy wound is grievous."

Regime Change

JANUARY 20, 2005

IN HIS SECOND TERM, President Bush is determined on regime change. The country whose order he seeks to overthrow is not ruled by mullahs or Baathists. But members of his administration have compared its system to communism. The battle will be "one of the most important conservative undertakings of modern times," wrote the deputy to Karl Rove, the White House political chief, in a confidential memo. Since the election, the president has spoken often of the "coming crisis," and he has mobilized the government to mold public opinion for the conflict ahead. The nation whose regime he is set on toppling is the United States.

Since the New Deal, the American social contract has been built on acceptance of its reforms. When Dwight Eisenhower became the first Republican president after Franklin Roosevelt and Harry Truman, he never challenged the New Deal, but instead solidified the political consensus that has prevailed for decades. Now Bush has launched an assault on the social contract in earnest, seeking to blast away at its cornerstone, Social Security, which disburses pensions to the elderly and payments to the disabled.

The end of the election marked the start of Bush's new campaign, stumping relentlessly to replace this "flat bust, bankrupt" system by siphoning Social Security funds into private stock-market accounts. His motive was best explained by his political aide, Peter Wehner, in a memo circulated through the White House: "For the first time in six decades, the Social Security battle is one we can win," Wehner wrote triumphantly in the afterglow of the election victory. "And in doing so, we can help transform the political and philosophical landscape of the country."

To achieve this conservative dream, the public must first be convinced that Social Security is bankrupt. The administration, Wehner writes, must "establish an important premise: the current system is heading toward an iceberg. We need to establish in the public mind a key fiscal fact: right now we are on an unsustainable course." Moreover, Wehner states, the private accounts are simply a wedge for future benefit cuts, though he does not advocate that the administration stress that point.

And so Bush and Cheney insist that Social Security will soon be "flat bust." A political front group run by one of Rove's protégés, which produced the television commercials that trumpeted defamations about John Kerry's military record, is spinning out new ads on Social Security. The Social Security Administration itself has been dragooned into sending out millions of letters telling recipients that the system is in "crisis."

Despite Bush's furious animadversions, the Social Security actuaries in their most sober assessments report that the current system will issue full benefits without any changes until 2042. Very slight modifications then would guarantee complete solvency into the indefinite future. Thus the "iceberg" melts before the facts.

"It's a badly, badly flawed plan," Robert Rubin, the former secretary of the treasury and current Citigroup director, told me. "From a fiscal point of view, it's horrendous. It adds to deficits and federal debt in very large numbers until 2060." He calculates that the transition costs of Bush's plan for the first ten years will be at least $2 trillion, and $4.5 trillion for the second ten years. The exploding deficit would have an "adverse effect on interest rates, an adverse effect on consumption and housing prices, reduce productivity and growth, and crowd out debt capital to the private sector. Markets could begin to lose confidence in fiscal policy. The soundness of Social Security will be worse."

Rubin adds that the stock market is hardly a sure bet. "You are not making Social Security more secure by subjecting people's retirement to equity risk. If you look at the Nikkei in Japan, you get a sense of what can happen."

Behind the pomp and circumstance of the inauguration, the display of might and rhetoric of right, lie the fear and trembling of the Republican Party. If the defeated, disheartened Democrats can maintain a modicum of discipline, the Republicans will alone be forced to defend Bush's Social Security proposal. Enough of them realize that attacking the fundament of the social contract may let loose political furies against them. Already the powerful chair of the House Ways and Means Committee, Bill Thomas, has called Bush's plan "a dead horse." But Bush appears intent on regime change at home. In his first term, he promised "compassionate conservatism." In his second term, he pledges casino conservatism, the restoration of boom and bust, which he calls "the ownership society." He has gambled his presidency on it.

"A Broken Force"

JANUARY 27, 2005

THE MOST PENETRATING CRITIQUE of the realism informing President Bush's second inaugural address, a trumpet call of imperial ambition, was made one month before it was delivered, by Lieutenant General James Helmly, chief of the U.S. Army Reserve.

In an internal memorandum, he described "the Army Reserve's inability under current policies, procedures and practices . . . to meet mission requirements associated with Operation Iraqi Freedom and Enduring Freedom. The Army Reserve is additionally in grave danger of being unable to meet other operational requirements and is rapidly degenerating into a broken force."

These "dysfunctional" policies are producing a crisis "more acute and hurtful" as the Reserve's ability to mobilize troops is "eroding daily."

The U.S. force in Iraq of about 150,000 troops is composed of a "volunteer" army that came into being with the end of military conscription during the Vietnam War. More than 40 percent are National Guard and reserve troops, most of whom have completed second tours of duty and are being sent out again.

The Pentagon has maintained the force level only by "stop-loss" orders that coerce soldiers to remain in service after their contractual enlistment expires—a back-door draft. Reenlistment is collapsing, dropping by 30 percent last year. The Pentagon justified this de facto conscription by telling Congress that it is merely a short-term solution until Iraq stabilizes and an Iraqi security force fills the vacuum. But this week the Pentagon announced that the U.S. force level would remain unchanged through 2006.

"I don't know where these troops are coming from. It's mystifying," Representative Ellen Tauscher, a ranking Democrat on the House Armed Services Committee, told me. "There's no policy to deal with the fact we have a military in extremis."

Bush's speech calling for "ending tyranny in all the world" was of consistent abstraction uninflected by anything as specific as the actual condition of the military that would presumably be deployed on various global missions.

But the speech was aflame with images of destruction and vengeance. The neoconservatives were ecstatic, perhaps as much at their influence in inserting their gnostic code words into the speech as the dogmatism of the speech itself.

For them, Bush's rhetoric about "eternal hope that is meant to be fulfilled" was a sign of their triumph. The speech, crowed the neocon journalist William Kristol, who consulted on it, was indeed "informed by Strauss"—a reference to Leo Strauss, a philosopher of obscurantist strands of absolutist thought, mentor and inspiration to some neocons who believe they fulfill his teaching by acting as tutors to politicians in need of their guidance.

Informed is hardly the precise word to account for the manipulation of Bush's impulses by cultish advisers with ulterior motives. Even as the neocons reveled in their influence, Bush's glittering generalities, lofted on wings of hypocrisy, crashed to earth. Would we launch campaigns against tyrannical governments in Pakistan, Egypt, Saudi Arabia, or China? Of course, as the White House briefed reporters, Bush didn't mean his rhetoric to suggest any change in strategy.

Unfortunately for Condoleezza Rice, such levels of empty abstraction could not glide her through her Senate confirmation as secretary of state without abrasion. With implacable rigidity, she stood by every administration decision. There was no disinformation on Saddam Hussein's development of nuclear weapons of mass destruction; any suggestion that she had provided misleading information in the rush to war was an attack on her personal integrity. The light military force for the invasion was just right. And it is still just right.

Contrary to Senator Joseph Biden of the Foreign Relations Committee, who stated that there are only 14,000 trained members of the Iraqi security forces, she insisted there are 120,000. Why, Secretary of Defense Rumsfeld had told her so.

Then, implicitly acknowledging the failure to create a credible Iraqi army, the Pentagon announced that the U.S. forces would remain at the same level for the next two years. Rice's Pollyanna testimony was suddenly inoperative. The administration has no strategy for Iraq or for the coerced American army plodding endlessly across the desert.

Representative Tauscher wonders when the House Armed Services Committee, along with the rest of the Congress, will learn anything from the Bush administration that might be considered factual: "They are never persuaded by the facts. Nobody can tell you what their plan is, and they don't feel the need to have one."

On the eve of the Iraqi election, neither the president's soaring rhetoric nor the new secretary of state's fantasy numbers touch the brutal facts on the ground.

The March of Folly

FEBRUARY 3, 2005

PRESIDENT BUSH'S State of the Union address adds an element of euphoria to the utopianism of his inaugural speech. Coming between the two speeches, the Iraqi election has given him a significant event over which to drape his universal abstractions. Who would not want it to be true that the courageous people of Iraq, as one body, have defied bloodthirsty fanatics in order to establish a thriving democracy that will be a beacon to the rest of the Middle East, and that the glow from that fire will truly light the world?

The Iraqi election went more or less as anticipated. The Kurds voted in overwhelming numbers, and an exit poll reported that they overwhelmingly endorsed independence. The Shia, the majority suppressed throughout the history of Iraq, turned out in large numbers to celebrate their inevitable empowerment. The Sunnis, who have always ruled, but whom the election ratified as a minority and who were allotted no part in a new government, hardly voted at all. Most of the Sunnis are sympathetic to the insurgency. Yet all the parties campaigned on ending "the occupation," as even members of Prime Minister Iyad Allawi's cabinet call the coalition forces. Integrating the Sunnis has been made more difficult by a centrifugal election process.

The morning after, the Iraqi state received the nod of legitimacy from other governments, but it is no more capable than before of providing security or basic public services. It remains utterly dependent on "the occupation" for the indeterminate future. Nor is this democracy any more protective of liberal values. Just days before the election, Human Rights Watch reported that the Iraqi government engages in systematic torture of detainees.

The Shia victory was a quiet victory for Iran, whose leaders, unlike Bush, did not claim credit. The Iranian Shia government has invested more than $1 billion in Iraqi Shia political parties, organizations, and media. The Qods Force, the extraterritorial arm of Iran's Islamic Revolutionary Guards, has trained Shia militias, and its intelligence agents have honeycombed the Iraq government and Shia parties.

Before the election, King Abdullah of Jordan warned of a "Shia crescent" dominated by Iran that could stretch through Iraq to southern Lebanon. Though Abdullah praised the balloting in Iraq, the governments of Saudi Arabia and Egypt share his anxiety about Iranian influence in Iraq.

The Iraqi election is the culmination of the long Iran-Iraq war that Iran has won without lifting a finger. Its neighbor has been replaced by a Shia ascendancy atop a weak state that cannot threaten it, but is subject to its influence in many ways. When the mist of elation lifts, the shadow of Iran looms.

The Bush policy consists of paralysis interrupted by fits of saber rattling. The responsibility to rein in Iran's development of nuclear weapons has been assumed by the United Nations and the European Union. Led by Mohammed ElBaradei, head of the U.N.'s International Atomic Energy Agency, the European Union has negotiated Iran's agreement for now to allow inspection of its facilities and to freeze its production of fissionable material. For his good deed (and for declaring before the Iraq war that there were no weapons of mass destruction there), the Bush administration has attempted to oust ElBaradei.

Despite their promise, these negotiations are unlikely to succeed unless the United States enters into them; for only the United States can offer the big carrots: lifting the sanctions, recognition, and perhaps entry into the World Trade Organization. The presence of 150,000 troops next door has not prevented Iran from suppressing its reform movement. Opening Iran to liberalization, while containing its nuclear ambition, would appear to be an obvious win-win situation for the West. But some in the administration want the negotiations to fail.

Vice President Cheney fantasizes about an Israeli air strike on Iranian nuclear facilities. Seymour Hersh of the *New Yorker* reports that there are clandestine special-operations teams inside Iran trying to identify suitable targets for U.S. bombing. Two Republican senators, Rick Santorum and John Cornyn, have introduced a bill that would authorize the funding of Iranian exile groups and stipulate "regime change" as official U.S. policy. Yet the United States is overstretched militarily, and it is not certain that all Iranian nuclear facilities would be eliminated by an Osirak-like strike. If attacked, Iran could create untold mischief within Iraq. But the dream world of ideology trumps the national interest. Thus, toward the Europeans' greatest diplomatic initiative on the country whose fate is most closely linked with Iraq, Bush's policy, on the eve of his trip to Europe, is a vacuum.

Blinding bursts of triumphalism are characteristic of a march of folly, and they quicken its pace. True, just as paranoids have real enemies, the euphoric can experience a high from events that actually occur. But the insistence on euphoria, as those who grapple with reality know, is symptomatic of a disorder that can dangerously swing in mood.

Spending Political Capital

FEBRUARY 10, 2005

FEAR MADE GEORGE BUSH'S PRESIDENCY, gave him his "mission," and allowed him to remain in office. Before September 11, he had drifted to the lowest approval rating ever for a president after just eight months on the job.

Throughout the 2004 campaign, Republicans hammered out "September 11," "terrorism," and "Saddam Hussein" like an anvil chorus. Bush got his victory in the narrowest win of any second-term president since Woodrow Wilson in 1916, but he acts as if it is the moment of deliverance Republicans have been waiting for since Herbert Hoover lost the White House.

Because fear created Bush's "political capital," he sees no reason why it should fail him now. His attempt to transfer fear from the war on terrorism to the war on the New Deal may seem straightforward to him, but the truth is that only fear generated in foreign policy has protected him politically from his unpopular positions on domestic issues. Since September 11, without variation, Bush's poll numbers have paralleled the quantity of news stories about terrorism. The more terrorism dominates the media, the higher his ratings; and whenever terrorism reporting declines, he begins to sink. The war on terrorism is his meta-narrative. But what happens when the ground shifts?

In the Middle East, the Israelis and Palestinians have declared a ceasefire. The progress of negotiations will depend in large part on an increased U.S. role. Can Bush continue to act as the innocent bystander? In Iraq, since the election there, even military operations against the Sunni insurgency have moved into the context of internal politics. Does Kurdish ambition have any bounds? Will the Kurds be permitted to control oil-rich Kirkuk or the presidency, both of which threaten the NATO relationship with Turkey?

Is the U.S. military the enforcer of Islamic law imposed by the Shias, including polygamy and mandatory chadors? More broadly, is the United

States the internal security force for Iran's interest in Shia ascendancy? (The Iranian ambassador to the United Kingdom, Seyed Mohammad-Hossein Adeli, said in a speech last week: "Thanks to American adventurism, we have got rid of both the Taliban and Saddam.") And, having now encouraged European engagement with Iran on nuclear development, will the United States join in order to bring it to a successful conclusion?

The secretary of state, Condoleezza Rice, declared in Paris: "It is time to turn away from the disagreements of the past." But whose past did she mean? Her next statement gave the answer: "The key to our future success lies in getting beyond a partnership based on common threats, and building an even stronger partnership based on common opportunities, even those beyond the transatlantic community."

Rice's pronouncement is nothing less than a break with Bush's threat-based approach. Without ambiguity or nuance, she said U.S. foreign policy must now be rooted not in the war on terrorism, but in "opportunities."

While Rice was on her grand tour, Bush rushed from his State of the Union address to rallies in the West and South to stump for Social Security privatization. Despite research by the Social Security actuary and the Congressional Budget Office to the contrary, he insists the system is collapsing. As he jetted across the United States, Republican representatives and senators either announced their opposition or reserved judgment.

At his rallies, the crowds cheered his words against terrorism as though they were a nostalgic reenactment of his campaign and then fell into befuddled silence.

His explanations of the Social Security proposal were so convoluted that Bush confessed: "Does that make any sense to you? It's kind of muddled. Look, there's a series of things that cause the . . . like, for example, benefits are calculated based upon the increase of wages, as opposed to the increase of prices. Some have suggested that we calculate . . . the benefits will rise based upon inflation, as opposed to wage increases. There is a reform that would help solve the red if that were put into effect. In other words, how fast benefits grow, how fast the promised benefits grow, if those . . . if that growth is affected, it will help on the red. OK, better? I'll keep working on it."

A week after the address, the White House has admitted it has no timetable for proposing a plan. The urgent centerpiece of Bush's second term is indefinitely on hold.

Bush's gibberish on Social Security is not the sign of a man without qualities. Bush can be articulate, a master of his talking points and highly focused. His inability so far to sell his latest case of fear, however, may presage growing political incoherence. The momentum of events, abroad and at home, has carried him to an unknown place, where complications may ambush him at every turn. The consequences of George W. Bush are the greatest threat to George W. Bush.

A Hireling, a Fraud, and a Prostitute

FEBRUARY 17, 2005

THE WHITE HOUSE PRESSROOM has often been a cockpit of intrigue, duplicity, and truckling. But nothing challenges the most recent scandal there.

The latest incident began with a sequence of questions for President Bush at his January 26 press conference. First, he was asked whether he approved of his administration's payments to conservative commentators. Government contracts had been granted to three pundits who had tried to keep the funding secret. "There needs to be a nice, independent relationship between the White House and the press," said the president as he called swiftly on his next questioner.

Jeff Gannon, Washington bureau chief of Talon News, rose from his chair to attack Democrats in the Congress. "How are you going to work— you said you're going to reach out to these people—how are you going to work with people who seem to have divorced themselves from reality?"

For almost two years Gannon had been called on by press secretary Scott McClellan in the daily White House press briefings to break up difficult questioning from the rest of the press. On Fox News, one host hailed him as "a terrific Washington bureau chief and White House correspondent." Gannon was frequently quoted and highlighted as an expert guest on right-wing radio shows. But who was he? His strange nonquestion to the president inspired inquiry. Talon News is a wholly owned subsidiary of a group of Texas Republicans. Gannon's most notable article had asserted that John Kerry "might some day be known as 'the first gay President.'"

Gannon also got himself entangled in the investigation into the criminal disclosure of the identity of the covert CIA operative Valerie Plame. Plame is the wife of the former U.S. ambassador Joseph Wilson, who was sent by the Bush administration to discover whether Saddam Hussein was procuring uranium in Niger for nuclear weapons. He learned that the suspicion was bogus; appalled that the administration lied about nuclear WMD to justify the Iraq war, he wrote an article in the *New York Times* about his role after the war.

In retaliation, administration officials blew Plame's CIA cover. Gannon had called up Wilson to ask him about a secret CIA memo supposedly proving that his wife had sent him on the original mission to Niger, prompting the special prosecutor in the case to question Gannon about his "sources."

Gannon's real name, it turns out, is James Dale Guckert. He has no journalistic background whatsoever. His application for a press credential to cover the Congress was rejected. But at the White House, the press office arranged for him to be given a new pass every single day, a deliberate evasion of the regular credentialing that requires an FBI security check. It was soon revealed that "Gannon" owned and advertised his services as a gay escort on more than half a dozen websites with names like Militarystud.com, MaleCorps.com, WorkingBoys.net, and MeetLocalMen.com, which featured dozens of photographs of "Gannon" in dramatic naked poses. One of the sites was still active this week.

Thus a phony journalist, planted by a Republican organization, used by the White House press secretary to interrupt questions from the press corps, protected from FBI vetting by the press office, disseminating smears (some of them homophobic) about its critics and opponents, was unmasked not only as a hireling and fraud but as a gay prostitute, at enormous risk for blackmail.

The Bush White House is the most opaque—allowing the least access for reporters—in living memory. Every news organization has been intimidated, and reporters who have done stories the administration finds discomfiting have received threats about their careers. The administration has its own quasi-official national TV network in Fox News; hundreds of right-wing radio shows, conservative newspapers, journals, and Internet sites coordinate with the Republican apparatus.

Inserting an agent directly into the White House press corps was a daring operation. Until his exposure, Gannon proved useful for the White House. But the ploy highlights the Republican effort to sideline an independent press and undermine its legitimacy. Spin now seems quaint. "In this day and age," said Press Secretary McClellan, waxing philosophical about the Gannon affair, "when you have a changing media, it's not an easy issue to decide or try to pick and choose who is a journalist." It is not that the White House press secretary cannot distinguish who is or is not a journalist: it is that there are no journalists, just the gaming of the system for the concentration of power. The undercover agent in the press corps has given spin a new level of meaning.

The Plot against the New Deal

MARCH 3, 2005

THE COMING DEFEAT of President Bush on Social Security will be the defining moment in domestic policy and politics for his second term and for the future of the Republican Party. It will be a central, clarifying event because Bush alone chose to start this fight.

Campaigning in 2004 on the trauma of September 11, he won by the smallest margin of any incumbent president in American history. The Electoral College map was little changed from the deadlock of 2000. Although Bush barely took two states he had lost before (Iowa and New Mexico), he lost New Hampshire to John Kerry. Bush's political adviser, Karl Rove, had forecast a fundamental realignment that would establish Republican dominance, but Bush's desperate political position required a series of tactics of character assassination against the Democratic candidate and culture-war gambits on gay marriage, organized around the fear factor of September 11. The outcome was a strategic victory but not a structural one, and Bush's campaign further polarized the country.

In the chasm between his meager win and his grandiose ambition, Bush might have decided to form a government containing some moderate Republican and Democratic cabinet members, claiming that the gravity of foreign crisis demanded national unity. But the thought apparently never occurred to him. Instead, he charged ahead in the hope of realizing the realignment that eluded him in the election.

Not since 1928, when Herbert Hoover was elected in a landslide, have the Republicans held the White House and such clear majorities in both the House of Representatives and the Senate. Bush acts with the urgency of a president for whom political advantage must be seized now or lost forever. So he has decided to swing a sledgehammer at the cornerstone of the New Deal and the Democratic Party. The gamble would pay off in closely tying to the Republican Party the Wall Street banks that would finance the transition costs of privatization and the bond houses and stock firms that would be flush with new investments. But, most important, it would unravel the fact and idea of government entitlement programs providing for the needs of the people as a whole. Once Social Security was cut into pieces, the Democrats would be left defensively representing the least politically powerful and most vulnerable—literally the lame and the halt, poor single mothers ("welfare queens"), and minorities. The Democrats would be drawn and quartered on the wheel of broken entitlements.

Bush launched his initiative to privatize Social Security with a bang, promoting it in his State of the Union address and stumping the country at rallies. Rove has been put in charge of organizing the campaign as an extension of the 2004 effort. From the White House, Rove directs the lobbyists of K Street in Washington and the U.S. Chamber of Commerce, the National Rifle Association, and the religious right. Suddenly, the Swift Boat Veterans for Truth have reappeared as warriors against the pro–Social Security AARP, smearing the seniors' organization as antimilitary and pro–gay marriage. And Tony Feather, a Republican consultant with long-time ties to Rove, has reemerged with a war chest of millions to spend through a front group called Progress for America, just as he did against Kerry.

Even the Social Security Administration has been inducted into the campaign. Five years ago, it sent out a routine annual booklet titled *The Future of Social Security: Will Social Security Be There for You? Absolutely.* Now a new booklet has been mailed to tens of millions, warning: "Social Security must change to meet future challenges." And it suggests that Social Security should not be regarded as a "foundation on which to build your financial future."

And yet the more the public has learned of Bush's plan, the more that plan has buckled. Poll after poll reveals that increased information about it leads to heightened resistance. Growing majorities oppose Bush's program, Bush's favorability rating has plunged to the lowest level of any president at this point in his second term, and trust in the Democrats has steadily risen.

In the face of public rejection, Bush retreats and attacks at the same time. He has announced that he is uncertain when or even if he will propose his own bill before Congress, while the White House says that the president will stage new rallies for a Social Security initiative that has yet to take any practical form.

Republican leaders have become studies in hesitation and anxiety. The Senate majority leader, Bill Frist, declares that the "pacing" should be "determined by the American people." In a statement as fuzzy as he could manage, he explained, "In terms of whether it will be a week, a month, six months, or a year as to when we bring something to the floor, it's just too early."

The House majority leader, Tom DeLay, rhetorically echoing Saddam Hussein's reference to the "mother of all battles," called Social Security the "mother of all issues." He added: "And it is going to take a lot of dialogue with the American people." When Tom "the Hammer" DeLay, who hangs a whip on his wall, pleads for understanding, the problem must be that the American people understand too much already.

To Bush and the Republicans, the problem is one of salesmanship. If only they hone the pitch and convince the wary customers that they really mean well, saving people from a bad investment and delivering a bargain, they will clinch the deal. Frank Luntz, a Republican consultant who has made a specialty out of wordplay, has advised them on how to make friends and influence people. In a memo circulated among the Republican leadership last month, he urged that Republicans appeal to emotions, not facts. The public, Luntz writes, wants "empathy rather than statistical declarations. . . . It is tempting to counter-attack using facts and figures. Resist the temptation." He reemphasizes: Social Security "is a difficult subject because there are many obscure facts and figures. Stay away from them!!!" No fewer than three exclamation points!!!

Republicans, says Luntz, should never use the word *privatized*. They should substitute *personalized*. "And PLEASE remember that you are NEVER talking about privatizing Social Security, nor are you advocating INDIVIDUAL accounts. You are talking about creating PERSONAL retirement accounts." Republicans should talk about "personalized accounts" as being about "the future," he says, and also remind people that "Social Security was built for a different America."

Another problem, Luntz instructs Republicans, is that the public is familiar with the gyrations of the stock market. "There is a difficulty . . . in talking too much about the stock market. The American people are sensitive to the ups and downs of the stock market." So, he urges, Republicans should claim that that Social Security is at "larger risk" if it is not "personalized."

When all else fails, Republicans should simply resort to the fear factor: "September 11th changed everything. So start with September 11th. This is the context that explains and justifies why we have $500 billion deficits, why the stock market tanked, why unemployment climbed to 6 percent . . . Without the context of September 11th you will be blamed for the deficit. . . . Link the war on terror to the economy."

But Luntz's rhetorical twists and turns, adopted by Bush and the Republicans, are hardly innovative. They are as ancient as the earliest arguments made by Republicans against Social Security when it was first introduced. Social Security is in crisis, Social Security will not be there, only the Republicans can save the system by privatizing it—all these themes were advanced in the 1936 Republican Party platform. This yellowing document reads like the most recent Republican declaration: "Society has an obligation to promote the security of the people, by affording some measure of protection against involuntary unemployment and dependency in old age. The New Deal policies, while purporting to provide Social Security, have, in fact, endangered it." The 1936 Republican platform claimed that the federal government would not be able to meet its financial obligations to pay retirement benefits, and two-thirds of the people would be deprived. It also insisted that "the fund will contain nothing but the government's promise to pay" and was "unworkable."

The Republican candidate for president against Franklin D. Roosevelt that year, Alf Landon, governor of Kansas, was the first to run on "reforming" Social Security, which he dubbed a "hoax." Roosevelt's victory seemingly settled the question of Social Security and the basic programs of the New Deal. In every election afterward, the GOP split internally between conservatives, who rallied behind their standard-bearer, Senator Robert Taft, and those who called themselves modern Republicans. When Dwight Eisenhower defeated the eternally disappointed Taft for the 1952 nomination, the conservatives crawled to a corner, embittered and despairing. Conservatives were convinced that overthrowing the New Deal must be accomplished through a long march through the Republican Party, also overthrowing modern Republicanism.

At last, in 1964, the conservatives grabbed the Republican nomination, and their candidate, Barry Goldwater, thrilled them by declaring his opposition to Social Security. Goldwater advocated privatization to deal with what he claimed was the system's crisis: "It promises more benefits to more people than the incomes collected will provide," he said.

In the closing days of the 1964 campaign, as Goldwater faced overwhelming defeat, his campaign purchased television time to broadcast a speech by a Goldwater supporter who was felt to be a more convincing salesman than the candidate: Ronald Reagan. This speech was Reagan's debut on the national stage and the effective launch of his political career. The image remains; the words are mostly forgotten.

In fact, much of his talk was devoted to making the well-worn case against Social Security. It faced "fiscal shortcomings." It was not "insurance" but really a "welfare program." It was deeply in debt. Young workers could "take out a policy that would pay more than Social Security. Now are we so lacking in business sense that we can't put this program on a sound basis, so that people who do require those payments will find they can get them when they're due—that the cupboard isn't bare? . . . Can't we introduce voluntary features?" To conclude his argument, Reagan warned that a medical program in France was bankrupt and that the same fate would befall Social Security: "They've come to the end of the road."

But when Reagan became president, he jettisoned his denunciation of Social Security. In 1983, he signed a bipartisan tax and benefits bill extending its solvency until 2060. The ultimate conservative had used anti–Social Security rhetoric to galvanize his conservative base to gain office, but as president he joined his Republican predecessors in supporting the system. With that, he took the issue off the table for years. Campaigning in 1996, Senator Bob Dole never said a word against Social Security, proud of having been a cosponsor of the 1983 bill Reagan had signed.

Now, George W. Bush has sought what Ronald Reagan would not. Only Bush as president has attempted to make good on the reactionary rhetoric against Social Security since its inception. He has tried to dress up his effort as a "reform," as a "new idea," but the language, on historical examination, turns out to be recycled from the 1936 Republican platform, the Landon and Goldwater campaigns, and words that Reagan discarded as president.

Bush's impending defeat on Social Security is no minor affair. He has made this the centerpiece of domestic policy of his second term. It is the decades-long culmination of the conservative wing's hostility against Social Security and the Democratic Party. Projecting images of Roosevelt and Kennedy cannot distract from Bush's intent to undermine the accomplishments of Democratic presidents. The repudiation of Bush on Social Security will be fundamental and profound and will shake the foundations of conservative Republicanism. Bush's agony is only beginning, if the Democrats in the Senate can maintain their discipline.

Orwell's Clock

MARCH 10, 2005

IN THE HEAT OF THE BATTLE over the Florida vote after the 2000 U.S. presidential election, a burly, mustachioed man burst into the room where the ballots for Miami–Dade County were being tabulated, like John Wayne barging into a saloon for a shoot-out. "I'm with the Bush-Cheney team, and I'm here to stop the count," drawled John Bolton. And those ballots from Miami-Dade were not counted.

Now that same John Bolton has been named by President Bush as the U.S. ambassador to the United Nations. "If I were redoing the Security Council today, I'd have one permanent member, because that's the real reflection of the distribution of power in the world," Bolton once said. Lately, as undersecretary of state for arms control, he has wrecked all the nonproliferation diplomacy within his reach. Over the past two decades he has been the person most dedicated to trying to discredit the United Nations. George Orwell's clock of 1984 is striking thirteen.

The euphoria (at least among some European elites) that Bush's European trip marked a conversion on the road to Brussels is fading. It was Bush himself who decided to reward Bolton with a position where he could continue his crusade as a "convinced Americanist" against the "globalists," especially those at the United Nations and the European Union.

Bolton made a play to become deputy secretary of state after the 2004 election, but Condoleezza Rice, who understood that his love of bureaucratic infighting would have undermined her authority, blocked him. Dick Cheney privately promised Bolton that if all else failed he would give Bolton a job on his vice-presidential staff, but that proved unnecessary when Bush nominated him to the U.N. post. Rice announced his appointment, symbolically demonstrating that he reports to her. But Bolton has deep support within the White House, whereas Rice is very much a work in progress. With Bolton's appointment, the empire strikes back.

Bolton is an extraordinary combination of political operator and ideologue. He began his career as a cog in the machine of Senator Jesse Helms of North Carolina, helping Helms's political action committees evade legal restrictions and federal fines. Helms, the most powerful reactionary in the Senate, sponsored Bolton's rise to Reagan's Justice Department. "John Bolton," Helms said, "is the kind of man with whom I would want to stand at Armageddon, or what the Bible describes as the final battle between good and evil."

Bolton is often called a neoconservative, but he is more a neocon ally, implementer, and agent. His roots are in Helms's Dixiecrat Republicanism, not the neocons' airy Trotskyism or Straussianism.

Bolton is a specimen of the "primitives," as Truman's secretary of state, Dean Acheson, called the unilateralists and McCarthyites of the early Cold War. Through his political integration into the neocon apparatus, Bolton might be classified a neoprimitive.

At the State Department, Bolton was Colin Powell's enemy within. In his first year, he forced the U.S. withdrawal from the Anti–Ballistic Missile Treaty, destroyed a protocol on enforcing the Biological Weapons Convention, and ousted the head of the Organization for the Prohibition of Chemical Weapons. He scuttled the Comprehensive Nuclear Test Ban Treaty and the U.N. Conference on the Illicit Trade in Small Arms and Light Weapons. And he was behind the renunciation of the U.S. signature on the 1998 Rome statute creating the International Criminal Court. He described sending his letter notifying the U.N. secretary general, Kofi Annan, as "the happiest moment of my government service."

Bolton's meddling in diplomacy on nonproliferation with North Korea and Iran guaranteed that the allies had no unified position and encouraged the Koreans and Iranians to play the nuclear card. Bolton's response to these crises has been to lead the charge to remove the head of the U.N.'s International Atomic Energy Agency, Mohamed ElBaradei. In late November, Bolton denounced the Blair government and the Europeans negotiating with the Iranians as "soft" for attempting "diplomatic means."

Bolton might be granted the integrity of his primitivism, a true believer who imagines Fortress America besieged by the United Nations and Europeans: "Americanists find themselves surrounded by small armies of globalists, each tightly clutching a favorite new treaty or multilateralist proposal." But Bolton's coarse ideology is advanced by sophisticated campaigns of disinformation, and not only on Iraq and North Korea. His leaks of falsehoods that Syria and Cuba had developed weapons of mass destruction sparked internal revolts by intelligence professionals and the foreign service.

For Bolton, as for his neoconservative allies, the ends justify the means. But, unlike them, he has no use for romantic rhetoric about the "march of freedom" and "democracy," as he demonstrated so effectively in Florida. And now he has the job he sought above all from the beginning.

The Brilliant Career of Jack Abramoff

MARCH 17, 2005

As "Still the One" boomed from the loudspeakers, shaking the silverware in the Washington Hilton ballroom Tuesday, the most powerful Republican in Congress, House Majority Leader Tom DeLay, appeared on the stage before more than a thousand Republican faithful—a martyr scourged and flayed by evildoers for his purity of heart. It was his enemies who had the dirty hands. The Democrats are "without power" and "have put style above substance, politics over people, and partisanship over everything." Immediately after being cheered, DeLay held a press conference to denounce the press as purveyors of "fiction and innuendo."

The uncertain fate of the majority leader, known as the "Hammer" and to the Republican members and lobbyists in Washington as "the concierge of Capitol Hill," threatens to undermine not only the Bush administration's agenda but also the political machine DeLay has built by allying special interests, lobbyists, and Republicans, and the Republican dominance of Congress. The conservative leader Paul Weyrich pronounced that defending DeLay is a life-or-death matter—"spiritual warfare."

Not once at this Republican conference on tax reform did DeLay mention that he had just minutes earlier escaped from another of his ethical travails. On a party-line vote, the House had just defeated a Democratic measure to create a bipartisan task force "to restore public confidence in the ethics process."

Three times last year DeLay was rebuked by the House Ethics Committee. But DeLay has more to worry about. Three of his closest aides in Texas are standing trial for criminal campaign-finance violations involving funneling $2.5 million in illegal corporate money from his political action committee to Republican candidates for the state legislature. (After the election, the legislature redistricted congressional seats to eliminate Democrats and consolidate Republican control of the House.)

In response to the possibility that he may face trial himself, DeLay tried to force the House to abolish a GOP rule that requires leaders to step down temporarily if indicted. But members faced uproar from their constituents, and DeLay had to abandon his gambit. As the web of grand juries and trials entangling his closest political associates spreads, his self-protective tactics have become more frantic. Last month, he purged those Republicans from the House Ethics Committee who had any Hamlet-like hesitations about suppressing further investigations into his activities.

DeLay's troubles reveal the anatomy of his power, known from Texas to Washington as DeLay, Inc. By controlling the majority in the House, DeLay has been able to enforce discipline on the vast army of lobbyists, law firms, and trade associations in Washington. His K Street Project, named after the nondescript street where many of the lobbyists maintain their offices, attempts to ensure that Democrats will not be hired by lobbyists and law firms, which will kick in maximum campaign contributions or else let their clients suffer the consequences.

In 1999, DeLay received a "private rebuke" from the House Ethics Committee for punishing the Electronic Industries Alliance when it hired a Democrat to head its Washington office. DeLay sabotaged trade bills that would have benefited the EIA, and soon the group hired a former House Republican staffer, who arranged contributions to DeLay's political action committee. One prominent Republican lobbyist confided to me that DeLay personally upbraided him for hiring a Democrat into his firm. The Republican majority is thus financially supported through strong-arm tactics and quid pro quos, and it pursues policies that always serve the demands of special interests: the pharmaceutical companies on Medicare, credit card firms on bankruptcy, and oil, gas, and coal companies on energy.

But DeLay's methods are being exposed. In a civil trial filed by defeated Democratic congressional candidates in Texas against DeLay's political action committee, new documents revealed last week proved he had created the PAC and was directly involved in raising corporate donations that are illegal under Texas law. At a recent press conference DeLay tried to brush aside the indictments of his aides by the Travis County prosecutor as "frivolous" and a "joke." But the prosecutor, when asked, has refused to rule out indicting DeLay.

Meanwhile, the Justice Department has impaneled a federal grand jury to hear testimony into possible fraud and public corruption by one of the Washington lobbyists closest to DeLay, Jack Abramoff, and his business partner, the public relations executive Michael Scanlon, DeLay's former press secretary. That investigation might yet encompass two other DeLay allies: the former Christian Coalition leader Ralph Reed, another business partner of Abramoff's, and Grover Norquist, a lobbyist who organizes the conservative groups behind DeLay's initiatives and who has also profited from his dealings with Abramoff. Stalled before the House Ethics Committee is an investigation into trips DeLay took to South Korea and Britain, the latter financed by Abramoff. Both those investigations involve the central figure of DeLay's former chief of staff (now a lobbyist), Ed Buckham.

"I go about my job," DeLay told reporters, trying to distance himself. "Jack Abramoff has his own problems. Any other questions?" In an earlier statement, obviously crafted by his attorneys, DeLay said, "If anybody is trading on my name to get clients or to make money, that is wrong, and they should stop it immediately." He's shocked, shocked!

DeLay's suggestion that Abramoff is his most casual acquaintance was belied by his fulsome tribute to Abramoff on the occasion of DeLay's trip in 1995 to the Northern Mariana Islands, a U.S. protectorate in the Pacific and one of Abramoff's clients. Abramoff lobbied for garment factories there to be exempt from U.S. labor laws guaranteeing the federal minimum wage. After Abramoff arranged an all-expenses-paid visit, DeLay led the successful charge to make island sweatshops safe from wage, hour, and immigration laws. DeLay wrote Abramoff's client: "When one of my closest and dearest friends, Jack Abramoff, your most able representative in Washington, D.C., invited me to the islands, I wanted to see firsthand the free-market success and the progress and reform you have made." Years later, an investigation by the Marianas public auditor discovered that Abramoff's law firm had operated "without a valid contract."

Abramoff's connection to DeLay was forged the instant Republicans won the Congress in 1994. DeLay declared he would run for party whip, and Abramoff backed him. "He's someone on our side," said Buckham. "He has access to DeLay." And it was none other than Buckham who had brought in Abramoff.

In 2000, Abramoff paid for DeLay and his wife, Christine, and Buckham and his wife to visit London and stay at the Four Seasons Hotel. A year later, Buckham got the Korea-U.S. Exchange Council to pay for a trip to Seoul by DeLay and his wife. Buckham, a registered foreign agent was in fact the founder of the council, whose address is the same as his lobbying firm. It is illegal for House members to accept travel expenses from either registered foreign agents or lobbyists. Both these trips are awaiting investigation before the paralyzed House Ethics Committee.

Buckham is not only DeLay's former chief of staff but also his personal pastor. (Buckham, a nondenominational evangelical, doesn't preside at a church.) DeLay's wife was put on Buckham's lobbying firm's payroll from 1998 to 2002. And Buckham has also hired Tony Rudy, DeLay's former general counsel and deputy chief of staff, and Karl Gallant, formerly the executive director of DeLay's political action committee.

I first encountered Jack Abramoff in 1985 when I was a national staff reporter for the *Washington Post*. He was then the executive director of a conservative organization called Citizens for America, created by Lewis Lehrman, the drugstore mogul, who had been defeated in the race for governor of New York against Mario Cuomo in 1982. President Reagan's backers encouraged Lehrman to build a group that would campaign for his program. Using this vehicle, Lehrman believed he could become a Republican powerhouse. He hired former leaders of the College Republicans to run it: Abramoff and his pal, Grover Norquist. But, as I reported in the *Washington Post*, Lehrman belatedly discovered that he had been "boxed out of the bookkeeping." The $3 million budget had been "gutted," as one of the group's officers explained to me. Abramoff and Norquist had held "one big party" and "gone hog wild." They were fired, and the group went under. It was the beginning of Abramoff's brilliant career.

A year later, in 1986, Abramoff emerged as chair of the International Freedom Foundation, which was secretly financed with $1.5 million a year from the pro-apartheid South African government. He also produced a pulp anticommunist action movie, *Red Scorpion*. By 1994, with the Republicans triumphant in Congress, the law firm of Preston Gates announced Abramoff as a lobbyist who "maintains strong ties to Speaker Newt Gingrich, Majority Leader Dick Armey, Majority Whip Tom Delay and [House] Republican Policy Committee Chairman Chris Cox and their staffs." Thomas Edsall wrote in the *Washington Post:* "In less than a decade, Abramoff's ties to Republican congressional leaders and powerbrokers in the conservative movement catapulted him into the highest ranks of Washington lobbyists. By 2003, Abramoff's clients—including the Business Roundtable, Atofina Chemicals, Humana, Primedia Inc. and tribal clients—paid his law firm $11.57 million in fees, one of the highest such sums in Washington." Norquist and DeLay were among Abramoff's biggest promoters. "What the Republicans need is 50 Jack Abramoffs," Norquist said in 1995. "Then this becomes a different town."

Teaming up with DeLay's former press secretary, Scanlon, Abramoff charged Indian tribes seeking help for their casinos a total of $66 million in fees. He directed them to funnel money to a variety of Republican groups, including Norquist's Americans for Tax Reform and DeLay's political action committee. With Indian money flowing into Republican coffers, DeLay declared in 1995 that "people recognize that Jack Abramoff has been an important part of this transition." Abramoff also turned for help to another old College Republican friend, Ralph Reed, who was paid $4.2 million between 2001 and 2003 to organize, through his consulting firm (Century Strategies), Christian constituencies against Indian gambling interests that competed with Abramoff's Indian clients. (Reed's front groups also received funds from Indians.)

One tribe, the Tigua in Texas, whose casino was under siege from Reed's lobbying, felt compelled to seek help from the main Republican lobbyist for Indian tribes, Abramoff. On February 6, 2002, Abramoff e-mailed Scanlon under the subject line "I'm on the phone with Tigua": "Fire up the jet, baby, we're going to El Paso!" Scanlon replied: "I want all their MONEY!!!" Abramoff e-mailed Reed: "I'd love us to get our mitts on that moolah!!" When the *El Paso Times* ran a story titled "450 Casino Employees Officially Terminated," Scanlon e-mailed it to Abramoff: "This is the front page of today's paper while they will be voting on our plan!" Abramoff wrote back: "Is life great or what!!!!" The Tigua paid $1.8 million in fees, but in the end Abramoff and Scanlon failed to get their casino reopened. "A rattlesnake will warn you before it strikes," said the Tigua leader. "They did everything behind our backs."

When the Senate Committee on Indian Affairs launched an investigation last year and Abramoff took the Fifth Amendment at its hearings, his law firm fired him. Still, Abramoff was honored by the Bush campaign as a "Pioneer" for raising more than $100,000 in 2004.

But the revelations continue. Last week *Newsweek* reported that the FBI is investigating $2.5 million that passed through a conservative think tank to the bank accounts of Abramoff and Scanlon. According to *Newsweek*, "The payments to the National Center for Public Policy Research were meant for a PR campaign promoting Indian gaming, center officials said." DeLay, who has signed fundraising letters for the center, was also the recipient of its largesse: two lavish foreign trips, one of them costing $70,000 to play golf at St. Andrews in Scotland. As it happens, he was accompanied on the trip by Abramoff, a member of the center's board.

The federal grand jury has been calling witnesses in the Tigua case for months. The FBI is looking into the curious case of the National Center for Public Policy Research. The Senate Indian Affairs Committee continues its inquiries. The civil case against DeLay's operation in Texas proceeds. The first of several criminal cases in Travis County focusing on his political action committee has begun. The House Ethics Committee has standing complaints before it about DeLay's foreign trips. Meanwhile, the corruption of public ethics is defied by sanctimonious appeals to the higher morality of "spiritual warfare."

A Confederacy of Shamans

MARCH 14, 2005

THE POLITICS OF PIETY were transparently masked by Republicans attempting to make capital over the fate of Terri Schiavo, the brain-damaged woman who has been locked in a persistent vegetative state for fifteen years and whose feeding tube was ordered removed by a Florida state judge at the request of her husband.

At last, the case that had been considered by nineteen judges in seven courts and three times appealed to the Supreme Court, which refused to hear it, seemed resolved. But Republican congressional leaders and President George Bush seized on the court ruling as the moment for "a great political issue," as a memo circulated among Senate Republicans put it. The Democrats, it declared, would find it "tough" and the conservative "pro-life base will be excited." The president, who had hesitated for three days before making a statement on the tsunami in December, rushed from his Texas ranch back to the White House to sign the legislation.

The Schiavo case is unique among medical cases, including those of the thirty-five thousand other people in persistent vegetative states. It is the only one in which the parents, who are not legal custodians, have been granted by an act of Congress and the president a federal court review of state court rulings. Wresting jurisdiction from the state judiciary is an unprecedented usurpation, a travesty of the federal system that displaces the Constitution with an ill-defined faith-based "culture of life," enthroning by edict theology above the law.

In 1999, as governor of Texas, Bush signed a state law permitting hospitals to cease artificial life support when doctors decide reasonable hope is gone, even if the patient's family objects. Now, two months into his second term as president, his major domestic initiative to privatize Social Security is doomed, his budget dead on arrival, and his poll ratings down to a new low of 45 percent approval.

His brother, Governor Jeb Bush of Florida, has campaigned for years on the Schiavo crusade and has hired a prominent religious right-wing leader as the lawyer to represent the state in the case. In their legal battle, the agonized Schiavo parents have made themselves the financial dependents of two conservative groups, one antiabortion, the other with a stated mission to "confront and challenge the radical legal agenda advocating homosexual behavior."

The Senate majority leader, Bill Frist of Tennessee, is a leading candidate for the Republican presidential nomination in 2008. For him, the Schiavo case is the beginning of the struggle for Bush's succession. He was a heart surgeon before his entry into politics, and the nameplate on the front door to his Capitol Hill office reads "William H. Frist, M.D." He signs correspondence "Bill Frist, M.D."

Amid the debate, after watching snatches of videotape of Schiavo, he proclaimed a diagnosis that she was not vegetative, contrary to diagnoses of the neurologists who have personally examined her. This is not the first unusual medical opinion he has voiced. Several months ago, in a national TV interview on ABC, Frist refused to acknowledge that saliva and tears cannot transmit HIV/AIDS, one of the shibboleths of the religious right.

The House majority leader, Tom DeLay of Texas—who has been thrice rebuked by the House Ethics Committee and has now paralyzed the committee to prevent it from considering new, more serious charges against him, whose closest aides are on trial in Texas for corruption, and who has taken measures to try to hold onto his political position if he is indicted— explained at a meeting of a right-wing group that the Schiavo case was divinely inspired to rescue conservatives from martyrdom. "One thing God has brought to us is Terri Schiavo," said DeLay. "This is exactly the issue that's going on in America, the attacks on the conservative movement against me and many others. . . . This is a huge, nationwide, concerted effort to destroy everything we believe in . . . and we have to fight back." Like Frist, DeLay plays doctor. "She talks and she laughs and she expresses likes and discomforts," he declared.

"Come down, President Bush," said the anguished husband, Michael Schiavo. "Come talk to me. Meet my wife. Talk to my wife and see if you get an answer. Ask her to lift her arm to shake your hand. She won't do it."

Terri Schiavo cannot speak or gesture, but to true believers, she is making sounds only they can hear. They see what they want in order to believe, and they believe in order to see. For the first time public policy in the United States is being made on the basis of pitting invisible signs against science.

As in tribal cultures, a confederacy of shamans—Bush, Frist, and DeLay —have appeared to conduct rites of necrophiliac spiritualism. Only the shamans can interpret for the dying and control their spirits, hovering between heaven and earth. The public opinion polls show overwhelming disapproval of the Republican position. But these polls are just so much social science. In this operation, for the tribe, there is no way of proving failure.

The Passion of the Culture War

MARCH 31, 2005

THE BUSH ADMINISTRATION doesn't have a faith-based initiative; it *is* a faith-based initiative. When President Bush rushed back to the White House from his Texas ranch to sign the congressional bill prolonging life support for Terri Schiavo, who died Thursday at forty-one, he demonstrated his faith in the infallibility of his political strategy. Just months earlier, in the 2004 presidential election, he had proved its efficacy. By nailing the flag to the cross, Bush's campaign linked the war on terrorism to the culture war. Under these banners, Bush marched as the crusader king against barbarian hordes without and within.

In unprecedented numbers, evangelical Protestants and conservative, self-described "faithful" Catholics flocked to the polls to vote for him. Ballot initiatives against gay marriage in eleven swing states helped magnetize these constituencies. By a simple symbolic gesture in the Schiavo case, Bush would again become the transcendent holy warrior, suddenly lifted by "values" from the slough of despond into which his Social Security privatization scheme had cast him. It never dawned on him or his Cardinal Richelieu (Karl Rove) that the polls, like the heavens, would come crashing down on him.

The entry of a host of political actors transformed the private tragedy into a public drama. Its grotesque unfolding has revealed scenes of ambition and hypocrisy, the inner politics of religious fanaticism, and the limits of the Republican strategy that was launched by Richard Nixon and has now reached its apotheosis under George W. Bush.

It was almost inevitable that the biographies of the politicians who used the Schiavo case as a platform would be examined for their own decisions about the medical care of their family members or patients. The House majority leader, Tom DeLay, bedeviled by ethical scandals, forced the Schiavo bill through the House while comparing his political embattlement to the effort to reattach her feeding tube. In 1988, according to the *Los Angeles Times*, DeLay decided, along with other members of his family, to pull the

162

plug on his father, Charles Ray DeLay. There was no chance he would recover from injuries sustained in a tram accident, and he would "basically be a vegetable," according to DeLay's aunt. The instructions on his chart read: "Do not resuscitate." DeLay filed a wrongful-death lawsuit against the tram manufacturer and settled for $250,000, after which he became a leading opponent of such lawsuits.

The Senate majority leader, Bill Frist, M.D., who offered a positive prognosis for Schiavo on the basis of having viewed clips of videotape and called for her "rescue," had as a doctor pulled the plug on a "regular basis," his staff acknowledged. And in 1989, Frist published a book, *Transplant*, in which he stated that anencephalic infants, suffering the same condition as the cortex-dead Schiavo, should be classified as "brain-dead."

Even the Franciscan Brothers of Peace, a ministry numbering only ten monks, two of whom have appeared as personal counselors to Schiavo's parents, confronted a crisis when the founder of their group suffered a heart attack and severe brain damage. He was kept alive and fed through a tube, but in 2003, after a dozen years, the monks decided to withdraw his life support. Their inconsistency in doing one thing while encouraging others to do another is best left for them to explain. More important, their presence is a small indicator of a larger political crackup.

Bush believes that he won his reelection in great part on the basis of "values" and that all he needs to do to refresh his power is to invoke them. But in signing a private bill by Congress that could not stand constitutional scrutiny for the sake of gratifying a faction of the Republican base, he has exposed and inverted the raw politics of the culture war. Instead of being blinded by the light of his shining faith, the public was repelled by what it saw as crass exploitation.

After a week of damage, the White House was quietly leaking to the press that Bush had not wanted to return from Texas after all. His effort to distance himself from the corrosive Schiavo issue had the effect of depicting him as ambivalent and indecisive—the negative image he had sought to ascribe to John Kerry.

Bush had no instinct that he was overreaching. He did not grasp that the case would become for the Republican Party something like what the gay-marriage decision of the Massachusetts Supreme Judicial Court has been for the Democratic Party. In both incidents, the parties have been pushed to their marginal bases. Bush's problem is that he has helped move the religious right to the heart of his party.

Bush's strategy was early formulated by Richard Nixon, who sought to absorb discontented Southern Democrats and urban ethnic Catholics into the Republican Party. Both traditional Democratic constituencies were alienated by the civil rights movement and the liberalization of social mores, including demands for women's rights, among the younger generation. (George Wallace, the former governor of Alabama, initially gathered support from these disaffected groups with a classic pseudo-populist appeal tinged with racism.)

A year after Nixon's election, one of his political strategists, Kevin Phillips, published *The Emerging Republican Majority*, laying out the details of how to realign the coming cycle of American politics. In the South, the Republicans should not oppose civil rights but enforce them, a move which would prove "essential if southern conservatives are to be pressured into switching to the Republican Party." In the North, as the Democratic Party became "a vehicle for Negro advancement," Republicans should build "a new populist coalition" around law and order and against "experimental residential, welfare and educational programming."

Thus Nixon's "silent majority" strategy used what was euphemistically called the "social issue" to unite Southern Baptists and conservatives with Northern Catholics. The 1972 election appeared to fulfill his plan. While Nixon carefully assimilated these constituencies, the Democratic candidate, George McGovern, was overwhelmed by raucous minorities, women's liberationists, and antiwar protesters, whose chaotic behavior only illustrated the points Nixon was making. (According to Vice President Spiro Agnew, the Democratic Party was the party of "acid, amnesty, and abortion.") But Watergate short-circuited Nixon's strategy. And his successor, Gerald Ford, was a rock-ribbed Republican who believed in the Equal Rights Amendment and was pro-choice on abortion. It was hardly surprising that he drew a primary challenge in 1976 from the right and its new champion, Ronald Reagan, that he barely managed to survive.

In 1980, Reagan anointed the religious right as ministers of the "social issue." "You can't endorse me, but I endorse you," he told the Religious Roundtable. The Reagan White House helped direct the conservative takeover of the Southern Baptist Convention, radically altering its theological positions. The SBC had previously upheld the right of abortion and the strict separation of church and state, and was against mandatory prayer in schools. By 1982, all these tenets had been reversed.

In 2004, evangelical Protestant churches and conservative Catholic bishops were crucial in mobilizing voters on Bush's behalf. Ohio, Iowa, and New Mexico were among the states that tipped to Bush under their influence. To the conservative Catholic bishops, Kerry represented their worst nightmare—a liberal Catholic as the most powerful man in the world—and they donned inquisitors' robes to issue maledictions that he should not receive communion.

In the beginning of his involvement in the Schiavo case, Bush acted on faith that it was a political gift. Why not? The politics of "values" had always enabled him to gain the offensive. For Reagan, it was morning again in America. Now it would be deathwatch in America. But Bush miscalculated the public response and lost control. Bush isn't using the religious right; it is using him.

The culture war has imploded inside the Republican Party. The religious fanatics and political freebooters who have flocked to the Schiavo deathwatch can never lose, no matter how extreme their pronouncements. Schiavo has given the religious right an invaluable lever with which to pressure Bush and the Republicans, who can never fully satisfy its demands if they are to sustain a national majority. The inviolability of marriage, states' rights, limited government, respect for the law—even these conservative principles must be cast aside in the struggle for power. Moreover, the Catholic right, a minority within both the American church and the religious right, has used this event to flex its muscles before evangelical Protestants as never before.

The battle over Schiavo is only proximately about Schiavo. The more spectacularly ghoulish the antics surrounding the Florida hospice, the more threatening the message sent to Bush. A bigger prize looms. The shadow of political blackmail hangs over Bush's Supreme Court nominations. Bush's appointment of justices who meet the approval of the religious right, even if he had intended to appoint them all along, must be interpreted as its triumph in the Schiavo struggle. If he flouts its will, there will be hell for Republicans to pay. Bush has set himself up for appearing terrorized.

Politics under Red Robes

APRIL 7, 2005

PRESIDENT BUSH, a militant evangelical Protestant, has lowered the American flag to half-staff for the first time at the death of a pope. Also for the first time, a U.S. president will attend a papal funeral. Bush's political rhetoric is deliberately inflected with Catholic theological phrases, in particular "the culture of life," the words he used to justify his interference in the case of the brain-damaged Terri Schiavo, the removal of whose feeding tube was upheld nineteen times by state and federal courts.

In the 2004 election, Bush's campaign helped organize the attack on John Kerry's Catholic authenticity by conservative bishops who threatened to deny him communion. Inside the White House, policy and personnel are coordinated with right-wing Catholicism. Not only are issues like international population control, reproductive health, and women's rights vetted, but so also are appointments.

Since the accession of Pope John Paul II, the conservative mobilization within the American church has been a microcosmic version of the ascendancy of the conservative movement in the country generally. As the authority of the Vatican was marshaled on behalf of the conservatives, the Republican right adopted the Vatican's position as its own in order to capture Catholic votes. Now the social agendas of conservative Catholics and Republicans are indistinguishable.

John Paul II welcomed American democracy as a counter to communism, but he had no experience with democracy of any kind. He envisioned his mission as restoring the authority of the church. America appeared to him as a liberal inferno—its citizens, he lectured American bishops last year, were "hypnotized by materialism, teetering before a soulless vision of the world."

The Pope asserted his control over the American church in 1984 by naming the conservatives Bernard Law and John O'Connor as archbishops of Boston and New York. They became his chief agents. At the same time, the Vatican refused to deal with the elected officers of the U.S. Conference of Catholic Bishops, who were largely imbued with the spirit of Vatican II.

Cardinal Joseph Bernardin of Chicago was acknowledged as the leader of the bishops and represented the broad progressive tradition of the American church. He articulated the concept of Catholicism as a "seamless garment" in which abortion was only one among many important issues. In 1994 he announced a common-ground initiative, titled Church in a Time of Peril, calling on the church to overcome its polarization and suppression of discussion on the issues tearing it apart—from women's changing roles to the fact that many Catholics did not accept most church teachings on sexuality to the declining numbers of priests. Bernardin was a consensus builder and believed he had touched all bases with the Vatican before unveiling his project. But the same day, Cardinal Law, clearly acting with Vatican authority, denounced it: "The fundamental flaw in this document is its appeal for 'dialogue' as a path to 'common ground.'"

Bernardin died months later and was replaced by a protégé of Law's. In 2002, the *Boston Globe* ran the first of more than 250 stories on the molestation of children and teenagers by parish priests. Law resisted investigating the sex scandal and faced potential criminal prosecution for his cover-ups. The pope rescued him with a sinecure in the Vatican. Following these revelations, conservatives under siege lashed out more ferociously. As they saw it, their failure to overturn the law on abortion demonstrated that they had not been hard-line enough. Thus the sex scandal set the stage for the right-wing Catholic offensive on behalf of Bush in the 2004 campaign.

With the pope's death, American Catholics yearn for openness. According to a poll by Gallup, 78 percent want the next pope to allow Catholics to use birth control; 63 percent say he should let priests marry; 59 percent believe he should have a less strict policy on stem cell research; and 55 percent say he should allow women to be priests.

But the Republicans are moving aggressively on the conservative social agenda. This week, in Kansas, gay marriage was banned in a referendum. Four states have passed bills permitting pharmacists to refuse to fill prescriptions for contraceptives if doing so conflicts with their own beliefs. The governor of Illinois has issued an emergency order to ensure that pharmacists fill all prescriptions. California's legislature is debating a similar law.

By consolidating power, the pope believed that he was strengthening the church. Now the conservatives want a post–John Paul papacy to extend his stringency. Others want moderation, openness, and discussion. Catholics in America do not now hold the same principle of hope. No one monitors the church's crisis more closely than the White House, and no one plots to exploit its division more ruthlessly. Religion is politics under red robes. So Bush travels to Rome.

The Keys of the Kingdom

APRIL 21, 2005

PRESIDENT BUSH TREATED his final visit with Pope John Paul II
in Vatican City on June 4, 2004, as a campaign stop. After enduring a public rebuke from the pope about the Iraq war, Bush lobbied Vatican officials
to help him win the election. "Not all the American bishops are with me,"
he complained, according to the *National Catholic Reporter*. He pleaded
with the Vatican to pressure the bishops to step up their activism against
abortion and gay marriage in the states during the campaign season. It appeared that he had been rebuffed by Angelo Cardinal Sodano, the Vatican
secretary of state.

However, about a week later, Cardinal Joseph Ratzinger sent a letter to
the U.S. bishops, pronouncing that those Catholics who were pro-choice
on abortion were committing a "grave sin" and must be denied communion. He pointedly mentioned "the case of a Catholic politician consistently
campaigning and voting for permissive abortion and euthanasia laws"—
an obvious reference to John Kerry, the Democratic candidate and a
Roman Catholic. If such a Catholic politician sought communion,
Ratzinger wrote, priests must be ordered to "refuse to distribute it." Any
Catholic who voted for this "Catholic politician," he continued, "would be
guilty of formal cooperation in evil and so unworthy to present himself
for Holy Communion." During the closing weeks of the campaign, a pas-
toral letter was read from pulpits in Catholic churches repeating the omi-
nous suggestion of excommunication. Voting for the Democrat was nothing less than consorting with the forces of Satan, collaboration with "evil."

In 2004 Bush increased his margin of Catholic support by 6 points
from the 2000 election, rising from 46 to 52 percent. Without this shift,
Kerry would have had a popular majority of a million votes. Three
states—Ohio, Iowa, and New Mexico—moved into Bush's column on the
votes of the Catholic faithful. Even with his atmospherics of terrorism and
September 11, Bush required the benediction of the Holy See as his saving
grace. The key to his kingdom was turned by Cardinal Ratzinger.

With the election of Ratzinger to the papacy, his political alliances with conservative politicians can be expected to deepen and broaden. Under Benedict XVI, the church will assume a consistently reactionary activism it has not pursued for two centuries. And the new pope's crusade against modernity has already joined forces with the right-wing culture war in the United States, prefigured by his interference in the 2004 election.

Europe is far less susceptible than the United States to the religious wars that Ratzinger will incite. Attendance at church is negligible; church teachings are widely ignored; and the young generation is least observant of all. But in the United States, the Bush administration and the right wing of the Republican Party are trying to batter down the wall of separation between church and state. Through court appointments, they wish to enact doctrinal views on the family, women, gays, medicine, scientific research, and privacy as public policy—battlefields in the larger Kulturkampf, or culture war.

Joseph Ratzinger was born and bred in the cradle of the Kulturkampf. Roman Catholic Bavaria was a stronghold against northern Protestantism during the Reformation. In the nineteenth century the church opposed the unification of Italy and Germany into nation-states, fearing that they would diminish the church's influence over the shambles of duchies and provinces that had followed the breakup of the Holy Roman Empire. The church promulgated the doctrine of papal infallibility in 1870 to tighten its grip on Catholic populations against the emerging centralized nations and to sanctify the pope's will over that of mere secular rulers.

In response, Otto von Bismarck, the German chancellor, launched what he called a Kulturkampf to break the church's hold. He removed schools from the control of the church, expelled the Jesuits, and instituted civil marriage ceremonies. Bismarck lent support to Catholic dissidents opposed to papal infallibility, who were led by the German theologian Johann Ignaz von Dollinger. Dollinger and his personal secretary were subsequently excommunicated. His secretary was Georg Ratzinger, great-uncle of the new pope, who became one of the most notable Bavarian intellectuals and politicians of the period. This Ratzinger was a champion against papal absolutism and church centralization and an advocate for the poor and working class—and also an anti-Semite.

Joseph Ratzinger claims his Kulturkampf to be a reaction to the student revolts of 1968. Should Joschka Fischer, a former student radical and now the German foreign minister, have to answer entirely for Ratzinger's Weltanschauung? Pope Benedict's Kulturkampf bears the burden of the church's history and that of his considerable family. He represents the latest incarnation of the long-standing reaction against Bismarck's reforms—which began with the assertion of the invented tradition of papal infallibility—and, ironically, against the positions on the church held by his famous great-uncle. But the roots of his reaction are even more profound.

The new pope's burning passion is to resurrect medieval authority. He equates the Western liberal tradition (that is, the Enlightenment) with Nazism and denigrates it as "moral relativism." He suppresses all dissent, discussion, and debate within the church and concentrates power within the Vatican bureaucracy. His abhorrence of change (a trait he shares with George W. Bush) runs back beyond 1968 to the revolutions of 1848, the "springtime of nations," and 1789, the French Revolution. But, even more momentously, the alignment of the pope's Kulturkampf with the U.S. president's culture war has also set up a conflict with the American Revolution.

For the first time, an American president is politically allied with the Vatican in its doctrinal mission (except, of course, on capital punishment). In the messages and papers of the presidents from George Washington until well into those of the twentieth century, there was not a single mention of the pope, except in one minor footnote. Bush's lobbying trip last year to the Vatican reflects an utterly novel turn, and Ratzinger's direct intervention in American electoral politics ratified it.

The right wing of the Catholic Church is as mobilized as any other part of the religious right. It is seizing control of Catholic universities, exerting influence at other universities, stigmatizing Catholic politicians who fail to adhere to its conservative credo, pressing legislation at the federal and state levels, seeking government funding and sponsorship of the church, and vetting political appointments inside the White House and the administration—imposing, in effect, a religious test of office. The Bush White House encourages these developments under the cover of moral uplift as it forges a political machine uniting church and state—as was done in premodern Europe.

The American Revolution, the Virginia Statute on Religious Liberty, the U.S. Constitution, and the Bill of Rights were fought for explicitly to uproot from American soil any traces of ecclesiastical power in government, which the Founding Fathers to a man regarded with revulsion and foreboding.

The Founders were the ultimate representatives of the Enlightenment. They were not antireligious, though few if any of them were orthodox or pious. Washington never took communion and refused to enter the church, although his wife did so. Benjamin Franklin believed that all organized religion was suspect. James Madison thought that established religion did as much harm to religion as it did to free government, twisting the word of God to fit political expediency and thereby throwing religion into the political cauldron. And Thomas Jefferson, allied with his great collaborator, Madison, conducted decades of sustained and intense political warfare against the existing and would-be clerisy. His words, engraved on the Jefferson Memorial, are a direct reference to established religion: "I have sworn upon the altar of God eternal hostility against every form of tyranny over the mind of man."

But now the Republican House majority leader, Tom DeLay, threatens the federal judiciary, saying: "The reason the judiciary has been able to impose a separation of church and state that's nowhere in the Constitution is that Congress didn't stop them." And the Senate majority leader, Bill Frist, will participate through a telecast in a rally on April 24 in which he will say that Democrats who refuse to rubber-stamp Bush's judicial nominees and uphold the filibuster are "against people of faith."

But what would Madison say? This is what Madison wrote in 1785: "What influence in fact have ecclesiastical establishments had on Civil Society? In some instances they have been seen to erect a spiritual tyranny on the ruins of the Civil authority; in many instances they have been seen upholding the thrones of political tyranny; in no instance have they been seen the guardians of the liberties of the people. Rulers who wished to subvert the public liberty may have found an established Clergy convenient auxiliaries. A just Government instituted to secure & perpetuate it needs them not."

What would John Adams say? This is what he wrote to Jefferson in 1815: "The question before the human race is, whether the God of nature shall govern the world by his own laws, or whether priests and kings shall rule it by fictitious miracles?"

Benjamin Franklin? "The way to see by faith is to shut the eye of reason."

And Jefferson, in *Notes on the State of Virginia*, written in 1782:

It is error alone which needs the support of government. Truth can
stand by itself. Subject opinion to coercion: whom will you make your
inquisitors? Fallible men; men governed by bad passions, by private as well
as public reasons. And why subject it to coercion? To produce uniformity.
But is uniformity of opinion desireable? No more than of face and stature.
Introduce the bed of Procrustes then, and as there is danger that the large
men may beat the small, make us all of a size, by lopping the former and
stretching the latter. Difference of opinion is advantageous in religion. The

several sects perform the office of a Censor morum over each other. Is uniformity attainable? Millions of innocent men, women, and children, since the introduction of Christianity, have been burnt, tortured, fined, imprisoned; yet we have not advanced one inch towards uniformity. What has been the effect of coercion? To make one half the world fools and the other half hypocrites. To support roguery and error all over the earth.

The Republican Party was founded in the mid-nineteenth century partly as a party of religious liberty. It supported public common schools, not church schools, and public land-grant universities independent of any denominational affiliation. The Republicans, moreover, were adamant in their opposition to the use of any public funds for any religious purpose, especially involving schools.

A century later, in 1960, there was still such a considerable suspicion of Catholics in government that the Democratic candidate for president, John F. Kennedy, felt compelled to address the issue directly in his famous speech before the Houston Ministerial Association on September 12.

What did Kennedy say?

I believe in an America where the separation of church and state is absolute—where no Catholic prelate would tell the President (should he be Catholic) how to act, and no Protestant minister would tell his parishioners for whom to vote—where no church or church school is granted any public funds or political preference. . . . I believe in an America that is officially neither Catholic, Protestant nor Jewish— where no public official either requests or accepts instructions on public policy from the Pope, the National Council of Churches or any other ecclesiastical source—where no religious body seeks to impose its will directly or indirectly upon the general populace or the public acts of its officials.

Now Bush is attempting to create what Kennedy warned against. He claims to be conservative, but he seeks a rupture in our system of government. The culture war, which has had many episodes, from the founding of the Moral Majority to the unconstitutional impeachment of President Clinton, is entering a new and far more dangerous phase. In 2004 Bush and Ratzinger used church doctrine to intimidate voters and taint candidates. And through the courts the president is seeking to codify not only conservative ideology but religious doctrine.

When men of God mistake their articles of devotion for political platforms, they will inevitably stand exposed in the political arena. When politicians mistake themselves for men of God, their religion, however sincere, will inevitably be seen as contrivance.

As both president and pope invoke heavenly authority to impose their notions of tradition, they have set themselves on a collision course with the American political tradition. In the name of the Declaration of Independence, the Constitution, and the Bill of Rights, democracy without end. Amen.

"Serial Abuser"

APRIL 14, 2005

ONCE AGAIN, PRESIDENT BUSH is conducting a grand experiment in cognitive dissonance, testing whether his asserted "truths" can prevail over new and obvious facts. This psychological phenomenon was first defined in 1957 by the sociologist Leon Festinger and a team of social scientists who studied the behavior of members of a UFO cult under duress when aliens failed to land on Earth as predicted. Some in the cult dropped out when the announced deadline came and went; others redoubled their conviction in the face of contrary evidence.

Bush's latest experiment involves his appointment of John Bolton as ambassador to the United Nations. The cognitive dissonance being tested goes beyond the nominee's oft-stated contempt for the United Nations and extends to his blatant efforts to twist intelligence. Bush's guinea pigs are the Senate Foreign Relations Committee and, as always, the American people.

On Tuesday, John Negroponte, nominated as the first director of national intelligence, pledged in his confirmation hearings before the Senate Intelligence Committee that he would attempt to ensure reliable information, unlike that provided in the run-up to the Iraq war. "Our intelligence effort has to generate better results," said Negroponte. "That is my mandate, plain and simple. . . . The things that need to be done differently will be done differently."

At the same time, Carl W. Ford Jr., the former assistant secretary of state for intelligence and research, was testifying in the Bolton confirmation hearings before the Foreign Relations Committee that Bolton was "a serial abuser" of intelligence and intelligence officers. Ford described Bolton as "an ill-suited nominee to become ambassador to the United Nations . . . a quintessential kiss-up, kick-down kind of guy" who "stands out" as he "abuses his authority with little people" in his efforts to subvert the intelligence process for his own political purposes.

With the Bolton hearings, we are at last getting a glimpse of how the

Bush administration's political leadership has been systematically brow-beating and threatening the intelligence community to ideologically driven conclusions. We are also learning that the national security team of the first term was sharply and bitterly divided, with Secretary of State Colin Powell unable to impose his views even on his own undersecretary. Bolton waged his war against the intelligence professionals within the State Department as a fifth column, constantly and flagrantly undermining his own chain of command. His efforts to coerce the State Department's Intelligence and Research Bureau (INR) to rubberstamp his political imperatives "prompted the Secretary of State to intervene," according to Ford's testimony. Powell felt compelled to speak to INR analysts in order to "assure employees that they should continue to 'speak truth to power.' " But his extraordinary step did not stop Bolton's relentless campaign of intimidation. In case after case—Iraq, Cuba, and North Korea—Bolton personally bullied INR analysts, berated them, screamed at them, and sought to destroy their careers if they did not do his bidding, even when it flew in the face of the facts, disregarded professional procedures, and contradicted the stated policy of the secretary of state.

The discrepancy between the reckless record of John Bolton and the anodyne promises of John Negroponte is not the only factor that points to the use of cognitive dissonance. Two reports on Bush-era failures of intelligence—one by the Senate Intelligence Committee, the other by the President's Commission on Intelligence Capabilities Regarding Weapons of Mass Destruction—carefully avoided studying the political manipulation of information. Instead, both blamed the intelligence community alone, as though it acted in a vacuum. Despite orchestrated criticism before the Iraq war by conservatives that the intelligence agencies were not alarmist enough about Iraq's WMD, both reports have excoriated the agencies for being too alarmist. But the Senate Intelligence Committee report of last year attributed the failure to the intelligence community's "groupthink." In fact, INR was not part of any such "groupthink" and proved in retrospect to have been consistently correct on WMD in Iraq and elsewhere, despite being subjected to the pressures of Bolton the "serial abuser."

The cognitive dissonance has been further elevated by Republican Senator Lincoln Chafee, of Rhode Island, the swing vote on the Foreign Relations Committee. At first he indicated skepticism about voting to confirm Bolton and asked questions that elicited information highlighting Bolton's abusive conduct. But then he denied the hearings had produced anything that would lead him to vote against Bolton. If Chafee votes against Bolton, the committee will be deadlocked in a nine-to-nine tie, and the nomination will not be able to move to the Senate floor.

"It was strong testimony from Mr. Ford. He used strong language," Chafee conceded. But, he added, "it's all focused on this one incident. We're not really seeing a pattern." Then the Senate's Hamlet swung the other way. "From the evidence we've heard, he's a difficult man to work for," Chafee said on Wednesday. Bolton, he continued, was "absolutely not" the best man for the job. "It's not my style," he said. Here, with infinite jest, Chafee was playing Yorick, but he swiveled back into character as Hamlet. "I don't endorse it, but that doesn't mean it can't be successful for some people." Thus Chafee wrestled with cognitive dissonance: Should he acknowledge the reality that contradicts the false picture before him? To be or not to be?

On Wednesday, Democratic Senator Christopher Dodd of Connecticut asked Bolton to explain why he had requested intercepts from the National Security Agency of other U.S. officials' communications, a highly irregular act. And the committee's vote on Bolton was postponed until next week. Will new information surface between now and then about this or another matter?

The pattern that has emerged so far in the hearings is inescapable. Ever the realist, Brent Scowcroft, the elder Bush's national security adviser, lately fired by President Bush from the Foreign Intelligence Advisory Board, remarked last week at a Washington think tank: "How [Bolton] performs will depend on two things—the instructions he gets—and whether he will carry them out."

Consider, first, the case of Iraq's WMD. The Senate Intelligence Committee report states that in early October 2002, the deputy director of the CIA informed the Senate that the intelligence community did not believe British intelligence reports of enriched uranium sales by Niger to Iraq. Then the CIA director, George Tenet, told the deputy national security adviser the same thing. The president, Tenet urged, should not be a "fact witness" to a claim for which evidence was lacking.

This assessment was consistent with that of State's own intelligence office, INR. Yet, in December 2002, the first State Department report on Iraq's WMD declaration included the falsehood that Iraq was seeking enriched uranium in Niger. This lie was inserted by none other than Bolton, only to be subsequently scrubbed from official documents and the State Department website after his superiors realized he was gaming the system.

Despite these efforts by the CIA and the State Department to accurately represent the facts, President Bush uttered the now-infamous sixteen words in his 2003 State of the Union address, lending his imprimatur to the lie. The national security adviser, Condoleezza Rice, claimed she never reviewed the statement before it came out of the president's mouth. Her deputy, Stephen Hadley, who had been told only three months earlier by Tenet that it was false, took responsibility. (Both, of course, have since been promoted in Bush's second term.) A White House spokesman was trotted out in July 2003 to acknowledge that "the sixteen words did not rise to the level of inclusion in the State of the Union address."

Undoubtedly, Powell and his deputy, Richard Armitage, were keenly aware of Bolton's disloyal act. The evidence is unmistakable: Powell did not use the claim in his February 2003 speech to the United Nations that made the case for Iraqi WMD, one week after the State of the Union. But neither Powell nor Armitage was formally interviewed by the Senate Intelligence Committee for its report. Nor have they been called to testify before the Senate Foreign Relations Committee on Bolton's confirmation.

Consider, next, the case of North Korea. From the beginning of the administration, Bolton has been a key figure in the manipulation of intelligence in a conservative network stretching from the Office of the Vice President to the Defense Department's Office of Special Plans to Bolton's own office as an undersecretary in the State Department. This political operation has also depended on Republican senators and outside conservative groups for support at crucial moments. Bolton acted like a rogue, but he was not unilateral. Powell distrusted him but could not remove him, mainly because of Dick Cheney's protection for Bolton's subversive campaigns.

Over the six-party talks with North Korea to curb its production of nuclear weapons, Powell and Bolton fought a running battle. Bolton continually attempted to sabotage Powell's negotiations by making antagonistic remarks to upset the North Koreans. Finally, in 2003, Powell instructed his special envoy and chief negotiator, Charles Pritchard, to inform the North Koreans that only the president and the secretary of state—and their designated representative (meaning Pritchard)—had authority. This communication was specifically aimed at Bolton.

Bolton's speeches were combed over by INR and others in the State Department—"taken on line by line," according to a direct source quoted by Steve Clemons, a fellow at the New America Foundation, on his website, Washington Note. "There was always a fight." In July 2003, Bolton submitted a speech to be delivered in Seoul, South Korea. Forty-three "line items" were "challenged and expunged," Clemons reports. Bolton left for Seoul without having his speech approved. On landing, he demanded that the

South Korean government provide him a venue at which to speak, but, after consulting with the State Department, it refused. Then Bolton forced the U.S. embassy staff to locate a forum. On July 31, he gave his inflammatory speech, titled "A Dictatorship at the Crossroads" and calling the North Koreans "extortionist," without having received final clearance from the State Department. The North Koreans' response was immediate and exactly what Bolton must have hoped for. They called him "human scum." With that, the negotiations threatened to blow up.

Pritchard tried to calm North Korea by reiterating Powell's injunction about who spoke for the U.S. government. Infuriated, Bolton struck back. In August 2003, Republican Senator John Kyl of Arizona sent a letter to Vice President Cheney and the State Department calling for "corrective action" against Pritchard for being out of step with administration policy. Kyl claimed that Pritchard had attacked Bolton by telling the North Koreans that his speech reflected only Bolton's "private view." Pritchard replied that he had not mentioned Bolton by name at all. "According to those who have read the diplomatic notes on the meeting," Clemons reports, "Pritchard never mentioned Bolton's name in the meeting and focused on his objective—which was to keep the North Koreans committed to the scheduled first meeting of talks in Beijing." Nonetheless, a week later, Pritchard resigned his post. Bolton had won.

Consider, finally, the case of the elusive Cuban WMD, the incident that led Ford, after some "soul-searching," to testify at Bolton's confirmation hearings. In February 2003, as the Bush administration was making its closing arguments before going to war that Iraq possessed WMD, Bolton decided he would give a speech stating that Cuba also had WMD. His text appeared on the desk of INR's chief expert on chemical and biological warfare, Christian Westerman. He checked Bolton's claims against the existing intelligence and concluded that they were untrue. Enraged, Bolton summoned the analyst to his office.

Westerman testified before the Foreign Relations Committee about what happened next: "He was quite upset that I had objected and he wanted to know what right I had trying to change an undersecretary's language. . . . And he got very red in the face and [was] shaking his finger at me and explained to me that I was acting way beyond my position, and for someone who worked for him. I told him I didn't work for him." Of course, Westerman worked directly for Carl Ford—and for the U.S. government. "And so, he basically threw me out of his office."

Bolton angrily called Thomas Fingar, principal deputy assistant secretary of state, to his office. "What did Mr. Bolton say to you?" Fingar was asked by the Foreign Relations Committee. He replied: "That he was the president's appointee, that he had every right to say what he believed, that he wasn't going to be told what he could say by a midlevel INR munchkin analyst." Then Bolton told Fingar "that he wanted Westerman taken off his accounts. I said, 'He's our CW/BW [chemical and biological weapons] specialist, this is what he does.' He expressed again, as I remember it, that he was the president's appointee, [and] he could say what he wanted."

In the end, Bolton did not give the speech, and Westerman was not reassigned or fired. Questioned about the episode, Bolton remarked: "I didn't seek to have these people fired. I didn't seek to have them discharged. I said I lost my trust in them."

By exposing a handful of Bolton's manipulations, the hearings have exposed the politicization of intelligence that has been studiously ignored by the Senate Intelligence Committee and the President's Commission. The Republican chair of the committee, Senator Pat Roberts of Kansas, has been a reliable tool of the White House in suppressing any talk of the political distortion of intelligence. Not only has he reneged on his commitment to Democratic senators on his committee that it would conduct an investigation, but he has avoided looking into the obvious cases of abuse of intelligence beyond that of WMD in the rush to war—and has thus laid the onus entirely on the intelligence community. Roberts conceives his chairmanship as blind support of the Bush White House, at the expense of his constitutional duty in the Senate. He has been a principal enabler of the abuse.

After three days of testimony, the pattern of Bolton's efforts to bend information, intimidate the intelligence community, and willfully subvert his superiors was firmly established. Yet Senator Chafee wavered about whether there was indeed a pattern. "Chafee's comment that it is an exception is inaccurate," a senior State Department official told me. "Bullying, bombastic, screaming 'I'm going to crush you,' that's typical."

Bolton's methods are hardly unknown to the White House. It can only be assumed that they are what the president wants in his ambassador to the United Nations. But Bolton will be confirmed only if the senators voting for him believe that the evidence their own hearings have unearthed cannot possibly be true. In that event, Bush's use of cognitive dissonance again will have triumphed.

The Good Soldier's Revenge

APRIL 28, 2005

FROM THE REDOUBT of his retirement, former secretary of state Colin Powell is beginning to exact revenge. His sterling reputation was soiled after he lost most of his important battles within the administration during Bush's first term. While he lamented that he had been "deceived" into presenting false information before the United Nations to justify the Iraq war, he was the good soldier to the end, giving every sign of desiring to fade away.

But now he has reemerged to conduct a campaign to defeat President Bush's nomination of the conservative hard-liner and former undersecretary of state, John Bolton, as U.S. ambassador to the United Nations.

In seeking to prevent the bullying and duplicitous ideologue from representing the United States before the international organization, Powell is engaging in hand-to-hand combat with his successor. Secretary of State Condoleezza Rice's first true test has not arrived from abroad. Caught by Powell's flanking movement, she is trapped in a crisis of credibility, which she herself is deepening.

Powell's closest associate, his former deputy Richard Armitage, is orchestrating much of the action. Wavering senators are directed to call Powell, who briefs them on Bolton's demerits. Powell's former chief of staff, Lawrence B. Wilkerson, has surfaced to give an interview to the *New York Times,* declaring that Bolton would be "an abysmal ambassador."

Other former foreign-service officers have queued up to provide ever-uglier details of Bolton's career as a "serial abuser" and "a quintessential kiss-up, kick-down sort of guy," as Carl W. Ford Jr., the former director of intelligence at the State Department, described him before the Senate Foreign Relations Committee.

Rice's response to the seemingly endless stream of witnesses has been to order State Department senior staff to stanch the flow of adverse stories.

"This whole building knows how Bolton dealt with people," a dismayed senior State Department official told me. "If she is sending a different signal than Powell sent, that will be difficult. The muzzle is being put on, the damage is being done. To the extent it's buttoned up here, it's dangerous for the secretary. Powell and Armitage created an environment of accountability about treatment of the staff. Any kind of allegation that you did things like Bolton did was death in the foreign service. Persons were removed. Now she's trying to be a team player, trying to support someone Powell ostracized."

Indeed, last year Powell and Rice clashed over an allegation that a National Security Council officer close to Rice, Robert Blackwill, had physically assaulted a female foreign-service officer. Initially, Rice tried to protect him, but Powell and Armitage presented the evidence to her and told her that if she didn't discipline Blackwill, the matter would be made public. Blackwill was forced to resign.

And after Bolton attempted to coerce a State Department intelligence officer to agree to an unfounded report about nonexistent Cuban WMD, Powell personally assembled the entire intelligence staff to instruct them to ignore Bolton. When the British foreign secretary, Jack Straw, complained to Powell that Bolton was obstructing negotiations with Iran on the development of nuclear weapons, Powell ordered Bolton to be cut out of the process, telling an aide: "Get a different view." The British also objected to Bolton's interference in talks with Libya, and again Powell removed Bolton. But, as much as he may have wanted to, Powell could not dismiss him because of his powerful patron, Vice President Cheney.

The Bolton confirmation hearings have revealed his constant efforts to undermine Powell on Iran and Iraq, Syria and North Korea. They have also exposed a most curious incident that has triggered the administration's stonewall reflex. The Foreign Relations Committee has discovered that Bolton made, and was granted, a highly unusual request for ten intercepts by the National Security Agency of conversations involving past and present government officials. Whose conversations did Bolton secretly secure, and why?

Staff members on the committee believe that Bolton was probably spying on Powell, his senior advisers, and other officials reporting to him on diplomatic initiatives that Bolton opposed. If so, it is also possible that Bolton was sharing this top-secret information with his neoconservative allies within the Pentagon and the Office of the Vice President, with whom he was in daily contact and who were known to be working in league against Powell.

If the intercepts are released, they may disclose whether Bolton was a key figure in a counterintelligence operation run inside the Bush administration against the secretary of state, which would put him in the role of the hunted character played by Will Smith in *Enemy of the State*. Both Republican and Democratic senators have demanded that the State Department, which holds the NSA intercepts, turn them over to the committee. But Rice so far has refused. What is she hiding by her cover-up?

Rice's rise has been dependent on her unwavering devotion to the president; in the Bolton case, she is again elevating loyalty to her leader above all else. Will Powell lose once more? But this episode points beyond the general's revenge, Rice's fealty, Bolton's contempt, or even presidential prerogative, to a gathering storm over constitutional government.

The Incredible Shrinking President

MAY 5, 2005

ON THE NINETY-NINTH DAY of his second term, one day short of the fabled hundred days used to mark a president's progress since Franklin D. Roosevelt's whirlwind beginning of the New Deal, President Bush held a press conference to explain how far he had gotten in undoing the New Deal.

Bush had allotted sixty days for a nationwide tour to sell his plan for privatizing Social Security. Insisting that the system was in imminent danger of collapse, he proposed a vague scheme for carving out private retirement accounts. He did not acknowledge that the deficit, ballooned by his regressive tax cuts for the wealthy, might have anything to do with the government's solvency. Of course, he did not advocate rescinding his top-rate giveaway; nor did he suggest raising the levy on the rich or the limit on income subject to Social Security taxation (currently $90,000), the solutions favored by large majorities of the public. Nor did he propose any detailed plan, though he tried to goad the Democrats into doing so, on his terms. But the more Bush campaigned on his proposal, the less support it received. By the end of his tour, 58 percent disapproved of it and only 35 percent approved, according to a CNN/*USA Today*/Gallup poll.

Rather than admit defeat, Bush upped the ante. He unveiled a new idea at his press conference, "progressive indexing," that would slash benefits for the middle class and affluent but purportedly not those for the poor. The poll numbers rolled in instantly: 54 percent disapproved, and 38 percent approved. Even Senator Trent Lott of Mississippi, lately deposed as majority leader, dismissed Bush's plan as little more than "a welfare system." Indeed, transforming it into a means-tested welfare system from a universal one is its intent.

The day after the 2004 election, Bush claimed that he had achieved a mandate. "When you win there is a feeling that the people have spoken and embraced your point of view, and that's what I intend to tell the Congress, that I made it clear what I intend to do as president." Even last

184

week, as Bush was replacing one unpopular Social Security panacea with another, Karl Rove, his chief political adviser, was taking another victory lap, this time in Ohio, to declare before a gathering of Republican faithful that Bush was making a lasting political "realignment."

An autodidact and amateur history buff, Rove, a University of Utah dropout, has beguiled younger members of the Washington press corps since 2000 with billowing visions of realignment. He regularly compares Bush's campaign with William McKinley's in 1896, which ushered in a long period of Republican dominance. "A successful party," he told his reportorial transcribers, "had to take its fundamental principles and style them in such a way that they seemed to have relevance to the new economy, the new nature of the country, and the new electorate." The analogy also contains a self-serving implication, with Rove casting himself as the modern version of Mark Hanna, the Republican kingmaker behind McKinley. (Rove's assertions about realignment have always been little more than a press strategy. They may reflect his wishful thinking, but the only actual constituencies he has in mind for this talk are reporters and pundits.)

In the 2004 election, Bush's victory gave him a legitimacy he did not have in the 2000 election, when he lost the popular vote and was handed the presidency by the Supreme Court (in a decision notable for Justice Antonin Scalia's claim that counting the votes in Florida would call into question Bush's "legitimacy"). But the shift from illegitimacy to legitimacy is not a mandate for realignment. In 2004, the country made a decision by a narrow margin to stick with Bush as a defender against terrorism. Bush won no mandate to dismantle the legacy of the New Deal, and during the campaign he went out of his way to deny that he would ever do that. Now a majority of evangelical Protestants who voted for Bush, his strongest constituency, are awakening to his position on Social Security, and they disapprove, according to a Democracy Corps poll. The more Bush openly pushes his domestic agenda, the more his base disintegrates.

In 2004, Rove field-marshaled a campaign that targeted anxious working-class women ("security moms"), conservative Catholics, evangelicals, and white married men. With the launching of the Social Security tour, Rove hoped to duplicate this tactical success, peeling off enough marginal constituencies to frighten a few Democrats into backing the Bush plan and thereby shatter Democratic unity, force the proposal through, and herald realignment. But the process Rove set in motion during the campaign is now operating in reverse, as distress among evangelicals over a change in Social Security suggests.

Rove's claim to be the advance man of realignment bears superficial plausibility mainly because he was a key operative when realignment in Texas accelerated in the 1990s. But there the cards had already been already dealt. Although his smarmy dirty tricks helped undermine a number of prominent Democrats, and he latched on to the rising star of George W. Bush, Texas had already drifted a long way toward Republicanism, following the classic Southern pattern on a slightly delayed schedule.

In the first hundred days of Bush's second term, Rove's magisterial vision of realignment, undergirded by the movement of tectonic social forces, is being obviously eclipsed by Tom DeLay's undisguisedly brutal leadership. The defining sensibility of the Bush administration—50 percent plus one equals 100 percent—is represented by the mindset of the Republican House. Following Majority Leader DeLay's edict, Speaker Dennis Hastert enshrined the operating principle that the "majority of the majority" governs the entire body. The minority has no rights, no consultative role, no say whatsoever.

By also attempting to eliminate the Senate filibuster for judicial nominations, overriding the constitutional prerogative of "advise and consent," the Republicans are trying to turn the more deliberative upper body into a reflection of the lower one. Thus Bush is running his second term under the political assumptions of the Republican leadership of the House. It should not be forgotten in the rush to eviscerate Senate rules that Vice President Dick Cheney was once the House whip and that it was he who acted as the patron and protector of Newt Gingrich in his rise to leadership.

Bush's new proposal on Social Security has both a policy and a political content. The two are one and the same. Bush's "progressive indexing" would destroy Social Security as a universal old-age pension and disability program, transforming it into a politically vulnerable welfare supplement solely for the poor. "Under the proposed reductions," the *New York Times* observed, "young workers who now earn about $36,000 would face a 16 percent cut; those earning about $58,000 would face a cut of 25 percent, and those earning $90,000, 29 percent. People not yet in the work force would face even larger reductions."

But there's worse news. The economist Brad DeLong calculates just how Social Security as we know it would end for the middle class. Bush's proposal, he writes,

> turns Social Security from a program in which benefits rise with incomes to one in which nearly everybody's benefit is roughly the same: about

1,900 of today's dollars a month. [It] caps the maximum Social Security retirement benefit at roughly $22,500 a year (adjusted for inflation). Bush's private-accounts plan—which would allow people to contribute 4 percent of their wages—makes retirees repay the taxes they diverted into private accounts out of their standard Social Security benefit. Medicare premiums are already deducted from your Social Security check. Deduct the claw-back for the private-accounts diversion as well, and by late in this century the odds are that—at least for the upper middle class—the standard Social Security check would be zero.

As a political matter, the Bush plan for de facto abolition of Social Security is a desperate ploy to re-create the right-wing, pseudo-populist appeal of the Nixon and Reagan eras. Social Security would become a program that unfairly taxes the middle class, which would receive short shrift on benefits, as the taxes they paid go to the poor. The poor, of course, are disproportionately minorities, black and Hispanic, and Social Security would become tainted as a "minority" program.

The program would foster a new code language. Once again, the poor would be stigmatized as undeserving, purportedly not having worked as hard for what they earned. The middle class would be "victimized by unfair discrimination" (language used in the 1980 Republican Party platform to denounce affirmative action). As under Nixon and Reagan, minorities would be tagged as greedy "special interests" and not among mainstream American "groups." (Reagan's acceptance speech at the Republican convention in 1984 was masterful for its use of coded rhetoric: "Is there any doubt that they will raise our taxes? . . . We're here to see that government continues to serve the people and not the other way around. . . . We don't lump people by groups or special interests.")

Under Bush's program, "taxes" would become a code word for the expropriation of resources from the middle class by the federal government to fund undeserving minorities and the work-shirking poor. "The government" would become the central villain—indifferent to the plight of the middle class, preying on it like a vampire, the instrument that "bleeding-heart liberals" use to salve their misplaced sense of morality—by forcibly transferring taxpayer dollars to lazy, cheating, criminal, and licentious freeloaders and "welfare queens." And "values" would become the ultimate word to invest social and economic inequality with moral legitimacy.

As the late Lee Atwater, Rove's mentor in pseudo-populism, explained in 1984 to the *Washington Post* reporter Thomas Edsall: "In the 1980 campaign, we were able to make the establishment, in so far as it is bad, the government. In other words, big government was the enemy, not big business. . . . If the people are thinking that the problem is that taxes are too high and government interferes too much, then we [Republicans] are doing our job." The best story, Atwater continued in his candid disquisition, was of a welfare recipient who "fills his den with liquor using food stamps."

Such is the vision of Social Security as a wedge issue for a Republican realignment. For now, however, what the Bush White House has conceived as a wedge issue against the Democrats has become a wedge whose sharp edge is pointed at the Republicans.

Still, even as Republicans become ever more divided, their leaders in Congress contrive new devices to advance Bush's proposal. Perhaps they might even turn the Social Security scheme into an amendment to a reconciliation bill on tax cuts. Many twists and turns lie ahead.

But, having stopped waving the banner of the war on terrorism to obscure all else, Bush is becoming the incredible shrinking president. The election provided an event around which Bush could claim his indispensability in combating terrorism. But now he is left simply with the endless civil strife in Iraq, whose chief beneficiary is Iran. (Fifty-seven percent of Americans now believe it was not worth going to war, compared with 41 percent who say it was, according to the latest Gallup poll—a fall of 9 points in support since February.)

Bush's pretense that he gained a mandate in the 2004 election is being stripped away. But the loss of his political sheen only incites his arrogance. A week before he altered his Social Security plan, Bush held a meeting at the White House to pressure members of Congress. The president pulled aside Representative Charles Rangel, the Democrat from Harlem, and told him that his sixty-day tour was going very well and those who opposed him on Social Security would pay the price in the 2006 midterm elections. Rangel replied with dry wit: "I told him if he is right, the press has not been very kind to him."

Whether suffering delusions of grandeur or not, Bush's attitude is to bludgeon his way out of the corner he is backing himself into. Hurling threats, he's looking for a barroom brawl. Some realignment.

Damage

MAY 12, 2005

TONY BLAIR'S near-fatal political strategy in the British election inadvertently but inevitably exposed the dilemma of his special relationship with George Bush. Blair had attempted to wage a campaign that skirted Iraq, the issue voters cited as the overriding cause for their disillusionment, with about only one-third willing to say that they trusted the prime minister. But his invitation to the voters to vent their frustration at the beginning of the campaign—the so-called masochism strategy—naturally brought their anger over Iraq to the surface. Once he had raised the level of political toxicity, Blair simply froze.

Blair had achieved the extraordinary feat of persuading the Labour party to transform itself into a party that wins power. But this time his ability to persuade was exhausted. When confronted with the criticism that he had summoned, he offered no argument. Instead, he pushed voters away with a defiant exasperation that provoked their resistance as he challenged them to judge him. Why wouldn't Blair persuade? Was it just weariness, or ambivalence?

Blair knew that arguing the case for intervention in Iraq would blot out his effort to discuss his program for a third term. But his tongue was tied for other reasons as well. As the head of government, he could not speak of his disagreements with Bush. Out of loyalty to an ally, the national interest, and protocol, he couldn't acknowledge that he had urged alternative policies on Bush. Blair never mentioned how he had wrung a commitment (honored or not) out of Bush to restart the Middle East peace process. He could not discuss the way the Bush administration had systematically ignored the British representative in Iraq, Jeremy Greenstock. He did not note that Downing Street was spitting blood over the depredations visited on it by the bullying John Bolton and the rest of the neoconservative cabal. He did not allude to his national security team's consternation over Condoleezza Rice's incompetence. He did not reveal the many ways he had supported Colin Powell in his struggles with Donald Rumsfeld and Dick

Cheney. Blair's stalwart refusal to be transparent about his own good faith and positive actions contributed to his image as dishonest and furtive.

Blair's interlocutor within the Bush administration, Colin Powell, was in the same quandary, and they were bonded, exploited, and tarnished together. Of course, if Blair had not joined with Bush, he would have opened a large window of opportunity for the Conservative Party. But, like Powell, Blair convinced himself that going along in public was essential to his efforts to influence Bush behind closed doors. Like Powell, every time Blair made a slight gain, he reinforced his delusion of influence. Both overvalued their leverage.

Blair knew that Bush had no practical post-invasion scenario, other than the neoconservative fantasy of a flower-strewn parade. "There was little discussion in Washington of the aftermath after military action," according to a memo from Richard Dearlove, the head of MI6, to the prime minister on July 23, 2002. After that, Powell presented the State Department's seventeen-volume *Future of Iraq* prospectus to the Bush administration but was ruthlessly shoved aside; Blair, cornered, felt compelled to go to war without a plan. Thus, although regime change was botched from the start, the failure was a subject he could hardly discuss in the campaign. He was perpetually cornered.

British prime ministers have misjudged American presidents to their detriment before: Churchill and Roosevelt over the fate of the British Empire, Eden and Eisenhower over the Suez Canal. The special relationship has been fraught with prime ministers intent on maintaining its veneer. Rumsfeld crudely drew attention to the inherently unbalanced nature of this alliance on the eve of the Iraq war, when he declared that British military forces were unnecessary: "There are workarounds."

In his relationship with Bush, Blair apparently misread the outward signs of American culture and interpreted them through British eyes. Bush can be so amiable and informal dressed in his blue jeans that his manner can be mistaken for openness and cooperation, when in fact it conceals a particular type of American class superiority and indifference. Bush, after all, seems so friendly compared with the glowering Cheney, who clawed his way upward. It's not easy for someone who's never traveled in America to grasp the evolution of the Bush family from Northeast patricians into Texas Tories, and the dissolution of the New England character along the way—especially its sense of responsibility, duty, and humility.

Bush's amiability toward Blair merely demonstrates his acceptance of the prime minister into his fraternity, his private club. But even if Blair read Bush exactly right in every nuance, the outcome remains the same. (Gordon Brown and Bush are a car crash waiting to happen. Bush has an instinctive revulsion for serious intellectuals unwilling to engage in the locker-room banter that is his mode of condescension.)

The underlying events that produced the British election result provide a harsh, cautionary, and unsettling lesson, and not only for Blair. Prime ministers to come will take the story of Blair's embrace of a powerful but mendacious ally, and Blair's subsequent loss of public trust, as a warning. Future American presidents will be regarded with underlying suspicion far into the future. By chastening Blair, the British voters have applied the only brake they have on Bush's foreign policy. But the damage done to the U.S.-U.K. relationship could have incalculable long-term, negative consequences for the world.

Guantánamo

MAY 19, 2005

MICHAEL ISIKOFF HAS BECOME the Lynndie England of the Washington press corps. For inadequately sourcing a story reporting that the Koran of a detainee at the Guantánamo Bay prison had been flushed down a toilet, the Bush administration has turned the *Newsweek* reporter into a scapegoat for the disastrous consequences of its torture policy.

In a blurred sequence of events, the story traveled rapidly from Washington to Afghanistan and back again, from tragedy to farce. Relying on a single anonymous source, *Newsweek* had before publication dutifully passed the article along for comment by the Pentagon, which declined to refute it. Appearing as a squib in the Periscope section of the magazine, it was seized on by demagogues who exploited it to arouse bands of Islamists and other opponents of Hamid Karzai's government in Afghanistan.

After riots in which seventeen people died, the Bush administration pointed the finger of blame at *Newsweek*. The White House imposed a series of demands on the magazine, as though it were a defeated rogue state. First, *Newsweek* had to accept responsibility for its error. *Newsweek*'s single source had suddenly decided he was not a profile in courage and informed the reporter that he was no longer certain of his previous assertion. Second, *Newsweek* had to apologize profusely and retract the article. Third, it had to explain to the world that it alone was responsible for the anger of the Muslim world and that official U.S. policy dictated respect for the Koran.

In short, *Newsweek* has had to do everything that the Bush administration has refused to do about its torture policy. It is *Newsweek* that is at fault for the utter absence of U.S. prestige and credibility; *Newsweek*'s editors who must engage in rituals of accountability at the behest of an administration that disdains accountability for itself; *Newsweek* that must demonstrate transparency about its internal procedures; *Newsweek* that must use its resources to explain to a wary world that the Bush administration has clean hands.

The White House and Pentagon press secretaries have competed in their excoriations of *Newsweek*, topped with flourishes of double-talk and self-contradiction. At the White House, Scott McClellan insisted that *Newsweek* could rectify itself only "by talking about the way they got this wrong and pointing out what the policies and practices of the United States military are when it comes to the handling of the holy Koran." Asked if he was giving orders to the magazine, the deadpan McClellan replied: "It's not my position to get into telling people what they can and cannot report."

At the Pentagon, Lawrence Di Rita batted down allegations by numerous detainees at Guantánamo that the Koran had been defiled. Instead, he declared, "It's possible detainees themselves have done [this] with pages of the Koran—and I don't want to overstate that either because it's based on log entries that have to be corroborated." Thus in denying the allegations and shifting blame to the detainees, Di Rita helpfully pointed out that his claim was no more "corroborated" than theirs.

While the administration faults *Newsweek* for relying on a flawed source, it has refused to respond specifically to the reports of the Senate Select Intelligence Committee and the Commission on the Intelligence Capabilities of the United States regarding Weapons of Mass Destruction that in constructing its case for going to war in Iraq it relied on disinformation from bogus Iraqi émigré sources, especially the agent dubbed Curveball, who was exposed as a duplicitous alcoholic. While demanding a retraction and an apology from *Newsweek*, nobody in the administration has ever bothered to respond to the statement by the former secretary of state, Colin Powell, that he was deceived in delivering his February 2003 speech before the United Nations Security Council about WMD in Iraq, which contained twenty-six major errors. By this standard, perhaps the president should reward Isikoff with the Medal of Freedom that he has bestowed on the architects of "catastrophic success."

In fact, the allegation published by *Newsweek* has been made by many former detainees at Guantánamo. The *New York Times* rightly reports that these have not been "authenticated." They cannot be. In the absence of the due process of law, denied to detainees in the floating netherworld of this gulag, absolutely nothing can be "authenticated."

The controversy about the desecrated Koran touches on merely one technique of abusing Guantánamo inmates. Many other methods of torture have been "authenticated," including the persistent abuse of Islam. *Newsweek*'s item appeared soon after a new book providing just such a firsthand account was published: *Inside the Wire,* by Erik Saar, a former Army interpreter at Guantánamo, with Viveca Novak, a correspondent for *Time* magazine. Saar witnessed provocatively attired female interrogators rubbing their genitals in front of chained detainees and then smearing them with red liquid they were told was menstrual blood. Saar also documents that detainees were forced to view pornographic videos and magazines. "Had someone come to me before I left for Gitmo and told me we would use women to sexually torment detainees to try to sever their relationships with God, I probably would have thought that sounded fine," he writes. "But I hated myself when I walked out of that room. . . . We lost the high road. . . . There wasn't enough hot water in all of Cuba to make me feel clean."

Newsweek's story also follows the publication last month of a report by Human Rights Watch, *Getting Away With Torture? Command Responsibility for the U.S. Abuse of Detainees.* The report discusses at length why "shocked" FBI agents have been ordered not to be present at torture sessions conducted by CIA agents and military interrogators: "There is growing evidence that detainees at Guantánamo have suffered torture and other cruel, inhuman, or degrading treatment. Reports by FBI agents who witnessed detainee abuse—including the forcing of chained detainees to sit in their own excrement—have recently emerged, adding to the statements of former detainees describing the use of painful stress positions, extended solitary confinement, use of military dogs to threaten them, threats of torture and death, and prolonged exposure to extremes of heat, cold and noise."

The Human Rights Watch report provides more irrefutable detail:

> In particular, agents of the Federal Bureau of Investigation express their shock at techniques used on detainees. In one email, an FBI agent wrote: "Here is a brief summary of what I observed at GTMO. On a couple of occassions [*sic*], I entered interview rooms to find a detainee chained hand and foot in a fetal position to the floor, with no chair, food, or water. Most times they had urinated or defacated [*sic*] on themselves and had been left there for 18, 24 hours or more. On one occassion, the air conditioning had been turned down so far and the temperature was so cold in the room that the barefooted detainee was shaking with cold. When I asked the [military police] what was going on, I was told that interrogators from the day prior had ordered this treatment, and the detainee was not to be moved. On another occassion, the A/C had been

turned off, making the temperature in the unventilated room probably well over 100 degrees. The detainee was almost unconscious on the floor with a pile of hair next to him. He had apparently been literally pulling his own hair out throughout the night. On another occassion, not only was the temperature unbearably hot, but extremely loud rap music was being played in the room, and had been since the day before, with the detainee chained hand and foot in the fetal position on the tile floor." Another FBI agent reported seeing a detainee "sitting on the floor of the interview room with an Israeli flag draped around him, loud music being played and a strobe light flashing."

The *Newsweek* item was published just days after the travesty that has been the trial of Specialist Lynndie England. The learning-disabled National Guard private from rural Appalachia was tried for the various humiliations visited on prisoners in Abu Ghraib in Iraq. She was depicted in infamous photographs gleefully posing next to piled bodies of naked Iraqis, leading a prisoner by a leash, and engaging in other cruelties. Her lawyer arranged for a reduced sentence in exchange for an admission of guilt. But the former lover of the pliable England, Specialist Charles Graner, a seductive and abusive character convicted in January of nine counts of abuse at Abu Ghraib, testified that the photographs of the naked pyramid were intended for use in training other guards. The military judge promptly threw out England's plea bargain, entered a plea of not guilty, and ordered a new trial. "You can't have a one-person conspiracy," said the judge.

The Pentagon, however, has ruled that any criminal acts of torture are confined to a conspiracy among the likes of England and Graner—and Brigadier General Janice Karpinski, who was in charge of Abu Ghraib and who was cited on May 5 (as *Newsweek* was going to press) for dereliction of duty and shoplifting (for good measure). "I believe I was a convenient scapegoat," she remarked. Everyone else up the chain of command was exonerated, including Lieutenant General Ricardo Sanchez, whose decisions facilitated the torture policy. Nor was Major General Geoffrey Miller, the former commandant at Guantánamo, held culpable, though it was he who, on Pentagon orders, arranged the export of torture techniques from Guantánamo to prisons in Iraq.

Nor were there rebukes for anyone who devised the policy exempting the United States from the Geneva Conventions restrictions on torture—perhaps because President Bush signed the order. The White House legal counsel, Alberto Gonzales, who had called the Geneva Conventions "quaint" in a memo to the president, was rewarded by being named attorney general.

Nor was there any setback for Jay Bybee, assistant attorney general for the Office of Legal Counsel, who wrote the key torture memo, arguing that the president as commander in chief was not bound by existing law and that approved torture could be anything short of "organ failure, impairment of bodily function or even death." Bybee was awarded a judgeship on the U.S. Court of Appeals for the Ninth Circuit.

Nor was Secretary of Defense Donald Rumsfeld, who bears responsibility for his department, ever held to account. Rumsfeld, whose handwritten annotations on memos recommend particular techniques of "stress and duress," makes a point of demonstrating his lack of accountability and his ignorance. When asked if he had read the report by Major General Antonio Taguba on torture at Abu Ghraib, he answered, "Whether I have read every page, no. There is a lot of references and documentation to laws and conventions and procedures and requirements, but I have certainly read the conclusions and other aspects of it."

Nor was Lieutenant General William Boykin, the officer sent from Guantánamo to Iraq to "Gitmo-ize" its prisons, removed from his position as assistant to the undersecretary of intelligence in the Pentagon. In 2003, Boykin, in uniform, gave a notorious PowerPoint presentation to a church group in which he explained that our enemy in the war on terrorism is "Satan"; that "they're after us because we're a Christian nation"; that, compared to a Muslim believer, "my God was bigger than his. I knew that my God was a real God, and his was an idol"; and that Bush was divinely ordained as president: "Why is this man in the White House? The majority of Americans did not vote for him. Why is he there? And I tell you this morning that he's in the White House because God put him there for a time such as this." Boykin was very quietly chastised for his remarks, but he kept his post, where he remains to this day. The refusal to remove Boykin is widely seen in the Muslim world as proof that the United States is officially engaged in a religious crusade against Islam.

The *Newsweek* story is one of those journalistic incidents that are wrong in their sourcing but may well be right about the truth of the matter. Allegations of abuse by detainees (not "authenticated," as the *New York Times* reminds us) go beyond the contempt shown for the Islamic religion. Such abuses have in fact been widely "authenticated" by the Pentagon's own Fay/Jones report, the Church report, the Ryder report, the Taguba report, the Schlesinger report, the Schmidt report, and reports by nongovernmental organizations such as the Association of the Bar of the City of New York Committee on International Human Rights, Amnesty International, the American Bar Association, the International Committee of the Red Cross, the Center for Constitutional Rights, and Human Rights Watch.

Former detainees have given highly detailed accounts of their captivity and torture. They may be seeking revenge; they may indeed be Islamist terrorists. But these claims have also been recorded by their lawyers as part of the effort to create actual trials, to bring detainees like them to justice before the law, which the Bush administration is fighting tooth and nail.

One of the most graphic accounts of brutality is provided by those known as the Tipton Three, three men from the West Midlands of Britain who were captured in Afghanistan in 2001, held in Guantánamo, and released to Britain in March 2004 without being charged with any crimes. After their release, in June 2004, the Supreme Court ruled that the U.S. court system has the authority to decide whether foreign nationals held at Guantánamo are wrongfully imprisoned. The Tipton Three recounted their horrific travails to lawyers for the Center for Constitutional Rights, who represented them before the Supreme Court and produced a 115-page composite statement. In one of the many gruesome descriptions, a former detainee says: "The behavior of the guards towards our religious practices as well as the Koran was also, in my view, designed to cause us as much distress as possible. They would kick the Koran, throw it into the toilet and generally disrespect it."

Before the *Newsweek* mistake, there had been several such reports in the American press. The *Washington Post,* on March 26, 2003, reported several incidents of abuse of the Koran: "Merza Khan, who had been captured in northern Afghanistan while fighting for the Taliban, said Americans in Kandahar tied him up and alternately forced him to lie face down on the ground, then squat with his hands on his head for hours. He also said he saw American soldiers throw the Koran on the ground and sit on it while in Kandahar."

Knight Ridder Newspapers reported on March 6, 2005:

Captives at the Guantánamo Bay prison are alleging that guards kicked and stomped on Korans and cursed Allah, and that interrogators punished them by taking away their pants, knowing that would prevent them from praying. Guards also mocked captives at prayer and censored Islamic religious books, the captives allege. And in one incident, they say, a prison barber cut a cross-shaped patch of hair on an inmate's head. Most of the complaints come from the recently declassified notes of defense lawyers' interviews with prisoners, which Guantánamo officials initially stamped 'secret.' Under a federal court procedure for due-process appeals by about 100 inmates, portions are now being declassified.

The *Los Angeles Times,* on April 15, 2005, quoted a former detainee: "He said their Korans were taken and handled disrespectfully. . . . Al-Mutairi recalled three prisoner hunger strikes. . . . A third came after the Korans were mishandled."

The *New York Times,* on May 1, 2005, reported: "A former interrogator at Guantánamo, in an interview with *The Times,* confirmed the accounts of the hunger strikes, including the public expression of regret over the treatment of the Korans."

Overexcited and undersourced, *Newsweek* rushed into print with a story similar to those that other major news organizations have published without a murmur of protest from the Bush administration. When *Newsweek*'s story was used as a propaganda device by Islamists in Afghanistan, the Bush administration turned the tables on *Newsweek,* holding it responsible for the hostility of the Muslim world. The Bush administration has been successful in this single endeavor of journalistic criticism, detecting one unsound story among many unchallenged ones. But no amount of abject apology by *Newsweek*'s editors for shoddy journalism can undo the damage done by Bush with his torture policy.

The Truth about Torture

JUNE 1, 2005

PRESIDENT BUSH'S press conference on Tuesday, at which he denounced Amnesty International's annual report, containing allegations of torture by the United States, as "absurd" and dismissed all such allegations as inspired by terrorists, was the crescendo of a concerted administration campaign to stifle the rising clamor on its torture policy.

Amnesty International released its report on human rights on May 25. Among other findings, it documents that some five hundred detainees are being held at the Guantánamo military base. The Supreme Court ruled six months ago in *Rasul v. Bush* that they are entitled to legal counsel and due process, but Amnesty noted that the detainees have not been provided with lawyers in secret administrative reviews held to determine whether they are "enemy combatants." And the more than fifty thousand detainees being held in twenty-five prisons in Afghanistan and seventeen prisons in Iraq are "routinely denied access to lawyers and families." An unknown number of people have disappeared into secret prisons—having been "rendered" to U.S. allies like Uzbekistan, where torture is routine. The Amnesty report called this shrouded network "the gulag of our time" and concluded that the administration's methods are counterproductive: "The 'war on terror' appeared more effective in eroding international human rights principles than in countering international 'terrorism.' "

The Amnesty report followed on the heels of the Bush administration's blaming *Newsweek* magazine for provoking anti-American riots in Afghanistan, which resulted in seventeen deaths, by its publication of a story that a Koran had been flushed down a toilet at Guantánamo. After the anonymous Pentagon source for the item hesitated about his certainty, the Defense Department, through its press secretary, Lawrence Di Rita, demanded that *Newsweek* apologize, and *Newsweek*'s editor, Mark Whitaker, abased himself elaborately for its error. But a week afterward the Pentagon disclosed that there had indeed been five incidents involving abuse of the Koran, though not a toilet flushing. (Some further clarification may be helpful on this fine point: as it happens, the detainees don't have flush toilets, but buckets.) At a press conference on the same day the Amnesty report was issued, Di Rita was asked, in light of the acknowledged Koran abuses and the apology he had insisted that *Newsweek* make, "Mr. Di Rita, as the Department of Defense, are you going to present your apologies to the Arab world?" Di Rita replied: "For what?"

A day later, on May 26, in a suit brought by the American Civil Liberties Union seeking information about detainees, the federal district court judge Alvin Hellerstein ruled that 144 photographs of abuse at Abu Ghraib prison in Iraq must be publicly released. The judge stated that the "photographs present a different level of detail and are the best evidence the public can have of what occurred."

Immediately the Bush administration launched a ferocious counteroffensive to obscure any debate about its torture policy, discrediting Amnesty's report, which was largely based on previously released official documents. The seriousness with which the administration regards the torture issue—as a political matter—was reflected by the seniority of those sent forth to deny the allegations. The questions were not left to the likes of press secretaries Di Rita or Scott McClellan. All the voices sang in a choir from a common book of talking points. Secretary of State Condoleezza Rice hit Amnesty's report as "absurd." The Joint Chiefs of Staff chair, General Richard Myers, called the report "absolutely irresponsible." And Vice President Cheney took umbrage at the insult: "Frankly, I was offended by it. For Amnesty International to suggest that somehow the United States is a violator of human rights, I frankly just don't take them seriously." He added that the "allegations of mistreatments" came from "somebody who had been inside and released to their home country and now are peddling lies."

The Wurlitzer of the conservative media was playing the same songs, but in a higher octave. On May 27, before the administration heavyweights made their statements, the *Wall Street Journal*'s editorial page declared that the human rights report is "one more sign of the moral degradation of Amnesty International," which it labeled a "highly politicized pressure group" whose reports "amount to pro–al Qaeda propaganda."

The *National Review* chimed in with an article titled "Amnesty Unbelievable," charging that Amnesty's report "says much more about the nature of Amnesty International—and the agenda of similar left-wing nongovernmental organizations—than it does about the human-rights record of the United States."

By the time Bush held his press conference, every nuance of his response on the issue had been carefully configured and rehearsed by Cheney, Rice, Myers, and the rest of the team. "I'm aware of the Amnesty International report, and it's absurd," the president began. Then he repeated himself: "It's an absurd allegation." The country, he declared, is virtuous, and therefore, he suggested, his motives must be innocent. "The United States is a country that is—promotes freedom around the world." Under Bush, the rule of law prevails: "When there's accusations made about certain actions by our people, they're fully investigated in a transparent way."

He repeated himself again: "It's just an absurd allegation." Once again, he claimed nothing had gone amiss. "In terms of the detainees, we've had thousands of people detained. We've investigated every single complaint against the detainees." Every complaint, he assured his audience, was false, because the motives of the detainees are as evil as his are pure: "It seemed like to me they based some of their decisions on the word of—and the allegations by—people who were held in detention, people who hate America." Here, Bush turned lexicographer: "People that had been trained in some instances to disassemble—that means not tell the truth." In conclusion, he banged again on his drum: "And so it was an absurd report. It just is."

It may be of minor, ironic interest that before the invasion of Iraq, the Bush administration cited Amnesty International's reports on Saddam Hussein's violations of human rights as unimpeachable texts. Secretary of Defense Donald Rumsfeld often claimed Amnesty as his ultimate authority. Now, inexplicably, Amnesty has gone over to the side of the devil. (On Wednesday, Rumsfeld assailed Amnesty as "reprehensible" and losing "any claim to objectivity or seriousness." But he admitted that some detainees have been mistreated, "sometimes grievously." Thus, according to the secretary of defense, they were not all "disassembling.")

Bush's press-conference talking points apparently did not prepare him to engage with the particulars of the new Amnesty report: that even after the Supreme Court ruling in *Rasul v. Bush,* "no detainee had had the lawfulness of his detention judicially reviewed"; that in Afghanistan, "the International Committee of the Red Cross (ICRC) had access only to some detainees in Bagram and Kandahar air bases"; and that "refusal or failure of the U.S. authorities to clarify the whereabouts or status of the detainees, leaving them outside the protection of the law for a prolonged period, clearly violated the standards of the U.N. Declaration on the Protection of

All Persons from Enforced Disappearance." For Bush, it seems, the devil is not in the details.

By training his fire on Amnesty, the new enemy, Bush seeks to obscure those who opposed the implementation of his torture policy: Colin Powell, then secretary of state; the senior military; the Judge Advocate General's Corps of the military; and the FBI.

The conflict over that policy has pitted Bush's civilian ideologues against much of the military and the national security apparatus. The policy was developed after September 11, 2001, by a small group of political appointees clustered in the Office of Legal Counsel of the Department of Justice and the Office of the White House Counsel. All were part of the tight-knit network of the right-wing Federalist Society and shared contempt in principle for international law. These legal cadres produced a stream of memos arguing that the United States was not bound by the Geneva Conventions on torture, that torture even unto death was an acceptable technique, and that the president, as commander in chief, was beyond the confines of legal restrictions in war.

Powell, former chair of the Joint Chiefs of Staff and representing the military's position as well as that of the Department of State, strenuously objected. His legal adviser, William H. Taft IV, argued in a memo on February 2, 2002, that the United States should adhere to the Geneva Conventions because "it demonstrates that the United States bases its conduct not just on its policy preferences but on its international legal obligations." He emphasized that withdrawing from the conventions in Afghanistan "deprives our troops there of any claim to the protection of the Convention in the event they are captured and weakens the protections accorded by the Conventions to our troops in future conflicts." The White House legal counsel, Alberto Gonzales, however, sent a memo to the president denigrating the Geneva Conventions as "quaint." Powell lost the battle.

The application of the torture policy also stirred sharp objections from the Judge Advocate General's Corps, whose members are present at the interrogations of prisoners. A delegation of JAG officers brought their detailed information about torture to the Association of the Bar of the City of New York. The officers were highly agitated that they were being turned into accomplices of a policy they regarded as a violation of international law, contrary to American traditions and potentially threatening to U.S. soldiers in the field. They told Scott Horton, a partner at Patterson, Belknap, Webb, and Tyler and chair of the bar association's Committee on International Law, that Pentagon officials were pushing the torture policy and creating an "atmosphere of legal ambiguity." The JAG officers related their alarm that Douglas Feith, the neoconservative undersecretary of defense for policy, had called the Geneva Conventions "law in the service of terrorism." But their uniform objections did not stop the policy.

The latest of many official government investigations into torture—all of which, beginning with the Taguba report on Abu Ghraib, have documented abuses—was provoked by the objections of the FBI to incidents of torture its "shocked" agents were forced to observe. FBI agents have now been ordered by the bureau not to participate in this policy. Slivers of the new report, still being drafted by Lieutenant General Randall Schmidt of the Air Force, have seen the light of day as a result of the ACLU suit. The FBI internal memos describe, among other details, shackled detainees who had "urinated or defecated on themselves" and one detainee "almost unconscious on the floor with a pile of hair next to him. He had apparently been literally pulling his own hair out throughout the night."

In the week before his press conference, and as the Amnesty report was released, Bush expounded on his theory of communications. "See," he said, "in my line of work you got to keep repeating things over and over and over again for the truth to sink in, to kind of catapult the propaganda." His statement was an axiom to place alongside that of his chief of staff, Andrew Card, who explained in the summer of 2002, before the invasion of Iraq, why there had been a lull in presidential public relations: "From a marketing point of view, you don't introduce new products in August."

But Bush's statement at his press conference on his torture policy is more than a case study of how his White House markets its "products." It reveals his fundamental misunderstanding of the political dimension of the war on terrorism and his failure to grasp the full range of instruments available to advance America's national interest. Bush imagines that his high-flown rhetoric about the "march of democracy" amounts to international diplomacy, but he has no concern for how people abroad can be expected to react to the continuing reports on torture. For him, any opposition becomes further proof of the righteousness of his cause. Bush has faith that he can dictate what should be perceived as fact even when it collides with facts on the ground. The talking points about his virtue, prepared by his staff, play to his vanity. But as he postures for the domestic political market, he undermines America's national interest in the world.

Deep Throat's Lessons

JUNE 9, 2005

THE UNVEILING OF THE IDENTITY of Deep Throat—Mark Felt, the former deputy director of the FBI—seemed to affirm the story of Watergate as the triumph of the lone journalist supported from the shadows by a magically appearing secret source. Shazam! The outlines of the fuller story we now know, thanks not only to Felt's self-unmasking but to disclosures by the *Albany Times Union* of upstate New York, unreported so far by any major outlet. Felt was not working as "a disgruntled maverick . . . but rather as the leader of a clandestine group" of three other high-level agents to control the story by collecting intelligence and leaking it. For more than thirty years the secrecy around Deep Throat diverted attention to *who* Deep Throat was rather than *what* Deep Throat was—a covert FBI operation in which the *Washington Post* reporter Bob Woodward was almost certainly an unwitting asset.

When the FBI director, J. Edgar Hoover, died on May 2 1972, Felt, who believed he should be his replacement, was passed over. The Watergate break-in took place a month later. As President Nixon sought to coerce the CIA and FBI to participate in his increasingly frantic efforts to obstruct justice, Felt, who had access to raw intelligence files, organized a band of his most trusted lieutenants and began a campaign of strategic leaking. The Felt op, in fact, was part of a widespread revolt of professionals throughout the federal government against Nixon's threats to their bureaucratic integrity.

Nixon's grand plan was to concentrate executive power in an imperial presidency, politicize the bureaucracy and crush its independence, and invoke national security to wage partisan warfare. He intended to "reconstitute the Republican party," staging a "purge" to foster "a new majority," as his aide William Safire wrote in his memoir. Nixon declared in his own memoir that to achieve his ends, the "institutions" of government had to be "reformed, replaced or circumvented. In my second term I was prepared to adopt whichever of these three methods—or whichever combination of them—was necessary."

But now George Bush is building a leviathan beyond Nixon's imagining. The Bush presidency is the highest stage of Nixonism. The commander in chief has declared himself by executive order above international law, the CIA is being purged, the Justice Department is deploying its resources to break down the wall of separation between church and state, the Environmental Protection Agency is being ordered to suppress scientific studies, and the Pentagon is subsuming intelligence and diplomacy, leaving the United States with blunt military force as its chief foreign policy.

The three main architects of Bush's imperial presidency gained their formative experience amid Nixon's downfall. Donald Rumsfeld, Nixon's counselor, and his deputy, Dick Cheney, served as successive chiefs of staff to Nixon's successor, Gerald Ford, both opposing congressional efforts for more transparency in the executive.

With perfect Nixonian pitch, Cheney remarked in 1976: "Principle is OK up to a certain point, but principle doesn't do any good if you lose." During the Iran-contra scandal, Cheney, a Republican leader in the House of Representatives, argued that the congressional report denouncing "secrecy, deception and disdain for the law" was an encroachment on executive authority.

The other architect, Karl Rove, Bush's senior political aide, began his career as an agent of Nixon's dirty trickster Donald Segretti—one of the "ratfuckers," as Segretti called his boys. At the height of the Watergate scandal, Rove operated through a phony front group to denounce the lynch-mob atmosphere created in this city by the *Washington Post* and other parts of the Nixon-hating media.

Under Bush, the Republican Congress has abdicated its responsibilities of executive oversight and investigation. When the Republican senator John Warner, chair of the Armed Services Committee, held hearings on Bush's torture policy in the aftermath of the Abu Ghraib revelations, the White House set rabid House Republicans to attack him. There have been no more such hearings. Meanwhile, Bush insists that the Senate vote to confirm John Bolton as U.S. ambassador to the United Nations while refusing to release essential information on Bolton's unaccounted use of National Security Agency intercepts requested by the Senate Foreign Relations Committee.

One of the chief lessons learned from Nixon's fall was the necessity of muzzling the press. The Bush White House has neutralized the press corps and even turned some reporters into its own assets. The disinformation about WMD in the rush to war in Iraq, funneled into the news pages of the *New York Times,* is the most dramatic case in point. By manipulation and intimidation, encouraging an atmosphere of self-censorship, the Bush White House has distanced the press from dissenting professionals inside the government.

Mark Felt's sudden emergence from behind the curtain of history evoked the glory days of the press corps and its modern creation myth. It was a warm bath of nostalgia, and cold comfort.

A Broken Body

JUNE 16, 2005

THE HOUSE OF REPRESENTATIVES of the 109th Congress suffers the classic symptoms of a decadent ancien régime. It seems an eon ago that the Republicans swept into power in 1994, after forty years in the wilderness, on a "Contract with America" whose preamble promised: "To restore accountability to Congress. To end its cycle of scandal and disgrace."

Day by day, week by week, spectacles unfold in its august chambers that reveal new incidents of corruption, unaccountability, and chaos. The Republican clamor for "democratic deliberation" faded long ago, even as a distant echo, as the screws of centralized power tightened. The Democrats have been prevented from debating legislation, attaching amendments, and participating in conferences. Any gesture of dissent is gaveled out of order. Republican members too have been relegated to the sidelines, rubber-stamping what the leadership dictates.

"Gutless chicken shit," Tom DeLay shouted seven years ago at a reporter asking questions about his ethics violations. Today, the Republican majority leader frantically maneuvers to quash any investigation by the House Ethics Committee into three foreign trips paid for by his close friend, the lobbyist Jack Abramoff, who is himself under a Department of Justice probe for fleecing Indian tribes of tens of millions of dollars. (It is illegal for members of Congress to accept foreign trips from lobbyists.)

Since the House has been in session this year, the Ethics Committee has met for exactly one day. On that day, in May, it decided under intense public pressure to reverse its fail-safe scheme to thwart any investigation of DeLay. The committee had announced rules by which a deadlock would lead to dismissal of any charge. Because the committee is the only one equally divided between majority and minority members, a deadlock was guaranteed, and so, therefore, was DeLay's escape.

But last week DeLay designed a new device to frustrate an investigation. The rules of the committee stipulate that its staff must be nonpartisan. However, another rule allows the chair and the ranking minority member each to appoint a staff member without the other's approval. The chair, Representative Doc Hastings, Republican of Washington State, seized on that rule to name his longtime chief of staff as director of the committee. With that move he succeeded in throwing a wrench into the works. Predictably, the Democrats protested, and the process ground to a halt; unless it is somehow unstuck, the investigation of DeLay has been stalled indefinitely.

Although it is DeLay's tactics that have paralyzed the Ethics Committee, he blames the Democrats for the consequences of his own actions. "They don't want an Ethics Committee," DeLay complained. "They would like to drag this out and have me and others before the Ethics Committee in an election year." Hastings, for his part, has been exposed as having his own web of relationships with Abramoff, who boasted to a client that his ties to Hastings were "excellent."

So long as the Ethics Committee is in effect defunct, it cannot investigate any new cases, such as that involving Representative Randy "Duke" Cunningham, Republican of California, which emerged in the past week. Cunningham, an influential member of the House Defense Appropriations Subcommittee, has helped a defense contractor named Mitchell Wade and his company, MZM Inc., win tens of millions of dollars in contracts. In 2003, Wade paid Cunningham $1.67 million for his house in Del Mar, California, and then resold it for $700,000 less than he paid Cunningham. The discrepancy suggested a neat and deliberate overpayment with the appearance of a bribe. The real estate agent involved, however, stated that $1.67 million was a fair price. But then it emerged that she and two of her family members had made eighteen financial contributions to Cunningham's campaigns, totaling $11,500 since 1997. Normally, the Ethics Committee would have taken up Cunningham's gamey situation. But for all intents and purposes, there is no Ethics Committee. Corruption cannot be acknowledged, much less investigated and rebuked.

While DeLay was orchestrating the latest plot turn in the Ethics Committee, Representative James Sensenbrenner, Republican of Wisconsin, continued his chairmanship of the Judiciary Committee as circus act. On June 10, he presided over a morning's hearing on the renewal of the PATRIOT Act, with testimony from witnesses invited by the Democratic minority. It was the one occasion when the Democrats were allowed under the rules to give critics of the bill an official forum. Sensenbrenner, whose routine demeanor is peeved and bilious, was on a hair trigger. He did not permit the ranking Democrat, John Conyers of Michigan, to finish his opening statement. He refused to recognize Democrats on their points of order. Finally, he declared the hearings over. "Much of what has been stated is not irrelevant," he announced absurdly. "Point of order," said Representative Sheila Jackson Lee, of Texas. "No, I will not yield," said Sensenbrenner. He cut off the microphones of Democrats as their words hung in the air: "Will the gentleman yield?" and "Point of order, Mr. Chairman." Sensenbrenner stormed out the door.

Sensenbrenner's high-handedness was hardly exceptional. This spring he barred Democrats from consultation on legislation that made drivers' licenses into national identification cards—in effect backdoor immigration legislation that could lead to sweeps against illegal immigrants with licenses. Indeed, no hearings whatsoever were held before the bill's passage.

At the same time, in April, Sensenbrenner rammed through a bill called the Child Interstate Notification Act, which applies federal criminal penalties to adults aiding and abetting minors who leave a state with parental-notification laws in order to get an abortion in another state. When Democrats on the Judiciary Committee submitted amendments, Sensenbrenner and his staff rewrote their captions in the official record without informing them. In every case, Sensenbrenner's language presented Democrats as defending "sexual predators." One caption of an amendment by Jerrold Nadler, Democrat of New York, for example, read: "Mr. Nadler offered an amendment that would have exempted sexual predators from prosecution under the bill if they were grandparents or adult siblings of a minor."

Right-wing Republicans like to posture as middle-class populists who are only reacting to the intrusions on individual liberty by liberal elites. But Sensenbrenner, the epitome of Republican arrogance, is the pampered heir to the Kotex fortune, whose sense of entitlement is exceeded only by his rancor.

DeLay's system of centralization has Washington in its grip. Republican House members are factotums of the leadership group he dominates. The regular operation of House committees has been overthrown. Decisions are handed down by DeLay and his lieutenants. Lobbyists convene with lawmakers in private to write legislation. What's more, lobbying firms are ordered to kick in campaign contributions and are under threat of losing preference if they hire Democrats. The speaker of the House, Dennis Hastert, DeLay's sock puppet, opened the 109th Congress by declaring that legislation had to meet the approval of "the majority of the majority"— DeLay's rule for right-wing control.

On about 80 percent of the bills before the House, amendments are prohibited as a result of what are called "closed rules." By manipulation of so-called suspension bills—for example, those that name federal buildings and praise civic groups—the business of the House has become a playpen of trivialities. Instead of substantive debate, two-thirds of all the time on the House floor is devoted to these meaningless measures. By this means, the leadership concentrates power and frustrates the House from acting as deliberative body. The schedule of the House has been reduced to something like that of a small state legislature of the nineteenth century, with many of its lollygagging members turning up for work on Tuesday and leaving on Thursday.

The efforts to suppress the proper workings of the House on inquiries of corruption and to quell uneasy questions about legislation from Democrats are only increasing the public pressure on the Republican leadership. Ever more rigid control is producing sharper and deeper fissures in its façade. The desperation for order fosters greater disorder. Such is the state of the American democracy that the rest of the world is encouraged to emulate.

Blinded by the Light
at the End of the Tunnel

JUNE 23, 2005

ON JUNE 21, network news reported that the Pentagon had claimed that forty-seven enemy operatives had been killed in Operation Spear in western Iraq. Last month, the Pentagon declared that 125 had been killed in Operation Matador, near the Syrian border. "We don't do body counts on other people," Donald Rumsfeld, the secretary of defense, stated in November 2003.

On January 29 of this year, the day before the Iraqi election, President Bush announced the "turning point" of the situation in Iraq. On May 2, 2003, he stood on the deck of the USS *Abraham Lincoln* before a banner saying "Mission Accomplished" and the next day proclaimed that "the mission is completed." On June 2 of this year, he declared: "Our mission is clear there, as well, and that is to train the Iraqis so they can do the fighting."

Last week, Bush retreated to his ultimate justification, that Iraq was invaded because Saddam Hussein was involved with the terrorists behind the September 11 attacks, a notion believed by a majority of those who voted for him in 2004: "We went to war because we were attacked."

On March 16, 2003, Dick Cheney, the vice president, prophesied: "We will, in fact, be greeted as liberators. . . . I think it will go relatively quickly." Only last month, Cheney assured us that the insurgency in Iraq is in "the last throes." On June 18, General William Webster, the U.S. commander in Baghdad, said: "Certainly saying anything about 'breaking the back' or 'about to reach the end of the line' or those kinds of things do not apply to the insurgency at this point."

The war has reached a tipping point—not in Iraq, but in the United States. Every announcement of a "turning point" heightens the rising tide of public disillusionment. Every reference to September 11 strains the administration's credibility. The revelation of how "the intelligence and facts were being fixed around the policy" for war, as in the now-famous Downing Street memo, reflecting a discussion on the Bush administration's intention to invade Iraq conducted by Prime Minister Tony Blair with his

211

senior advisers on June 23, 2002, shatters even some Republicans' previously implacable faith.

On June 21, a Gallup poll reported that Bush's approval rating was collapsing along with support for the war. Only 39 percent of Americans now support it. "The decline in support for the war is found among Republicans and independents, with little change among Democrats." (Since March, Republican support has fallen 11 points, to 70 percent.)

"They're starting to talk numbers again," Pat Lang remarked to me about the return of body counts. Lang is the former chief at the Defense Intelligence Agency for the Middle East, South Asia, and counterterrorism. "They were determined not to do that. But they can't provide a measurement to tell themselves they're doing well. As you know, it means nothing."

Lang, who served as an intelligence officer in Vietnam, observes: "For almost all of the war, Vietnam was a better situation than Iraq. During the conduct of the war, the security situation was far better than this." The Iraqi elections are "irrelevant to the outcome of the war because the people who voted were the people who stood to gain."

Iran is the long-term winner. "Iran intends to pull the Shia state of Iraq into its orbit. You can be sure that Iranian revolutionary guards are honeycombed throughout Iraq's intelligence to make sure things don't get out of hand." About the "euphoria" said to have followed the election, a claim faithfully echoed by the press corps, Lang simply says: "Laughable, comical, pathetic."

Bush's Iraq syndrome is a reinvention of Lyndon Johnson's Vietnam syndrome. In December 1967, Walt Rostow, LBJ's national security adviser, famously declared about the Vietcong and the North Vietnamese: "Their casualties are going up at a rate they cannot sustain. . . . I see light at the end of the tunnel." The official invitation to the New Year's Eve party at the U.S. embassy in Saigon read: "Come see the light at the end of the tunnel." The Tet offensive struck a month later.

"Even when what happened was really more positive than it seemed to be—the Tet offensive in 1968 was a military disaster for the Vietcong and North Vietnamese army—no one believed it because there was no light at the end of tunnel," Harry McPherson, who was President Johnson's counsel in the White House, told me. For a modern instance, McPherson cited the statement this week by Chuck Hagel, a Republican senator from Nebraska: "The White House is completely disconnected from reality. It's like they're just making it up as they go along. The reality is that we're losing in Iraq."

Bush's light-at-the-end-of-the-tunnel vision can only accelerate the cycle of disillusionment. His instinctive triumphalism inevitably has a counterproductive effect. His refusal to insist on responsibility for blunders—indeed, his readiness to reward and honor their perpetrators—enshrines impunity and hubris.

His doctrine of presidential infallibility, the election being his only "moment of accountability," can no longer be sustained by reference to September 11. His defense of the abuse and torture of detainees at Guantánamo and other prisons in violation of laws formerly upheld by the United States blots out his attempts to explain the purity of his motives.

In *The Quiet American,* Graham Greene's 1955 novel on the wages of naive arrogance in Vietnam, the world-weary British journalist Fowler remarks to Pyle, the U.S. agent with the best of intentions: "Oh, I know your motives are good, they always are. . . . I wish sometimes you had a few bad motives, you might understand a little more about human beings. And that applies to your country too, Pyle."

"The Last Throes"

JUNE 30, 2005

"THEY'RE JUST WRONG about our strategy. We've had a strategy from the beginning," said President Bush on May 13, 2003. It was only thirteen days since he had made his triumphant tailhook landing in an S-3B Viking on the USS *Abraham Lincoln* ("I flew it"), stood before the sailors in a flight suit, and declared the Iraq conflict concluded as a large banner behind him proclaimed "Mission Accomplished."

Then he flicked off pesky congressional critics of the immediate postwar transition policy. "Jerry Bremer is running the strategy, and we are making very good progress about the establishment of a free Iraq." Appointed by Bush as the head of the Coalition Provisional Authority, Bremer had disbanded the Iraqi army and was purging the Baath Party, acts that convinced the Sunnis that the United States intended to exclude them from any new arrangement. "And the person who is in charge is me," Bush continued. "Look, I just don't make decisions on polls, and I can't worry about polls."

A year later, on June 28, 2004, Iraq's new prime minister, Iyad Allawi, projected optimism as the CPA handed over authority to his government. "In a few days, Iraq will radiate with stability and security," he promised.

A year after that, on June 20, Vice President Dick Cheney assured us that the insurgency is in "the last throes." But on June 26, Secretary of Defense Donald Rumsfeld explained that the Iraqi insurgency could last "five, six, eight, ten, twelve years." The next day, the new Iraqi prime minister, Ibrahim al-Jaafari, sought to create a more upbeat assessment. "I think two years will be enough, and more than enough to establish security."

By then the White House had announced that President Bush would deliver an address to the nation on Iraq. There was no particularly momentous event in the field to compel it—no overwhelming offensive by insurgents, no political breakthrough by the Iraqi government. But the steady accretion of U.S. military fatalities (eighty in May, seventy-seven so far in June), the daily pictures of carnage on TV, and the seepage of reports on the Downing Street memo had eroded Bush's domestic support. It was the crisis on the home front that prompted him to explain the crisis abroad. The president who earlier claimed he wasn't worried about polls needed to lift his sagging ratings.

His appearance was preceded on June 22 by a bombing run by his chief political adviser, Karl Rove, to soften up the targets. "Conservatives saw the savagery of 9/11 in the attacks and prepared for war; liberals saw the savagery of the 9/11 attacks and wanted to prepare indictments and offer therapy and understanding for our attackers," he said. Rove's remarks signaled that Bush's strategy remains organized around control of the image of 9/11. Maintaining support for Bush's foreign policy demands relentless domestic polarization—including defining critics as giving aid and comfort to the enemy. What worked in the campaign would continue to work.

On Tuesday night Bush marched before hundreds of troops attired in red berets at Fort Bragg, North Carolina. The live audience poised at attention stood in for the public before their commander in chief. Their silence suggested obedience to orders. The only interruption for applause came at the end, when the presidential advance team began clapping to the line: "We will stay in the fight until the fight is won."

Five times Bush mentioned 9/11. Terrorism was mentioned twenty-nine times. We are in Iraq, in short, because of 9/11. "And we fight today because terrorists want to attack our country and kill our citizens, and Iraq is where they are making their stand." Bush was not articulating a policy so much as conflating 9/11 with Iraq to restore his popularity.

The novelty in Bush's speech came not from his militarized stagecraft but from his approving quotation of Osama bin Laden: "Some wonder whether Iraq is a central front in the war on terror. Among the terrorists, there is no debate. Here are the words of Osama bin Laden: 'This third world war is raging in Iraq. The whole world is watching this war.' He says it will end in victory and glory or misery and humiliation."

By citing Bin Laden, Bush raised him to the stature of a foreign leader. But he went further, embracing Bin Laden's understanding of the war's dynamics as a crusade. By endorsing Bin Laden's notion of a "third world war," the American president lent the prestige of his office to the terrorists' vision. Using Bin Laden's statement to justify his own course, Bush legitimated their war.

By mixing 9/11 and Iraq, Bush jumbled the actual logic of cause and effect. In the rush to war, Bush, Cheney, & Co. had suggested that Saddam Hussein was allied with terrorists, connecting the dots to 9/11. But the CIA now reports that Iraq has become a terrorist training center only since the failed postwar reconstruction.

Rather than make his case by admitting the administration blunders that led to the current crisis, explaining his proposed correction of course, and realistically discussing Iraq's current political or military situation or any empirical factor on the ground, Bush sought to recapture his past standing by repeating his past rhetoric.

Bush's strategy rests on more than sheer avoidance of facts, however; it depends on willful ignorance of the history of Mesopotamia.

From the creation of the Iraqi state in 1921 to the army's coup of 1958, Iraq had fifty-eight governments. In 1968, the Baathist Party led by Saddam Hussein staged another coup. Some periods of this prolonged chaos were less unstable than others, but the instability was chronic and profound. The overthrow of Saddam appears to have returned Iraq to its "natural" unstable state. But in fact the instability runs even deeper.

The Baathists, of course, were Sunnis. Saddam was a Sunni. Before him, the monarchs, beginning with Faisal I, were Sunnis. Before Faisal, the Ottomans, whose rule began in the fifteenth century, were Sunnis. Shiites have never ruled the country until now. Why should the Sunnis, after six hundred years of control, accede to the dominance of Shiites? In Vietnam, the root motivation against the United States was nationalism, as it was against the French. It even trumped communism in the national liberation struggle. In Iraq, religion and ethnicity are often ascribed as the root motivations of conflict. But to the extent that nationalism may exist as a factor, its ownership does not and cannot reside in the current Iraqi state.

The present Iraqi government is a ramshackle affair of Shiites and Kurds. The Kurds have no interest in a central authority; they play the game only to solidify their autonomy. The Shiites are maintained as dominant only by the presence of the U.S. Army and their sectarian militias. They will never disband those militias in favor of a national army unless they can run the army like an expanded version of the Shiite militias. Prime Minister al-Jaafari and the other Shiite leaders, including Deputy Prime Minister Ahmed Chalabi, have all been Iranian agents or allies, recipients of Iranian largesse in one form or another. Shiite Iraqis are natural friends and allies of Shiite Iran. Iraq under the Shiites does not have to be remade in Iran's image to serve Iranian interests. Whether or not sharia (Islamic law) is imposed, Iraqi Sunnis will never see Shiites as Iraqi patriots or nationalists but, only as being in league with Iraq's traditional and worst enemy.

These suspicions are hardly abstract. The militia of the largest Shiite faction, the Badr Brigade of SCIRI (the Supreme Council of Islamic Revolution in Iraq), was trained and armed by Iran's Islamic Revolutionary Guards and is heavily infiltrated and directed by Iranian agents today. Yet Bush has invested American blood and treasure in the proposition that a Shiite-dominated government, which now inevitably means an Iranian-influenced regime, can serve a second master in the United States and present itself to the Sunnis as national saviors.

Bush did not acknowledge this underlying assumption of his policy. Perhaps he does not know it is his assumption. Bush was insistent in disdaining any "timetable" for withdrawal from Iraq. He made no reference to Rumsfeld's twelve-year calculation. But Rumsfeld, who has demanded precise indexes for progress, is the only, and the highest, official in the administration who has offered any metric. How did he arrive at the estimate of twelve years? What analyses have been done by the Department of Defense to inform his statement? And what is the view of the Joint Chiefs of Staff? Has Rumsfeld presented his analysis before the principals of the National Security Council? Has he, or the national security adviser, or the director of national intelligence, briefed the president on it? If not, why not? Has he briefed the Armed Services Committees of the House and Senate?

Given Rumsfeld's twelve-year timetable, what plan has he formulated for troop rotation in Iraq? How many tours of duty will units serve? How will the army be replenished over twelve years? What effect will the prospect of twelve years of war have on the recruitment rate, down 40 percent this year despite $40,000 enlistment bonuses?

When will Rumsfeld propose his twelve-year budget? At the current rate of $1 billion a week spent on Iraq (a low estimate; some experts believe the true figure is double that), the cost over twelve years would be $4.38 trillion. But that estimate does not include hidden costs such as replacement materiel, special benefits, and reenlistment bonuses. And will the budget be reviewed by the Department of Defense, the White House Office of Management and Budget, or the Treasury? Furthermore, the war is financed through supplemental budget requests. Once enacted by Congress, the money is raised by selling Treasury bills, mostly to Chinese and other Asian banks. The Chinese use the interest to finance their military modernization, which the United States has told them is not permitted. Where are the Department of Defense analyses justifying this strategic tradeoff?

On the question of a timetable, either the president or the secretary of defense lacks credibility. If it's the secretary, and there are no analyses, no metrics behind his comment, then the president must immediately repudiate his statement. In his speech, Bush failed to clarify his administration's internal confusion. Until he does, the administration cannot claim to speak with a single voice.

In his call for "sacrifice," Bush strove to sound somber, but his tone was more gladiatorial than anguished. His speech superficially recalled the Vietnam speeches of Lyndon Johnson, another president who tried to muster public support for a war that increasingly resembled a quagmire. But Johnson's speeches were filled with a sense of the sobriety of the venture and moment. Even as he urged patience, as Bush did, and said the nation was being tested in Vietnam, as Bush did about Iraq, he spoke of moral ambiguities. In his State of the Union address of 1967, for example, Johnson said of the Vietnam War: "No better words could describe our present course than those once spoken by the great Thomas Jefferson: 'It is the melancholy law of human societies to be compelled sometimes to choose a great evil in order to ward off a greater.'" And Johnson warned the country against "arousing the hatreds and the passions that are ordinarily loosed in time of war."

Johnson was an anguished president, a reluctant warrior, personally devastated by the loss of life and fully aware of the costs of the war to himself, his presidency, and the nation. Vietnam was a war he inherited; he had made not a single decision to go to war. From the beginning, he knew he presided over a disintegrating policy. He believed that if he withdrew from Vietnam, he would provoke a right-wing backlash as virulent as McCarthyism and sacrifice his Great Society programs. Johnson grappled with bad and worsening prospects. He was always skeptical about the war and tended toward pessimism. He gathered as much information as he could and reached out to the most informed people he could. He especially sought out senators he respected who had serious reservations, like Richard Russell and Mike Mansfield.

"You can't listen to those tapes of Johnson without hearing a man in utter agony, knowing he's trapped," I was told by Leslie Gelb, the director of the Pentagon Papers project inside the Defense Department during the Johnson administration and president emeritus of the Council on Foreign Relations. "Bush doesn't think he's trapped. Bush has reduced everything to will. I've never seen any self-doubt or agonizing, or anyone who works with him suggest that."

From the thoroughly favorable political position of national unanimity after 9/11, Bush pursued a war of choice in Iraq, relying on shaky, distorted, and false intelligence. Skeptics were driven into a corner and punished. The administration became an echo chamber.

Immediately after the invasion, Cheney, Rumsfeld, and their neoconservative deputies systematically excluded knowledgeable experts from participation in reconstruction. The State Department's extensive Future of Iraq project was sidelined, and Rumsfeld refused to permit the new U.S. Office of Reconstruction to hire thirty-two State Department experts, as David L. Phillips, a member of the State Department's project, recounts in *Losing Iraq: Inside the Postwar Reconstruction Fiasco.* Phillips's firsthand account is a chronicle of epic disaster. He reveals that it was not only the State Department and the intelligence services that were ignored. On the question of disbanding the Iraqi army, it was the U.S. military's senior experts who were shunted aside: "The Bush administration had committed one of the greatest errors in the history of U.S. warfare," he writes.

In his speech, Bush said that once the Iraqi army is re-created, we will leave. Iraqification has become the linchpin of U.S. policy. "To me the reason we didn't win in Vietnam isn't that we failed to arm the South Vietnamese armed forces or give them air cover at the end," said Gelb. "The reason they lost is that they didn't have a government they felt was worth defending and dying for. Without that, no army is going to fight. It won't take twelve years, it will take forever."

The crisis in Iraq has been produced by deliberate decisions taken by the Bush administration against the advice of the State Department, the military, and others. "Their lack of planning was criminally irresponsible, grounds for impeachment," said Gelb. "Of the things that have happened to the U.S. in warfare, this was the single greatest dereliction of duty. It wasn't as if the military wasn't telling them they needed more troops. They still don't know what they are doing."

Bush's speech did not mark a new foreign policy. It did not resolve the political conundrums of Iraq. It cannot advance the combat-readiness of the feeble Iraqi army. Rather, his speech was an exercise in public relations to retrieve his own political situation.

Unlike Lyndon Johnson, he does not grasp the tragic dimensions of his war. Like Johnson, he is giving hostages to fortune. Everything he says can and will be used against him in the court of public opinion. His fortitude appears as recklessness, his determination as cluelessness.

The Supreme Chance of a Lifetime

JULY 7, 2005

EVER SINCE FRANKLIN D. ROOSEVELT breached the conservative fortress of the U.S. Supreme Court, Republicans have dreamed of restoration. Every Republican president has attempted to fill the court with judges who would stall, overcome, and even reverse change in the law and in American society. President Eisenhower felt that appointing Earl Warren as chief justice was the "biggest damn-fool mistake I ever made." Warren became the leader of liberal jurisprudence, using the law to advance social equality and rights. "Impeach Warren!" became the cry of the right.

President Nixon attempted to pack the court with two Southern segregationists who were rejected by the Senate. His choice for chief justice, Warren Burger, as conservative as he was, disappointed him, and he took to calling him "a dumb Swede." At last he selected William Rehnquist, the farthest-right candidate he could find, a judge who had personally intimidated blacks and Hispanics from voting at polling places and written a memo in favor of segregation. Before his confirmation hearing, Nixon instructed him to "be as mean and rough as they said you were."

Rehnquist's consistent conservatism made him President Reagan's natural choice for chief justice. Reagan, too, hoped to pack the court with justices who would play well with Rehnquist. He appointed Antonin Scalia, even farther to the right than Rehnquist, and nominated Robert Bork, perhaps even to Scalia's right, a dyspeptic reactionary rejected by the Democratic Senate. And Reagan named Sandra Day O'Connor, thereby gaining credit for appointing the first woman justice. She also happened to be a conservative former state senator from Arizona, such a close friend of her fellow Arizonan Rehnquist that they had once dated.

President George H. W. Bush believed that he was filling the court with traditional conservatives, but he played two wild cards. David Souter has aligned himself with the moderates and liberals. Clarence Thomas has been consumed with a conservative fervor fed by rage and resentment; he appears not to have recovered from his confirmation hearing, where he was accused of sexual harassment and which he decried as a "high-tech lynching." Initially Thomas followed in the shadow of Scalia, but he has emerged on an even farther shore of the right.

With only two out of nine justices appointed by a Democratic president, the Republican right still considered the court a bastion of betrayal and temple of the left. O'Connor often turned out to be the swing vote in decisions going five to four against the conservatives. She is a classic literal conservative who believes that tradition and precedent have their own claims. She is small-bore, resting her decisions on evidence and case law, while Rehnquist, Scalia, and Thomas veer erratically in hot ideological pursuit of the "original understanding" of the Constitution as they divine it, through a mystical séance summoning shades of the Founding Fathers who bear little resemblance to their historical selves. With O'Connor, *Roe v. Wade*, guaranteeing the right to abortion, has been preserved; affirmative action and campaign-finance reform have been upheld.

Conservatives' frustration at their inability to remake the country through Republican domination of the Supreme Court has risen exponentially during O'Connor's ascendance. The Federalist Society, a tightly knit group of conservative lawyers created during the Reagan period, now operates as a controlling network throughout the Bush administration. There is not a single presidential appointee in a position of legal responsibility who is not a card-carrying member. Among them, the regnant doctrine is that of the "Constitution in exile"—a belief that the true Constitution has been suppressed since Franklin D. Roosevelt and can be restored by the uniform appointment of "originalists" to the court.

With O'Connor's retirement, the Republican counterrevolution sees the opportunity of a lifetime to shift the court once and for all. While the fate of legal abortion has aroused the most controversy, national security will undoubtedly involve the court even more deeply in making new law. A host of new questions are unresolved. What power does the president have to keep information secret? What is the extent of executive privilege as applied to war powers? Should free speech be infringed when national security is supposedly at risk? What is the president's power to detain? Can due process be suspended? What is the president's power to torture?

Indeed, the notion of torture is alive in the executive branch. Bush's lawyers in the Office of Legal Counsel of the Justice Department have concluded that the president "enjoys complete discretion," and any limitation on his power to torture is unconstitutional. Justice Clarence Thomas concurs. In his dissenting opinion in *Hamdi v Rumsfeld*, Thomas argued that detainees have no right to due process of law; he would assign "unique" powers to the executive in national security and none to Congress, contrary to the Constitution. The extremity of advocating legalisms for the suspension of rights and for torture is not unrelated to a broader extremism.

The spirit animating the Bush administration and the conservatives on the court is the illusion of omnipotence. It is the opposite of that of Justice John Paul Stevens (a Republican appointed by President Gerald Ford, who recently expressed his pride in that appointment). In his dissent last year in *Rumsfeld v. Padilla*, Stevens argued that an American citizen could not be detained without due process. "Even more important than the method of selecting the people's rulers and their successors," he wrote, "is the character of the constraints imposed on the executive by the rule of law."

Rove's War

JULY 14, 2005

THIS IS KARL ROVE'S WAR. From his command post next to the Oval Office in the West Wing of the White House, he is furiously directing the order of battle. The Republican National Committee lobs its talking points across Washington; its chairman forays into the no-man's-land of CNN. Rove's lawyer, Fox News, and the *Wall Street Journal* editorial board are sent over the top. Newt Gingrich and Tom DeLay man the ramparts, defending Rove's character.

For two years, since the appointment of an independent counsel to investigate the disclosure of the identity of an undercover CIA operative, President Bush and his press secretary, Scott McClellan, have repeatedly denied the involvement of anyone in the White House. "Have you talked to Karl, and do you have confidence in him?" a reporter asked Bush on September 30, 2003. "Listen, I know of nobody," he replied. "I don't know of anybody in my administration who leaked classified information. If somebody did leak classified information, I'd like to know it, and we'll take the appropriate action."

Bush backed himself into that corner because of a sequence of events beginning with the ultimate rationale he offered for the Iraq war. Public support for the war had wavered until the administration asserted unequivocally that Saddam Hussein was seeking to acquire and build nuclear weapons. Its most incendiary claim was that he had tried to purchase enriched yellowcake uranium in Niger. An Italian magazine, *Panorama,* had received documents appearing to prove the charge. The former ambassador Joseph Wilson was secretly sent by the CIA to investigate, and he found no evidence to substantiate the story. The CIA subsequently protested against the inclusion of the rumor in a draft of a Bush speech, and Bush delivered the speech on October 7, 2002, without it.

But a month earlier, a British white paper had mentioned the Niger rumor. And in his January 2003 State of the Union address, Bush said: "The British government has learned that Saddam Hussein recently sought significant quantities of uranium from Africa." By then these six-teen notorious words had already been proved false, debunked by three separate reports from administration officials, which were apparently ig-nored ahead of Bush's speech. On March 7, 2003, the International Atomic Energy Agency announced that the Niger documents were "not authentic." The following day, the State Department concurred that they were forger-ies. The invasion of Iraq began on March 20.

After the war began, the administration refused to acknowledge the lie . To set the record straight, Wilson wrote an op-ed article on July 6, 2003, in the *New York Times,* titled "What I Didn't Find in Africa." It was the first crack in the credibility of the administration's case for the war, sug-gesting that the underlying intelligence had been abused, distorted, and even forged. National Security Adviser Condoleezza Rice later admitted, "It was information that was mistaken." And the CIA director, George Tenet, said the lines "should never have been included in a text written for the president."

On July 14, about a week after Wilson's op-ed piece appeared, the con-servative columnist Robert Novak wrote that Wilson's "wife, Valerie Plame, is an Agency operative on weapons of mass destruction. Two senior admin-istration officials told me Wilson's wife suggested sending him to Niger to investigate the Italian report." The revelation of Plame's identity may be a violation of the Intelligence Identities Protection Act of 1982—a felony car-rying a ten-year prison sentence. Apparently the release of Plame's identity was political payback against Wilson by a White House that wanted to shift the public focus from the Iraq war to Wilson's motives.

On July 30, the CIA referred a "crime report" to the Justice Department. "If she was not undercover, we would not have a reason to file a criminal referral," a CIA official said. On December 30, the Justice Department ap-pointed Patrick Fitzgerald, U.S. attorney for northern Illinois, as the spe-cial prosecutor.

Fitzgerald's investigation stalled when two reporters he subpoenaed, Matthew Cooper of *Time* magazine and Judith Miller of the *New York Times,* initially refused to testify, citing their professional obligation to protect their sources. But *Time* handed over Cooper's notes on his conver-sation with Rove to the prosecutor, and Cooper eventually decided to co-operate. Miller chose to remain in contempt of court and has been impris-oned until the grand jury is dissolved.

With the publication of Cooper's memo of July 11, 2003 to his editors two weeks ago, which substantiated that Rove leaked Plame's name and identity to him and not the other way around, as Rove had claimed, the White House was asked about whether the president would adhere to its own "highest standards," as McClellan had put it, and fire anyone involved in outing Plame. But since Monday both McClellan and Bush have refused to comment on the investigation. While the White House stonewalls, Rove has license to run his own damage-control operation. His surrogates argue that if Rove did anything, it wasn't a crime. There's no cause for outrage, except at Joe Wilson, and now, in a turn of the screw, Matt Cooper. The inhabitants of the political village should busy themselves with their arts and crafts. No one's status will be endangered or access withdrawn, it is implied, if they do nothing rash. They should simply accept that exposing undercover CIA operatives is part of politics as usual. Return to your homes. Stay calm.

Rove is fighting his war as though it will be settled in a court of Washington pundits. Brandishing his formidable political weapons, he seeks to demonstrate his prowess once again. His corps of agents raises a din in which their voices drown out individual dissidents. His frantic massing of forces dominates the capital by winning the communications battle. Indeed, Rove may succeed momentarily in quelling the storm. But the stillness may be illusory. Before the prosecutor, Rove's arsenal is useless.

Can the special counsel be confounded by manipulation of the Washington chattering class? What's the obligation of a reporter to a source in this case? What game are Rove and his surrogates playing? What are the legal vulnerabilities of Rove and others in the White House?

Wilson's article provided the first evidence that the reasons given for the war were stoked by false information. But to attack Wilson by outing his wife is superficially perplexing. Even if the allegation were true that she "authorized" his mission, as Rove told Cooper, it would have no bearing whatsoever on the Niger forgeries, or on any indictment. But Rove's is a psychological operation intended to foster the perception that the messenger is somehow untrustworthy and therefore his message is, too. The aim is to distract and discredit. By trying to taint Wilson's motives, Rove has constructed an elaborate negative image.

The *Wall Street Journal* editorial of July 13 best reflected the through-the-looking-glass Rovian defense and projection: "For Mr. Rove is turning out to be the real 'whistle-blower' in this whole sorry pseudo-scandal. . . . In short, Mr. Rove provided important background so Americans could understand that Mr. Wilson wasn't a whistleblower but was a partisan trying to discredit the Iraq War in an election campaign."

In order to untangle this deceptive web, it's essential to return to the beginning of the long disinformation campaign triggered by the publication of Wilson's op-ed piece. The facts illuminate not only the mendacity of the smears but also the seeming quandary of the reporters who have become collateral damage.

In early 2002, Valerie Plame was an officer in the Directorate of Operations of the CIA task force on counterproliferation, which dealt with weapons of mass destruction, including Saddam's WMD programs. At that time, as she had been for almost two decades, she was an undercover operative. After training at the "Farm," the CIA's school for clandestine agents, she became what the agency considers among its most valuable and vulnerable operatives—a NOC, an agent who works under non-official cover. Because NOCs travel without diplomatic passports, if they are captured as spies they have no immunity and can be imprisoned or even executed. As a NOC, Plame helped set up a front company, Brewster-Jennings, whose cover has now been blown and whose agents and contacts may be in danger still. After marrying Wilson in 1998, she took Wilson as her last name.

When the Italian report on Niger uranium surfaced, Vice President Cheney's office contacted the CIA's counterproliferation office to look into it. Such a request is called a "tasker." It was hardly the first query the task force had received from the White House, and such requests were not made through the CIA director's office but directly. Plame's colleagues asked her if she would invite her husband out to CIA headquarters at Langley, Virginia, for a meeting to assess the question.

Wilson had already performed one secret mission to Niger for the CIA, in 1999, and he was trusted. Wilson had also had a distinguished and storied career as a foreign-service officer. He served as acting ambassador in Iraq during the Gulf war and was hailed by the first President Bush as a "hero." Wilson was an important part of the team and highly regarded by Secretary of State James Baker and National Security Adviser Brent Scowcroft. Wilson was also an Africa specialist. He had been a diplomat in Niger, the U.S. ambassador to Gabon, and senior director for Africa on the National Security Council during the Clinton administration. (I first encountered Wilson then, and we have since become friends.) No professional was better suited for this CIA mission.

Plame's superiors asked her to cable the field officers in Africa for routine approval of an investigation of the Niger claim. At Langley, Wilson met with about a dozen officers to discuss the situation. Plame was not at the meeting. Afterward, Wilson informed his wife that he would be traveling to Niger for about ten days. She was not particularly enthusiastic, having recently given birth to twins, but she understood the importance of the mission. She had no authority to commission him: she was not the responsible senior officer. Nor, if she had been, could she have done so unilaterally. Neither Joe nor Valerie Wilson stood to gain personally from the mission. He undertook the trip out of a long-ingrained sense of government service.

CIA officers debriefed Wilson the night of his return at his home. His wife greeted them but excused herself from the discussion. She later read a copy of his debriefing report, but she made no changes in it. The next they spoke of Niger uranium was when they heard President Bush's mention of it in his 2003 State of the Union address.

Attributing Wilson's trip to his wife's supposed authority became the predicate for a Rove-orchestrated campaign against his credibility. Seven months after the appointment of the special counsel, in July 2004, the Republican-dominated Senate Select Committee on Intelligence issued its report on flawed intelligence leading up to the Iraq war. The blame for failure was squarely put on the CIA for "groupthink." (The Republicans quashed a promised second report on political pressure on the intelligence process.) The three-page addendum by the ranking Republicans followed well-worn attack lines: "The plan to send the former ambassador to Niger was suggested by the former ambassador's wife, a CIA employee."

The CIA subsequently issued a statement, as reported by *New York Newsday* and CNN, that the Republican senators' conclusion about Plame's role was wholly inaccurate. But the *Washington Post*'s Susan Schmidt reported only the Republican senators' version, writing that Wilson was "specifically recommended for the mission by his wife, a CIA employee, contrary to what he has said publicly." Schmidt quoted the senators' account of a CIA official who stated that Plame had "offered up" Wilson's name in a memo. Plame's memo, in fact, was written at the express directive of her superiors, two days before Wilson was to come to Langley for his meeting, to describe his qualifications in a standard protocol to receive "country clearance." Unfortunately, Schmidt's article did not reflect this understanding of routine CIA procedure. The CIA officer who wrote the memo that originally recommended Wilson for the mission— who was cited anonymously by the senators as the only source who said that Plame was responsible—was deeply upset at the twisting of his testimony, which was not public, and told Plame he had said no such thing.

The CIA spokesman Bill Harlow told Wilson that the Republican Senate staff never contacted him for the agency's information on the matter.

Curiously, the only document cited as the basis for Plame's role was a State Department memo later debunked by the CIA. The *Washington Post* reported on December 26, 2003 that "CIA officials have challenged the accuracy of the . . . document, the official said, because the agency officer identified as talking about Plame's alleged role in arranging Wilson's trip could not have attended the meeting. 'It has been circulated around,' one official said." Even more curious, one of the outlets to which the document was circulated was Talon News Service and its star correspondent, Jeff Gannon (aka Guckert). Talon was revealed to be a partisan front for a Texas-based operation called GOPUSA, and Gannon was exposed as a male prostitute, without previous journalistic credentials yet with easy and unexplained access to the White House. According to the *Post*, "the CIA believes that people in the administration continue to release classified information to damage the figures at the center of the controversy."

Fitzgerald sought testimony from Matthew Cooper because he had published an article on the Wilson case that cited anonymous White House sources. Miller had published no article on the Plame issue at all. Apparently, another witness gave up Miller's name to the prosecutor under questioning. Who that witness might be and under what circumstances he or she cited Miller is unknown. (In the run-up to the war, Miller's articles on WMD were crucial in creating a political atmosphere favorable to the administration's case. But her articles were later revealed to be false, based on disinformation, and the *Times* published a long apology.)

Both Cooper and Miller claimed journalistic privilege to protect their sources, but the court ruled against them. U.S. District Court Judge Thomas Hogan's opinion suggested that the prosecutor's case had deepened and widened.

In discussing the sealed affidavit filed by Fitzgerald, and not revealed to the defendants, Hogan stated that the "Special Counsel outlines in great detail the developments in this case and the investigation as a whole. The ex parte affidavit establishes that the government's focus has shifted as it has acquired additional information during the course of the investigation. Special Counsel now needs to pursue different avenues in order to complete its investigation." Judge Hogan concluded that "the subpoenas were not issued in an attempt to harass the [reporters], but rather stem from legitimate needs due to an unanticipated shift in the grand jury's investigation."

Now Miller languishes in jail, and Cooper has testified before the grand jury. Is Miller protecting her sources, or does the prosecutor seek to question her as a disseminator of information? Should a journalist protect a source if that person has not provided information that is true to the best of their knowledge, but disinformation? What is the obligation of reporters to protect people who have misled them?

In the best-case scenario for Miller, Bill Kovach believes that any pledge she may have made to a source should be invalid. Kovach is the former Washington bureau chief of the *New York Times,* a former curator of the Nieman Foundation for Journalism at Harvard University, and a founding director of the Committee of Concerned Journalists. He describes the internal policy set within the *Times* on sources. "By the 1980s, we decided that we had to set some limits because reporters had been misled, and the credibility of the news reports had been damaged by misleading sources. When I was chief of the bureau in Washington, we laid down a rule to the reporters that when they wanted to establish anonymity, they had to lay out ground rules that if anything the source said was damaging, false, or damaged the credibility of the newspaper, we would identify them."

In the Plame matter, Kovach sees no obligation of the reporters to false sources. "If a man damages your credibility, why not lay the blame where it belongs? If Plame were an operative, she wouldn't have the authority to send someone. Whoever was leaking that information to Novak, Cooper, or Judy Miller was doing it with malice aforethought, trying to set up a deceptive circumstance. That would invalidate any promise of confidentiality. You wouldn't protect a source for telling lies or using you to mislead your audience. That changes everything. Any reporter that puts themselves or a news organization in that position is making a big mistake."

Obviously, in its present crisis the *Times* is not following these rules. Are its editors unaware of the underlying facts and falsehoods? Do the editors have a responsibility to determine who is a fair source and who is a deceiver? Has anyone fully debriefed Miller? For now, the *Times* is frozen in its heroic defense of the First Amendment.

Washington, meanwhile, is an echo chamber of Rove's agents. His lawyer, Robert Luskin, has trashed Cooper: "By any definition, he burned Karl Rove." The Republican National Committee chair Ken Mehlman has appeared on talk shows, given newspaper interviews, and circulated a three-page memo of talking points to Republican surrogates. In one brief statement, for example, Mehlman said: "The fact is Karl Rove did not leak classified information. He did not, according to what we learned this past weekend, reveal the name of anybody. He didn't even know the name. . . . He tried to discourage a reporter from writing a story that was false."

Mehlman's farrago of lies and distortions may be a fair representation of Rove's fears. Is it a "fact" that Rove didn't leak classified information? Plame's identity, of course, was classified; that is why the CIA referred the matter to the Department of Justice for investigation. But is Mehlman disclosing yet another Rove worry? The prosecutor can indict under any statute, including simply leaking classified information. Is Rove afraid of being indicted under that law, not just the law that makes it a crime to identify Plame? Mehlman raises a further Rove anxiety. No, Rove didn't "reveal the name." But the law doesn't cite that as a felony; it only specifies revealing the "identity" of an operative as a crime. Rove spoke of "Joe Wilson's wife." That qualifies as an "identity." Rove seemed to know that much—her identity.

Helpfully guiding a reporter to the truth and away from "a story that was false"? Indeed, Rove was planting two false stories, not just one. The first was that "Joe Wilson's wife" had sent him on his mission; the second was to suggest that Wilson was wrong and that there would be new information to support the original Bush falsehood. In fact, the White House admitted that Wilson was correct and that Bush's sixteen words asserting the Iraq-Niger connection were wrong. Yet Rove attempted to insinuate doubt in the mind of the reporter to discourage him from writing a story that was true.

At one point, on CNN, Wolf Blitzer asked Mehlman if he had attended meetings at the White House on how to deal with Wilson. Suddenly, the voluble Mehlman constricted. "I don't recall those meetings occurring," he said. Has the prosecutor inquired about such meetings and their participants?

The sound and fury of Rove's defenders will soon subside. The last word, the only word that matters, will belong to the prosecutor. So far, he has said very, very little. Unlike the unprofessional, inexperienced, and weak Ken Starr, he does not leak illegally to the press. But he has commented publicly on his understanding of the case. "This case," he said, "is not about a whistle-blower. It's about a potential retaliation against a whistle-blower."

Tunnel Vision

JULY 21, 2005

"THE WAR ON TERROR GOES ON," proclaimed President Bush
on the day of the London terrorist bombings, July 7. Throughout the 2004
campaign, Bush's winning theme was terror. He achieved the logic of a
unified-field theory connecting Iraq to Afghanistan by threading terror
through both, despite the absence of evidence. In almost every city and
town, Bush insisted that if we didn't fight the terrorists there, we would be
fighting them at home. In January of this year, the CIA's think tank, the
National Intelligence Council, issued a report describing Iraq as the mag-
net and the training and recruiting ground for international terrorism.
The false rationale for the invasion had become a self-fulfilling prophecy.
But with his popularity flagging, Bush returned to the formulations that
had succeeded in his campaign.

In Bush's "global war on terror," Iraq and Afghanistan present one extended battlefield against a common enemy, and the strategy is and must
be the same. So far as Bush is concerned, it's always either the day after 9/11
or the day before the Iraq invasion. Time stands still at two ideal political
moments. But the consequences since then have been barely managed
chaos.

"I was horrified by the president's last speech on the war on terror [on
June 28]—so much unsaid, so much disingenuousness, so many half-
truths," James Dobbins told me. Dobbins was Bush's first envoy to
Afghanistan and is now the director of international programs at the Rand
Corporation, a defense think tank. Afghanistan is now the scene of a Taliban revival, chronic Pashtun violence, dominance by U.S.-supported war-
lords (who have become drug lords, exploiting the exploding traffic in
opium poppies), and a human rights black hole. "Afghanistan is going better than Iraq," Dobbins said. "That's not much of a standard."

From the start, he said, the effort in Afghanistan was "grossly under-
funded and undermanned." The military doctrine was the first error. "The
U.S. focus on force protection and substitution of firepower for manpower

231

creates significant collateral damage." But the faith in firepower sustained the illusion that the mission could be "quicker, cheaper, easier." And that justification fit with recasting Afghanistan as a mere sideshow to Iraq.

At the same time, according to Dobbins, there was "a generally negative appreciation of peacekeeping and nation building as components of U.S. policy, a disinclination to learn anything from the previous [administration's experience] in Bosnia and Kosovo."

What's more, lack of accountability began at the top and filtered down. On the day of the Afghan president Hamid Karzai's inauguration in December 2001, Dobbins met General Tommy Franks, the head of Central Command, at the reopened Afghan airport. As they drove to the ceremony, Dobbins informed Franks of press reports that U.S. planes had mistakenly bombed a delegation of Afghan tribal leaders traveling to Kabul for the inauguration and killed perhaps several dozen people. "It was the first time he heard about it. When he got out of the car, reporters asked him about it. He denied it happened. And he denied it happened for several days. It was classic 'deny first, investigate later.' It turned out to be true. It was a normal reflex."

Democracy was at best an afterthought for the Bush administration, much less democracy for Afghans. At the conference in Bonn, Germany, establishing international legitimacy for the new Afghan government, "the word *democracy*," Dobbins points out, "was introduced at the insistence of the Iranian delegation."

Democracy, now the overriding rationale for the global war on terror, does not, however, include support for human rights, at least in Afghanistan. "In terms of the human rights situation," said Dobbins, "Karzai is well-meaning and moderate and thoroughly honorable. But he's overwhelmed, he's not a great manager, he has few instruments of power."

Donald Rumsfeld's Pentagon and the White House removed restraints on torturing prisoners—in Guantánamo Bay, Afghanistan, and Iraq. "These were command failures, not just isolated incidents, in that we dismantled systems designed to protect us from these kinds of events. You didn't have the checks and balances. They've had consequences in terms of public image," Dobbins said.

In April, the United States succeeded, after refusing to cooperate for two years with the United Nations rapporteur on human rights for Afghanistan, in abolishing the office altogether. The U.N. representative, Cherif Bassiouni, a distinguished expert on international law who has helped train hundreds of judges in Afghanistan, told me, "Karzai was in favor of keeping the mandate. But the U.S. was quite adamant. The U.S. came to the conclusion they needed to kill the messenger with hope the message would die. The tactics are contrary to any valid strategy. If the strategy is to stabilize Afghanistan, have a democratic regime, cut narco-trafficking and terrorism, what is being done is precisely the opposite."

Dobbins believes that the operation in Afghanistan has improved, but that the U.S. administration "hasn't readily acknowledged its mistakes and has corrected them only after losing a good deal of ground, irrecoverable ground." For all the problems there, "most of the violence is not al Qaeda type, but Pashtun sectarian violence. It's not international terrorism."

For Bush, however, facts on the ground cannot alter his stentorian summons to the global war on terror. "I've never liked the term *war*," said Dobbins. "This is a campaign conducted primarily, [as it] should be, by law-enforcement, diplomatic, and intelligence means. The militarization of the concept is a theme that mobilizes the American public effectively, but it's not a theme that resonates well in the Middle East or with our allies elsewhere in the world. I think some reconceptualization would be helpful. But the White House probably doesn't. Karl Rove doesn't spend a lot of time worrying about the impact of his strategies in the Muslim world."

"We're taking the fight to the terrorists abroad so we don't have to face them here at home," Bush declared in June—and repeated endlessly. His doublethink relieves any fear of cognitive dissonance. London, like Iraq and Afghanistan, is apparently "there," not "here."

"The Meaning of Words"

JULY 28, 2005

NEVER BEFORE has a president suddenly discarded his self-proclaimed "mission." But after declaring himself the commander in chief in the "global war on terror," President Bush has tossed the catchphrase aside in an elusive search for a new one. The "global war on terror" was his slogan to link the war in Afghanistan to the invasion of Iraq, the battle supposedly being one and the same. The quest for a new slogan is more than a public-relations gesture. It reflects not only the failure but also the vacuum of his strategy.

In Bush's speech at Fort Bragg, North Carolina, on June 28, for which the White House asked for and received national television coverage, he reaffirmed "fighting the global war on terrorism," mentioned "terror" or "terrorism" twenty-three more times, and compared this "global war on terrorism" with the Civil War and World War II. Since then, however, his administration has simply dropped the words that more than any others Bush has identified as the reason for his presidency.

Throughout July, administration officials have substituted new words for the old. Instead of trumpeting the "global war on terrorism," Secretary of Defense Donald Rumsfeld and General Richard Myers, chair of the Joint Chiefs of Staff, have sounded the call to "a global struggle against violent extremism." Medals stamped "Global War on Terror" have been awarded to brave U.S. soldiers. Will new medals now be minted?

Myers's change in language involves considerable historical and policy revisionism. He had gone along with Rumsfeld in policies opposed by senior military figures such as the former Army chief of staff, General Eric Shinseki, who was publicly derided by Paul Wolfowitz, then deputy secretary of defense, for worrying about invading Iraq with a light force. But now Myers presents himself as a secret dissident. In a speech before the National Press Club on Monday, he claimed he "objected to the use of the term 'war on terrorism' before, because if you call it a war, then you think of people in uniform as being the solution."

Myers also reveals himself now to be an ardent internationalist who believes that though the military is carrying the burden, future conflicts demand "all instruments of our national power, all instruments of the international communities' national power." In effect, Myers is repudiating the Bush doctrine of "preemptory self-defense" enunciated in the "National Strategy to Combat Weapons of Mass Destruction" in December 2002 to provide justification for the Iraq war.

"It is more than just a military war on terror," Stephen Hadley, the national security adviser, told the New York Times in an interview this week. "It's broader than that. It's a global struggle against extremism. We need to dispute both the gloomy vision and offer a positive alternative."

The imperative for a "positive alternative," however, is not to disperse something as nebulous as a "gloomy vision." It has not suddenly dawned on the Bush national security apparatus that the phrase *war on terror* describes a never-ending battle against a tactic. Dropping the signature phrase of the Bush presidency is part of an effort to cobble together some sort of expedient political solution that will allow U.S. troops to be drawn down before disaster strikes the Republicans in the midterm elections of 2006. *Shock and awe* has been replaced by *stunned and confused*. By stuffing the old slogan down the memory hole, the Bush administration has withdrawn credibility from its neoconservative policy. Unfortunately, ideology has consequences.

The new U.S. ambassador to Iraq, Zalmay Khalilzad, has arrived on the bloody scene to warn of impending civil war. But U.S. intelligence does not have an accurate sense of either the number of insurgents or their composition. "That would not be a worthwhile metric," Pentagon spokesman Lawrence Di Rita said recently. Thus Rumsfeld's assistant secretary for public affairs acknowledges that he doesn't know precisely who the enemy is.

Some of the insurgents are Sunni Arabs opposed to Shiite and Kurdish domination of a country they ruled from the time of the Ottoman Empire until the U.S. invasion. Some are former members of Saddam Hussein's Baath Party's secret police. Others are jihadists who operate like mobile mafias.

"My answer is, bring them on," Bush challenged Iraqi attackers on July 2, 2003. Since then there have been more than five hundred suicide attacks in Iraq. Saudi Arabian intelligence interrogated about three hundred Saudis captured on their way to fight or detonate themselves in Iraq; a Saudi study revealed that few if any of them had previous contact with al

Qaeda and that most were motivated by the U.S. occupation. A similar study of 154 foreign fighters by the Israeli Global Research in International Affairs Center reached the same conclusion.

In the face of relentless suicide bomber attacks, U.S. forces have withdrawn as much as possible in the past few weeks to the safety of their bases, drastically reducing their "operational tempo" and cutting casualties to about half those in June.

The insurgents' strategy is not to create another Vietnam. Their forces are not analogous to the hierarchical armies of the North Vietnamese and Viet Cong. Some responsible Sunni sheikhs and leaders may be drawn to participate in writing a new constitution, but there can be no full representation of insurgents. Apart from the nearly insuperable obstacles of getting Sunnis to endorse a Shiite Islamic republic and Kurdish autonomy, ultimately there is no "them" there to negotiate with. The insurgents have no concrete program: their game plan, after all, is a bloodbath. If they cannot strike at Americans, garrisoned in their forts, they will kill soft targets such as Iraqi policemen, local officials, and even children. Their strategy is to perpetuate anarchy, perhaps triggering a civil war: the worse it is, the better for them. Their models are Lebanon and Somalia.

"Bush is in a tough spot, one of his own making," the retired three-star Marine general Bernard Trainor told me. "Bush has to try to make the best of a bad hand. This administration did not really pose the what-if and what-then questions in planning. Now I hope they are. I haven't seen evidence of it yet. I'd like to think that people in the second and third tier understand. Whether the top three understand—the president, Cheney, and Rumsfeld—I don't know. It's hard to say. If you look at the evidence of the first administration, the answer would be no."

While other administration officials tried out the new post–war on terror slogans, Bush's longtime packager, Karen Hughes, nominated as undersecretary of state for public diplomacy, testified in her confirmation hearing before the Senate last week. Her rhetoric was filled with high-flown abstractions about "limits on the power of the state" and "respect for women," and phrases against "tyrants" and in favor of "freedom."

But U.S. diplomats in Iraq must attempt to negotiate through Iraqi ethnic, religious, and sectarian politics to help produce a settlement that "doesn't quite live up to Jeffersonian principles," said Trainor. Women's rights, for example, will almost certainly be undercut in the new constitution. And Shiites are insistent that the new state be Islamic. "Right now the goal is to get the Iraqi national security forces into some sort of reasonable shape and draw down our forces. Our presence is an irritant, but perhaps it's a lesser of evils, at least for the time being. These are the things that should have been discussed early on."

In the closing days of the 2004 election campaign, President Bush returned time and again to the theme that aroused the most fervent support for him. "The outcome of this election will set the direction of the war against terror, and in this war there is no place for confusion and no substitute for victory." He ridiculed his Democratic opponent, Senator John Kerry: "His top foreign policy adviser has questioned whether it's even a war at all, saying that's just a metaphor, like the war on poverty," Bush said. "I've got news: Anyone who thinks we are fighting a metaphor does not understand the enemy we face and has no idea how to win the war and keep America secure."

But that "war," like the campaign, is over, and it has been rebranded. A new metaphor has been ordered up for duty. Just as Bush has leapt from reason to reason for the Iraq war, from weapons of mass destruction to the "march of freedom," so he now jumps from slogan to slogan. His changeability, in the short run, according to Trainor, may be a hazard. "Bush has to keep up a brave front. If he shows any signs of changing course perceptually, that could be a problem for him not only domestically but also on the battlefront. Any backing off from the hard position has a strong chance of giving encouragement to those who wish us ill. What happens when you aren't seen as exercising control? What happens when you are seen as less than all-powerful? That's the position they are in right now."

The undermining of democracy by sacrificing credibility to justify endless war was early described by the historian Thucydides in his *History of the Peloponnesian War:* "The meaning of words had no longer the same relation to things, but was changed by them as they thought proper. Reckless daring was held to be loyal courage; prudent delay was the excuse of a coward; moderation was the disguise of unmanly weakness; to know everything was to do nothing. Frantic energy was the true quality of a man."

Above the Rule of Law

AUGUST 5, 2005

Just months before the London bombings, on visiting the Guantánamo Bay prison, British counterterrorism officials were startled that they did not meet with legal authorities, but only military personnel; they were also disturbed to learn that the information they gathered from the CIA was unknown to the FBI counterterrorism team and that the British were the only channel between the two U.S. agencies. The New York City Police Department's counterterrorism unit was better synchronized with British methods and aims than the U.S. government was.

The Italian counterterrorism operation that was essential in the capture of one of the alleged terrorists fleeing London is itself in open conflict with Bush's "war." Last month, an Italian prosecutor filed indictments against thirteen CIA operatives who allegedly betrayed their Italian intelligence colleagues in the surveillance of an Egyptian Muslim cleric, using their information but not telling them that they had "rendered" the suspect to Egypt (that is, kidnapped him) rather than permitting his arrest in Italy. Now the CIA agents are fugitives from Italian justice.

International counterterrorism is running afoul of Bush's imperatives for what has become a dirty war. Though *war on terrorism* is a phrase the Bush administration declared obsolete last month (only to have Bush reinstate it), the dirty war remains very much in place. Since September 11, Bush has drawn a sharp dichotomy between "war" and "law enforcement." In his 2004 State of the Union address, he ridiculed those who view counterterrorism as other than his conception of war: "I know that some people question if America is really in a war at all. They view terrorism more as a crime, a problem to be solved mainly with law enforcement and indictments. . . . The terrorists and their supporters declared war on the United States, and war is what they got."

During the presidential campaign, Vice President Dick Cheney contemptuously criticized the application of law enforcement rather than sheer military force as effeminate "sensitivity." In June of this year, Bush's deputy chief of staff, Karl Rove, attacked the very idea of "indictments" as a symptom of liberal weakness.

Against the strongest possible internal opposition—from senior U.S. military figures, the military's corps of lawyers, Secretary of State Colin Powell, and the FBI—Bush disdained the Geneva Conventions and avoided legalities, especially trials, to pursue a torture policy. He created a farflung system of prisons run by an unaccountable military chain of command separate from traditional counterintelligence. It has been operated clandestinely, removed from the oversight of Congress. And Bush has fought in the courts against the intrusions of due process in order to retain supreme presidential prerogative.

Yet Bush is increasingly embattled in the defense of his dirty war. The Pentagon has appealed against a federal judge's ruling to make public previously unreleased photographs and videos from Abu Ghraib depicting "rape and murder," according to a senator who has seen them. Meanwhile, the Pentagon has quashed the recommendation of military investigators looking into FBI reports of torture at Guantánamo Bay that its commander, Major General Geoffrey Miller, be reprimanded for dereliction of duty.

Last month, three top military attorneys from the Judge Advocate Generals' Corps for the army, air force, and marines testified before the Senate that they had objected from the start to the new, abusive techniques of interrogation of prisoners. One memo by Major General Jack Rives, deputy judge advocate general of the air force, said: "Several of the more extreme interrogation techniques, on their face, amount to violations of domestic criminal law."

In response, three Republican senators have proposed legislation that would in effect abolish Bush's dirty war. Their bill would prohibit "cruel, inhuman, or degrading treatment" of detainees, hiding prisoners from the Red Cross, and using methods not authorized by the army field manual. One of these senators, John McCain, himself a prisoner of war in Vietnam, released a letter signed by more than a dozen retired senior military generals and admirals as well as by former prisoners of war. It said: "The abuse of prisoners hurts America's cause in the war on terror, endangers U.S. service members who might be captured by the enemy, and is anathema to the values Americans have held dear for generations."

Cheney interceded to attempt to force the senators to withdraw the bill, claiming they are hurting the "war on terrorism," but they have refused. McCain declared that the debate was not about the terrorists, saying: "It's not about who they are. It's about who we are."

But the dirty war that damages the difficult work of counterterrorism continues unabated. It goes on for reasons beyond domestic political consumption. At its heart lies the drive for concentrated executive power above the rule of law.

Predictably, Bush's dirty war is having a counterproductive effect, just as dirty wars did in Vietnam, Algeria, and Argentina. For every militant abused or killed, a community of like-minded militants is inspired. Hatred, resentment, and vengeance are the natural outcomes. There has never been an ultimate victory achieved through a dirty war over these forces.

The Informer

AUGUST 11, 2005

THE TENSION of possibly being asked an impertinent question about Valerie Plame was unbearable for Robert Novak. Before it could be posed on CNN's August 4 episode of *Inside Politics*, Novak growled a vulgarity, tore off his microphone, and stalked off the set. Within an hour, a CNN spokesperson announced that the Washington columnist, who had been one of CNN's original marquee attractions, had engaged in "inexcusable and unacceptable" behavior and was suspended: "We've asked Mr. Novak to take some time off."

After his forty-nine years in Washington, rising to become a virtual institution unto himself, was this hasty exit the end for Bob Novak? He had operated for decades according to the rules and folkways of Washington as he understood them. He had worked and badgered and bullied his way to the top of the greasy pole. Novak was not just a reporter, or even a columnist who could make or break political careers, but a media celebrity. He was accepted as a charter member of the guild of Washington correspondents. Until now, his status insulated him from the consequences of any error or offense.

CNN executives and producers had reached a breaking point in their recent discussions about their Novak problem. Ever since he had written a column on July 14, 2003, revealing the identity of an undercover CIA operative, citing "two senior administration officials" as his sources, he had become a principal figure in a major news story. On July 6, 2003, the former U.S. ambassador Joseph Wilson IV wrote an opinion piece in the *New York Times*, disclosing that he had been sent on a secret mission by the CIA before the Iraq war to assess whether Saddam Hussein was seeking to purchase enriched yellowcake uranium in Niger. Wilson had concluded that Saddam was not. Despite Wilson's finding, confirmed by two other reports to the CIA, Bush declared in his 2002 State of the Union address that Saddam was seeking Niger uranium to produce nuclear weapons. That fear became the ultimate rationale for the invasion of Iraq. "We don't want the smoking gun to be a mushroom cloud," said the national security adviser, Condoleezza Rice.

Wilson's op-ed piece was the first revelation that the justification for war was based on false information. The administration reflexively sought to strike back at Wilson's credibility by suggesting that his wife, Valerie Plame Wilson, a CIA operative, had been responsible sending him on that mission. The original assignment, however, came from Vice President Dick Cheney's office, and others in the CIA had authorized Wilson's trip. Robert Novak was the first person to expose Plame's identity.

Soon a special prosecutor was appointed to investigate whether the Intelligence Identities Protection Act of 1982, stipulating a ten-year prison sentence for violations, had been contravened as a result of the leak to Novak or whether any other law had been broken. As fingers were pointed in the direction of Bush's senior political adviser, Karl Rove, and Cheney's chief of staff, I. Lewis "Scooter" Libby, the prosecutor questioned the president and vice president as well as other White House officials.

The prosecutor then turned his gaze on reporters who might have had information. He subpoenaed Matt Cooper of *Time* magazine and Judith Miller of the *New York Times*. Cooper eventually agreed to testify, while Miller refused and was jailed for contempt of court. Both had argued that revealing their sources was a breach of their First Amendment rights as journalists.

While Cooper and Miller were embroiled in legal proceedings (Miller is now locked in a federal prison in Alexandria, Virginia), Novak, who wrote the initial story, remained silent about whether he had testified and what he knew. He had become the man of mystery.

Miller's sentencing tightened the ring around Novak. He had covered numerous politicians in trouble, but being in the spotlight himself was a new experience. Appearing on C-SPAN just before Miller went to jail, he expressed irritation at her and Cooper for objecting to testifying about their sources. "I don't know why they're upset with me," Novak said. "They ought to worry about themselves. I worry about myself."

Over the past two years, he has offered several conflicting accounts of the circumstances surrounding the information he received about Plame's identity. "I didn't dig it out; it was given to me," he told *Newsday* in his first explanation. "They thought it was significant, they gave me the name, and I used it." Then, on September 29, 2003, the day the criminal investigation was formally announced, Novak declared on CNN, "Nobody in the Bush administration called me to leak this." Rather than tell his audience what he knew, he engaged in a show of bravado. "It looks like the ambassador [Wilson] really doesn't know who leaked this to me," he said. He turned to a guest on the show, Representative Harold Ford, Democrat of Tennessee, and asked, "Do you know whether my source was in the White House? Do you know that at all?"

Two days later, back on CNN, Novak decried the investigation. "This kind of scandal . . . is Washington at its worst," he said. Three days after that, he appeared again on CNN to defend his source as someone who "is not a partisan gunslinger." Then he fell into radio silence, declining to answer questions on his counsel's advice.

But, according to the *Washington Post*, on July 27, 2005, the former CIA spokesman Bill Harlow

> testified last year before a grand jury about conversations he had with Novak at least three days before the column was published. He said he warned Novak, in the strongest terms he was permitted to use without revealing classified information, that Wilson's wife had not authorized the mission and that if he did write about it, her name should not be revealed. Harlow said that after Novak's call, he checked Plame's status and confirmed that she was an undercover operative. He said he called Novak back to repeat that the story Novak had related to him was wrong and that Plame's name should not be used. But he did not tell Novak directly that she was undercover because that was classified.

Soon, an obviously upset Novak broke through his wall of silence. Five days later, on August 1, he wrote a column that reflected his internal churning. He began by noting that his lawyer "urged me not to write this" but that he felt compelled to defend "my integrity." He insisted that he had used "suggesting," not "authorizing," to describe Plame's role, and that Harlow's statements in any case were "meaningless." He explained: "Once it was determined that Wilson's wife suggested the mission, she could be identified as 'Valerie Plame' by reading her husband's entry in 'Who's Who in America.' "

But Novak raised more questions than he answered. Had he in fact learned Plame's identity from *Who's Who?* What happened to those "two senior administration officials"? Most important, Novak still would not reveal whether he had testified and what he had said. Under the circumstances, it is unimaginable that he has not cooperated with the prosecutor. Had he not done so, he would have been subjected to the same subpoenas and contempt proceedings as Cooper and Miller. He also would have had to appear before the grand jury. It seems almost certain that his attorney arranged for Novak to give his testimony under oath in an interview with the prosecutor. This arrangement, unlike an appearance before the grand jury, allows a witness to have an attorney present. Matt Cooper's detailed account of his grand jury testimony, published in *Time*, continued to fuel the question of what Novak told the prosecutor.

At CNN, Novak's August 1 column created something of a crisis. For some time, the news director and producers had tried to ask Novak about his knowledge of the Plame affair. How could the network claim to be a serious news organization if it gave Novak a free pass? Now they decided that Novak had to be asked about *Who's Who*. Is that where he learned about Valerie Plame? Or was he diverting attention from where he really got the information?

The CNN anchor Ed Henry placed a copy of *Who's Who* on the desk in front of Novak as he prepared to parry with his usual opponent, the Democratic political consultant James Carville. The proximate subject was the Senate candidacy of Republican Representative Katherine Harris of Florida. "Don't be too sure she's going to lose . . . all the establishment's against her and I've seen these Republican anti-establishment candidates who do pretty well," Novak said. Carville attempted to make a comment, but Novak cut him off. "Just let me finish what I'm going to say, James. Please, I know you hate to hear me, but you have—" Carville replied that Novak has "got to show these right-wingers that he's got backbone, you know. It's why the *Wall Street Journal* editorial page is watching you. Show 'em you're tough." "Well, I think that's bullshit!" spat back Novak. "And I hate that." He turned to Henry, glancing at the volume of *Who's Who*, and said, "Just let it go." With that, he removed his microphone and departed.

"I'm sorry as well that Bob Novak obviously left the set a little early," Henry explained to viewers. "I had told him in advance that we were going to ask him about the CIA leak case. He was not here for me to be able to ask him about that. Hopefully we'll be able to ask him about that in the future." But perhaps not for a long time, until CNN decides when to lift Novak's suspension, which some at CNN have suggested to me may not be until the Plame imbroglio is entirely resolved.

Just last year, the investigation was a laughing matter for Novak. He appeared onstage at the annual dinner at the Gridiron Club, the exclusive inner circle of the Washington press corps, of which he is a long-standing member. As a gag, Novak was attired as the former diplomat Wilson, wearing top hat and cutaway coat, singing to the tune of "Once I Had a Secret

Love": "Novak had a secret source who lived within the great White House . . . / so he outed a girl spy the way princes of darkness do . . . / Now John Ashcroft asks Bob who and how / could be headed to the old hoosegow." He belted out his last line with panache: "Cross the right wing you may try, / Bob Novak's coming after you." The press corps hooted and clapped. They loved that Bob.

Novak began in one era of journalism and helped pioneer another. His career spanned the transformation of the Washington correspondent into media star, from front-page grub to buck-raking showboat. Novak came to Washington from the hinterlands in 1956 as a young man to report on the Associated Press's congressional beat. The *Wall Street Journal* snatched him up as its Senate reporter, drawing the eye of Rowland Evans, a writer on the *New York Herald Tribune*. Evans was looking for a partner, what journalists call a "legman," to produce a syndicated column. Novak, the wire-service machine, fit the bill.

Evans and Novak's column was highly successful, and together they coauthored valuable books on the presidencies of Lyndon Johnson and Richard Nixon. (Their later book on Ronald Reagan was a rush job that was not of the same quality, as Evans freely admitted to me.) The polished, Yale-educated Evans was a smooth social presence within the Georgetown set. Novak was someone he worked with every day but rarely if ever saw in the evening. The two men were an odd couple, not because of any divergence of political perspective, but because of class.

Novak did not truly come into his own until cable television altered the character of the Washington press corps. Once the archetype of the old-fashioned shoe-leather reporter and political inside-dopester, Novak's identity changed overnight when he appeared on CNN on its opening week in 1980. The raw no-name network saw in Novak a symbol of credibility and authority. In addition to appearing frequently on news programs, he and Evans were given a weekly interview show. Two years later, Novak became a regular on *The McLaughlin Group*, which broke the mold of TV talk shows. It was not a calm, modulated, informative roundtable of polite reporters but a food fight. Novak thrived in the format, emerging as a vituperative, dismissive, and mean-spirited bully, a cartoonlike character who attracted and repelled viewers. CNN promptly rewarded him with another show, *Crossfire*, after the departure of the initial conservative host, Pat Buchanan. The liberal side of the program was filled with a shifting cast, while Novak was its constant conservative centerpiece.

Although both Novak and John McLaughlin (host of *The McLaughlin*

Group) were conservatives, they had an abrasive relationship. In the final analysis, Novak was jealous that McLaughlin was the sole proprietor of the show and reaped the profits. So Novak pulled aside the other figures on the program—his friends Al Hunt, then bureau chief of the *Wall Street Journal,* and Mark Shields, the syndicated columnist—and made them an offer to join a new talk show. Novak cut a deal with CNN that made him the executive producer and star of *The Capital Gang.*

Novak had now become a cottage industry. Evans retired, but Novak's column remained syndicated to more than three hundred newspapers, including the *Washington Post.* The Evans and Novak show turned into *The Novak Zone.* Novak was ubiquitous on CNN. "He's Novak—he can do what he wants," a CNN source told me. He was also a frequent guest on the political panel of NBC's *Meet the Press.* He continued the political newsletter he had begun with Evans, an important stream of income. He charged high fees to business executives to attend his retreats, which featured leading politicians who appeared at Novak's beck and call. They understood the implicit exchange of these appearances for positive media coverage.

Novak's columns always play favorites, ranging from the neoconservative Richard Perle to the supply-sider Richard Gilder. Gilder, who has run the Club for Growth, a conservative political action committee, also happens to be Novak's investment adviser. Twice, Karl Rove was dismissed from George H. W. Bush's campaign, in 1980 and 1992, respectively, for leaking information to Novak. Those who agree to serve as sources for him, however, receive protection from his wrath and an outlet when their interests and Novak's coincide. "Look, I'm not David Broder," Novak told Amy Sullivan of the *Washington Monthly,* about the quintessentially moderate columnist for the *Washington Post.* "I'm not one of the real good guys. They try to make things nicer. That's not my deal."

Novak lives and breathes politics, so it was somewhat startling when he publicly converted to Catholicism from Judaism in 1998. He was raised as a Jew in Joliet, Illinois, but his columns have been almost uniformly hostile to Israel. No one had ever seen his spiritual side before. His conversion ceremony at St. Patrick's in Washington was packed with invited guests, liberals and conservatives alike, with whom he has appeared on talk shows.

There was more to Novak's conversion than met the eye,: it brought him into Washington's tight-knit, far-right Catholic coterie. Andrew Sullivan, the conservative Catholic writer, observed: "Perhaps the least-known aspect of Robert Novak's public persona is that he is a convert not just to

Catholicism but to its most hard-line sect, Opus Dei. It helps explain Novak's occasional, weird digressions into defenses of the most far-right social causes, and also why those columns appear, without this context, to be, well, slightly unhinged."

Just as the children of many notables in Washington land jobs in politics or government, so Novak's son Alex surfaced as the marketing director of Regnery Publishing, the conservative book imprint. Since Alex has held his position, his father has promoted four Regnery books in his columns and on TV shows. During the 2004 campaign, Novak went all out to hype Regnery's big product of the season, *Unfit for Command*, a smear job of John Kerry's war record, by the Swift Boat Veterans for Truth. Regnery's owner, Tom Phillips, also owns Eagle Publishing, which is the distributor of Novak's newsletter.

For years, Novak has used his various platforms to promote whatever causes and individuals he deems fit. Along the way, he has fostered any number of false assertions, accusations, and innuendos without any consequences to his standing in Washington. In 1989, he published a malicious rumor promoted by members of the Republican National Committee about the supposed sexual orientation of the House majority leader, Tom Foley, referring to "the alleged homosexuality of one Democrat who might move up the succession ladder." Foley felt obliged to declare: "I am, of course, not a homosexual."

After the death of I. F. Stone, the iconoclastic, independent journalist of the left, Novak said on CNN that Stone had been a paid agent of the KGB. The author Eric Alterman, a columnist for the *Nation* and a friend of Stone's, wrote, "Since Stone was dead by this time, however, Novak was free to make his McCarthyite accusation without fear of a libel suit. I wrote to the president of CNN shortly thereafter to ask for a correction, but received no response."

Throughout 1997, Novak relied on a source who had in fact been in the pay of the KGB, the FBI agent Robert Hanssen, who was apprehended and convicted of spying for the Soviet Union. Novak used Hanssen as his principal source for stories attempting to prove that Attorney General Janet Reno was covering up Clinton campaign finance scandals. The innuendo that Novak published turned out to be a flow of disinformation. In 2002, he wrote a column divulging his dependence on the spy. "To be honest to my readers, I must reveal it."

But none of this caused any disquiet at the newspaper that syndicates his column, the *Chicago Sun-Times;* at CNN; or at his most important outlet, the *Washington Post*. His friends and acquaintances continued their celebration of Novak the celebrity. In 2001, he was the honored guest at one of Washington's major charity roasts. When the media stars had finished their mild ribs, he took the stage. Above all, he said, he had learned one primary lesson from his long Washington experience: "There are two kinds of people in this town—sources . . . and targets, and you better make up your mind which you are."

For Novak, the Plame leak was business as usual. The only extraordinary wrinkle was the appointment of a special prosecutor. But immediately after Patrick Fitzgerald was named to the post, Novak's colleagues rallied to his defense. Wolf Blitzer, the CNN anchor, declared: "All of us who know Bob Novak know he's one of the best reporters in the business and has been for nearly half a century." The editor of the *Chicago Sun-Times*, Steve Huntley, reminded everyone that Novak remains "one of the best reporters in this country." But no testimonial, Gridiron Club dinner, or charity roast had the power to lift the pressure that drove Novak from the set of his beloved CNN last week.

As Novak now attempts to fend off his pursuers, he resorts to his old bullying; he brandishes his status, invents new stories, and tries to shave the facts. With each failed effort, he has become more frantic, racing from television talk show to syndicated column, tossing off ever more illogical and tortured alibis that only heighten suspicion of him. By plying more tricks of the trade, his patented tidbits of disinformation, he confirms the impression of petty squalor. Instead of escaping through the fog of his distortions, he rivets searchlights on his desperate flight.

The self-described "prince of darkness" appears blinded by the light. He cannot see himself as everyone else does. He has called so much attention to himself that he casts no shadow at all. He is completely exposed. He has become a fugitive who cannot find a safe house in the town that he thought was his bailiwick. His craven torment and wild flailing at his inability to halt his self-destruction might cast him as a Dostoevskian figure. But his absence of doubt deprives him of the depth of existential crisis. Bob Novak now resembles Gypo Nolan, the Judas of John Ford's classic 1935 movie *The Informer*—an IRA traitor on the run, used to the comfort of matey sycophants, but whom no one will shield and who unwittingly betrays himself in the end.

Unhappy Holiday

AUGUST 18, 2005

HOME ON THE RANGE, more than the deer and the antelope play. Near a drainage ditch by the road leading to Prairie Chapel, President Bush's Texas ranch, the mother of a dead soldier has pitched a tent. Cindy Sheehan has refused to leave until she is granted an audience with the president. Her son, twenty-four-year-old Army Specialist Casey Sheehan, a Humvee mechanic, was killed in Baghdad's Sadr City on April 4, 2004, and she calls her makeshift memorial vigil "Camp Casey."

Her previous meeting with Bush only impelled her to seek the satisfaction of another one. "He didn't even know Casey's name. Every time we tried to talk about Casey and how much we missed him, he would change the subject."

Bush has sent out emissaries, including his national security adviser, Stephen Hadley, to reason with her, but she remains adamant. Her emotional drama and outspoken opposition to the Iraq war have become daily news. Every twist in her standoff provides grist for expanded coverage.

Other bereaved parents of dead soldiers have suddenly begun speaking out and receiving respectful media attention. In Ohio, Paul Schroeder, the father of Lance Corporal Edward Schroeder II, killed two weeks ago with sixteen other troops from Ohio, called a press conference in front of his Cleveland home. "Our comments are not just those of grieving parents," he said. "They are based on anger, Mr. President, not grief. Anger is an honest emotion when someone's family has been violated." Before Sheehan's vigil, public support of Bush's Iraq policy had plummeted to 34 percent.

From the administration come conflicting statements about strategy in Iraq. The recent fiasco over the attempted rebranding of the "war on terrorism" as the "global struggle against violent extremism" reflects internal tension. While Bush proclaims that he will "stay the course," military sources leak stories that the vaunted objectives of the Iraq war—democracy and civil order—are chimerical. Pentagon briefings suggest that U.S.

forces may be drawn down soon, but the projections do not flow from any new strategy.

Iraq's confounded constitution writing has further illuminated its centrifugal forces and the visible hand of Iran. It is becoming undeniable that the outcome of the war will be an Islamic republic closely allied with Iran.

For the American public, this news melds in their daily lives with the rise of oil prices. The Iraq invasion was supposed to guarantee cheap oil. The price boost has erased wage gains and flattened consumer demand; but this oil crisis is more than a tale of statistics. Like oil crises in the past, it strikes at American feelings of independence, mobility, and exceptionalism. Not since the oil crisis of 1979 that provoked President Carter's "malaise" speech have such frustrations surfaced.

Sandstorms by the banks of the Euphrates swirl to the Waco River, and the presidential vacationer, besieged by marches, has turned querulous. As his crusade is overtaken by a sense of futility, Bush explained why he would not meet Sheehan: "I think it's also important for me to go on with my life, to keep a balanced life." This week he's planned a bicycle ride with Lance Armstrong.

Question Time

AUGUST 25, 2005

PRESIDENT BUSH TOOK A BRIEF BREAK this week from his month-long vacation to deliver speeches in Utah and Idaho urging the nation to the course in Iraq. Because American soldiers have died there, we must continue. "We will finish the task that they gave their lives for," Bush said in Salt Lake City on Monday.

Meanwhile, he moved his vacation to the Tamarack Resort in Donnelly, Idaho, where he made a short statement to the traveling White House press corps. He described the drafting of the Iraqi constitution as an "amazing event" in its guarantees of democracy and women's rights, and compared its deliberations to those at the Philadelphia convention that gave rise to the U.S. Constitution. "We had a little trouble with our own conventions writing a constitution," he said. Then he took a few questions.

"She expressed her opinion. I disagree with it," Bush said about Cindy Sheehan, the mother of a twenty-four-year-old soldier killed in Iraq, who had camped outside the president's ranch asking for a meeting to hear her critical comments on the war. "I met with a lot of families. She doesn't represent the view of a lot of the families I have met with. And I'll continue to meet with families."

Later, Bush asked, "We've got somebody from Fox here, somebody told me?"

"Does the administration's goal—I'll ask you about the Iraqi constitution. You said you're confident that it will honor the rights of women."

"Yes."

"If it's rooted in Islam, as it seems it will be—is there still the possibility of honoring the rights of women?"

"I've talked to Condi, and there is not—as I understand it, the way the constitution is written is that women have got rights, inherent rights recognized in the constitution, and that the constitution talks about, you know, not 'the religion,' but 'a religion.' Twenty-five percent of the assembly is going to be women, which is a—is embedded in the constitution. OK. It's been a pleasure."

"What else are you going to do? Are you going to bike today?"

"I may bike today. Been on the phone all morning. Spent a little time with the CIA man this morning, catching up on the events of the world. And, as I said, I talked to Condi a couple of times. And tonight I'm going to be dining with the governor and the delegation from Idaho, spend a little quality time with the first lady here in this beautiful part of the world. May go for a bike ride."

"Fishing?"

"I don't know yet. I haven't made up my mind yet. I'm kind of hanging loose, as they say." With that, the questions ended, and the vacation continued.

While Bush has allowed the press only abbreviated and controlled access, he has been coddled by the Republican Congress, despite the spike in public disapproval of his conduct of the Iraq war.

In February 1966, Senator J. William Fulbright, chair of the Foreign Relations Committee, held the first hearings on the Vietnam War, which were televised nationally for six days. The public was riveted by the penetrating questioning of administration officials and the debates among the members of the committee. Fulbright had been a friend of President Lyndon Johnson for years. Johnson, after all, had been the Senate majority leader, and Fulbright was a fellow Southerner. But the escalation of the war and the absence of a clear strategy of resolution prompted Fulbright to call the hearings. He held additional hearings in August 1966, in October and November 1967 and, when Richard Nixon became president, eleven days of hearings in April and May 1971. Fulbright believed that it was his constitutional duty to exercise oversight of the executive.

No similar Senate hearings on the origins, conduct, and strategy of the Iraq war have been held. During the Johnson period, the Democrats controlled both chambers of the Congress. But Fulbright did not feel that submitting to partisan discipline under the whip of the White House was a higher principle for the legislative branch than performing as a check and balance. Fulbright was a Democrat raising pointed questions about the policy of a Democratic president. No Republican Senate committee chair has seen fit to follow the Fulbright example. The one-party Republican rule of the Congress has resulted in the stifling of inquiry. Abandoning its powers and duties, the Republican Senate as a body refuses to hold the executive accountable.

The Democrats, suffering the debilities of the minority, are a congressional party without the authority to initiate committee hearings. They cannot set an agenda or command television cameras. Their Republican colleagues have shunted them to the sidelines; the White House is deaf to their entreaties. Senator Joseph Biden of Delaware, the ranking Democrat on the Foreign Relations Committee, after fact-finding missions to Iraq, has offered numerous ideas to the administration, none of which have been accepted. Biden's good-faith effort at offering helpful practical advice has been utterly ignored.

The opposition party cries in the wilderness. On Iraq, the administration will heed no Democratic position other than blind support. Democrats are criticized for offering no substantial alternative policies; but it is impossible for them to propose solutions to problems about which they, like the public, have been denied essential information. Why should Democrats produce polished answers when the administration won't or can't explain itself? Developing hard-and-fast positions on particular difficulties in Iraq will not make the White House hear them. The Democrats' greatest potential strength now is simply to ask questions.

The questions of consequence that might be asked, if there were a responsible Congress to pose them, are many, extending from Iraq to Iran, from public diplomacy to intelligence, and to the fate of our military.

On Iraq: Why was it necessary for the Bush administration to impose an arbitrary deadline on the drafting of the Iraqi constitution, the single most important document for a new Iraq? The constitution appears to undermine the administration's commitment to a unitary state and to democracy, and it enshrines Islamic law as a basis of government legitimacy. Why didn't the administration allow the Iraqi communities to attempt to reach acceptable compromises on their own timetable?

Recent reports, including articles in the *Washington Post,* document the growth of sectarian militias that engage routinely in abductions, assassinations, and other violence against domestic opponents. In many towns and cities, these militias have supplanted or taken over national security and police forces. What plans does the administration have to contain or disband them? Are there any plans for integrating these militias into national security forces so that they lose their sectarian identity and command structure? If there are no such plans, what analyses has the administration done to determine the future effectiveness of an Iraqi national security force in this environment?

On the U.S. military: The retired four-star general Barry McCaffrey, reflecting the views of many senior officers, has stated that "the wheels are going to come off" the military in Iraq in twenty-four months and that the

Reserve and National Guard systems are approaching meltdown. What is the administration's strategy for ensuring combat readiness and preparedness? Are the various conflicting statements by administration and military commanders on the withdrawals of some troops dictated by this meltdown or by some assessment, not yet publicly articulated, of the security conditions in Iraq?

General Peter Schoomaker, the chief of staff of the army, has declared that U.S. troops may be stationed in Iraq for at least four more years. Where will these troops be found?

As of May 2005, the U.S. military has plans to build four large bases in Iraq, each designed to hold a brigade-size combat team, aviation units, and other support personnel. Does the administration intend to establish these as permanent U.S. bases? What is the long-term strategy behind their construction? How will the current levels of U.S. forces in the region affect other potential security contingencies if they are maintained over a period of years?

On Iran: When asked about military action, President Bush has stated that all options are on the table regarding Iran. Has the administration drawn up military options? What are the assessments of military analysts of likely outcomes in exercising such options?

The administration has emphasized that Iran is a proliferator of weapons of mass destruction, a major supporter of terrorism, and a notorious violator of human rights. Recent reports in the press have documented that Iran is the principal funder of the leading Shiite political parties and militias in Iraq. Iran has also expanded its influence in Lebanon through Hezbollah's gains in legislative elections. What assessments has the administration made about Iran's response to any U.S. military action against it?

The German chancellor Gerhard Schroeder has declared he would not support such an action. Which allies have agreed to support the administration's military option in Iran? What responses has the administration planned to deal with a military action against Iran within international bodies, including the United Nations Security Council and NATO?

On U.S. intelligence: Has the administration commissioned a National Intelligence Estimate for military options against Iran? Has the new director of national intelligence, John Negroponte, assured the intelligence community that its objectivity and integrity will be protected from any political pressure? Will the DNI prominently raise caveats from intelligence analysts where there are disagreements? Will any new NIE be shared with the Congress in a timely fashion before any debate of any action is undertaken?

The administration has used Republican members of the House of Representatives in the past to attack senators of both parties for raising serious questions about the administration's policies. (Representative Duncan Hunter's attack on Senator John Warner for conducting hearings on Abu Ghraib is a notable example.) Will the president take steps to ensure that the oversight responsibilities of the Congress are not compromised or inhibited? Will he make every effort to inform his political aides that they are not to interfere with the congressional oversight process so that information and analysis are not twisted by political criteria?

On oil: The president recently signed an energy bill that provided no new measures for lessening U.S. dependence on foreign oil. In the absence of a commitment to achieve more energy independence, what measures does the administration propose to guarantee a steady supply and stable price of oil from Arab nations? The administration's advocacy of opening the Arctic National Wildlife Refuge to oil exploration would have only a marginal and transient impact. What energy-conservation measures does the administration propose?

On U.S. alliances: A number of member states in the coalition involved in the Iraq war and occupation have withdrawn their troops. Has the administration drawn up plans for our military to fill these gaps now and in the future? What policies does the administration plan to create a more cooperative environment, especially within the Western alliance? Does the president plan to consult fully with the nation's historic allies on military options in the future? Has the administration discussed its military options involving Iran with key allies? If the administration does not plan to change its policies on extralegal actions, such as going to war without advance consultation, how does it propose to strengthen our traditional alliances? With Iran and Iraq under the sway of Shia fundamentalism, how does the administration plan to encourage the cooperation of other Arab nations in the region?

On public diplomacy: Bush's longtime political aide, Karen Hughes, has recently been confirmed as undersecretary of state for public diplomacy and public affairs. Two previous appointees have resigned this post in frustration. With U.S. prestige at an all-time low throughout the world, according to several polls conducted by independent organizations such as the Pew Trust and the German Marshall Fund's Transatlantic Institute, what policies does the administration plan to change to reverse this trend?

Given that the draft Iraqi constitution enshrines Shiite Islamic law restricting the rights of women, how does the new undersecretary explain the administration's acquiescence in such an obviously undemocratic development? How does the undersecretary explain the administration's goal of spreading democracy in the Middle East, given that the process of drafting the Iraqi constitution has alienated secular Iraqis, Sunnis, and Kurds and aligned the United States with the dominant Shiite factions heavily influenced by Iran? In pursuing its stated goal of democratization, the administration has focused on Sunni-ruled nations—Egypt, Saudi Arabia, Jordan, and Syria. What does the undersecretary offer as incentives to these nations in the light of the administration's failure to protect the rights of Sunnis and women in Iraq?

The Pentagon continues to block a federal court order to publicly release photographs and videotapes of torture committed at the Abu Ghraib prison. The president has threatened to veto the military appropriations bill if an amendment sponsored by three Republican senators (John McCain, Lindsey Graham, and John Warner) that would outlaw torture and abuse of prisoners is attached. How does the administration foresee any change in the international perception of the U.S. image if it continues to follow these policies?

The president's policy has involved his abrogation of U.S. adherence to the Geneva Conventions that protect prisoners against torture. Will the administration pledge to comply with these conventions in the future? Will the administration permit the International Committee of the Red Cross unfettered access to all prisoners under U.S. supervision?

These are only some of the pressing questions that might be asked by members of Congress. The Republican Congress has left a vacuum of responsibility. Raising these matters would not merely foster necessary public debate. It would stir to life the legislative branch and begin to show what an energetic Democratic majority might do on the public's behalf.

Senator Fulbright was the first to criticize the pathology of the imperial presidency that he called "the arrogance of power." He also stands as a political exemplar. Fulbright's fearlessness, skepticism, and precision present a historical model for the Democrats, even if they lack his authority as chair of a committee.

Only by asking questions can the Democrats hope to determine the substance of Bush's increasingly evanescent and futile policies, to which they are supposed to respond. Only by asking questions can they demonstrate that they understand the nature of the Congress and should be granted control in it. Question time is their opportunity and obligation.

PART THREE

NEMESIS II

"HECK OF A JOB":
FROM THE LANDFALL OF HURRICANE
KATRINA TO THE REVOLT OF THE GENERALS

Hurricane Katrina

AUGUST 31, 2005

BIBLICAL IN ITS RAGE and scope, Hurricane Katrina has left millions of Americans to scavenge for food and shelter and hundreds or thousands reportedly dead. With its main levee broken, the evacuated city of New Orleans has become part of the Gulf of Mexico. But the damage wrought by the hurricane may not be entirely the result of an act of nature.

A year ago, the U.S. Army Corps of Engineers proposed to study how New Orleans could be protected from a catastrophic hurricane, but the Bush administration ordered that the research not be undertaken. After a flood killed six people in 1995, Congress created the Southeast Louisiana Urban Flood Control Project, in which the Corps of Engineers strengthened and renovated levees and pumping stations. In early 2001, the Federal Emergency Management Agency issued a report stating that a hurricane striking New Orleans was one of the three most likely disasters in the United States, along with a terrorist attack on New York City. But by 2003 the federal funding for the flood-control project had essentially dried up as money was drained into the Iraq war. In 2004, the Bush administration cut by more than 80 percent the funding requested by the New Orleans district of the U.S. Army Corps of Engineers for holding back the waters of Lake Pontchartrain. Additional cuts at the beginning of this year (for a total reduction in funding of 44.2 percent since 2001) forced the New Orleans district of the Corps to impose a hiring freeze. The Senate had debated adding funds for fixing New Orleans's levees, but it was too late.

The New Orleans *Times-Picayune,* which before the hurricane had published a series on the federal funding problem, and whose presses are now underwater, reported online: "No one can say they didn't see it coming. . . . Now in the wake of one of the worst storms ever, serious questions are being asked about the lack of preparation."

The Bush administration's policy of turning over wetlands to developers almost certainly also contributed to the heightened level of the storm surge. In 1990, a federal task force began restoring wetlands surrounding

New Orleans. Every two miles of wetland between the Crescent City and the Gulf reduces a surge by half a foot. Bush had promised "no net loss" of wetlands, a policy launched by his father's administration and bolstered by President Clinton. But he reversed his approach in 2003, unleashing the developers. The Army Corps of Engineers and the Environmental Protection Agency then announced they could no longer protect wetlands unless they were somehow related to interstate commerce.

In response to this potential crisis, four leading environmental groups conducted a joint expert study, concluding in 2004 that without wetlands protection, New Orleans could be devastated by an ordinary hurricane, let alone a category 4 or 5 storm. "There's no way to describe how mindless a policy that is when it comes to wetlands protection," said one of the report's authors. The chair of the White House's Council on Environmental Quality dismissed the study as "highly questionable" and boasted, "Everybody loves what we're doing."

"My administration's climate change policy will be science-based," President Bush declared in June 2001. But in 2002, when the Environmental Protection Agency submitted a study on global warming to the United Nations reflecting its expert research, Bush derided it as "a report put out by a bureaucracy," and excised the climate-change assessment from the agency's annual report. The next year, when the EPA issued its first comprehensive *Report on the Environment,* stating, "Climate change has global consequences for human health and the environment," the White House simply demanded removal of the line and all similar conclusions. At the G8 meeting in Scotland this year, Bush successfully stymied any common action on global warming. Scientists, meanwhile, have continued to accumulate impressive data on the rising temperature of the oceans, which has produced more, and more severe, hurricanes.

In February 2004, sixty of the nation's leading scientists, including twenty Nobel laureates, warned in a statement titled *Restoring Scientific Integrity in Policymaking:* "Successful application of science has played a large part in the policies that have made the United States of America the world's most powerful nation and its citizens increasingly prosperous and healthy. . . . Indeed, this principle has long been adhered to by presidents and administrations of both parties in forming and implementing policies. The administration of George W. Bush has, however, disregarded this principle. . . . The distortion of scientific knowledge for partisan political ends must cease." Bush completely ignored this statement.

In the two weeks preceding the storm in the Gulf, the trumping of science by ideology and expertise by special interests accelerated. The Federal Drug Administration announced that it was postponing sale of the morning-after contraceptive pill, despite overwhelming scientific evidence of its safety and its approval by the FDA's scientific advisory board. The United Nations special envoy for HIV/AIDS in Africa accused the Bush administration of responsibility for a condom shortage in Uganda—the result of the administration's evangelical Christian agenda of preaching "abstinence." When the chief of the Bureau of Justice Statistics in the Justice Department defied a White House order to delete its study showing that African Americans and other minorities are subject to racial profiling in police traffic stops, he was forced out of his job. When the Army Corps of Engineers' chief contracting oversight analyst objected to a $7 billion no-bid contract awarded for work in Iraq to Halliburton (the firm of which Vice President Cheney was formerly CEO), she was demoted, despite her superior professional ratings. At the National Park Service, a former Cheney aide, a political appointee lacking professional background, drew up a plan to overturn past environmental practices and prohibit any mention of evolution while allowing sale of religious materials through the Park Service visitor centers and gift shops, including those at the Grand Canyon National Park.

On the day the levees burst in New Orleans, Bush delivered a speech in Colorado comparing the Iraq war to World War II and himself to Franklin D. Roosevelt: "And he knew that the best way to bring peace and stability to the region was by bringing freedom to Japan." Bush had boarded his very own streetcar named desire.

"What Didn't Go Right?"

SEPTEMBER 8, 2005

THE BUSH ADMINISTRATION's mishandling of Hurricane Katrina stands as the pluperfect case study of the Republican Party's theory and practice of government. For decades conservatives have funded think tanks, filled libraries, and conducted political campaigns to promote the idea of limited government. Now, in New Orleans, the theory has been tested. The floodwaters have rolled over the rhetoric.

Under Bush, government has been "limited" only in certain weak spots, like levees, while in other spots it has vastly expanded into a behemoth subsisting on the greatest deficit spending in the nation's history. Rather than being empowered, state and local governments have been rendered impotent in the face of circumstances beyond their means, in which they have desperately requested federal intervention. Experienced professionals in government have been forced out, tried-and-true policies discarded, expert research ignored, and cronies elevated to senior management.

Before Katrina, the Republican theory was given its most apposite formulation by Grover Norquist, a prominent lobbyist and close adviser to the House majority leader, Tom DeLay, who said about government that he wanted to "drown it in the bathtub." In New Orleans, Norquist's wish has come to pass.

In the light of recent events, only two people have had the audacity to articulate a defense of the Republican idea of government. House Speaker Dennis Hastert, asked about rebuilding New Orleans, volunteered: "It doesn't make sense to me." He elaborated: "I think federal insurance and everything that goes along with it . . . we ought to take a second look at that." Thus Hastert upheld rugged individualism over a modern federal union. Just a month earlier, as it happened, Hastert had put out a press release crowing about his ability to win federal disaster relief for drought-stricken farmers in his Illinois district. Although he was too preoccupied attending a campaign fundraiser for a Republican colleague to travel to Washington to vote for the $10.5 billion emergency appropriation to deal with Katrina's aftereffects, he did finally return to the capital to push for even more drought aid from the Department of Agriculture. Hastert's philosophy is not undermined by his stupendous hypocrisy, for hypocrisy is at the center of the Republican idea. Hastert simply has the shamelessness of his convictions.

The second defender was Michael Brown, director of the Federal Emergency Management Agency, a position for which he was qualified by a résumé that includes being fired from his previous job as commissioner of the International Arabian Horse Association and, more important, having been the college roommate of Joe Allbaugh, President Bush's 2000 campaign manager and Brown's predecessor at FEMA. On September 1, Brown stated: "Considering the dire circumstances that we have in New Orleans, virtually a city that has been destroyed, things are going relatively well." Brown was unintentionally Swiftian in his savage irony. The next day, President Bush patted him on the back: "Brownie, you're doing a heck of a job." Brown exemplifies the Bush approach to government, a blend of cynicism, cronyism, and incompetence presented with faux innocence as well-meaning service and utter surprise at things going wrong.

Even as the floodwaters poured into New Orleans, unimpeded by any federal effort to stanch the flow, the White House mustered a tightly coordinated rapid response of political damage control. Karl Rove assumed emergency management powers. The strategy was to dampen any criticism of the president, rally the Republican base, and cast blame on the mayor of New Orleans and the governor of Louisiana, both Democrats. It was a classic Bush ploy against the backdrop of crisis. The object was to polarize the nation along partisan lines as swiftly as possible. While policy collapsed, politics reigned. Once again, Bush the divider, not the uniter, emerged.

The White House released a waterfall of themes. No matter how contradictory, administration officials maintained message discipline. The first imperative was to disclaim and deflect responsibility. White House Press Secretary Scott McClellan admonished the press corps, "This is not a time to get into any finger-pointing or politics or anything of that nature." Everyone from the president down to the lowliest talk-show hosts echoed the line that criticism during the crisis and reporting its causes were unseemly and vaguely unpatriotic.

After establishing that line, the White House laid out other messages to duck responsibility. Bush declared, "I don't think anybody anticipated the breach of the levees." From his bully pulpit, he intended to drown out the reports trickling into the print media that he had cut the funding for rebuilding the levees and for flood control. Then Bush assumed the pose of the president above the fray, sadly calling the response "unacceptable." Meanwhile, he praised "Brownie."

After September 11, there was an external enemy, "evildoers" against whom to incite fear and fervor. Now, instead, the flood has brought to the surface the deepest national questions of race, class, and inequality. On August 30, the day after the hurricane hit, the Census Bureau released figures showing that the numbers of poor had increased for the fourth year in a row, by 1.1 million since 2003, to 12.7 percent of the population: blacks and Hispanics were the poorest, and the South remained the poorest region. Since Bush has been in office, poverty has grown by almost 9 percent. (Under President Clinton, poverty fell by 25 percent.) As these issues began to receive serious attention for the first time in years, Bush reiterated that it was inappropriate to "play the blame game."

Meanwhile, his aides sought to blame Ray Nagin, the mayor of New Orleans, and Kathleen Blanco, the governor of Louisiana. On September 3, the *Washington Post*, citing an anonymous "senior administration official," reported that Blanco "still had not declared a state of emergency." *Newsweek* published a similar report. Within hours, however, the *Post* published a correction: the report was false. In fact, Blanco had declared an emergency on August 26 and sent President Bush a letter on August 27 requesting that the federal government declare an emergency and provide aid; and, in fact, Bush did make such a declaration, thereby accepting responsibility. Nonetheless, these facts have not silenced White House aides sounding the drumbeat that state and local officials—but, curiously, not the Republican governors of Mississippi and Alabama, which also suffered severe damage—are ultimately to blame.

Yet others operated off message, casting aspersions on the hurricane's victims. The president's mother, Barbara Bush, interviewed on American Public Media's *Marketplace* program, said of the displaced from Louisiana who are temporarily housed in Houston's Astrodome: "What I'm hearing, which is sort of scary, is they all want to stay in Texas. Everyone is so overwhelmed by the hospitality. And so many of the people in the arena here, you know, were underprivileged anyway, so this—this is working very well for them."

And Senator Rick Santorum, Republican of Pennsylvania, suggested that the residents of New Orleans who failed to escape the flood should be punished. "I mean, you have people who don't heed those warnings and then put people at risk as a result of not heeding those warnings. There may be a need to look at tougher penalties on those who decide to ride it out and understand that there are consequences to not leaving."

The White House sought to turn back the rising tide of anger among blacks by deputizing Secretary of State Condoleezza Rice to the publicity effort. During the early days of the hurricane and flood, she had been vacationing in New York, taking in Monty Python's *Spamalot* and spending thousands on shoes at Ferragamo on Fifth Avenue. In the store, a fellow shopper reportedly confronted her, saying, "How dare you shop for shoes while thousands are dying and homeless!"—prompting security men to bodily remove the woman. A week after the hurricane, Rice mounted the pulpit at a black church in Whistler, Alabama. "The Lord Jesus Christ is going to come on time," she preached, "if we just wait." One hundred and ten years after Booker T. Washington counseled patience and acceptance to the race in his famous "Atlanta Compromise" speech in the aftermath of Reconstruction's betrayal, the highest African American official in the land updated his advice of forbearance.

After a Cabinet meeting on Tuesday, Bush warned against the "blame game" as he pointed his finger: "Bureaucracy is not going to stand in the way of getting the job done for the people." His aides briefed reporters that "bureaucracy" of course referred to state and local officials. That night, at the White House, Bush met with congressional leaders of both parties, and the House minority leader, Nancy Pelosi, urged Bush to fire Brown. "Why would I do that?" the president replied. "Because of all that went wrong, of all that didn't go right last week," she explained. To which he answered, "What didn't go right?"

Bush's denigration of "bureaucracy" raises the question of the principals responsible in his own bureaucracy. Within hours of the president's statement, the Associated Press reported that Michael Brown had waited five hours after the hurricane struck to request one thousand workers from the Homeland Security Department secretary, Michael Chertoff. Part of their mission, he wrote, would be to "convey a positive image" of the administration's response.

The New Orleans *Times-Picayune* disclosed that Max Mayfield, head of the National Hurricane Center, briefed Brown and Chertoff on Katrina's potentially disastrous consequences before the hurricane made landfall. "We were briefing them way before landfall," Mayfield said. "It's not like this was a surprise. We had in the advisories that the levee could be topped." The day after Bush's cabinet-room attack on bureaucracy, the *St. Petersburg Times* revealed that Mayfield had also briefed President Bush in a video conference call. "I just wanted to be able to go to sleep that night knowing that I did all I could do," Mayfield said.

After its creation in 1979, FEMA became "a political dumping ground," according to a former FEMA advisory board member. Its ineffective performance after Hurricane Hugo hit South Carolina in 1989 and Hurricane Andrew struck Florida in 1992 exposed the agency's shortcomings. Back then Senator Fritz Hollings of South Carolina called it "the sorriest bunch of bureaucratic jackasses." President Clinton appointed James Lee Witt as the new director, the first one ever to have had experience in the field. Witt reinvented the agency, setting high professional standards and efficiently dealing with disasters.

FEMA's success as a showcase federal agency made it an inviting target for the incoming Bush team. Allbaugh, Bush's former campaign manager, became the new director, and he immediately began to dismantle the professional staff, privatize many functions, and degrade its operations. In his confirmation hearing testimony in 2001 before the Senate, Allbaugh attacked the agency he headed as an example of unresponsive bureaucracy: "Many are concerned that Federal disaster assistance may have evolved into both an oversized entitlement program and a disincentive to effective State and local risk management. Expectations of when the Federal Government should be involved and the degree of involvement may have ballooned beyond what is an appropriate level. We must restore the predominant role of State and local response to most disasters."

After September 11, 2001, FEMA was subsumed into the new Department of Homeland Security and lost its cabinet rank. The staff was cut by more than 10 percent. Since then, the budget has been cut every year and most of its disaster-relief efforts disbanded. "Three out of every four dollars the agency provides in local preparedness and first-responder grants go to terrorism-related activities, even though a recent Government Accountability Office report quotes local officials as saying what they really need is money to prepare for natural disasters and accidents," the *Los Angeles Times* reported.

After retiring from FEMA in 2003, handing over the agency to his deputy and college roommate, Brown, Allbaugh set up a lucrative lobbying firm, the Allbaugh Company, which mounts "legislative and regulatory campaigns" for its corporate clients, according to its website. After the Iraq war, Allbaugh established New Bridge Strategies to facilitate business for contractors there. He also created Diligence, a firm to provide security to private companies operating in Iraq. Haley Barbour, the former chair of the Republican National Committee and now governor of Mississippi, helped Allbaugh start all his ventures through his lobbying and law firm, Barbour Griffith and Rogers. Indeed, the entire Allbaugh complex is housed at Barbour Griffith and Rogers. Ed Rogers, Barbour's partner, has become a vice president of Diligence. Diane Allbaugh, Allbaugh's wife, went to work at Barbour Griffith and Rogers. And Neil Bush, the president's brother, received $60,000 as a consultant to New Bridge Strategies.

On September 1, the Pentagon announced the award of a major contract for repair of damaged naval facilities on the Gulf Coast to Halliburton, the firm formerly headed by Vice President Dick Cheney and whose chief lobbyist is Joe Allbaugh.

Hurricane Katrina is the anti-9/11 in its divisive political effect, its unearthing of underlying domestic problems, and its disorienting impact on the president and his administration. Yet, in other ways, the failure of government before the hurricane struck is reminiscent of the failures leading up to 9/11. The demotion of FEMA resembles the demotion of the counterterrorism czar Richard Clarke. In both cases, the administration ignored clear warnings.

In a conversation with a former diplomat with decades of experience, I raised these parallels. But the Bush administration response evoked something else for him. "It reminds me of Africa," he said. "Governments that prey on their people."

"Heck of a Job"

SEPTEMBER 15, 2005

BUSH's AMERICA is gone with the wind. It lasted just short of four years, from September 11, 2001, to August 29, 2005. The devastation of New Orleans was the meteorological equivalent of a dirty bomb, but Hurricane Katrina approached the homeland with advance warnings, scientific anticipation, and a personal briefing of the president by the director of the National Hurricane Center about a possible breaching of the levees. It was as predictable as though Osama bin Laden had phoned in every detail of an impending attack to the television networks. No terrorist attack would or could be as completely foreseen as Katrina.

Bush's entire presidency and reelection campaign were organized around one master idea: he stood as the protector and savior of the American people under siege. On this mystique he built his persona as a man of conviction and action. In the 2004 election, a critical mass of voters believed that because of his unabashed patriotism and unembarrassed religiosity, he would do more to protect the country than John Kerry would. They also believed that his fervor must be strength. Criticisms that Bush was overzealous, simplistic, and single-minded only served to reinforce his image.

The deepest wound is not that he has shown himself incapable of defending the country but that he lacks the will to do so. In Bush's own evangelical language, he revealed his heart.

Overnight, the press disclosed a petulant, vacillating president it had not noticed before. It was as if there was a new man in the White House. *Time* magazine described a "rigid and top-down" White House where aides are petrified to deliver bad news to a "yelling" president. *Newsweek* reported that two days after the hurricane, top White House aides, who "cringe" before the "cold and snappish" president, met to decide which of them would be assigned the miserable task of telling Bush he would have to cut short his summer vacation. "The [hurricane's] reality, say several aides who did not wish to be quoted because it might displease the president, did not really sink in until Thursday night."

With each of his three trips (so far) to survey the toxic floodwaters of New Orleans, Bush drifted farther out to sea. On his most recent voyage on Monday, asked about his earlier statement—"I don't think anybody anticipated the breach of the levees"—he said, "When that storm came through at first, people said, Whew. There was a sense of relaxation." In fact, the first failures of the levees came even before the brunt of the storm hit the city. On Monday, queried about the sudden resignation of the Federal Emergency Management Agency director, Michael "Heck of a Job" Brown, Bush told the press, "Maybe you know something I don't know." On Tuesday, all else having failed, he tried a novel tactic to deflect the "blame game," as he called it. "To the extent that the federal government didn't fully do its job right," he declared, "I take responsibility." "Extent" was the loophole allowing his magnanimity to be bestowed on the distant abstraction of government.

It was easier for Bush to renounce alcohol at age forty than ideology at almost sixty. Bush had radicalized Ronald Reagan's conservatism, but never has Reagan's credo from his first inaugural rung so hollow: "Government is not the solution to our problem." Yet social Darwinism cannot protect the homeland. That twenty thousand mostly poor blacks were locked in the New Orleans Convention Center without food and water for several days without the knowledge of Michael Brown is not an urban legend.

Poverty, previously unmentionable, has increased about 9 percent since Bush assumed office. The disparity between the White House's evangelical mission to democratize the world and its indifference at home is a foreign-policy crisis of new dimensions. Can Iraq be saved if Louisiana is lost? Bush's credibility gap is a geopolitical problem without a geopolitical solution. Assuming a new mission, Secretary of State Condoleezza Rice wears her racial identity to witness for Bush's purity of heart. So long as Bush could wrap himself in 9/11, his image was shielded; he could even justify invading Iraq by flashing the non sequitur to his base. But once another event of magnitude thundered over his central claim as national defender, the Bush myth crumbled. Only another event of this scale could begin to restore it. But it would also require a different set of responses from Bush. Now his evocation of 9/11 only reminds the public of his failed promise.

The rest of the Bush presidency will consist of his strained efforts to cobble his myth together again while others cope with the consequences of his damage. The hurricane has tossed and turned the country, but will not deposit it on firm ground for at least the three and half years remaining of the ruined Bush presidency.

From Gulf to Shining Gulf

SEPTEMBER 22, 2005

EVEN THE WORDS are the same. On Iraq, President Bush declared on February 4, 2004, "We will do what it takes. We will not leave until the job is done." On post–Hurricane Katrina reconstruction, on September 15, he eerily echoed, "We will do what it takes. We will stay as long as it takes." It was reassuring for the nation to be told by the president in his televised address that he intends to "stay" in the United States and not cut and run. Perhaps a White House speechwriter hit the copy-and-paste function on his computer, or the word *stay* simply popped into the president's mind as he contemplated the crisis, straying into improvisation.

The jarring reverberation of this rhetoric suggested a presidency on a feedback loop. Analogies, of course, are imperfect. Bush's speech, which junked the whole of conservative ideology and channeled the spirit of Lyndon Johnson, might be taken as evidence that his frequent trips to New Orleans have worked some voodoo on him. But there are enough elements in common between the catastrophes in Iraq and New Orleans to point up the underlying similarities in the Bush approach from Gulf to shining Gulf.

Just as the Iraq war was predicated on the distortion, falsification, and suppression of intelligence, so was the administration's preparation for Katrina marked by the refusal to register and act on information contrary to its prefabricated beliefs. Bush's censoring and dismissal of science on global warming helped lull him into ignorance about the growing severity of hurricanes as a consequence. It was a possibility he did not want to know because it ran contrary to his dogmas. But his passivity extended to the eve of Katrina's landfall, when Max Mayfield, the director of the National Hurricane Center, briefed him by teleconference video about the likelihood that the raging storm would breach the levees of New Orleans. Under Bush, the Federal Emergency Management Agency had been reorganized from a professional and proficient operation into a political dumping ground, and since 2001 FEMA had been studiously ignoring precise warnings of a potentially disastrous hurricane hitting New Orleans.

Before the invasion of Iraq, Bush refused to listen to senior military commanders who argued that the light force deployed for attack would be insufficient to secure the country under occupation. Then Army Chief of Staff Eric Shinseki's Senate testimony on the dangers of the Bush planning earned him a publicly humiliating rebuke from Deputy Secretary of Defense Paul Wolfowitz (since rewarded by elevation to the presidency of the World Bank). Wolfowitz, a prominent neoconservative who had been advocating an invasion of Iraq from the earliest days of the administration, before September 11, and who entertained theories that Saddam Hussein might have been behind the bombing of the World Trade Center in 1993 and the Oklahoma City bombing in 1995, was acting as a point man for Bush in denying difficulty. Wolfowitz, along with the president, the vice president, and the secretary of defense, subscribed to the notion that the invasion would be a "cakewalk," a smiley face of a word affixed to the enterprise by Wolfowitz's friend and fellow neoconservative Ken Adelman. Dick Cheney waxed rhapsodic about the flowers that would be strewn in the path of U.S. soldiers.

Similarly, Bush, still on his month-long vacation in August, during which he devoted press appearances to explaining why he would not meet with Cindy Sheehan, a founder of Gold Star Families for Peace ("I think it's also important for me to go on with my life, to keep a balanced life"), greeted Katrina as a cakewalk. "When that storm came through at first, people said, Whew. There was a sense of relaxation," he said. The record, however, reveals Governor Kathleen Blanco of Louisiana frantically and unsuccessfully attempting to reach him or his chief of staff, and the levees being breached before the full force of Katrina hit New Orleans. Four days afterward, Bush's staff considered him so ill-informed on the basic facts that they prepared a video of network news reports for him to watch as Air Force One carried him back to Washington.

Going in light with the military in Iraq was replicated in New Orleans—to similar effect. "Stuff happens," remarked Donald Rumsfeld in response to the looting of Iraqi government ministries and the Iraqi National Museum. From the electric grid to oil pipelines, the infrastructure was trashed. In New Orleans, the National Guard was belatedly sent into the looted city, where the infrastructure had been wrecked by the storm. Unlike the Iraqi army, which simply disbanded, the New Orleans Police Department faced the struggle overstressed and undermanned. Lieutenant General Steven Blum, the top commander of the National Guard, told *USA Today*, "We were underequipped. We don't need tanks and attack helicopters and artillery, but we must have state-of-the-art radios and communications." The equipment needed was deployed in Iraq, and the administration had not planned for its use in natural disasters at home.

Amid the ruins, General Jay Garner was appointed the first head of the Coalition Provisional Authority in Iraq. From the start, the Pentagon curbed his authority while raising expectations of instant results in conformity with its scenario of liberation. When Garner was incapable of producing the desired pictures, he became the fall guy. Garner was poorly prepared for his mission, but he was not a thorough incompetent like the recently resigned FEMA director, Michael Brown. Whereas Bush defended "Brownie" as doing "a heck of a job," Garner was undercut. But both became scapegoats for the misfeasance of higher-ups—in Garner's case, the Pentagon, and in Brown's, his superior, the secretary of homeland security, Michael Chertoff. Throwing Garner and Brown overboard were attempts to foster impressions that they alone were responsible for the failures of policy.

Onto these fresh post-invasion, post-hurricane scenes of wreckage, the president swooped down, dressed in appropriate costumes. He alighted on the deck of the USS *Abraham Lincoln* in May 2003 attired as a fighter pilot while a banner arranged by the White House advance team gleamed behind him: "Mission Accomplished." That Thanksgiving, wearing an Army jacket, a jovial president turned up at a mess hall in Baghdad, hoisting a large turkey with all the trimmings for the troops. Only later was it reported that the turkey was a plastic decoration. In New Orleans's Jackson Square to deliver his major speech, Bush appeared in an open-collared shirt, sleeves rolled up, the man of the people ready for work. The square was brilliantly lit for his speech, but when he left, the electricity was turned off, and the deserted city was plunged again into darkness.

In 1787, Prince Grigori Potemkin, the chief minister of Catherine the Great of Russia, supposedly built façades of prosperous towns in the Crimea to impress her with his management. Historians now regard this story as apocryphal. But Bush's Potemkin villages are not legends. To the extent that he believes they represent his actual surroundings, his faith-based system of belief triumphs over the reality-based, and the president who poses in Potemkin villages has become the Potemkin villager.

Behind the high-flown rhetoric of "freedom on the march," the Coalition Provisional Authority imposed conservative nostrums such as the flat tax, and broke Iraqi labor unions. The CPA also served as a political clubhouse for right-wingers. It drew heavily upon the conservative think tank, the Heritage Foundation, as a resource for youthful, ideologically vetted and inexperienced applicants to fill important positions in Iraq. Now the Iraqi government has issued an arrest warrant for its former defense minister for stealing $1 billion, and an additional $8 billion is said to be missing. On HBO's *Bill Maher* show last week, the comedian interviewed Dan Senor, the former CPA press secretary, and asked him where the money went. "We didn't have first-world accounting standards when we distributed that money," Senor explained. He did not mention who exactly was in charge of the finances: Michael Fleischer, the brother of Ari Fleischer, Bush's former press secretary.

Like the former CPA chief L. Paul Bremer, Karl Rove, Bush's senior political adviser and deputy chief of staff, who has been appointed as head of the hurricane reconstruction effort, has drawn on the Heritage Foundation for ideas. The conservative think tank's hastily slapped-together policy compendium for the occasion, *From Tragedy to Triumph*, has become one of Rove's playbooks. Under cover of Bush's sudden acknowledgment in Jackson Square that "poverty has roots in a history of racial discrimination" and a sweeping promise to "rise above the legacy of inequality," the administration has promulgated a series of reactionary acts, from suspending affirmative action in granting contracts to cutting prevailing wages for construction to proposing the use of federal funds for vouchers to enable Katrina evacuees' children to reenroll in parochial and private schools.

Rove's appointment as reconstruction czar puts him in charge of distributing federal largesse. The budget for reconstruction is estimated at about $1 billion a day, for a total of at least $200 billion. With that treasure chest, Rove directs a gigantic K Street project, combining lobbyists and the administration. Already, firms with intimate ties to the Republican Party, such as Halliburton and Bechtel, are major beneficiaries, as they have been in Iraq. And Joe Allbaugh, the former FEMA director, Bush's chief of staff as governor of Texas and his 2000 campaign manager, acts as the middle man in the Gulf states.

With every speech, appearance, and policy announcing his good intentions, Bush compounds the law of diminishing returns. After his speech in Jackson Square, support for his reconstruction efforts fell by 4 percent. Every promise of a new government program angers his followers on the right; every hollow pledge alienates everyone else. The incredible shrinking domestic president can find no safety in reassuming his "war president" costume. Less than one-third of the American public now supports his policy in Iraq, according to a CNN/Gallup poll. The poll also reports that Americans have become bitterly pessimistic, with 54 percent saying they believe the United States "won't win."

In response, the Pentagon publicizes body counts of insurgents killed, the metric from the Vietnam War that Rumsfeld once said he would never use. Meanwhile, the Government Accountability Office reports that since the beginning of the cakewalk, the U.S. military has used 1.8 billion rounds of small-caliber ammunition.

None of these reality-based measurements discourages Rove, the architect of America's Potemkin villages. Last week, he attended a private conference of high rollers in Aspen, Colo., where he reportedly dismissed Bush's current standing as a problem of communication. "We have not been good at explaining the success in Iraq. Polls go up and down and don't mean anything," he was quoted as saying on the Huffington Post website. On the hurricane, while Bush was accepting "responsibility," Rove was conceding no error: "The only mistake we made with Katrina was not overriding the local government." And on public disillusionment with the Iraq war, he said: "Cindy Sheehan is a clown. There is no real antiwar movement. No serious politician, with anything to do with anything, would show his face at an antiwar rally."

Another minister of state perhaps best captured the state of mind reflected by Rove's comments. On the Bourbon kings, Charles Maurice de Talleyrand said, "They have learned nothing and forgotten nothing."

Karen Hughes Takes a Tour

SEPTEMBER 29, 2005

PRESIDENT BUSH has no adviser more loyal and less self-serving than Karen Hughes. As governor of Texas, he implicitly trusted the former Dallas television reporter turned press secretary with tending his image and words. She was the mother hen of his persona. In the White House, Hughes devoted heart and soul to Bush as his communications director, until she suddenly returned to Texas in 2002, citing her son's homesickness. There were reports that Karl Rove, jealous of power, had been sniping at her.

From her exile, Hughes produced a memoir, *Ten Minutes from Normal,* which is deeply uninteresting and unrevealing. Amid long stretches of uninformative banality lie unself-conscious expressions of religiosity, accounts of how she inserted Psalms 23 and 27 into Bush's speeches after September 11, 2001, and an entire page of small type reproducing a sermon she delivered on Palm Sunday aboard Air Force One. She quotes Condoleezza Rice, then national security adviser: "I think Karen missed her calling. She can preach."

After two undersecretaries of state for public diplomacy resigned in frustration in the face of the precipitous loss of U.S. prestige around the globe, Bush found a new slot for Hughes this year. She may be the most parochial person ever to hold a senior State Department appointment, but the president has confidence she can rebrand the United States.

This week, Hughes embarked on her first trip as undersecretary. Her initial statement resembled an elementary-school presentation: "You might want to know why the countries. Egypt is of course the most populous Arab country. . . . Saudi Arabia is our second stop. It's obviously an important place in Islam and the keeper of its two holiest sites. . . . Turkey is also a country that encompasses people of many different backgrounds and beliefs, yet has the—is proud of the saying that 'all are Turks.' "

Hughes appeared to be one of the pilgrims satirized by Mark Twain in his 1869 book, *Innocents Abroad,* about his trip on "The Grand Holy Land

Pleasure Excursion." "None of us had ever been anywhere before; we all hailed from the interior; travel was a wild novelty to us. . . . We always took care to make it understood that we were Americans—Americans!"

Hughes' simple, sincere, and unadorned language pellucidly reveals the administration's inner mind. Her ideas on terrorism and its solution are straightforward. "Terrorists," she said in Egypt at the start of her trip, "their policies force young people, other people's daughters and sons, to strap on bombs and blow themselves up." Somehow, magically, these evildoers coerce the young to commit suicide. If only they understood us, the tensions would dissolve. "Many people around the world do not understand the important role that faith plays in Americans' lives," she said. When an Egyptian opposition leader inquired why President Bush mentions God in his speeches, she asked him "whether he was aware that previous American presidents have also cited God, and that our Constitution cites 'one nation under God.' He said, 'Well, never mind.'"

With these well-meaning arguments, Hughes has provided the exact proof of what Osama bin Laden has claimed about American motives. "It is stunning . . . the extent [to which] Hughes is helping bin Laden," Robert Pape told me. Pape, a University of Chicago political scientist who has conducted the most extensive research into the backgrounds and motives of suicide terrorists, is the author of *Dying to Win: The Strategic Logic of Suicide Terrorism,* and recently briefed the Pentagon and the National Counterterrorism Center. "If you set out to help bin Laden," he said, "you could not have done it better than Hughes."

Pape's research debunks the view that suicide terrorism is the natural byproduct of Islamic fundamentalism or some "Islamo-fascist" ideological strain independent of certain highly specific circumstances.

Of the key conditions that lead to suicide terrorism in particular, there must be, first, the presence of foreign combat forces on the territory that the terrorists prize. The second condition is a religious difference between the combat forces and the local community. The religious difference matters in that it enables terrorist leaders to paint foreign forces as being driven by religious goals. If you read Osama's speeches, they begin with descriptions of the U.S. occupation of the Arabian Peninsula, driven by our religious goals, and that it is our religious purpose that must confronted. That argument is incredibly powerful not only to religious Muslims but secular Muslims. Everything Hughes says makes their case.

The undersecretary's blundering grand tour of the Middle East may be the latest incarnation of *Innocents Abroad*. "The people stared at us everywhere, and we stared at them," Twain wrote. "We generally made them feel rather small, too, before we got done with them, because we bore down on them with America's greatness until we crushed them."

The stakes, however, are rather different from what they were on The Grand Holy Land Pleasure Excursion. Hughes's trip "would be a folly," Pape says, "were it not so dangerous."

Twenty-First-Century Republicanism

OCTOBER 6, 2005

For THIRTY YEARS, beginning with the Nixon presidency, advanced under Reagan, stalled with the elder Bush, a new political economy struggled to be born. The idea was pure and simple: centralizing power in the hands of the Republican Party would ensure that the party never lost it again. Under George W. Bush, this new system reached its apotheosis. It is a radically novel social, political, and economic formulation that deserves study alongside capitalism and socialism. Neither Adam Smith nor Vladimir Lenin captures its essence, though it has far more elements of Leninist democratic centralism than Smithian free markets. Some have referred to this model as crony capitalism; others compare the waste, extravagance, and greed to the Gilded Age. Call it twenty-first-century Republicanism.

At its heart the system is plagued by corruption, an often unpleasant expense that greases its wheels. But now multiple scandals engulfing Republicans—from the suspended House majority leader, Tom DeLay, to the super-lobbyist Jack Abramoff to the White House political overlord Karl Rove—threaten to disrupt the system. Because it is organized by politics, it can be undone by politics. Politics, the greatest strength of Republicanism, has now become its greatest vulnerability.

The party runs the state. Politics drives economics. Important party officials are also economic operators. They thrive off their connections and rise in the party apparatus as a result of their self-enrichment. The past three chairs of the Republican National Committee have all been Washington lobbyists.

An oligarchy atop the party allocates favors. Behind the ideological slogans about the "free market" and "liberty," the oligarchy creates oligopolies. Businesses must pay to play. They must kick back contributions to the party, hire its key people, and support its program. Only if they give do they receive tax and regulatory breaks and helpful treatment from government professionals.

Those professionals in the agencies and departments who insist on adhering to standards other than those imposed by the party are fired, demoted, and blackballed. The oligarchy wages war against these professionals to bend government purely into an instrument of oligopolies.

Corporations pay fixed costs in the form of legal graft to the party in order to suppress the market, drastically limiting competitive pressure. Then they collude to control prices, create cartels, and reduce long-term planning primarily to the political game. The larger consequences are of no concern whatsoever to the corporate players, so long as they maintain access to the political players.

The lobbying expenses of every industry, from financial services to computers, are staggering. Broadcast media firms spent $35.88 million in 2004 alone on lobbyists in Washington, according to the Center for Public Integrity. Telephone companies spent $71.97 million, cable and satellite TV corporations $20.22 million. The drug industry during the same period shelled out $123 million to pay 1,291 lobbyists, 52 percent of them former government officials. The results have been direct: the Food and Drug Administration has been reduced to a hollow shell, and Medicare is banned from negotiating lower drug costs with pharmaceutical companies. In the 2004 election cycle, the drug industry paid out $87 million in campaign contributions for federal officials, 69 percent of them flowing to Republicans.

Whereas almost all lobbying before the Bush era was confined to Capitol Hill, now one in five lobbyists approaches the White House directly. Consider the success story of one Kirk Blalock, a former aide to Karl Rove, as deputy director of the Office of Public Liaison, where he coordinated political links to the business community. Now, one year out of the White House, he's a senior partner in the lobbying firm of Fierce, Isakowitz, and Blalock. Of thirty-three major clients, he lobbies for twenty-two among his former colleagues in the White House. Indeed, the Bush White House boasts twelve former lobbyists in responsible positions, from Bush's chief of staff, Andrew Card (American Association of Automobile Manufacturers), on down.

"The number of registered lobbyists in Washington has more than doubled since 2000 to more than 34,750," reports the *Washington Post*, "while the amount that lobbyists charge their new clients has increased by as much as 100 percent."

Macro- and microeconomic policies are subordinate to the circular alliance of oligarchy and oligopoly. Government expenditures increased faster under Bush than at any time since Lyndon Johnson's Great Society. But this time the spending is not intended to prime the economic pump. Nor is it invested mainly in public goods such as infrastructure or schools, or used to improve the standard of living of the middle and working classes, whose incomes and real wages are rapidly shrinking. Instead it is poured into military contracts and tax cuts heavily weighted to favor the very wealthiest, who do not in turn invest in productive capital. As a result, the largest budget surplus in U.S. history has been transformed into the largest deficit. U.S. Treasury bonds are principally held by Asian banks, a shift that presages a strategic tilt of global power and long-term threat to national security. The illusion that, as the post–Cold War unipolar power, the United States faces no countervailing forces is undermined by the administration's constantly draining deficits. Thus twenty-first-century Republicanism reverses the policies that brought about the American century.

Under Ronald Reagan, supply-side economics had unanticipated consequences: tax cuts, instead of fostering increased government revenues, blew a hole in the budget. Under Bush, such deficits have been an instrument in a conscious policy following the Reagan lesson. The reason is to apply fiscal pressure on government, making its regulations more pliable in the interest of oligopoly and therefore of the Republican political class. Just as macroeconomic policy is the plaything of politics, so is microeconomic policy. Environmental degradation, declining public health, and urban neglect are insignificant byproducts.

The Republican system is fundamentally unstable. Bush has no economic policy other than Republicanism. As the economic currents run toward an indefinable reckoning, the ship of state drifts downstream.

In stable systems, individuals are replaceable parts. Republicanism as constructed under Bush is a juggernaut that cannot afford to scrape an iceberg.

The Republican scandals converge on operators who are at the center of the oligarchy. Their own relationships are complicated and mutually entangled. But the outcome of the scandals affecting these major actors will inevitably unravel the Republican project.

On Monday, Tom DeLay was indicted by a Texas grand jury for laundering corporate contributions through his political action committee, a crime that carries a life sentence. DeLay had resigned on September 28 as House majority leader after being handed his first indictment for felony conspiracy. Even as DeLay proclaimed himself a victim of injustice—"I am indicted just for the reason to make me step aside as majority leader"—he proclaimed that he would rule "with or without the title."

As DeLay shouts defiance, federal prosecutors close in on one of DeLay's "closest and dearest friends," Jack Abramoff, whose largesse to DeLay over the years, including lavish trips to Korea and Britain, is part of the investigation. Abramoff's bilking of millions from Indian tribes has brought other Republican figures, including the lobbyist Grover Norquist, a key DeLay adviser, and Ralph Reed, a central character in the religious right, under legal scrutiny.

At the same time, the special prosecutor, Patrick Fitzgerald, investigating the exposure by senior administration officials of the identity of CIA operative Valerie Plame, has completed his inquiry by receiving the testimony of the *New York Times* reporter Judith Miller, and must issue any indictments before his grand jury expires on October 28. Within the White House, Karl Rove, feverishly mustering wavering conservative support for Bush's nomination to the Supreme Court of Harriet Miers, his personal lawyer and the White House legal counsel, awaits the result.

Bush never much liked DeLay. DeLay criticized Bush's father, for which there can be no forgiveness (only Bush is allowed to rebel against his father), and DeLay criticized him, too. When DeLay wanted to slash the earned-income tax credit, Governor Bush, beginning his presidential campaign in 1999 and seeking to establish his bona fides as a "compassionate conservative," said DeLay wanted to balance the budget "on the backs of the poor." DeLay was a useful foil.

DeLay, the former exterminator from Sugar Land, Texas, a suburb of Houston, who had called the Environmental Protection Agency "the Gestapo," rose from the Texas Legislature to the U.S. Congress. Once known as "Hot Tub Tom" for his boisterous reveling, he was born again, and his right-wing politics always had a forbidding, punitive undercurrent. When he became Republican whip, he hung a whip on his office wall. He relished his new nickname, "the Hammer." Asked to put out his cigar in a restaurant because it violated the nonsmoking rule, he roared, "I am the federal government!"

DeLay never really respected Newt Gingrich, who had led the Republicans out of their forty-year sojourn in the wilderness to control of Congress and became speaker of the House. Despite Gingrich's penchant for vituperative personal attacks on Democrats, DeLay thought he was soft. There was something of the lost boy about Gingrich, who collected dinosaur bones, loved to visit zoos, and speculated about outer space. DeLay also felt that Gingrich had fallen under the seductive spell of President Clinton and conceded too much to him. DeLay plotted coups against Gingrich and finally succeeded in deposing him after the Republicans lost seats in the 1998 midterm elections. Worried that Gingrich would weaken in the struggle to impeach and remove Clinton, DeLay saw Gingrich as doubly vulnerable because his mistress was on the House payroll. DeLay coerced House Republicans to impeach Clinton, threatening moderates that he would fund their opponents in primary elections and deny them advantageous committee assignments. Without DeLay, there would have been no impeachment. After the Senate acquitted Clinton, DeLay preached at his local church that Clinton had been impeached because he had "the wrong worldview."

The center of DeLay's operation was the K Street Project, the pay-to-play system by which businesses and lobbyists kicked funds back to the Republican Party in exchange for legislation. He kept a little black book noting which lobbyists were good and which were bad, who deserved favors and who punishment. One reporter, believing that the story about the black book was apocryphal, asked DeLay, who proudly showed it to him.

Of all the lobbyists on the "good" list, Jack Abramoff ranked at the top. Abramoff's provenance as a scion of Beverly Hills, California, could not have been more fortuitous for a career in the Republican Party. His father was president of the Diners Club franchises, owned by Alfred Bloomingdale, a member of Ronald Reagan's kitchen cabinet. Abramoff parlayed his connections and money into a campaign that gained him the chairmanship of the College Republicans in 1981, Year 1 of the Reagan era.

Abramoff's campaign manager was a radical right-winger named Grover Norquist, and the two of them recruited a zealous younger activist, Ralph Reed, to carry out their orders. Reed required College Republicans to recite a speech from the movie *Patton,* replacing the word *Nazis* with *Democrats:* "The Democrats are the enemy. Wade into them. Spill their blood! Shoot them in the belly!"

Norquist was the first to point out the political potential of evangelical churches to Reed, envisioning that they could be turned into Republican clubhouses. During the week of George H. W. Bush's inauguration, Reed encountered Pat Robertson, the right-wing televangelist, who recruited him on the spot to run the Christian Coalition. "I want to be invisible," Reed explained. "I do guerrilla warfare. I paint my face and travel at night."

You don't know it's over until you're in a body bag. You don't know until election night."

Norquist himself underwent a metamorphosis from gadfly to player with the Republican takeover of Congress. His Wednesday meeting became a place where conservative groups from the National Rifle Association to the Christian Coalition plotted strategy. Norquist opened it up to lobbyists, who paid exorbitant fees to be part of the action. They, too, were then coordinated. Norquist was especially close to Gingrich, a relationship he used to build up his own lobbying business behind front groups such as Americans for Tax Reform. Once Gingrich was toppled, Norquist used Abramoff to link him tightly to DeLay.

Karl Rove, who began his political career as chair of the College Republicans in 1971, had been well acquainted with the Abramoff circle for years by the time he started planning George W. Bush's presidential campaign. He was not enamored of the antitax crusader Norquist, who had made a grandstand gesture of assailing Governor Bush in the mid-1990s for suggesting raising taxes to support schools. But, for the campaign, Rove made peace with him.

In 1997, Reed left the Christian Coalition to found his own lobbying firm, Century Strategies. He sent Abramoff an e-mail: "Hey, now that I'm done with the electoral politics, I need to start humping in corporate accounts! I'm counting on you to help me with some contacts." Rove soon recruited Reed for the upcoming Bush campaign, setting him up as a consultant for Enron.

When Senator John McCain defeated Bush in the Republican primary in New Hampshire, Reed came into play. South Carolina was Armageddon. Suddenly, McCain was beset by a series of vicious accusations, including racial slurs about an adopted East Asian daughter and other campaign dirty tricks.

Marshall Wittman, who had worked as director of the Christian Coalition under Reed, had joined McCain's staff, though Reed had attempted to recruit him to the Bush campaign. "Ralph was very, very, very close to Rove," Wittman told me. "Ralph asked me in 1997 if I wanted to work on the Bush campaign. Rove was operating everything. Rove parked Ralph at Enron. Ralph told me before the New Hampshire primary that he would do what it took to eliminate McCain as an opponent if he posed a challenge to Bush. He would do whatever it took, that means below the radar, paint his face. Ralph has a dual personality, Dr. Jekyll and Mr. Hyde, charming in public and then ruthless and vicious."

Abramoff grew ever closer to DeLay, helping DeLay's former aides who had become lobbyists and who also assisted his business. Abramoff took millions from various Indian tribes and then pitted other lobbyists against them so that they would have to pay him more. When Norquist complained to Abramoff about a "$75K hole in my budget from last year," his pal put him in the deal. Reed was hired to use the religious right to campaign against the casino that the Tigua tribe had contracted Abramoff to help them open. Meanwhile, Abramoff forced the Choctaw tribe, another client, to kick back $1.5 million to the Alabama Christian Coalition. Norquist acted as the go-between for the money, ultimately funneling it to Reed's efforts.

Eventually, the Senate Indian Affairs Committee exposed the various scams; it does not seem ironic that the committee's chair is McCain. Soon, the Justice Department was investigating. Norquist and Reed have both appeared in front of the grand jury. Reed is running for lieutenant governor of Georgia. "Ralph has notions he'll be president of the United States," said Wittman.

Abramoff is under investigation by a grand jury in Guam for illegal contracts and money laundering, and another grand jury in Fort Lauderdale, Florida. In that case, a former business partner in the SunCruz casino boat company, with whom Abramoff had had a dispute, was allegedly murdered by three hit men, who have been indicted for the crime. Abramoff's business partner, Adam Kidan, paid $30,000 in company funds to one of the killers' daughters, who performed no services for the company, and $115,000 to a firm the hit man owned. Reportedly, Abramoff is not under suspicion for the murder, but he was indicted in August for bank fraud in the case.

Last month, another player in the ring was arrested—David Safavian, a Bush White House official, director of the Office of Federal Procurement Policy, in charge of overseeing $300 billion in federal contracts. Safavian had been Abramoff's lobbying partner in the mid-1990s, before he became Norquist's lobbying partner. Before he was elevated to his sensitive post in the White House, he had been chief of staff at the General Services Administration, where he tried to help Abramoff grab two federal properties in Washington. On Wednesday, Safavian was indicted on five counts of perjury and obstruction of justice. (Safavian's wife, Jennifer, is chief counsel on the House Government Operations Committee, overseeing the investigation into the Bush administration's response to Hurricane Katrina.)

Meanwhile, the grand jury in the Valerie Plame case prepares to conclude its work. In August, it called Rove's assistant, Susan Ralston, to testify. As it happens, she had formerly been Abramoff's assistant. And it was revealed that before she allowed people to meet with Rove, she cleared them with Norquist. Rove, for his part, often used Abramoff and Norquist as his conduits to DeLay.

Now all the investigations are coming to a climax. Will it mean the decline and fall of the Rovian empire? "Rove is the ultimate center of everything," said Wittman. "All roads lead to Rove. If it's Rove, everything collapses. People say there is no indispensable man. That's not true."

But more than the fate of one man or even a ring around him is at stake. For decades, conservatives created a movement to capture the Republican Party and remake it in their image. Under Bush, Republicanism as a system dominates.

With astonishing arrogance and bravado, the Republican oligarchy wired politics and business so that they would always win. But in believing that they actually possessed absolute power, they overreached. Now their project teeters on the brink.

Judy d'Arc

OCTOBER 12, 2005

From the steakhouses of the lobbyists to the cloakrooms of the Senate, from book launch parties to news bureaus, the main subject in Washington is who will be indicted and when. As the inquiry of the independent counsel, Patrick Fitzgerald, into the leaking of the identity of CIA operative Valerie Plame approaches its deadline of October 28, the cast of characters appears for final performances before the grand jury. Trailing clouds of mystery, they disappear into the windowless chamber and emerge illuminating nothing. Fitzgerald's airtight office, leaking to no reporter, only fuels the fires of rumor by its silence.

Once again, on Tuesday, the New York Times reporter Judith Miller was summoned to the prosecutor's sanctum. Miller was the stovepipe for disinformation from the administration and Ahmad Chalabi (self-proclaimed "hero in error") directly onto the front page of the Times in the run-up to the invasion of Iraq. When the former ambassador Joseph Wilson, in his Times op-ed piece of July 6, 2003, "What I Didn't Find in Niger," debunked the tale that Saddam Hussein had sought enriched uranium for nuclear weapons, he exposed more than the falsity of the president's claim; his account was also a blow to the credibility of Miller's stories. Ten months later, the Times published an extraordinary retraction saying that some of its coverage was "not as rigorous as it should have been." Miller's identity went unmentioned.

After spending eighty-five days in prison for contempt of court, protecting the anonymity of the source already revealed for a story she never wrote about Wilson and his wife, Plame, Miller extracted a fig leaf from that source. Vice President Cheney's chief of staff, I. Lewis Libby, reminded her that he had given her a waiver a year ago. Frantically, she raced out of jail and appeared before the grand jury. If she had not hastily flipped, she might have faced indictment for criminal contempt and obstruction of justice.

The Times, unlike the Washington Post, NBC News, and Time magazine, whose reporters all testified in the case, had decided Miller's fight was an essential defense of freedom of the press. Inevitably, her cause was deflated. Journalists, after all, are citizens, and they must testify if they witness crimes, according to a 1972 Supreme Court decision that the courts were bound to uphold. Miller's adamantine martyrdom, for which she had the full support of the *Times*, obliterated the customary privilege of reporters that had existed solely in deference to the now-punctured status of the press. The *Post*'s lawyers anticipated the result beforehand and counseled cooperation, but the *Times* decided instead to accept Miller at her word and her refusal as a principled stand, and to force an issue it was destined to lose.

After her first appearance before the grand jury, Miller suddenly discovered notes of a conversation with Libby, having previously declared that she had no such notes. That conversation, about Wilson, took place on June 23, 2003, two weeks before Wilson's op-ed article was published. Two people I spoke with who visited Miller in prison report that she appeared completely convinced of her stance as press martyr. But rumor-plagued Washington has divided into two camps: was Miller a self-deluded dupe or a co-conspirator?

The *Times*, meanwhile, has subordinated its news coverage to her legal defense, withholding reportage on what she has told the grand jury, though the newspaper promises a full account. Will it include her colleagues' recollections of how livid she was that the *Times* published Wilson's op-ed piece?

Unlike Watergate, which was largely advanced by the press, this scandal has unfolded despite much of the press corps' efforts to avoid, belittle, or suppress the story until very recently. Also unlike Watergate, this case has seen major influences in the press aligning themselves with their sources in the administration, not with the professionals in the government acting as whistle-blowers. (One of Miller's sources, John Bolton, the U.S. ambassador to the United Nations, graciously paid her a visit in jail.) For his part, Bob Woodward, who has written two books describing events from the perspective of the Bush administration, supported the White House version of the Niger incident by charging in July 2004 that "there were reasonable grounds to discredit Wilson."

Even as Bush's popularity has crumbled over the past nine months, leading figures of the press have kept cheerleading for the political brilliance of Karl Rove, arguing that, like a superhero, he will rescue Bush. Indeed, a number of prominent journalists have received lucrative advances to write books extolling Rove's genius. Those panegyrics, however, may take unexpected twists in the late chapters. This week Rove is scheduled to testify before the grand jury for the fourth time.

Inside the West Wing, the lowering atmosphere of dread is like that of Edgar Allan Poe's "The Pit and Pendulum:" "Down—steadily down it crept."

The Conservative Revolt

OCTOBER 20, 2005

PRESIDENT BUSH is the most conservative president in modern times. He consciously modeled himself as the opposite of his father's split political personality. Fiercely attacked as a betrayer, the elder Bush was partially defeated by a conservative revolt. In a classic case of reaction formation, George W. Bush was determined never to make an enemy on the right.

President Bush brought the neoconservatives, banished by Ronald Reagan and Bush Sr., back into government and followed their scenario to the letter for remaking the Middle East through an invasion of Iraq, using 9/11 as the pretext. He meticulously followed the right-wing script on supply-side economics, enacting an enormous tax cut for the wealthy that fostered a deficit dwarfing Reagan's—the problem his father had tried to resolve through a tax increase that earned the right's hostility. And Bush has followed the religious right's line on stem cell research, abortion, and creationism.

For his vision of the world as black and white, his disdain for internationalism and international law, his tainting of the domestic opposition as unpatriotic, his unapologetic promotion of tax breaks and loopholes for the wealthy, and his religious zealotry, conservatives celebrated him. *The Right Man* was the title of a glowing hagiography by his former speechwriter, David Frum (also author of the Bush phrase "axis of evil," or at least "axis of ———"). "Bush's Greatness" was the headline of an article published in the neoconservative journal the *Weekly Standard* just before the 2004 election. Critics of Bush, it contended, were haters, and haters of Bush hated all "American conservatives and especially white, religious American conservatives."

For his second term, Bush took his narrow victory as a mandate to govern from the far right. At last he would begin the privatization of Social Security, rolling back the signature program of the New Deal. But he stumbled on a dirty little secret of conservatism: members of the public support conservative presidents only so long as they leave alone the liberal programs that benefit voters. The more Bush barnstormed the country to promote his Social Security scheme, the more the public understood it and opposed him.

Baffled and confounded, he plowed ahead, even as the Iraq war eroded his support. Then Hurricane Katrina blew the top off his administration's culture of cronyism. Meanwhile, the special prosecutor investigating the disclosure of a covert CIA operative's identity by senior administration officials has moved steadily and silently, like a submarine, toward his targets.

Bush's nomination of his White House legal counsel and former personal lawyer, Harriet Miers, for the Supreme Court was the hair trigger for a conservative revolt. Miers is demonstrably the least qualified nominee for the high court since Clarence Thomas. She has never been a judge or prominent public official and has no background in constitutional law. She appears on the White House website explaining how Bush plays horseshoes with his dog: "The president throws the horseshoes to Barney, and Barney runs after them."

In a meeting this week with the powerful chair of the Senate Judiciary Committee, Arlen Specter, who had said she needed a "crash course" in the law, Miers explained that she supported two court decisions that were the basis for *Roe v. Wade,* which legalized abortion. Then Miers took back her statement, reinforcing an image of incompetence and ignorance.

Conservatives see her nomination as a rebuke to the cadres of ideologues in the Federalist Society groomed for Republican upward mobility; right-wing pundits have outdone each other in denouncing her as a crony. Frum has launched a petition drive to force Bush to withdraw her nomination. "She once told me that the president was the most brilliant man she had ever met," the Bush iconographer sneered. Yet Bush nominated Miers in place of professional ideologues because he had fallen from grace as a consequence of his stubborn adherence to conservative policies; Bush calculated that the Senate would approve her, but not a right-wing judge with a well-delineated record. Had Bush's conservative policies succeeded, he might have been able to name a purebred ideologue.

Instead Bush finds himself the target of a right-wing campaign of intimidation. In response, he has declared that he chose Miers because of her religion, declaring and that the lapsed Roman Catholic turned evangelical Protestant would never change; he has thereby undercut her independence as well as violated the spirit of Article VI of the Constitution, which prohibits a "religious test" for public office.

Despite Bush's faithful implementation of conservative ideas, disloyal ideologues blame him personally in order to deflect attention from the failure of their ideas as they position themselves for whatever or whoever is next. Like Trotskyists for whom communism always remained an unfulfilled ideal, conservatives now claim that conservatism has not been tried, and that Bush is a "betrayer" and "impostor." In his attempt to avoid the nemesis of his father, he is reliving it.

The Indictment of Scooter Libby

NOVEMBER 3, 2005

ONE YEAR AFTER HIS REELECTION, President Bush governs from a bunker. "We go forward with complete confidence," he proclaimed in his second inaugural address. He urged "our youngest citizens" to see the future "in the determined faces of our soldiers" and to choose between "evil" and "courage." But as he listened to Bush that day, Vice President Dick Cheney knew that the election had been secured by a cover-up.

"I would have wished nothing better," declared Patrick Fitzgerald in his press conference of October 28, announcing the indictment on five counts of perjury and obstruction of justice of I. Lewis "Scooter" Libby, the vice president's chief of staff, "that, when the subpoenas were issued in August 2004, witnesses testified then, and we would have been here in October 2004 instead of October 2005. No one would have went to jail."

The indictment of Libby documents that it was Cheney who confirmed the exact identity of the covert CIA operative Valerie Plame to him. The indictment also describes a figure called "Official A," subsequently disclosed to be Karl Rove, the president's chief political adviser, who informed Libby that he had told the conservative columnist Robert Novak of Plame's secret status. The next day, July 12, 2003, Libby conferred with Cheney on how to handle the press on the matter. That same day, Libby revealed Plame's identity to two reporters, Judith Miller of the *New York Times* and Matthew Cooper of *Time* magazine. Then Libby falsely testified that he had learned Plame's name from reporters. On September 30, 2003, President Bush emphatically stated that he wanted anyone in his administration with information about the Plame leak to "come forward"; if anyone inside was involved, he wanted to know; and if anyone had violated the law, "the person will be taken care of." On June 10, 2004, he pledged that anyone on his staff who had leaked Plame's name would be fired.

When the Libby indictment was announced, Bush and Cheney praised him as a fine public servant. Still under investigation, Rove remains in the West Wing. But Cheney knew during the presidential campaign that he—Cheney—had discussed with Libby how to deal with Plame. Now Bush knows that Rove enabled Novak to publish her identity. But the president's promise to fire officials is suddenly inoperative. It is apparently acceptable for aides to deceive the president and compromise national security so long as they further his short-term political goals. Ever-shifting ends justify ever-shifting means.

Libby's alleged cover-up was undertaken in the spirit of neoconservative Leninism. The vanguard, which sets all policy and uses the party as its instrument, rationalizes any tactic. Libby was a deeply implanted neoconservative apparatchik, possessing long experience and great bureaucratic skill—an inside man, never seeking the spotlight for himself. He was a member of a small elite, not easily replaced. If he had testified truthfully in October 2004, the result would have consumed the final days of the campaign. His Leninist logic permitted him to protect the Republican cause, but he has tainted Bush's victory in history as surely as the Supreme Court decision in *Bush v. Gore* did in 2000.

Bush took his 2004 win as a resounding mandate for a right-wing agenda. His second term was to be the fulfillment of conservative dreams to roll back decades of liberalism. With each right turn, however, his popularity declined. Iraq accelerated his fall.

His nomination of his White House legal counsel, Harriet Miers, for the Supreme Court was an acknowledgment of his sharply narrowed political space. Bush believed he could thread the needle with her because her record was unknown. While the Republican masses supported him, the Leninist right staged a revolt. In Bush's cronyism and opportunism, they saw his deviation. With the prosecutor's indictment imminent, Bush withdrew the Miers nomination and caved. Broadly unpopular, he could not suffer a split right. His new nominee, the federal judge Samuel Alito, a reliable sectarian, is a testament to his bunker strategy.

Hostage to his failed fortune, Bush is a prisoner of the right. His administration has become its own little republic of fear. Libby's public trial will reveal the administration's political methods. Cheney, along with a host of others, will be called to testify. The specter of future calamities harries Bush to the right. "Disunity, dissolution and vacillation" are hallmarks of "the path of conciliation," as Lenin wrote in *What Is to Be Done?* The vanguard on "the path of struggle," criticized for being "an exclusive group," must oppose any retreat proposed by the "opportunist rearguard." "We are marching in a compact group along a precipitous and difficult path, firmly holding each other by the hand. We are surrounded on all sides by enemies, and we have to advance almost constantly under their fire."

Cheney's Trial

NOVEMBER 10, 2005

THE TRIAL OF SCOOTER LIBBY will also be the trial of Dick Cheney. Throughout his career in four Republican administrations, starting as an aide in the Nixon White House, Cheney has operated in the background and through back channels. But eventually the vice president will be called to the stand, perhaps as a witness for both the prosecution and the defense.

Cheney may request a sealed courtroom, ask for a redacted transcript of the proceedings, or assert executive privilege. But established legal precedent argues against a claim of executive privilege. The only basis on which he could refuse to testify would be to take the Fifth Amendment, protecting himself against self-incrimination. Of course, that would be political suicide because it would be perceived as a virtual admission of guilt. Indeed, Cheney has already waived that Fifth Amendment right, having submitted to an interview with the special prosecutor, Patrick Fitzgerald. And his testimony in the Libby trial opens a perjury trap if he contradicts anything he has previously said to the prosecutor.

In the trial, the prosecutor will attempt to penetrate Libby's cover-up, his obstruction of justice, which Fitzgerald has compared to throwing dirt in the eyes of an umpire. He will call a slew of White House aides, including a number of Cheney's, to break through Libby's bodyguard of lies. The truth about Cheney is to be found beyond the cover-up.

Since his indictment on five counts of perjury and obstruction of justice, Libby the loyalist, Cheney's Cheney, has moved swiftly to disabuse anyone of the notion that he will fall on his sword. The surest way for him to protect Cheney would have been to plead guilty to the charges, admit nothing, and go directly to jail. But Libby passed up his chance to plead in negotiations with the prosecutor before the indictment. He has hired a team of lawyers from three different firms who are making preparations for an aggressive defense. He has also begun raising money for his legal defense from Republican Party donors, whose names will be kept secret. To coordinate this fund and his public relations, he has hired Barbara Comstock, a longtime Republican Party operative and the communications director for the former attorney general John Ashcroft.

Libby is not a man in a hurry. His first legal maneuver was to waive his rights under the Speedy Trial Act, which requires a trial within 120 days. (The presiding federal judge, Reggie Walton of the U.S. District Court of the District of Columbia, scheduled the trial for January 2007.)

From the beginning, the White House has acted as though the Plame affair were a minor irritation that could be contained. Libby's elaborate stories to the grand jury, claiming he learned from journalists that Valerie Plame Wilson was a covert CIA operative, suggested supreme confidence that the journalists would not disclose their conversations with him. But only Judith Miller acted to shield him; she was sentenced to prison for eighty-five days before she agreed to testify. The others cited in the indictment, Matthew Cooper of *Time* magazine and Tim Russert of NBC News, had earlier undercut Libby's various accounts.

President Bush's insistence that he wanted to get to the bottom of the incident and that he would fire anyone involved in the leak was followed by studied inactivity. When the prosecutor revealed Libby and Rove as culpable for the leak, Bush made no gesture to fulfill his pledge. The Libby indictment, moreover, states that Libby learned of Plame's job from Cheney, though Cheney had publicly denied any knowledge or involvement. Yet Bush has taken no action and made no statement about his vice president's alleged deception.

In his October 28 press conference announcing the Libby indictment, Fitzgerald declared that he was "not done." Regardless of whether there are future indictments of Bush administration officials, the Libby trial itself will be a spectacle subjecting Republican candidates to vulnerability during the campaign season. A new poll by the Pew Research Center for the People and the Press shows that 79 percent believe that Libby's indictment is a matter of national importance. Cheney's legal exposure is also the Republicans' political exposure.

The prosecutor's cross-examination of Cheney need not be limited to the bits of information about him that are sprinkled in the Libby indictment. Cheney cannot be sure what the prosecutor has learned. He cannot, therefore, fully anticipate what he will be asked. He might be presented with surprises that test his veracity and challenge his poise. Fitzgerald may also have testimony that contradicts what Cheney might say on the stand, and may not necessarily reveal it to him.

Certainly, Cheney should expect to answer a series of questions similar to these: Mr. Vice President, you shared with Mr. Libby the information that Valerie Plame was a CIA employee, didn't you? You believed that revealing Plame's supposed involvement in her husband Joseph Wilson's mission to Africa would discredit him, isn't that true? What was your reaction when you learned of Robert Novak's column divulging the identity of Valerie Plame? You spoke to people about Mr. Novak's column after it appeared, didn't you? Please name them and describe those conversations.

Did you know the identity of the two senior administration sources cited in his column after you read it? If not, what efforts did you make to determine the identities of these individuals? When the White House press secretary, Scott McClellan, told the press corps in a briefing that neither Karl Rove nor Scooter Libby was involved in leaking Plame's identity, you knew that was false, but you never took any steps to inform McClellan or, more important, the president and the American people, did you?

What conversations did you have with Karl Rove or others on the White House staff about Joseph Wilson or Valerie Plame? You were present at meetings discussing Wilson's objections to the false Niger claims, weren't you? Did you discuss Plame with the president? What other critics of the administration did you ever discuss in meetings? Who else was present? Please tell us about those conversations. What conversations did you have about Valerie Plame or Joseph Wilson with the president?

Mr. Vice President, you knew from talking to Mr. Libby that he didn't obtain the information about Plame's identity from the press, didn't you? You knew Mr. Libby spoke with Tim Russert, Judith Miller, and Matthew Cooper, isn't that true? And you knew that he provided information about Plame to them, not them to him, didn't you? You were his source, not them, isn't that true?

Mr. Vice President, you are under oath.

Stab in the Back

NOVEMBER 17, 2005

ONE YEAR AGO, after his reelection, President Bush brashly asserted: "I earned capital in the campaign, political capital, and now I intend to spend it. It is my style." Twelve months later, Republicans were thrashed in elections for the governorships of Virginia and New Jersey. In St Paul, Minnesota, the Democratic mayor who endorsed Bush for reelection a year ago was defeated by another Democrat by 70 percent to 30 percent. Then the Republicans in the Congress split and failed to pass Bush's budget. That was followed by the Senate's rejection of Bush's torture and detainee policy by an 89 to 11 vote and by the overwhelming passage of a resolution stipulating that the president must submit a strategy on the withdrawal of U.S. forces from Iraq.

The turn against Bush in public opinion has been slow and considered, and is therefore also firm. A majority believe his administration manipulated prewar intelligence to lead the country into the Iraq war, and two-thirds disapprove of his policy on the war. His political capital already appears spent, and he has retreated from the ruins of his grandiose agenda into a defense of his past.

In the immediate aftermath of the Iraq war, Bush was the man of action who never looked back, openly dismissive of history. "History. We don't know. We'll all be dead." But his obsessive interest in the subject is not posthumous. The Senate's decision to launch an investigation into prewar disinformation has provoked a furious reaction.

On Veterans' Day (November 11), Bush addressed troops at an army base: "It is deeply irresponsible to rewrite the history of how that war began." He accused "some Democrats and anti-war critics" of lying in stating that "we manipulated the intelligence."

Later, Bush spoke before troops at an air force base, where he stated that the Democrats "now rewriting the past" are "sending mixed signals to our troops and the enemy." The soldiers "deserve to know that their elected leaders who voted to send them into war continue to stand behind them."

Unless "our will is strong," disunity will threaten "victory." While the "ruthless enemy determined to destroy our way of life" besieges us from without, the most insidious undermining comes from within. Thus an American president has updated the "stab in the back" theory of German General Erich Ludendorff, who stated in February 1919 that "the political leadership disarmed the unconquered army and delivered over Germany to the destructive will of the enemy."

The former Republican Speaker of the House, Newt Gingrich, always notable for his visions, has compared George Bush in his travails to Abraham Lincoln before Gettysburg. Gingrich, who has recently written a series of counterfactual novels of the Civil War, communicated his latest flight of fancy to a longtime former diplomat. "We are at war," insisted Gingrich. "With whom?" he was asked. "The Democrats," he apparently replied without hesitation. For Gingrich, ever the Republican guru, history is a plaything of the partisan present.

Bush's adoption of the Ludendorff strategy of blaming weak politicians for military failure and exalting "will" sets him at odds with liberal democracy. His understanding of history also clashes with the conservative tradition that acknowledges human fallibility and respects the past. Bush's presidency is an effort to defy history, not only in America but by treating the entire world as a blank slate. Now he wants to erase memory of his actual record, substituting a counterfactual history. "Fellow citizens, we cannot escape history," said Lincoln. Never mind.

The Long March of Dick Cheney

NOVEMBER 24, 2005

THE HALLMARK of the Dick Cheney administration is its illegitimacy. Its essential method is the bypassing of established lines of authority; its goal is the concentration of unaccountable presidential power.
When it matters, the regular operations of the CIA, Defense Department,
and State Department have been sidelined.

Richard Nixon is the model, but with modifications. In the Nixon administration, the president was the prime mover, present at the creation of
his own options, attentive to detail, and conscious of their consequences.
In the Cheney administration, the president is volatile but passive, firm
but malleable, presiding but absent. Once his complicity has been
arranged, a closely held "cabal"—as Lawrence Wilkerson, once chief of
staff to former Secretary of State Colin Powell, calls it—wields control.

Within the White House, the office of the vice president is the strategic
center. The National Security Council has been demoted to enabler and implementer. Systems of off-line operations have been laid to evade professional analysis and a responsible chain of command. Those who attempt to
fulfill their duties in the old ways have been humiliated when necessary,
fired, retired early, or shunted aside. In their place, acolytes and ambitious
careerists indistinguishable from true believers have been elevated.

The collapse of sections of the façade shielding Cheney from public
view has not inhibited him. His former chief of staff, I. Lewis Libby, indicted on five counts of perjury and obstruction of justice, appears to be withholding from the special prosecutor information about the vice president's
actions in the Plame affair. While Bush has declaimed, "We do not torture," Cheney lobbied the Senate to stop it from prohibiting torture.

At the same time, Cheney has taken the lead in defending the administration from charges that it twisted intelligence to justify the Iraq war and
misled the Congress even as new stories underscore the legitimacy of the
charges.

Former Senator Bob Graham has revealed, in a November 20 article in the *Washington Post,* that the condensed version of the national intelligence estimate titled *Iraq's Weapons of Mass Destruction Programs* that was submitted to the Senate days before it voted on the Iraq war resolution "represented an unqualified case that Hussein possessed [WMD], avoided a discussion of whether he had the will to use them and omitted the dissenting opinions contained in the classified version." The condensed version also contained the falsehood that Saddam Hussein was seeking "weapons-grade fissile material from abroad."

The administration relied for key information in the NIE on an Iraqi defector code-named Curveball. According to a November 20 report in the *Los Angeles Times,* it had learned from German intelligence beforehand that Curveball was completely untrustworthy and his claims fabricated. Yet Bush, Cheney, and, most notably, Powell in his prewar performance before the United Nations, which he now calls the biggest "blot" on his record and about which he insists he was "deceived," touted Curveball's disinformation.

In two speeches over the past week, Cheney has called congressional critics "dishonest," "shameless," and "reprehensible." He ridiculed their claim that they did not have the same intelligence as the administration. "These are elected officials who had access to the intelligence materials. They are known to have a high opinion of their own analytical capabilities." Lambasting them for historical "revisionism," he repeatedly invoked September 11. "We were not in Iraq on September 11th, 2001—and the terrorists hit us anyway," he said.

The day after Cheney's most recent speech, the *National Journal* reported that the president's daily brief prepared by the CIA ten days after September 11, 2001 indicated that there was no connection between Saddam and the terrorist attacks. Of course, the 9/11 Commission had made the same point in its report.

Even though experts and pundits contradict his talking points, Cheney presents them with characteristic assurance. His rhetoric is like a paving truck that will flatten all obstacles. Cheney remains undeterred; he has no recourse. He will not run for president in 2008. He is defending more than the Bush record; he is defending the culmination of his career. Cheney's alliances, ideas, antagonisms, and tactics have accumulated for decades.

Cheney is a master bureaucrat, proficient in the ways of the White House, the agencies and departments, and Congress. The many offices

Cheney has held add up to an extraordinary résumé. His competence and measured manner are often mistaken for moderation. Among those who have misjudged Cheney are military men—Colin Powell, Brent Scowcroft, and Wilkerson. As a result, they expressed surprise at their discovery of the ideological hard man. Scowcroft told the *New Yorker* recently that Cheney was not the Cheney he once knew. But Scowcroft and the other military men rose by working through regular channels; they were trained to respect established authority. They are at a disadvantage in internal political battles with those operating by different rules of warfare. Their realism does not account for radicalism within the U.S. government.

Nixon's resignation in the Watergate scandal thwarted his designs for an unchecked imperial presidency. It was in that White House that Cheney gained his formative experience as the assistant to Nixon's counselor, Donald Rumsfeld. When Gerald Ford acceded to the presidency, he summoned Rumsfeld from his posting as ambassador to NATO to become his chief of staff. Rumsfeld, in turn, brought back his former deputy, Cheney.

From Nixon, they learned the application of ruthlessness and the harsh lesson of failure. Under Ford, Rumsfeld designated Cheney as his surrogate on intelligence matters. Immediately after Watergate, Congress investigated past CIA abuses, and the press was filled with revelations. In May 1975, Seymour Hersh reported in the *New York Times* how the CIA had sought to recover a sunken Soviet submarine with a deep-sea mining vessel called the *Glomar Explorer*, built by Howard Hughes. When Hersh's article appeared, Cheney wrote memos laying out options ranging from indicting Hersh or getting a search warrant for Hersh's apartment to suing the *Times* and pressuring its owners "to discourage the NYT and other publications from similar action." "In the end," writes James Mann, in his indispensable book, *Rise of the Vulcans: The History of Bush's War Cabinet,* "Cheney and the White House decided to back off after the intelligence community decided its work had not been significantly damaged."

Rumsfeld and Cheney quickly gained control of the White House staff, edging out Ford's old aides. From this base, they waged bureaucratic war on Vice President Nelson Rockefeller and Henry Kissinger, a colossus of foreign policy, who occupied the posts of both secretary of state and national security adviser. Rumsfeld and Cheney were the right wing of the Ford administration, opposed to the policy of détente with the Soviet Union, and they operated by stealthy internal maneuver. The Secret Service gave Cheney the code name Backseat.

In 1975, Rumsfeld and Cheney stage-managed a cabinet purge called the "Halloween massacre" that made Rumsfeld secretary of defense and Cheney White House chief of staff. Kissinger, forced to surrender control of the National Security Council, angrily drafted a letter of resignation (which he never submitted). Rumsfeld and Cheney helped convince Ford, who faced a challenge for the Republican nomination from Ronald Reagan, that he needed to shore up his support on the right and that Rockefeller was a political liability. Rockefeller felt compelled to announce he would not be Ford's running mate. Upset at the end of his political career, Rockefeller charged that Rumsfeld intended to become vice president himself. In fact, Rumsfeld had contemplated running for president in the future and undoubtedly would have accepted a vice-presidential nod.

In the meantime, Secretary of Defense Rumsfeld undermined the negotiations for a new Strategic Arms Limitation Treaty being conducted by Kissinger. Fighting off Reagan's attacks during the Republican primaries, Ford was pressured by Cheney to adopt his foreign-policy views, which amounted to a self-repudiation. At the Republican Party Convention, acting as Ford's representative, Cheney engineered the adoption of Reagan's foreign-policy plank in the platform. By doing so he preempted an open debate and split. Privately, Ford, Kissinger, and Rockefeller were infuriated.

As part of the Halloween massacre, Rumsfeld and Cheney pushed out the CIA director, William Colby, and replaced him with George H. W. Bush, then the U.S. plenipotentiary to China. The CIA had been uncooperative with the Rumsfeld-Cheney antidétente campaign. Instead of producing intelligence reports simply showing an urgent Soviet military buildup, the CIA issued complex analyses that were filled with qualifications. Its national intelligence estimate on the Soviet threat contained numerous caveats, dissents, and contradictory opinions. From the conservative point of view, the CIA was guilty of groupthink, unwilling to challenge its own premises and hostile to conservative ideas.

The new CIA director was prompted to authorize an alternative unit outside the CIA to challenge the agency's intelligence on Soviet intentions. Bush was more pliant in the political winds than his predecessor. Consisting of a host of conservatives, the unit was called Team B. A young aide from the Arms Control and Disarmament Agency, Paul Wolfowitz, was selected to represent Rumsfeld's interest and served as coauthor of Team B's report. The report was single-minded in its conclusion about the Soviet buildup and cleansed of contrary intelligence. It was fundamentally a political tool in the struggle for control of the Republican Party, intended to destroy détente and aimed particularly at Kissinger. Both Ford and Kissinger took pains to dismiss Team B and its effort. (Later, Team B's report was revealed to be wildly off the mark about the scope and capability of the Soviet military.)

With Ford's defeat, Team B became the kernel of the Committee on the Present Danger, a conservative group that attacked President Jimmy Carter for weakness on the Soviet threat. The growing strength of the right thwarted ratification of SALT II, setting the stage for Reagan's nomination and election.

Elected to the House of Representatives in 1978, Cheney became the Republican leader on the House Intelligence Committee, where he consistently fought congressional oversight and limits on presidential authority. When Congress investigated the Iran-contra scandal (the creation of an illegal, privately funded, offshore U.S. foreign policy initiative), Cheney was the crucial defender of the administration. At every turn, he blocked the Democrats and prevented them from questioning Vice President Bush. Under his leadership, not a single House Republican signed the special investigating committee's final report charging "secrecy, deception and disdain for law." Instead, the Republicans issued their own report claiming there had been no major wrongdoing.

The origin of Cheney's alliance with the neoconservatives goes back to his instrumental support for Team B. On being appointed secretary of defense by the elder Bush, he kept Wolfowitz on as undersecretary. And Wolfowitz kept on his deputy, his former student at the University of Chicago, Scooter Libby. Earlier, Wolfowitz and Libby had written a document expressing suspicion of the Soviet leader Mikhail Gorbachev's liberalizing perestroika and warning against making deals with him, a document that President Reagan ignored as he made an arms-control agreement and proclaimed that the Cold War was ending.

During the Gulf war, Secretary of Defense Cheney clashed with General Colin Powell. At one point, he admonished Powell, who had been Reagan's national security adviser, "Colin, you're chairman of the Joint Chiefs . . . so stick to military matters." During the run-up to the war, Cheney set up a secret unit in the Pentagon to develop an alternative war plan, his own version of Team B. "Set up a team, and don't tell Powell or anybody else," Cheney ordered Wolfowitz. The plan was called Operation Scorpion. "While Powell was out of town, visiting Saudi Arabia, Cheney—again, without telling Powell—took the civilian-drafted plan, Operation Scorpion, to the White House and presented it to the president and the National Security Adviser," writes Mann in his book. Bush, however, rejected it as too risky. General Norman Schwarzkopf was enraged at Cheney's presumption. "Put a civilian in charge of professional military men and before long he's no longer satisfied with setting policy but wants to out-general the generals," he wrote in his memoir. After Operation Scorpion was rejected, Cheney urged Bush to go to war without congressional approval, a notion the elder Bush dismissed.

After the Gulf war victory, in 1992, Cheney approved a new "Defense Planning Guidance" document advocating U.S. unilateralism in the post–Cold War era. The final draft was written by Libby. Cheney assumed Republican rule for the indefinite future.

One week after Bill Clinton's inauguration, on January 27, 1993, Cheney appeared on CNN's *Larry King Live,* where he declared his interest in running for the presidency. "Obviously," he said, "it's something I'll take a look at. . . . Obviously, I've worked for three presidents and watched two others up close, and so it is an idea that has occurred to me." For two years, he quietly campaigned in Republican circles but discovered little enthusiasm. He was less well-known than he imagined and less charismatic than his former titles suggested. On August 10, 1995, he held a news conference at the headquarters of the Halliburton Company in Dallas, announcing that he would become its chief executive officer. "When I made the decision earlier this year not to run for president, not to seek the White House, that really was a decision to wrap up my political career and move on to other things," he said.

But in 2000, Cheney surfaced in the role of party elder, above the fray, willing to serve as the man who would help Governor George W. Bush determine who should be his running mate. Prospective candidates turned over to him all sensitive material about themselves, financial, political, and personal. Once he had collected it, he decided that he should be the vice presidential candidate himself. Bush said he had previously thought of the idea and happily accepted. Asked who vetted Cheney's records, Bush's aide Karen Hughes explained, "Just as with other candidates, Secretary Cheney is the one who handled that."

Most observers assumed that Cheney would lend experience and maturity to the administration, serving as surrogate father and elder statesman. Few grasped his deeply held views on presidential power. With Rumsfeld returned as secretary of defense, the position he had held during the Ford administration, the old team was back in place. Rivals from the past had departed, and the field was clear. The methods used before were implemented again. To get around the CIA, the Office of Special Plans was created within the Pentagon, yet another version of Team B. Senior military dissenters were removed. Powell was manipulated and outmaneuvered.

The making of the Iraq war, torture policy, and an industry-friendly energy plan has required secrecy, deception, and subordination of government as it previously existed. But these, too, are means to an end. Even projecting a "war on terror" as total war, trying to envelop the whole American society within its fog, is a device to invest absolute power in the executive.

Dick Cheney sees in George W. Bush his last chance. Nixon self-destructed, Ford was fatally compromised by his moderation, Reagan was not what was hoped for, the elder Bush ended up a disappointment. In every case, the Republican presidents were checked or went soft. Finally, President Bush provided the instrument, September 11 the opportunity. This time the failures of the past provided the guideposts for getting it right. The administration's heedlessness was simply the wisdom of Cheney's experience.

Bob Woodward's Cover-up

DECEMBER 1, 2005

In the beginning, seasoned political reporters at the *Washington Post* disdained the Watergate story as insignificant, implausible, and unserious. But two young journalists from the metro desk doggedly pursued every lead to expose a "cancer on the presidency" and help bring about Richard Nixon's resignation. Three decades later, after being dashingly portrayed on screen by Robert Redford and having published many revelatory best-sellers, Bob Woodward had come to embody the ultimate Washington insider, still burnished by the romance of Watergate and carrying the brand of the *Post*. Over the past month, however, he has personified the stonewalling and covering up he once penetrated and shattered to launch his brilliant career. His unraveling is as surprising and symptomatic a story of George W. Bush's Washington as his making was of Nixon's.

On October 27, the night before Vice President Cheney's chief of staff, I. Lewis "Scooter" Libby, was indicted on five counts of perjury and obstruction of justice, Woodward appeared on CNN's *Larry King Live*. The famous investigative reporter was asked about a rumor that he had a "bombshell" about the case. "I don't even have a firecracker," he replied, and then held forth.

"I'm quite confident we're going to find out that it started as a kind of gossip, as chatter. . . . There's a lot of innocent actions in all of this. . . . I don't know how this is about the build-up to the war." He expressed his sympathy in advance for those who might be indicted: "And you know, again, these are human beings. And what distresses me is, you know, so-and-so might be indicted, and so-and-so is facing. . . . And it is not yet proven." Woodward concluded with invective against Patrick Fitzgerald, calling him a "junkyard dog prosecutor."

On November 16, Woodward admitted that he had been called on November 3 to testify before the prosecutor, having been named by his source immediately after Libby's indictment. Woodward, it turned out, was the first journalist to learn the CIA operative Valerie Plame's identity, but he had maintained silence for more than two years. "I hunkered down," he told his own newspaper. "I'm in the habit of keeping secrets. I didn't want anything out there that was going to get me subpoenaed." Woodward claimed he heard about Plame in an interview he conducted in June 2003 for his book *Plan of Attack*, which appeared in April 2004 and failed to contain this startling information. While two other *Post* reporters testified before the prosecutor, Woodward hid his role as a material witness. With the disclosure, the storyteller lost the plot.

Woodward's fabled access has inspired comparisons with influential Washington journalists from before Watergate. But unlike Joseph Alsop or Walter Lippmann, he advocates no ideas and is indifferent to the fate of government. His access has been in the service of his technique of accumulating mountains of facts whose scale fosters an image of omniscience. As his best-sellers and wealth piled up, he lost a sense of journalism as provisional and inherently imperfect, viewing it instead as something engraved in stone. He had no point of view and felt no need to provide one because his point of view was the journalist as all-seeing god. But the method also made him particularly vulnerable to manipulation by cunning sources.

Woodward's 2002 book, *Bush at War*, based partly on dozens of selected National Security Council documents leaked to him at White House instruction, was especially invaluable to the administration for its portrait of Bush as strong, decisive, and in charge. Even with the hindsight of only three years, its omissions are as striking as its fragmentary facts, such as the absence of analysis of the disastrous military operation at Tora Bora in Afghanistan that allowed Osama bin Laden to escape. Woodward's sequel, *Plan of Attack*, includes intriguing shards of information about the twisting of intelligence to justify the war, but he failed to develop the material and theme.

By the time of the publication of *Plan of Attack*, Woodward was "hunkered down," shielding his "secrets" from his newspaper, its readers, and the Plame prosecutor. He cryptically told one of the *Post* reporters subpoenaed to testify to "keep him out of the reporting." He declared there were "reasonable grounds to discredit" the former ambassador Joseph Wilson, the whistle-blower. He asserted that a CIA assessment had determined Plame's outing had caused no damage, prompting the CIA to clarify that a damage assessment report has not yet been produced.

But when a source outed Woodward to the prosecutor, his cover-up was revealed. Above all, the extent of his credulity was exposed. It is more than paradoxical that the reporter who investigated Nixon and worked closely with professionals in government alarmed by the abuses should exhibit so little skepticism about Bush.

Condi's Tortuous Trail

DECEMBER 8, 2005

THE METAMORPHOSIS of Condoleezza Rice from the chrysalis of the protégé into the butterfly of the State Department has not been a natural evolution but has demanded self-discipline. She has burnished an image of the ultimate loyalist, yet she betrayed her mentor, George H. W. Bush's national security adviser, Brent Scowcroft. She is the team player, yet she carefully inserted knives into the back of her predecessor, Colin Powell, climbing them like a ladder of success. She is the person most trusted on foreign policy by the president and served as an enabler for Vice President Cheney and the neoconservatives. Now her public relations team at the State Department depicts her as a restorer of realism, builder of alliances, and maker of peace.

On her first trip to Europe early this year, she left a refreshing sensation by listening rather than lecturing. Flirting with power appeared to have a more seductive effect than arrogance. So the old face became a new face. But on this week's trip the iron butterfly emerged.

Rice arrived as the enforcer of the Bush administration's torture policy. She reminded the queasy Europeans that their intelligence services, one way or another, are involved in the rendition of hundreds of suspected terrorists transported through their airports for harsh interrogation in countries like Jordan and Egypt or secret CIA prisons known as "black sites." With her warnings, Rice recast the Western alliance as a partnership in complicity. In her attempt to impose silence, she spread guilt. Everybody is unclean in the dirty war, and nobody has any right to complain. "What I would hope that our allies would acknowledge," she said, "is that we are all in this together."

For the European leaders, facing public hostility to U.S. policy in Iraq and torture, Rice's visit was disquieting. In Italy, prosecutors have issued indictments of twenty-two current and former CIA operatives for their "extraordinary rendition" of an Egyptian suspect; among those indicted is the former Rome CIA station chief, who an Italian judge has ruled has no immunity from prosecution. The Italian foreign minister, Gianfranco Fini, asked about renditions, said, "We know absolutely nothing. We have not one single piece of knowledge." If the Italian government knew the facts, it would investigate, he added.

In Britain, the Foreign Office released a diplomatic disclaimer that it has "no evidence to corroborate media allegations about the use of U.K. territory in rendition operations." But upset members of the House of Commons have launched a parliamentary inquiry into whether the United Kingdom has violated the European Convention on Human Rights and the United Nations Convention against Torture. The foreign minister, Jack Straw, sent Rice a letter requesting any "clarification the U.S. can give about these reports in the hope that this will allay parliamentary and public concerns."

When the *Washington Post* reported on the eve of Rice's trip that CIA prisons holding U.S. detainees exist in Romania, Poland, and other Eastern European nations, it triggered an explosion. Even though Romania and Poland denied the report, the European Commission and the Council of Europe began investigations. The EC declared that for any member state to harbor a CIA prison would be "extremely serious" and bring down sanctions upon that country.

In Germany, Rice was greeted by the new chancellor, Angela Merkel, eager to repair relations with the Bush administration made awkward by former Chancellor Gerhard Schroeder's opposition to the Iraq war. Rice's visit was supposed to smooth over the conflicts of the past, but instead it revealed new ones indicating that the divisions between Germany—and Europe—and the United States are rooted in the Bush administration's fundamental policies.

Rice arrived in Berlin on the heels of a *Washington Post* report about the rendition, to a secret CIA jail in Afghanistan called the Salt Pit, of a German citizen, Khaled el-Masri, who was tortured and imprisoned for five months in a case of mistaken identity. After meeting with Rice, Merkel announced that Rice had acknowledged that the United States had made a "mistake" in the case. But Rice countered with a statement denying she had said that at all. The reconciliation with Germany was botched; Merkel was embarrassed; and Rice's credibility, at least in the German press, was left in tatters.

Rice had hoped to quell the controversy before she landed. On Monday, as she boarded her plane at Andrews Air Force Base in Washington, she delivered a lengthy statement on torture. Her speech was remarkable for its defensive, dense, and evasive tone. It was replete with half-truths, outright falsehoods, distortions, and subterfuges.

Her remarks can never sway or convince any European leader, foreign ministry, or intelligence service, which have the means to make their own judgments. In her effort to sway world opinion and reassure the American public, she raised the debate over torture to greater prominence and virtually invited inspection of her claims.

Rice has made memorably duplicitous statements in the past. There was her appearance before the 9/11 Commission, in which she had trouble recalling the CIA's presidential daily brief of August 6, 2001, titled "Bin Laden Determined to Strike in U.S.," and dismissed its significance. There were her many assertions about Saddam Hussein's weapons of mass destruction, including nuclear weapons: "We don't want the smoking gun to be a mushroom cloud." There was her attack on Richard Clarke, the former counterterrorism chief on the National Security Council, for his disclosure that neither Rice nor the president regarded al Qaeda as an urgent threat before September 11, 2001: she dismissed Clarke's assertion as a "scurrilous allegation." But her remarks on torture may turn out to be her most unforgettable full-length speech, tainting her tenure as secretary of state as indelibly as Colin Powell's speech, making the case for the Iraq war before the United Nations, blotted his.

"Torture is a term that is defined by law," said Rice. "We rely on our law to govern our operations." She neglected to explain that "torture," as she used the term, has been defined by presidential findings to include universally defined methods of torture, such as waterboarding, for which U.S. soldiers were court-martialed in 1902 and 1968 specifically on the basis of having engaged in torture.

But the Bush administration has rejected adherence to the Geneva Conventions as "quaint," in the term of Alberto Gonzales, then White House counsel and now attorney general; it rejects the definition of torture in the United Nations Convention against Torture (although the United States is a signatory); and it also rejects the definitions by other international expert bodies, including the European Human Rights Court, whose judgments are binding on the nations of the Council of Europe.

"The United States does not permit, tolerate, or condone torture under any circumstances," Rice insisted in her statement. "Moreover, in accordance with the policy of this administration: the United States has respected—and will continue to respect—the sovereignty of other countries." But was the kidnapping of the Egyptian suspect in Italy that has resulted in twenty-two indictments of CIA operatives a fiction? Have the Italian prosecutors been made aware that the event was a figment of their imaginations? Was holding el-Masri, the innocent German, not a violation of the sovereignty of another country?

Rice continued: "The United States does not transport, and has not transported, detainees from one country to another for the purpose of interrogation using torture. The United States does not use the airspace or the airports of any country for the purpose of transporting a detainee to a country where he or she will be tortured." But the German government was reported to have a list of four hundred flights over European airspace for the purpose of renditions. And Amnesty International reports that there have been eight hundred such flights. Once again, Rice relies upon her own definition of "torture" to deny it.

She went on: "The United States has not transported anyone, and will not transport anyone, to a country when we believe he will be tortured. Where appropriate, the United States seeks assurances that transferred persons will not be tortured." In fact, the United States receives assurances from those countries that it would be *unlikely* that the suspects will be tortured, a technical loophole that provides for a washing of hands. Everybody on all sides understands that there will be torture—as there has been.

Rice's legal interpretations were authoritative, bland, and bogus. It is hard to say whether they should be called Orwellian for their intentional falsity or Kafkaesque for their unintentional absurdity.

"International law allows a state to detain enemy combatants for the duration of hostilities," she said. But the administration has vitiated international law with its presidential findings. The "global war on terror" is a conflict without end; its duration extends into perpetuity. So long as terror is used as a tactic, or the threat of terror exists—which it always does—a state of war, such as it is, justifies indefinite detention.

Then Rice presented as the administration's position precisely the position it opposes: "Detainees may only be held for an extended period if the intelligence or other evidence against them has been carefully evaluated and supports a determination that detention is lawful. The U.S. does not seek to hold anyone for a period beyond what is necessary to evaluate the intelligence or other evidence against them, prevent further acts of terrorism, or hold them for legal proceedings." But the Bush administration has refused to place detainees within the criminal justice system. Instead, they have been kept in a legal limbo, denied the protections of both the U.S. justice system and the Geneva Conventions. The administration has hidden "ghost detainees" from the International Committee of the Red Cross. If the suspects are criminals, they have not been tried as criminals.

Rice cited two cases to make her point: Carlos the Jackal, the international terrorist captured in Sudan in 1994, and Ramzi Youssef, the 1993 World Trade Center bomber. But, unlike current detainees, both were put on public trial, Carlos in France, Youssef in the United States. And the European Commission on Human Rights issued a report that Carlos's rights were not violated. Both cases refuted in their particulars the larger argument Rice was making.

One case Rice did not cite was that of Ibn al-Shaykh al-Libi, a captured al Qaeda operative, whose claims about Saddam Hussein's possession of WMD were used by the administration to build the case for the Iraq war. "We've learned that Iraq has trained Al Qaeda members in bomb-making and poisons and deadly gases," President Bush said on October 7, 2002, drawing on al-Libi's information. Al-Libi also provided the basis for a dramatic high point of Secretary of State Powell's U.N. speech: "The story of a senior terrorist operative telling how Iraq provided training in these weapons to Al Qaeda. Fortunately, this operative is now detained, and he has told his story. I will relate it to you now, as he himself described it." But al-Libi had been tortured and repeated to his interrogators what they had suggested to him. The Defense Intelligence Agency reported in February 2002 that al-Libi's information was dubious, and the CIA also questioned its credibility in a report in January 2003—both reports that were made before the war. Rice's various statements created pandemonium across Europe that she tried to quiet with a clarification Wednesday in Ukraine. The policy she had just declared the United States did not follow, she announced, it would no longer pursue. "As a matter of U.S. policy, the United States' obligations under the CAT [U.N. Convention against Torture], which prohibits cruel, inhumane and degrading treatment—those obligations extend to U.S. personnel wherever they are, whether they are in the United States or outside of the United States," Rice said at a press conference with the Ukrainian president, Viktor Yushchenko.

Rice's erratic journey also raises the question of her own role in formulating and applying the policy. The *Washington Post* story on el-Masri reports that Rice intervened on the side of informing the German government, a disclosure that resulted in el-Masri's release. This fact suggests that Rice has a degree of authority and knowledge in the realm of detainees and "black sites."

Since 2003, Rice has repeatedly told representatives of Human Rights Watch and other similar organizations that the United States does not torture. There is no trail of memos tracing her involvement in the titanic struggle over U.S. torture policy between Powell and the senior military on one side and Dick Cheney, Donald Rumsfeld, and John Ashcroft's Justice Department on the other. Was the national security adviser completely out of the loop? On November 19, ABC News reported, "Current and former CIA officers tell ABC News there is a presidential finding, signed in 2002, by President Bush, Condoleezza Rice and then Attorney General John Ashcroft, approving the [harsh interrogation] techniques, including waterboarding."

That technique has its origin in the Spanish Inquisition. Indeed, in 1490, a baptized Christian who was a secret Jew, a converso named Benito Garcia, was subjected to water torture. The process drew out of him a confession of the ritual murder of a Christian child by crucifixion, purportedly to use his blood for a magic ceremony to halt the Inquisition and bring about Jewish control. The incident greatly helped whip up the fear that led to the expulsion of the Jews in 1492, as described by James Reston Jr. in his new book, *Dogs of God: Columbus, the Inquisition, and the Defeat of the Moors.*

Since the Inquisition, the method of waterboarding has been little refined. But Rice, like Bush, says we did not torture, do not torture, and will not torture anymore.

"The Law is King"

DECEMBER 22, 2005

PRESIDENT BUSH'S EXPLANATIONS of why he is justified in ordering domestic surveillance by the National Security Agency have shifted with every news cycle. He has sent out Attorney General Alberto Gonzales and Secretary of State Condoleezza Rice to bolster his justifications. (Rice averred that she was "not a lawyer" before repeating the talking points.) Bush personally tried to suppress disclosure by the *New York Times,* which had held the story for more than a year before breaking it, by summoning the *Times*' publisher, Arthur Sulzberger, and its editor, Bill Keller, to the Oval Office on December 6.

Bush invokes national security, the war on terror, and September 11 as though these phrases are enabling legislation. He has offered no sound legal basis for his evasion of the Federal Intelligence Surveillance Act, his dismissal of congressional oversight, and his abrogation of the Fourth Amendment. He has not presented any convincing reason why he decided not to seek warrants for surveillance from the special FISA court set up for that purpose. One of the eleven members of the FISA court, U.S. District Court Judge James Robertson, has quit in protest.

Bush claims to have briefed and received the approval of congressional leaders. But according to former Senator Bob Graham, Democrat of Florida, who was chair of the Senate Intelligence Committee when Bush began his spying, "There was no reference made to the fact that we were going to . . . begin unwarranted, illegal, and I think unconstitutional, eavesdropping on American citizens." After being informed of the president's actions in 2003, Senator Jay Rockefeller, the ranking Democrat on the Intelligence Committee, sent a handwritten note expressing his misgivings to Vice President Dick Cheney, who had briefed him. "Clearly, the activities we discussed raise profound oversight issues," he wrote. (Rockefeller's position on the Intelligence Committee kept him from making public what he knew.) The Republican chair of the Senate Judiciary Committee, Arlen Specter, has announced his disquiet and is planning to hold hearings.

Attorney General Gonzales and the former National Security Agency director, General Michael Hayden, have issued assurances that there was no purely domestic spying. "People are running around saying that the United States is somehow spying on American citizens calling their neighbors," Gonzales said. "Very, very important to understand that one party to the communication has to be outside the United States." But another *New York Times* report revealed that this claim was false and that there has been surveillance involving calls within the United States.

Bush has contradicted his previous statements that he sought warrants for all wiretaps and searches. "Now, by the way," he said on April 20, 2004, "anytime you hear the United States government talking about wiretap, it requires—a wiretap requires a court order. Nothing has changed, by the way." But the glaring contradiction between his statement then and his current ones does not deflect the president from stubbornly persisting.

Bush angrily called the leaking of his spying a "shameful act," expressing an emotion that contrasts with his obvious impassivity to the leaking of the identity of CIA operative Valerie Plame (an act under investigation by a special prosecutor, who has so far indicted the vice president's former chief of staff, I. Lewis "Scooter" Libby). For Bush, the whistle-blower who disclosed his surveillance is a traitor within. "The fact that we are discussing this program is helping the enemy," he said. And yet no one has really explained why the president mistrusts and bypasses the FISA court.

Since October 2001, Bush has personally authorized more than three dozen warrantless wiretaps. "We've got to be able to detect and prevent. I keep saying that, but this . . . requires quick action." But speed cannot be the reason for ignoring the FISA court, which has always acted expeditiously. From its inception in 1979 through 2002, covering the period when Bush began spying, the FISA court issued 15,264 warrants. In 2003, the court rejected four applications, and the next year it rejected none. In its entire history, those four are the only rejections.

William Rehnquist, the late chief justice of the Supreme Court, appointed all the sitting FISA judges. Nearly all are inclined to presidential prerogative. Its proceedings are ex parte—that is, secret. The FISA statute stipulates that the government can wiretap first and apply for a warrant later, within seventy-two hours. So long as it can provide "probable cause," the court will approve. In the light of the law and the court's record, the only reason to avoid it would be the fear that even a court that had acted almost as a rubber stamp would deny the government's requests.

The FISA court can reject an application on two grounds. The first is an absence of probable cause. The court must adhere to the law and cannot authorize dragnets. But Attorney General Gonzales has declared that any spying is triggered by "reasonable basis"—not probable cause. *Reasonable* means anything the government decides it is, requiring not a scrap of potential evidence. Second, the court can reject an application in which the evidence supporting "probable cause" has been produced by torture. But it is unlikely that the government would provide the court with details of the interrogation technique used. In any case, Bush apparently opted to launch trawling expeditions, lacking concrete evidence beyond lists of telephone numbers, and without the imprimatur of the court.

"The authorization I gave the National Security Agency after September the 11th . . . is fully consistent with my constitutional responsibilities and authorities," Bush said in his weekly radio address December 17. In other words, he is commander in chief and can act as he chooses. But the Supreme Court ruled in the 1952 Youngstown case, involving President Truman's seizure of a steel mill to stop a strike during the Korean War, that the commander in chief lacked the power to exceed the will of the Congress. "When the President takes measures incompatible with the expressed or implied will of Congress, his power is at its lowest ebb," wrote Justice Robert Jackson in his concurring opinion.

"I'm also using constitutional authority vested in me as commander in chief," Bush went on. But the Supreme Court ruled in the 2004 *Hamdan* case that the commander in chief could not imprison U.S. citizens without trial, no matter what the suspicion. "A state of war is not a blank check for the president when it comes to the rights of the nation's citizens," wrote Justice Sandra Day O'Connor.

"To fight the war on terror," Bush continued, "I am using authority vested in me by Congress, including the Joint Authorization for Use of Military Force, which passed overwhelmingly in the first week after September the 11th." But that congressional war resolution, authorizing Bush to take "necessary and appropriate force" against those responsible for the 9/11 attacks, did not intend presidential usurpation of all congressional and judicial powers in the name of national security. Indeed, after the AUMF, the administration sought amendments to FISA, understanding that congressional authority was required.

Gonzales provided yet another rationale, stretching the definition of al Qaeda: "Another very important point to remember is that we have to have a reasonable basis to conclude that one party to the communication is a member of al Qaeda, affiliated with al Qaeda, or a member of an organization affiliated with al Qaeda, or working in support of al Qaeda."

In other words, anyone can be tapped who is unknowingly connected by "working in support" of al Qaeda in any capacity.

Who would fall under the Bush guidelines? Consider the following case: A lawyer represents a man involved in an Islamic charity that turns out to be raising funds for al Qaeda. The lawyer theoretically could be wiretapped without a warrant, detained indefinitely without charges, imprisoned in isolation, and unable to consult legal counsel. In fact, there has been such a lawyer—who represented precisely such a client in New Jersey. The client was Dr. Magdy Elamir; the lawyer was Michael Chertoff, now the secretary of homeland security. Chertoff represented Elamir, who owned an HMO that was sued by the state of New Jersey for fraud. The FBI filed a report that he had skimmed money to support al Qaeda and that he financially supported the Al Salam mosque, which the "blind sheikh" Omar Abdel-Rahman used as a base of operations for the 1993 World Trade Center bombing. Elamir denied any involvement with al Qaeda but admitted funding the mosque.

The legal justification, such as it is, for the president's domestic surveillance policy rests in the arguments made in a memorandum of September 21, 2001, written by John Yoo, then deputy director of the Justice Department's Office of Legal Counsel. The commander in chief, he stated, could wiretap without court permission. "The government may be justified," Yoo wrote, "in taking measures which in less troubled conditions could be seen as infringements of individual liberties." Congress, he wrote in another memo four days later, could not put "limits on the president's determinations as to any terrorist threat, the amount of military force to be used in response, or the method, timing and nature of the response. These decisions, under our Constitution, are for the president alone to make."

Yoo is also the author of memos justifying torture. On January 9, 2002, he wrote a memo stating that the Geneva Conventions did not apply to detained terrorist suspects. On August 1, 2002, Yoo authored another memo, signed by his superior, Jay Bybee, defining torture as "equivalent in intensity to the pain accompanying serious physical injury, such as organ failure, impairment of bodily function, or even death."

These are the four known Yoo memos rationalizing expanded presidential authority. But there are at least a dozen of these documents, most of which have not yet come to light, sources close to attorneys at the Justice

Department tell me. The overriding theme of them all is that the president can ignore congressional acts.

Yoo, who left the Justice Department two years ago and is now a law professor at Boalt Hall at the University of California at Berkeley, was the writer of the documents. But he was not the author of the process. Nor was Gonzales, who was then the White House legal counsel. Then, as now, the driving force was Vice President Cheney.

Cheney's point man was David Addington, then his legal counsel and longtime aide (dating back to his time in Congress). Addington was the chief writer of a memo on torture policy that argued for unfettered presidential power. "In light of the president's complete authority over the conduct of war, without a clear statement otherwise, criminal statutes are not read as infringing on the president's ultimate authority in these areas," the memo stated. Prohibitions "must be construed as inapplicable to interrogations undertaken pursuant to his commander in chief authority." And Congress was relegated to the sidelines: "Congress may no more regulate the president's ability to detain and interrogate enemy combatants than it may regulate his ability to direct troop movements on the battlefield." Addington is now Cheney's chief of staff, having replaced Scooter Libby.

Aboard Air Force Two, on a trip back from Iraq, the prime mover granted an interview to the traveling press. "I believe in a strong, robust executive authority, and I think that the world we live in demands it," said Cheney. He explained that he has been anxious about "infringement on the authority of the presidency" since the Nixon White House, where he served as deputy to counselor Donald Rumsfeld. "Watergate and a lot of the things around Watergate and Vietnam, both during the '70s, served, I think, to erode the authority I think the president needs to be effective, especially in the national security area," he said.

But Cheney was even more revealing in an interview on CNN on Tuesday, responding to a question from the reporter Dana Bash, who sought to give the vice president every benefit of the doubt and an avenue of escape. "You talked about the fact that you briefed Congress voluntarily, that you do have a review process," said Bash. "But let's just say, in ten years or a few years, a president is elected who doesn't want to do those things, but you've given him this kind of power. What happens then?"

"Well," Cheney replied, "it will be up to him whether or not he uses it."

Cheney's idea of the head of state invested with absolute power is a venerable one. Bush's presidency is the latest experiment to achieve it.

Yoo's memos are the founding documents. But the idea lacks an American pedigree.

The original commentary on it appeared in a pamphlet published in 1776, *Common Sense,* written by Tom Paine:

> But where says some is the King of America? I'll tell you Friend, he
> reigns above, and doth not make havoc of mankind like the Royal Brute
> of Britain. Yet that we may not appear to be defective even in earthly
> honors, let a day be solemnly set apart for proclaiming the charter; let
> it be brought forth placed on the divine law, the word of God; let a crown
> be placed thereon, by which the world may know, that so far as we ap-
> prove as monarchy, that in America THE LAW IS KING. For as in absolute
> governments the King is law, so in free countries the law *ought* to be King;
> and there ought to be no other. But lest any ill use should afterwards arise,
> let the crown at the conclusion of the ceremony be demolished, and scat-
> tered among the people whose right it is.

Annus Horribilis

DECEMBER 29, 2005

IN HIS SECOND INAUGURAL ADDRESS, George W. Bush four times summoned the image of fire: "a day of fire," "we have lit a fire," "fire in the minds of men," and "untamed fire." In the first year of his second term, all four of the ancient Greek elements have wreaked havoc: the fire of war, and the "fire in the minds of men" of culture war; the air and water of Hurricane Katrina; and whirlwinds raging across the earth from Iraq to Florida, from Louisiana to Washington. Through obsession or obliviousness, rigidity or laziness, Bush has been singed, tossed about, engulfed, and nearly buried.

He began the year proclaiming "a turning point" in Iraq. In every crisis he faced, he assumed that everything would turn his way, as it always had in the past. He ended the year declaring "victory" within reach.

The first shift in his political fortunes came with his unprecedented intervention in the case of Terri Schiavo, a woman who had lain in a persistent vegetative state for fifteen years, and whose husband's effort to remove her feeding tube was upheld after fourteen appeals in Florida courts, five federal lawsuits, and four refusals by the U.S. Supreme Court to hear the case.

Bush had won the presidency in 2004 with an extraordinary outpouring of support from the religious right. So he rushed from his Texas ranch back to the White House in March to sign the bill transferring the Schiavo case from the state to the federal courts. Throughout the month, the Republicans strutted and the Democrats cowered. Then, on March 21, the spell that had carried over from the election campaign was suddenly broken in a single stroke. The deus ex machina that descended onto this fervent scene was an awakening public. An ABC News poll found that 63 to 28 percent backed the removal of Schiavo's feeding tube, and 67 to 19 percent believed that politicians urging that she be kept alive were demagogic and unprincipled.

By now, Bush's plan to privatize Social Security was for all intents and purposes moribund. He languished over his long summer vacation besieged by the mother of a U.S. soldier killed in Iraq, Cindy Sheehan. She camped out beside the road leading to the president's ranch, asking him to explain the "noble cause" for which her son had given his life. Bush refused to grant her an audience, his motorcade racing past her to a lunch with big party contributors.

After Hurricane Katrina hit New Orleans on August 29, Bush's aides held a fraught debate about which one of them would have to tell the president he should cut short his vacation. Four days after the hurricane landed, Bush left his ranch and, on Air Force One, watched a custom DVD of television news coverage assembled by his staff. He had not bothered to watch any of it on his own.

He praised his feckless chief of the Federal Emergency Management Agency, Michael Brown—"Brownie, you're doing a heck of a job"—and then nominated his former personal attorney and current White House legal counsel, Harriet Miers, for the Supreme Court. Though friends offered testimony of her evangelical religiosity, conservatives did not trust her because she had once made gestures supportive of women's and civil rights, and Bush pushed her to withdraw.

Bush hoped to erase the year's infamies with the election in Iraq on December 15, his ultimate turning point. He delivered five major speeches crafted by his new adviser on the National Security Council, Peter Feaver, a Duke University political scientist and coauthor of *Choosing Your Battles*, based on his public-opinion research showing that "the public is defeat phobic, not casualty phobic." In one speech, Bush mentioned "victory" fifteen times, against a background embossed with the slogan "Plan for Victory," and the White House issued a document titled *National Strategy for Victory in Iraq*.

On December 14, the president invited bipartisan groups of senators and representatives to White House briefings on the progress in Iraq that would follow the election. Among those assembled in the Roosevelt Room were the president, Vice President Dick Cheney, Secretary of State Condoleezza Rice, Secretary of Defense Donald Rumsfeld, National Security Adviser Stephen Hadley—and Peter Feaver, the polling expert. At the meeting with senators after the presentation, Bush called first on Senator John McCain, the Republican maverick, who gave an enthusiastic statement of support. A few more spoke. "Great, gotta go," said Bush. Afterwards, Feaver buttonholed senators to survey their opinions on the new approach.

Since the election of the Shiite slate that will hold power for four years, dedicated to an Islamic state allied with Iran, the president and his advisers have fallen eerily silent. As his annus horribilis draws to a close, Bush appears to have expended the turning points. Welcome to victory.

Bush's War on Professionals

JANUARY 6, 2006

NEW HORIZONS of secret government are emerging from the fog of war. The latest disclosure, by the *New York Times*, of domestic surveillance by the National Security Agency performed by evasion of the special Foreign Intelligence Surveillance Act (FISA) court, exposes a vast, hidden realm. But the NSA spying is not an isolated island of policy; it is connected to the mainland of Bush's expansive new national security apparatus.

At the beginning of the Cold War, the National Security Act of 1947 authorized the creation of new institutions of foreign policy and intelligence, including the National Security Council and the Central Intelligence Agency. But Bush has built a secret system, without enabling legislation, justified by executive fiat and presidential findings alone, deliberately operating beyond the oversight of Congress and the courts, and existing outside the law. It is a national security state of torture, ghost detainees, secret prisons, renditions, and domestic eavesdropping.

The arguments used to rationalize this system insist that the president as commander in chief is entitled to arbitrary and unaccountable rule. The memos written by John Yoo, a former deputy in the Justice Department's Office of Legal Counsel, constitute a basic ideology of absolute power.

Congress is regarded at best as a pest and at worst as an intruder on the president's rightful authority. The Republican chairs of the House Armed Services and Senate Intelligence committees, Representative Duncan Hunter of California and Senator Pat Roberts of Kansas, have been models of complicity in fending off oversight, attacking other members of Congress (especially Republicans) who have had the temerity to insist on it, using their committees to help the White House suppress essential information about the operations of government, and issuing tilted, partisan reports smearing critics. This is the sort of legislative involvement that the White House believes fulfills the congressional mandate.

During his first term, President Bush issued an unprecedented 108 statements on signing bills of legislation that expressed his own version of their content. He has countermanded the legislative history, which legally establishes the foundation of their meaning, by executive diktat. In particular, he has rejected parts of legislation that he saw as stepping on his power in national security matters. In effect, Bush engages in presidential nullification of any law he sees fit. He then acts as if his gesture supersedes the actions of Congress.

The political scientist Phillip Cooper, of Portland State University in Oregon, described this innovative grasp of power in a recent article in the *Presidential Studies Quarterly*. Bush, he wrote, "has very effectively expanded the scope and character of the signing statement not only to address specific provisions of legislation that the White House wishes to nullify, but also in an effort to significantly reposition and strengthen the powers of the presidency relative to the Congress." Moreover, these coups de main not only have overwhelmed the other institutions of government but have taken place almost without notice. "This tour de force has been carried out in such a systematic and careful fashion that few in Congress, the media, or the scholarly community are aware that anything has happened at all."

Not coincidentally, the legal author of this presidential strategy for accreting power was none other than the young Samuel Alito, in 1986 deputy assistant attorney general in the Justice Department's Office of Legal Counsel. Alito's view on unfettered executive power, many close observers believe, was decisive in Bush's nomination of him to the Supreme Court.

Last week, when Bush signed the military appropriations bill containing the amendment forbidding torture that he and Vice President Cheney had fought against, he added his own "signing statement" to it. It amounted to a waiver, authorized by Bush alone, that he could and would disobey this law whenever he chose. He wrote: "The executive branch shall construe Title X in Division A of the Act, relating to detainees, in a manner consistent with the constitutional authority of the President to supervise the unitary executive branch and as Commander in Chief and consistent with the constitutional limitations on the judicial power, which will assist in achieving the shared objective of the Congress and the President, evidenced in Title X, of protecting the American people from further terrorist attacks." In short, the president, in the name of national security, claiming to protect the country from terrorism, under war powers granted to him by himself, would follow the law to the extent that he decided he would.

Senator John McCain, the sponsor of the antitorture legislation, according to sources close to him, says that he has not determined how or when he might respond to Bush's "signing statement." McCain wishes to raise other issues, like ghost detainees, and he may wait to see how the administration responds to the new law. However, with responsibility for oversight moved from the Armed Services Committee to the Senate Intelligence Committee, chaired by the White House tool Pat Roberts, McCain and others have no reliable way of knowing whether the administration is complying. Once again, torture policy enters a shadow land.

Bush has responded to the latest exposures of the existence of his new national security apparatus as assaults on the government. It is these revelations, he said, that are "shameful." The passion he currently exhibits was something he was unable to muster for the exposure by members of his administration of the identity of CIA operative Valerie Plame. But there is a consistency between his indifference to discovering who was behind the outing of Plame and his furor over the reporting of warrantless NSA domestic spying. In the Plame case, the administration officials who spun her name to the conservative columnist Robert Novak and others intended to punish and intimidate the former ambassador Joseph Wilson for having revealed that a central element of the administration case for the Iraq war was bogus. In the NSA case, Bush is also attempting to crush whistle-blowers.

Bush's war on professionals has been fought in nearly every department and agency of the government, from intelligence to Interior, from the Justice Department to the Drug Enforcement Administration, in order to suppress contrary analysis on issues from weapons of mass destruction to global warming, from voting rights to the morning-after pill. Without whistle-blowers on the inside, there will be no press reports on the outside. The story of Watergate, after all, is not of journalists operating in a vacuum but is utterly dependent on sources internal to the Nixon administration. Deep Throat—Mark Felt, the deputy FBI director—whatever his motives, was a quintessential whistle-blower.

Now Bush's Justice Department has launched a "leak" probe, complete with prosecutors and grand jury, to investigate the disclosure of the NSA story. It is similarly investigating the *Washington Post*'s reportage of the administration's secret prison system for terrorist suspects. The intent is to send a signal to the reporters on this beat that they may be called before grand juries and forced to reveal their sources. (The disastrous legal strategy of the *New York Times* in defending Judy Miller as a Joan of Arc in the Plame case has crucially helped reinforce the precedent.) Within the bowels of government, potential whistle-blowers are being put on notice that they place their careers at risk for speaking to reporters in order to inform the public of what they consider wrongdoing.

State of War: The Secret History of the CIA and the Bush Administration, by James Risen, the *New York Times* reporter who broke the NSA story, offers new evidence of Bush's war on professionals in the intelligence community.

Risen writes that the administration created a secret, parallel chain of command to authorize the NSA surveillance program. While the professionals within the Justice Department were cut out, a "small, select group of like-minded conservative lawyers," such as John Yoo, were brought in to invent legal justifications. To the "small handful on national security law within the government" knowledgeable about the NSA program, the administration's debating points on the PATRIOT Act, which stipulates approval of eavesdropping by the FISA court, was a charade, a "mockery." Risen presents more witnesses and adds some episodes to familiar material —the twisting of intelligence and intimidation of professionals both before and after the Iraq war; a national security team commanded by Vice President Cheney in league with Secretary of Defense Rumsfeld; and neoconservatives contriving "stovepipe" intelligence operations to funnel disinformation from Ahmad Chalabi and other Iraqi exiles who were their political favorites.

Risen quotes a former top CIA official on Condoleezza Rice: a "very, very weak national security adviser. . . . I think Rice didn't really manage anything, and will go down as probably the worst national security adviser in history. I think the real national security adviser was Cheney, and so Cheney and Rumsfeld could do what they wanted."

Then director of the CIA, George Tenet, appears as an incorrigible courtier, trying to ingratiate himself with anecdotes of derring-do from the clandestine services. Rumsfeld, seeking to concentrate intelligence within the Pentagon, which controls 80 percent of the overall intelligence budget, was not amused. When Tenet told his entertaining James Bond stories, Rumsfeld asked him why they were relevant, and in one meeting made a point of humiliating Tenet by upbraiding him for using the F-word in the presence of a female official. A former CIA official who worked closely with Tenet is quoted: "George Tenet liked to talk about how he was a tough Greek from Queens, but in reality, he was a pussy. He just wanted people to like him."

While Rumsfeld was trampling Tenet, Deputy Secretary of Defense Paul Wolfowitz and Deputy Undersecretary Douglas Feith, the Laurel and

Hardy of neoconservatism, set up the Counter-Terrorism Evaluation Group "to sift through raw intelligence reports, searching for ties between Iraq and al Qaeda." CIA analysts were under unrelenting pressure to accept Chalabi's disinformation at face value. "They sent us that message a thousand times, in a thousand different ways," said one former senior CIA official. Tenet did nothing to halt the stream of pollution.

Risen reports that in April 2002, in a secret meeting in Rome, CIA case officers in Europe were told by the CIA's newly fortified Iraq Operations Group they had to get on the bandwagon for an Iraq war. "They said this was on Bush's agenda when he got elected, and that 9/11 only delayed it," one CIA officer who attended the conference is quoted as saying. "They implied that 9/11 was a distraction from Iraq."

Cheney not only intervened personally in attempting to force CIA analysts to rubber-stamp Chalabi's disinformation, Risen writes, but also directly interfered in CIA field operations. When the Netherlands declined to permit the CIA to attempt to recruit an Iraqi official there as an intelligence asset, Cheney called the prime minister of Netherlands to demand his approval, but was rebuffed.

Startlingly, Risen reports that on the eve of war, the CIA knew the United States had no proof of weapons of mass destruction, which were its casus belli, the justification for preemptive attack. The agency had recruited an Arab-American woman living in Cleveland, Dr. Sawsan Alhaddad, to travel to Baghdad to spy on her brother, Saad Tawfiq, an electrical engineer supposedly at the center of Saddam Hussein's nuclear weapons program. Once there, she won his trust, and he confided there was no program. He urged her to carry the message back to the CIA. On her return, she was debriefed, and the CIA filed the report in a black hole. It turned out that she was one of some thirty Iraqis who had been recruited to travel to Iraq to contact weapons experts there. Risen writes: "All of them . . . had said the same thing. They all reported to the CIA that the scientists had said that Iraq's programs to develop nuclear, chemical, and biological weapons had long since been abandoned."

Not willing to contradict the administration line, CIA officials withheld this information from the national intelligence estimate issued a month after Alhaddad's visit to Baghdad. The NIE stated conclusively that Iraq "is reconstituting its nuclear program." Risen writes: "From his home in Baghdad in February 2003, Saad Tawfiq watched Secretary of State Colin Powell's televised presentation to the United Nations about Iraq's weapons of mass destruction. As Powell dramatically built the American case for war, Saad sank further and further into frustration and despair. *They didn't listen. I told them there were no weapons.*"

When the CIA deputy director, John McLaughlin, raised questions about the fabled aluminum tubes that were supposedly a critical element of Saddam's nuclear program, Tenet waved McLaughlin's doubt aside. Skepticism was banished. When David Kay, chief of the Iraq Survey Group, discovered there were no WMD, he met with the ever-faithful Tenet, who told him: "I don't care what you say. You will never convince me they didn't have chemical weapons."

After the war, efforts within the CIA to dispel illusion and acknowledge reality in Iraq met with punishment. In November 2003, the CIA station chief in Baghdad submitted what is internally called an "aardwolf," a formal report on country conditions. "It pulled no punches in detailing how the new insurgency was gaining strength from the political and economic vacuum that the United States had allowed to develop in Baghdad," writes Risen. For his honesty, the station chief was subjected to "inflammatory accusations about his personal behavior, all of which he flatly denied," and he "quit the CIA in disgust." The destruction of his career led other CIA officers to hedge their reports, especially on Chalabi. The new station chief, in an aardwolf in late 2004, described the lethal conditions on the ground, and as a reward "his political allegiances were quickly questioned by the White House." Reality remained unwelcome.

Risen's book is one of a small and growing library that contains the strangled, usually anonymous cries of professionals. No doubt there will be other volumes to fill in more gaps and reveal yet new stories of the mangling of policy in the interest of ideology.

By attacking whistle-blowers and the press, Bush is rushing to protect the edifice he has created. He acts as if the exposure of one part threatens the whole. His frantic defense suggests that very little of it can bear scrutiny.

Meek, Mild, and Menacing

JANUARY 6, 2006

"IF THE PRESIDENT deems that he's got to torture somebody, including by crushing the testicles of the person's child, there is no law that can stop him?"

"No treaty," replied John Yoo, the former Justice Department official who wrote the crucial memos justifying President Bush's policies on torture, "war on terror" detainees, and domestic surveillance without warrants. Yoo made these assertions at a public debate in December in Chicago, where he also espoused the radical notion of the "unitary executive" —the idea that the president as commander in chief is the sole judge of the law, unbound by hindrances such as the Geneva Conventions, and possesses inherent authority to subordinate independent government agencies to his fiat. This concept is the cornerstone of the Bush legal doctrine.

Yoo's interlocutor, Douglass Cassel, a professor at Notre Dame Law School, pointed out that the theory of the "unitary executive" posits the president above the other branches of government: "Also no law by Congress. That is what you wrote in the August 2002 memo" (one of Yoo's memos justifying torture). "I think it depends on why the president thinks he needs to do that," said Yoo.

Unquestionably, Judge Samuel Alito's self-professed "strong" belief in executive power was one of his greatest credentials for Bush's nomination of him to the Supreme Court. The "unitary executive" is nothing less than "gospel," declared Alito in 2000, a theory that "best captures the meaning of the Constitution's text and structure."

In his manner before the Senate Judiciary Committee confirmation hearings this week, Alito has been punctilious, prosaic, and dutiful in repeating the talking points his political handlers have drilled him in. He seems like an understudy for the part of Willy Loman. But behind the façade of the supplicant, who wants to be liked, well liked, seethes a man out to settle a score.

331

Few public figures since Richard Nixon have worn their social resentment so obviously as Samuel Alito does. In his opening statement, trying to paint his self-portrait as a self-made man, the bland Alito made a brush stroke of hostility. The son of a middle-class civil servant in New Jersey, he attended Princeton and Yale Law School, which set him on a glide path to success. "Both college and law school opened up new worlds of ideas," he testified. "But this was back in the late 1960s and early 1970s. It was a time of turmoil at colleges and universities. And I saw some very smart people and very privileged people behaving irresponsibly." Despite all the "turmoil" around him, by all accounts Alito spent his university years undisturbed; there was no transforming incident in which he was rebuffed or insulted.

Alito further explained himself in his job application to the Reagan Justice Department. His interest in constitutional law, he wrote, was "motivated in large part by disagreement with Warren Court decisions," "particularly" in the area of "reapportionment." In fact, the Warren Court decisions in that area established the principle of "one person, one vote." Alito's career in the law has been a long effort to reverse the liberalism of the Warren Court.

When Alito served in the Justice Department, he argued that the federal government had no responsibility for the "health, safety and welfare" of the American people (a view rejected by President Reagan); that "the Constitution does not protect the right to an abortion"; that the executive branch should be immune from liability for illegal domestic wiretapping; that illegal immigrants have no "fundamental rights"; and that police had a right to kill an unarmed fifteen-year-old boy accused of stealing $10, a view rejected by the Supreme Court and every police group that filed briefs in the case. He also wrote a memo arguing that it would be legal for employers to fire staff and for the federal government to exclude from any of its funded programs people afflicted with AIDS because of "fear of contagion, whether reasonable or not."

As a judge, he has ruled consistently for employers against individual and civil rights, and for unbridled executive and police power. Against the majority of his court and six other federal courts, he argued that regulation of machine guns by the federal government was unconstitutional. He approved the strip search of a mother and her ten-year-old daughter although they were not named in a warrant, a decision denounced at the time by the federal judge Michael Chertoff, now secretary of homeland security, as a "cliché rubber stamp." Alito ruled in favor of a law requiring women to notify their husbands if they plan to have an abortion; that decision was overturned by the Supreme Court on the vote of Justice Sandra Day O'Connor, who stated, "A State may not give to a man the kind of dominion over his wife that parents exercise over their children."

Alito's decisions and dissents predictably flow from his politics. On the Supreme Court, as O'Connor's replacement, he will codify the authoritarianism of the Bush presidency even after it is gone.

The Republican System

HARDLY ANYONE in the Republican Party, in Congress, or at the White House seems to recall ever having met Jack Abramoff. Collective amnesia has suddenly descended on the capital. The super-lobbyist, whose plea bargain with prosecutors requires the extensive naming of names of members of Congress, staffers, ex-staffers, lobbyists, friends, colleagues and his own personal assistants, is spending his days racking his memory for details of their relationships that may become the basis for bills of indictment.

Abramoff, who pleaded guilty to fraud, tax evasion, and conspiracy to bribe public officials, has left a trail of hard evidence in addition to his sworn confessions. At the end of every business day, his assistant wrote a summary of all his contacts and their conversations, e-mailed it to him, and carefully saved it; these documents, mapping the days and ways of Jack Abramoff, are now in the hands of the prosecutors. (The assistant, Susan Ralston, moved seamlessly from his employ to the White House to become Karl Rove's assistant, where she regularly vetted supplicants to Rove through Grover Norquist, Abramoff's longtime political associate and business partner.)

Abramoff's appearance at the federal courthouse in Washington on January 3, attired in black fedora and black trench coat like an old-style "Mustache Pete" Mafioso, was bizarre but brilliant self-casting. He was not only his own producer but also his own dresser. In fact, Abramoff loved to recite lines from *The Godfather*. One of his favorite bits was Michael Corleone's reply to a politician seeking a cut of his illegal businesses: "Senator, you can have my answer now if you like. My offer is this: nothing."

Abramoff's theatricality is intertwined with his politics. The graduate of Beverly Hills High School is the son of the president of the franchises division of the Diners Club and close to Ronald Reagan's kitchen cabinet of California millionaires. The father financed young Jack's takeover of the College Republicans. After depleting the treasury of Citizens for America,

334

a conservative group founded by the drugstore mogul Lewis Lehrman, Abramoff produced a violence-packed, B-grade Cold War movie, *Red Scorpion*. With the capture of Congress by the Republicans in 1994, he hustled to Washington for the barbecue.

For more than a decade, Abramoff ran wild. From the offices of two major law firms, Preston Gates & Ellis and Greenberg Traurig, he traded in politicians and clients with abandon. To become wealthy and influential, he used false charities and phony think tanks, doled out all-expenses-paid trips, and opened his own Capitol Hill steakhouse, called Signatures, where he picked up congressmen's tabs. He moved effortlessly from being a "friend of Newt," the former Republican speaker of the House, Newt Gingrich, to being a "friend of Tom," the former Republican House majority leader, Tom DeLay. His associates from his College Republican days, Grover Norquist and Ralph Reed, were his musketeers. Reed, former president of the Rev. Pat Robertson's Christian Coalition, became Abramoff's instrument for buying and manipulating leaders of the religious right, one stratagem in his elaborate schemes to bilk Indian tribes that had hired him to help them win approval of their casinos. These were just a few of the Abramoff ploys now being untangled by prosecutors.

In his brazenness, extravagance, and heedlessness, Abramoff was one of a kind. Almost all lobbyists earning the kind of money he raked in follow the Washington rule of melting into the scenery. But Abramoff is not simply unique; he is also symptomatic. Abramoff's crimes are not illustrations of Washington generically gone haywire. He was not an accident waiting to happen. Nor was he just the latest in a dime-a-dozen scandals. Nor does he represent the vice of both parties. Above all, he is not a lobbyist who "bought Washington."

Abramoff has been an integral part of the Republican political machine that has flourished since the 1994 takeover. He has created vast slush funds at the disposal of DeLay (for example, the U.S. Family Network, a nonprofit front group financed by Russian oil tycoons), worked hand in glove with DeLay's political operatives, and supported the Republican congressional leadership with funds and favors. Abramoff's lobbying and politics are inextricable, one and the same, allowing him to simultaneously serve as a valuable member of the Republican machine and be out for himself. He was not the most significant player; nor were his tens of millions more money than bigger figures made. (Haley Barbour, formerly the chair of the Republican National Committee and a senior partner of a major Washington law firm, currently governor of Mississippi, comes to mind.) But

Abramoff, more than those with more influence or wealth, has the distinction of epitomizing the recent history of the Republican Congress.

The Abramoff affair is the greatest congressional scandal in American history since the Crédit Mobilier. In 1873, a congressional investigation revealed that the holding company of the Union Pacific Railroad had dispensed stock to thirty-some members of Congress; two were censured, none indicted. Undoubtedly, the punishments arising from the Abramoff affair will be more extensive than those from the Crédit Mobilier.

The latest Republican talking point on Abramoff is "I can't recall." DeLay had previously called him a "close personal friend." But an article last month in the *Washington Post* strangely reported: "The two met at a DeLay fundraiser on Capitol Hill in 1995, according to a former senior DeLay aide. The aide recalled that Edwin A. Buckham, then DeLay's chief of staff, told his boss: 'We really need to work with Abramoff; he is going to be an important lobbyist and fundraiser.' DeLay, a Christian conservative, did not quite know what to make of Abramoff, who wore a beard and a yarmulke. They forged political ties, but the two men never became personally close, according to associates of both men." The anti-Semitic undercurrent of DeLay's revisionism in his belated effort to distance himself is a piquant touch.

On Tuesday, in his first press conference of the new year, at his Capitol Hill office, Speaker Dennis Hastert described Abramoff as completely unfamiliar: "Well, you know, a year ago most people around Congress couldn't tell you who Jack Abramoff was and didn't know who his associates were or what connections there are." Meanwhile, that same day, at the briefing conducted by the White House, the press secretary, Scott McClellan, gave murky explanations of Abramoff's dealings at the Bush White House. Abramoff had been one of Bush's top fund-raisers (designated a "Pioneer" for raising more than $100,000 for the reelection campaign) and a member of the transition team for the Department of the Interior, and he had billed two tribal chiefs $25,000 for a White House lunch and meeting with President Bush. McClellan conceded that Abramoff had been invited to a couple of Chanukah parties. At his January 5 press briefing, when asked about Abramoff's participation in staff meetings, McClellan had said, "I'm making sure that I have a thorough report back to you on that. And I'll get that to you, hopefully very soon." Asked again by a reporter, "Who was in the staff meetings?" McClellan replied, "I don't get into discussing staff-level meetings." Thus Abramoff's history and that of the Republicans are being distorted, airbrushed, or stonewalled.

In 1994, the law firm of Preston Gates & Ellis sent out a press release hailing its new partner, Jack Abramoff, who "developed and maintains strong ties to Speaker Newt Gingrich." The *National Journal* reported: "The GOP victories in 1994 transformed [Abramoff] into a valuable asset as law firms recruited activists with connections to the new Gingrich team."

Gingrich, representing a congressional district of suburban white flight from Atlanta, touted himself as a cosmic thinker and Napoleonic military strategist. On a large easel, in one of his lectures, he described himself as "Teacher of the Rules of Civilization." Born Newt McPherson, Gingrich was the stepson of an abusive Army officer. He married one of his high-school teachers and later handed her divorce papers in her hospital room while she was recovering from cancer surgery. He left his position teaching at West Georgia College to enter politics. A secret 1960s wannabe, he identified the enemy as "the Great Society countercultural model" and the goal as a "conservative opportunity society" (the name of a group he founded).

The House Republican whip, Dick Cheney, quietly sponsored Gingrich's rise. Gingrich's method was to accuse congressional Democrats of scandal and manipulate the press into covering it. "I think one of the great problems we have in the Republican Party is that we don't encourage you to be nasty," he said. And he boasted, "We are engaged in reshaping the whole nation through the news media."

After Gingrich whipped up a commotion against the Democratic House speaker, Jim Wright, forcing his resignation over a union's bulk buying of copies of his memoir, Gingrich's staff was caught smearing the new speaker, the gentlemanly Tom Foley, as a closet gay, which he was not. Then Gingrich fostered a furor over the House members' bank, a kind of credit union from which they had always drawn loans against their paychecks. It was, as political scientist Nelson Polsby wrote in his book *How Congress Evolves*, "a comic-opera fiasco that the news media, skillfully abetted by a group of enthusiastic Republican members, pumped up into a Wagnerian Götterdämmerung." Several of Gingrich's Republicans were caught up in this pseudo-scandal and quit Congress, but he was willing to step over their bodies.

After the Republican sweep in 1994, Gingrich held a mad celebration featuring people dressed as the cartoon Power Rangers and Rush Limbaugh. One new Republican member, Sonny Bono, who had fallen from grace as a celebrity, warned Gingrich to guard against hubris.

The failed professor, now speaker, sent his aides and followers for training to U.S. Army training and doctrine centers at Fort Leavenworth,

Kansas, and Fort Monroe, Virginia., and called himself "CEO" of the House for which he was speaker. He suffered from extreme mood swings, bouncing from grandiose schemes to uncontrollable sobbing. He instructed his aides, "You guys have to tell reporters, if they're going to cover the Republicans now, they need a romantic view of history."

Almost at once, he took a $4.5 million book advance from Rupert Murdoch's publishing house, HarperCollins, and just as quickly in the resulting controversy was forced to give it back. For Murdoch, the ridiculously exorbitant advance was chump change, considering his stake in telecommunications legislation.

DeLay, a former exterminator from Sugar Land, Texas, who referred to the Environmental Protection Agency as the "Gestapo," was the new House Republican whip. What became the K Street Project, melding Republicans and lobbyists, was launched immediately, in January 1995. Initially, DeLay called it Project Relief. He gathered 350 industry lobbyists to work closely with his staff to write legislation to halt regulation. "They have the expertise," DeLay explained about the lobbyists who were recruited to draft bills he proposed. Even before the Republicans had won control in 1994, DeLay met for lunch with thirty or forty corporate lobbyists every Tuesday in the boardroom of the Independent Insurance Agents of America. These lobbyists financed his race for Republican whip, and even before the brand-new Congress met to vote on its leadership, DeLay had wrapped up his position. Among the Republican leaders, he was the only one with his own independent power base. And Project Relief made its power felt at once. Within a month after the new Republican Congress was sworn in, it voted for a hundred-day moratorium on all federal regulation of industry.

DeLay compiled a book that listed every industry political action committee, more than four hundred in all, as either "friendly" or "unfriendly," depending on their contributions. "See, you're in the book," he said to one lobbyist as he showed him his PAC listing. DeLay kept the book on a coffee table in his office. On the wall hung a bullwhip. He was the enforcer of Gingrich's rule: "If you want to play in our revolution, you have to live by our rules." In 1995, DeLay met privately with more than four hundred of the Fortune 500 companies, explaining why it was in their interest to abide by "our rules." By then, the Republicans had raised twice as much campaign money as the Democrats. The tobacco companies topped the big givers.

Project Relief morphed into the K Street Project. "We don't like to deal with people who are trying to kill the revolution," DeLay said. Law firms, trade associations, and industries that hired Democrats were ostracized. "You need to hire a Republican," DeLay told these Washington outfits. And the business groups also had to kick in campaign money, lots of it. DeLay personally sent letters to PACs telling them exactly how much money to contribute and to which Republican candidates and committees. The K Street Project merged corporate interests with the Republican Party; it served as an employment agency for activists and staffers, who were turned into lobbyists; and it converted lobbyists into writers of legislation, and the service sector of Washington into a bank for the party.

In November 1995, Gingrich demanded that President Clinton agree to massive cuts in Medicare and huge tax cuts for the wealthy. When Clinton refused, he shut down the federal government, for the first time in U.S. history. Medicare, he was quoted as saying, should "wither on the vine." Then, after reopening the government and conducting negotiations with Clinton, Gingrich forced another shutdown. "I don't care what the price is," he said. But the consequence was his discrediting. Most of the Contract with America, the manifesto the Republicans ran on in 1994, was never enacted.

In 1996, the House Ethics Committee found that Gingrich had made false statements to it in the course of an investigation, fined him $300,000, and issued an official reprimand. It was the most severe penalty ever levied against a speaker. Gingrich's scandal involved crossing the wires of his intellectual vanity with his special interests. And it was related to the government shutdown he had insisted on.

Gingrich used tax deductions to finance political operations run through his political action committee, GOPAC, and think tank, the Progress and Freedom Foundation. One of these operations was a lecture series he taped, titled "Renewing American Civilization." Among GOPAC's biggest donors was J. Patrick Rooney, chair of the Golden Rule Insurance Co. (Rooney's daughter served as GOPAC's deputy finance director.) Golden Rule sought the privatization of Medicare and its replacement by "medical savings accounts." In his "college course," Gingrich even included a promotional film for MSAs produced by Golden Rule.

In 1997, the other Republican leaders attempted a coup to replace Gingrich. DeLay gave his assent to the plot but stayed in the background. But the putsch failed, and Gingrich demanded that its leader, the rising star Representative Bill Paxon of New York, resign from the House. Days later, a bright young journalist, Sandy Hume, of the *Hill* newspaper, who had used Paxon as his source to disclose details of the coup, committed suicide. Hume, it was said, was despondent over having been arrested for drunken driving.

Gingrich, at a low ebb, grasped onto the impeachment of President Clinton as his lifeline. He pressed it as the number one issue in the 1998 midterm elections, but the Republicans lost five seats in the House. The public was simply opposed to an impeachment. Within two days, Gingrich resigned as speaker. The Republican leadership, especially DeLay, did not believe Gingrich was tough enough to push forward against Clinton. "I melt when I'm around him," Gingrich confessed to his second wife about Clinton. For more than a year Republicans sent a bodyguard, the hard-liner Richard Armey, to accompany Gingrich on all trips to the White House, fearing that Gingrich would compromise. Some of the Republicans also were privy to the information that Gingrich was personally vulnerable: his mistress was on the House payroll. And a few months after he quit as speaker, Gingrich told his second wife in a telephone call that he was leaving her.

Representative Robert Livingston of Louisiana became acting speaker, but not for long. On the day of the impeachment vote, December 19, 1998, he resigned when the pornographer Larry Flynt threatened to release sex tapes of his extramarital affairs. Livingston was a capable deal maker, but he was gone before he arrived.

The new speaker, Dennis Hastert, a former high school wrestling coach from Illinois, was DeLay's sock puppet. DeLay had coerced votes for impeachment, threatening hesitant moderates with far-right primary opponents, and the episode left his power among House Republicans unimpaired. If anything, it augmented his ability to intimidate members.

Governor George W. Bush of Texas positioned himself in his presidential campaign as a voice of reason and moderation, unblemished by the Republican Congress. He picked a strategic fight with DeLay over the earned-income tax credit for the working poor in order to assert his credentials as a "compassionate conservative." It was clear who was not compassionate.

Once Bush was elected, the Republican Congress, especially the House, became his essential prop. In today's House, there is no actual legislative process. The work week is typically only two days, as in a small state legislature. The Rules Committee forbids members from altering bills on the floor. Votes are blocked on bills that have bipartisan support, such as an extension of unemployment benefits that is opposed by a majority of the Republicans. Bills are crafted in the dead of night, behind closed doors, by a select group of Republican leaders, often without floor debate. The *Boston Globe,* in a 2004 series on the influence of lobbyists, reported that "on the Medicare and energy bills, businesses and other groups who reported lobbying on the two measures spent a staggering $799,091,391 in efforts to influence lawmakers, frequently employing former members of Congress, former staff members, and relatives of lawmakers to lobby on the bills." In addition, the *Globe* reported, the Republican Congress added "3,407 'pork barrel' projects to appropriations bills for this year's federal budget, items that were never debated or voted on beforehand by the House and Senate and whose congressional patrons are kept secret."

When it appeared that a Medicare bill would be defeated on the floor, Hastert kept debate open for three hours beyond its stipulated limit. DeLay twisted the arm of Representative Nick Smith of Michigan, promising him $100,000 in campaign contributions for his son, who was running for Congress, if he switched his vote. Smith confessed to the allegation of bribery and then withdrew the confession. Nonetheless, the Ethics Committee, which DeLay has attempted to shut down, delivered a "public admonishment" to DeLay.

This month, DeLay resigned his post as majority leader under the strain of his criminal trial in Texas and the Abramoff revelations. In Texas, DeLay has been indicted for illegally siphoning corporate funds into state political campaigns. By using his political action committee, Texans for a Republican Majority, as a conduit, he financed races in the Texas Legislature; then the Legislature, at his prompting, redrew congressional districts, removing Democrats from their seats and padding the Republican majority in the House. Last month, the *Washington Post* disclosed that Justice Department lawyers had found that DeLay's scheme violated the Voting Rights Act, disenfranchising black and Hispanic voters, but Bush administration officials overruled them.

In the battle to succeed DeLay, DeLayism will triumph. The leading candidate for majority leader, Representative Roy Blunt of Missouri, is so close to lobbyists that he left his wife to marry the lobbyist for Altria, the company that owns Philip Morris. In 2002, he inserted a provision into a homeland security bill to increase the penalties for selling stolen cigarettes. Blunt's son happens to be a lobbyist; his other son is the Republican governor of Missouri. He stands for nothing but business as usual. His challenger, Representative John Boehner of Ohio, runs a group called the K Street Cabinet. In 1995, on the floor of the House, Boehner handed out checks from tobacco lobbyists to Republican members, an act he says he regrets.

The House Republicans this week relaunched themselves as champions of reform, presenting a program to clean up the stain left by Abramoff and DeLay. Their proposal, however, would not prevent members from accepting meals and travel from lobbyists so long as they were linked to campaign fundraising. But such a program cannot deflect attention from the spectacle about to unfold.

The Abramoff affair is only at its start, and numerous members of the Congress and prominent Republican lobbyists and operatives may well and soon be ensnared. Behind closed doors, Abramoff and his partner Michael Scanlon, DeLay's former communications director, are singing.

Historians will examine the implications and nuances of the Abramoff affair, the K Street Project, and the trajectory of the Republican Congress from the dawn of its "revolution" to its Thermidorian dusk. For now, however, the matter is in the hands of the prosecutors.

The Proconsul's Apologia

JANUARY 26, 2006

In a curious juxtaposition, leading figures from the Bush administration have recently argued that the president is either omniscient or blind.

Karl Rove, Bush's political architect and deputy chief of staff, expert at arranging the smearing of the motives and patriotism of the president's critics, offered the first proposition. He remains under investigation by the special prosecutor for his potentially criminal involvement in the disclosure of an undercover CIA operative in order to tarnish the reputation of her husband, the former ambassador Joseph Wilson, who revealed that the rationale for the Iraq war was based on false evidence. Every day for the past two weeks, the White House press secretary, Scott McClellan, has stonewalled questions about Bush's and Rove's connections to the super-lobbyist Jack Abramoff, who has pleaded guilty to fraud and bribery and is cooperating with prosecutors. McClellan refuses to name the officials who attended "staff-level meetings" with Abramoff.

Under these clouds, Rove stepped to the lectern at the gathering of the Republican National Committee in Washington on January 20 to invoke the specter of September 11. Little else matters but that Bush grasps that 9/11 changed everything, and Democrats of course do not. "We need," Rove said, "a commander in chief and a Congress who understand the nature of the threat and the gravity of the moment America finds itself in."

As Rove spoke, L. Paul Bremer III, the former presidential proconsul in Iraq and head of the Provisional Coalition Authority, had begun his rounds of media interviews to promote his memoir, *My Year in Iraq*. "We really didn't see the insurgency coming," Bremer told NBC News. He also disclosed that he had argued for more troops but had been rebuffed by Secretary of Defense Donald Rumsfeld.

Rove's call to the faithful lacks the specificity of Bremer's confessions. For the political theme to remain vital, recent history must be obliterated; the image must prevail over the record. And for the moment, Rove appears not as the citizen under suspicion but as the cardinal of the Sacred Congregation for the Propaganda of the Faith.

The flaw with Bremer's apologia is that it too is challenged by the facts. In January 2003, Larry C. Johnson, a longtime CIA operative who was deputy director in the State Department's Office of Counter-Terrorism, where he served with Bremer, sent him a memo that accurately predicted an Iraqi uprising against the occupying forces, "no matter how benign or charitable," and the influence in Iraq of a "belligerent" Iran. "Bremer's reaction," Johnson told me, "was that this was off base, doesn't matter, we're going to war, don't undermine the effort. His mind was made up. There was no brooking any alternative analysis. This is the doctrine, the truth, either you admit to it or you're a heretic." When Bremer was appointed head of the CPA, Johnson tried to put him in touch with intelligence experts to brief him with information that the Bush administration had not considered, but Bremer did not "want to listen."

Bremer was modeling himself on his commander in chief. In fact, elder statesmen of the foreign policy establishment and the Republican Party repeatedly warned President Bush to his face of precisely the consequences of his planned actions. The former national security adviser, Brent Scowcroft, and the former secretaries of state James Baker and Lawrence Eagleburger, among others, "never thought the war would come off right," one of those who spoke to Bush told me. "We all felt that strongly. It was going to end with an Islamic republic dominated by Shia and influenced by Iran. There was no question they would have Iranian connections. If you know history, you don't have to be a genius." But Bush would not listen. "It's a sad story."

On the ruins, Rove once again is playing the patriot game to salvage Bush's short-term political position. This time he is attempting to turn Bush's warrantless domestic spying, contrary to the Foreign Intelligence Surveillance Act, into a false issue of whether Democrats support gathering intelligence on terrorists. Patriotism now demands dispensing with the law. The history of the Bush presidency underlines Rove's premise, but not as he wishes: "We need a commander in chief and a Congress who understand the nature of the threat and the gravity of the moment America finds itself in."

Bush's Brezhnev Period

FEBRUARY 6, 2006

THE MOST SIGNIFICANT and memorable statements in President Bush's lackluster State of the Union address, the phrases that most clearly and succinctly captured the state of his presidency after five years, were his heartfelt and hostile admonishments: "Hindsight alone is not wisdom. And second-guessing is not a strategy."

Bush did not claim to have learned any lessons from the past. Nor did he propose any new strategies. By assailing "hindsight" and "second-guessing," he attempted to deny legitimacy to critics and criticism. He banished analysis of his previous actions from consideration in formulating current or future policy. He denounced "isolationism" but asserted his own isolation. Anyone who does not adhere to the party line must be a dangerous and subversive revisionist. George Santayana (who observed that "those who cannot remember the past are condemned to repeat it") is uninvited.

By denigrating "hindsight," Bush made his mark alongside the line in the sand drawn the week before by his chief political adviser, Karl Rove. "At the core," said Rove, "we are dealing with two parties that have fundamentally different views on national security. Republicans have a post-9/11 worldview, and many Democrats have a pre-9/11 worldview." With these comments, Rove and Bush signaled the Republican midterm elections strategy, also a repetition of past plans. Democratic candidates should expect television commercials morphing their faces into Osama bin Laden's, like the spot used in 2002 to defeat then Senator Max Cleland of Georgia, the decorated triple-amputee Vietnam War veteran.

The latest NBC–*Wall Street Journal* poll, taken on the eve of Bush's speech, indicates unusually intense interest in the midterms, and such intensity at this early point suggests a large Democratic turnout. Bush's appeal that "our differences cannot be allowed to harden into anger" was an effort to soften his polarizing image. Meanwhile, evoking September 11, as always, he demarcated who was and was not truly patriotic and entitled to speak. At the low ebb of his presidency in public approval, he carefully orchestrated his biggest speech of the year to impose homogeneity, conformity, and the stifling of "second-guessing."

Bush's intent to stigmatize opposition was exemplified by the absurd removal from the visitors' gallery of the harmless and undisruptive Cindy Sheehan, a founder of the antiwar Gold Star Families for Peace, who had been given a ticket to the speech by a Democratic member of Congress. Her offense was wearing a T-shirt embossed with the number of U.S. military killed in Iraq: "2245 Dead. How many more?" She is not quite Santayana (or Brent Scowcroft), but any questioning of the price and burden of war is sufficient to merit removal from the president's sight.

Bush has entered his Brezhnev era of stagnation. Everything—from the latest five-year plan to the grandiose promise of world transformation—was repetitive and abstracted from grinding realities. His attempt to use the first year of his second term for permanent revolution at home, following Rove's script, has failed. Social Security privatization is now whittled down to a commission, the sort of gambit employed when a leader lacks support. But diminished prospects did not dim his extravagant rhetoric.

"We seek the end of tyranny in our world," Bush proclaimed. (In his 2005 State of the Union address, he pledged "the ultimate goal of ending tyranny in our world.") It would have demanded complicating "hindsight" to acknowledge that Hamas has attained power in Palestine; Hezbollah has greatly increased its influence in Lebanon; the Muslim Brotherhood has made unprecedented gains in Egypt; a Shiite extremist, Mahmoud Ahmadinejad, has become president of Iran; and theocratic Islamist Shiite factions aligned with Iran will govern Iraq, all through elections that no one has challenged as unfair (with the exception of those in Egypt). Just two days before Bush's speech, Secretary of State Condoleezza Rice admitted, "I don't know anyone who wasn't caught off guard by Hamas's strong showing." Of course, there had been many warnings issued by many serious people that fundamentalism is on the rise in the Middle East. Rice's confession of deafness and blindness, however, did not dim Bush's recurrent vision: Happy days are here again.

For every changed situation, he hoists tattered slogans. In Iraq, he said, "we are winning." Just before his speech, the University of Maryland Program on International Policy Attitudes released a study of Iraqis, reporting that 47 percent overall and 88 percent of Sunnis approve of "attacks on U.S.-led forces," and 80 percent want a timetable for U.S. withdrawal. In his speech, Bush did not define "winning." He simply asserted the word as though the certitude with which he uttered it would bring about whatever it is he means by it.

On the Palestinian elections, in his press conference on January 26, Bush's first response to Hamas's victory was to praise the election process: "I like the competition of ideas." (The first idea articulated in Hamas's charter: "Israel will exist and will continue to exist until Islam will obliterate it, just as it obliterated others before it.") But by ceasing the peace process, in the face of the second intifada, for more than a year after becoming president, humiliating the Palestinian president, Mahmoud Abbas, by refusing to meet with him on his first trip to Washington, and neglecting to help him make any tangible progress to show to his people, Bush's policies contributed to the overthrow of Palestinian moderates. In his State of the Union address, Bush urged Hamas to become something other than Hamas. If it fails to do so, he has no policy; this is the clueless approach already expressed by Rice.

On Iran, designated a member of the "axis of evil" in his 2002 State of the Union address, and currently developing its nuclear programs in defiance of the world community, Bush gropes for certainty. When he came into office he rejected diplomatic outreach to President Mohammad Khatami and the so-called reform elements, and then rejected feelers from the Iranian mullahs for assistance in dealing with the Taliban and al Qaeda and an overall settlement of U.S.-Iranian differences. He utterly miscalculated the increased influence of Iran as a consequence of the Iraq war. On the eve of the Iranian election last year, Bush denounced the extremist candidate Ahmadinejad, thereby predictably inciting support for him. Until 2005, Bush was reluctant to join the Europeans in containing Iran's nuclear programs. Now, he has no practical military or economic options. Unilateral action is too implausible even to pretend as a possibility. Bush is reduced to describing the Iranian people who elected Ahmadinejad as being "held hostage" and to calling on them to overthrow the regime. He has a scenario, but not yet a policy.

By his repeated denunciations of "radical Islam" in his speech, Bush cast his "war on terror" as a religious crusade, fitting exactly the perspective of al Qaeda and al Qaeda–like sects and providing the basic motivation for suicide terrorism, as the University of Chicago scholar Robert Pape has shown in his landmark study, *Dying to Win*. Bush appears more determined to enhance his stature in his own mind as a world hero battling barbarian hordes than to adopt careful language and strategy that might reduce and isolate radical Islamists.

With every phrase, Bush achieves the polar opposite of what he claims to intend. His orotund rhetoric about "freedom on the march," "democracy," "tyranny," and "evil" undermines itself. What happens when "democracy" does not advance democracy, and "freedom" is used to oppress? Bush's refusal to accept paradox, to see that his good motives may have unintended consequences, leads him to reject "hindsight." "Far from being a hopeless dream, the advance of freedom is the great story of our time," Bush said in his speech. Rather than reassess his own actions that have made his goals ever more distant—"second-guessing"—he clings to his self-image as a warrior and savior. But Bush may have become such a universally tainted figure that almost anything he says, especially in the language of idealism, is now discredited.

The Client

FEBRUARY 9, 2006

IN 1996, TEXAS GOVERNOR GEORGE W. BUSH received a summons to serve on a jury, which would have required admission that twenty years earlier he had been arrested for drunken driving. Already planning his presidential campaign, he did not want this biographical information disclosed. His lawyer at the time made the novel argument to the judge that Bush should not have to serve because "he would not, as governor, be able to pardon the defendant in the future." (The defendant was a stripper accused of drunken driving.) The judge agreed, and it was not until the closing days of the 2000 campaign that Bush's record surfaced. On Monday, the same lawyer, Alberto Gonzales, now U.S. attorney general, appeared before the Senate Judiciary Committee to defend "the client," as he called the president.

Gonzales was the sole witness called to explain Bush's warrantless domestic spying in obvious violation of the Foreign Intelligence Surveillance Act and circumvention of the special court created to administer it. The scene at the Senate was acted as though scripted jointly by Kafka, Mel Brooks, and John le Carré. After not being sworn in, the absence of oath taking having been insisted on by the Republicans, Gonzales offered legal reasoning even more imaginative than he had used to get Bush out of jury duty—a mélange of mendacity, absurdity, and mystery.

The attorney general argued that the FISA law did and did not apply, that the administration was operating within it while flouting it, and that it didn't matter. The president's "inherent" power, after all, allows him to do whatever he wants. It was all, Gonzales said, "totally consistent." But his explanation, observed Senator Arlen Specter, the Republican chair of the Judiciary Committee, "defies logic and plain English."

Congress, Gonzales elaborated, had no proper constitutional role, but in any case had already approved the president's secret program by voting for the authorization for the use of military force in Afghanistan, even if members didn't know it or, when informed years later that they had done so, objected that they hadn't. The law that was ignored, Gonzales declared, shouldn't be amended to bring this domestic spying under the law because the secret program is already legal, or might be legal, and anyway it doesn't matter whether Congress says it's legal. The all-powerful president should be trusted, but when Bush states wrongly that he goes to court for warrants, it's all right that he doesn't know what he is talking about. "As you know," Gonzales said, "the president is not a lawyer."

Who was or wasn't being spied on couldn't and wouldn't be explained. When Senator Dianne Feinstein, Democrat of California, asked whether the program could be used to "influence United States political processes, public opinion, policies or media," Gonzales replied, "Those are very, very difficult questions, and for me to answer those questions sort of off the cuff, I think would not be responsible." When Senator Joseph Biden, Democrat of Delaware, asked for assurances that only al Qaeda or suspected terrorists are subject to surveillance, Gonzales answered, "Sir, I can't give you absolute assurance."

Nor would he say what the program really is. "I am not comfortable going down the road of saying yes or no as to what the president has or has not authorized," Gonzales said. "I'm not going to respond to that," he said. "I'm not going to answer," he said.

Gonzales's ultimate argument was an appeal to history. George Washington, he pointed out in a display of erudition, "intercepted British mail," citing a 1997 CIA report on the subject. In the Civil War, the telegraph was wiretapped. And during World Wars I and II, communications were intercepted, too. Gonzales' ahistoricism about technology aside (George Washington had no cell phones to tap, no computers to hack), Washington, Lincoln, and Roosevelt could not break a law that did not exist.

Through his convoluted testimony, Gonzales once again served as the useful factotum representing "the client." But, in his tour of history, he neglected the disclosure by the Associated Press on February 3 of about two hundred pages of documents from the Gerald Ford's White House. These papers highlighted the objections of Ford's secretary of defense, Donald Rumsfeld, and chief of staff, Dick Cheney, to getting court warrants for domestic surveillance. It was partly to thwart such unaccountable executive power that Congress enacted the FISA in 1978.

Once again the power behind the throne, Cheney has found a way to relieve the frustrations of the past. But he is fulfilling more than the curdled dreams of the Ford and Nixon era. The Bush presidency is straining to realize a pre-Washington ideal—unconstitutional monarchy.

The Rules of the Game

FEBRUARY 15, 2006

IN THE ORIGINAL ACCOUNT authorized by Vice President Dick Cheney of his shooting of Harry Whittington, given by Katharine Armstrong, heiress and hunting companion, to the *Corpus Christi Caller-Times* and later elaborated on for other news outlets, the eleven members of the hunting party set off on the morning of February 11 in two trucks for the wilds of the fifty-thousand-acre Armstrong Ranch in search of quails. After lunch, whose menu was described as antelope, jicama salad, bread, and Dr Pepper, the hunters divided into two groups. Cheney went off with Armstrong, Whittington, and Pamela Pitzer Willeford, the U.S. ambassador to Switzerland and Liechtenstein.

At dusk, Whittington, a seventy-eight-year-old Austin lawyer and local Republican fixer, shot a bird and went behind the others to retrieve it. Hearing rustling in the bushes, Cheney, who has lately been using a cane in public and wearing two different shoes for comfort, reportedly quickly swiveled 180 degrees, 28-gauge shotgun in hand, and fired at what he believed were quails, but instead hit Whittington, thirty yards distant. "He got peppered pretty good," Armstrong said. "There was some bleeding, but it wasn't horrible. He was more bruised." The circumstances of this hunt were different from Cheney's previously celebrated 2003 hunt at the Rolling Rock Club in Pennsylvania, where he, Associate Supreme Court Justice Antonin Scalia, and eight others killed 417 pheasants and an unknown number of mallard ducks specifically raised for the purpose of being herded before the hunters to shoot. At that time, Cheney released to the press the information that he had personally killed seventy pheasants. At the Armstrong Ranch, the only known target he hit was Whittington.

The details of the story related by Armstrong, however, defied practical experience and were contradictory. Armstrong told NBC News that while she believed that no one was drinking alcohol, beer may have been served at lunch. "There may have been a beer or two in there," she said, "but remember, not everyone in the party was shooting." Armstrong's statement about beer appeared on the MSNBC website, but was subsequently and inexplicably scrubbed. Dr Pepper replaced beer in later versions of Armstrong's account. On the hunting accident and incident report form required by the Texas Parks and Wildlife Department, the shooter, Richard B. Cheney, checked the "No" box for the question, "Under the apparent influence of intoxicants or drugs?" But in an interview with Fox News Wednesday, Cheney admitted to having had a beer earlier in the day, contrary to his statement to Texas officials.

The murky method by which Cheney decided to handle the disclosure of the shooting was guaranteed to raise questions about the incident. He behaved secretively, evaded standard protocol, and brushed aside his obligations to the law. Unless Whittington dies, precipitating a grand jury probe that would require witnesses to testify separately under oath, the true story may never be known.

Whether or not the exact facts of the case are ever conclusively established, what happened at twilight in the south Texas brush has revealed the hierarchy of power within the Bush White House and the interests of those who wield that power. The surreptitious handling inside the White House of the shooting, moreover, cannot be understood apart from the society of Texas royalty and the ambitions of those, like Cheney and Karl Rove, who aspire to it. None of it is metaphoric.

About an hour after the shooting, an unidentified traveling aide of the vice president's called the White House Situation Room, which put him in touch with the chief of staff, Andrew Card. Why a call would be routed through the Situation Room, which receives and transmits only national security information, rather than the very capable and secure White House switchboard, remains mysterious. Card was deliberately misled, told only that there was an accident in Cheney's party, not that Cheney was involved. The vice president's staff apparently felt no need to inform the president's chief of staff of the true facts of the matter. Why Card was deceived is also mystifying, except insofar as it reflects the vice president's instinctive view of him as someone to be routinely stepped over and around. Card, acting responsibly, promptly called President Bush, who as a result was momentarily kept in the dark. Confusing Card was a way of managing Bush.

Enter Rove. Within minutes of the call to Card, the president's chief political adviser and deputy chief of staff spoke with Katharine Armstrong, an old friend of his, who told him that Cheney had shot Whittington. Who initiated this conversation is unknown. In any case, Rove, not the duped Card, informed the president of what had actually transpired.

The White House press secretary, Scott McClellan, was left out of the loop until the next morning. Instead, Armstrong, not anyone from the White House, disclosed to her local newspaper the news that the vice president had shot Whittington. It seems fair to infer that Cheney left to Rove the task of coaching her. Twenty hours after the accident, the *Corpus Christi Caller-Times* printed its report; then it slowly filtered to the national press corps, which was never alerted by the White House.

Armstrong's account, blaming the victim, bore the mark of a classic Rove-engineered statement. No one at the White House had yet to say a word. The president, though he was now well aware of events, made no query that would have ensured that in this extraordinary situation the White House was operating properly and according to the letter of the law. Whether ignorant or informed, he remained passive, deferring to Cheney and Rove.

Both the vice president and the deputy chief of staff, as it happens, owed their previous, lucrative jobs in the private sector to their relationships with the Armstrong family. Anne Armstrong, Katharine's mother, was on the board of Halliburton that made Dick Cheney its chief executive officer. Tobin Armstrong, Katharine's father, had financed Karl Rove & Co., Rove's political consulting firm. Katharine herself is a lobbyist for the Houston law firm Baker Botts, a major Texas power broker since it was founded in the nineteenth century by the family of James A. Baker III, the former secretary of state and close associate of George H. W. Bush.

Katharine Armstrong took up lobbying after her recent divorce. Her contracts include Parsons, a construction firm that has done work in Iraq and elsewhere. Her business partner, Karen Johnson, a close friend of Rove's, does extensive business with the State Department, the U.S. Agency for International Development, and defense contractors. But Armstrong's protestations to news media that she does not lobby Cheney should probably be taken at face value given her background.

Katharine Armstrong is linked to two family fortunes—those of Armstrong and King—that include extensive corporate holdings in land, cattle, banking, and oil. No one in Texas, except perhaps Baker, but certainly not the latecomer George W. Bush, has a longer lineage in its political and economic elite. In 1983, Debrett's Peerage Ltd., publisher of *Debrett's Peerage and Baronetage*, printed *Debrett's Texas Peerage*, featuring "the aristocrats of Texas," with the King family noted as the "Royal Family of Ranching." The King Ranch, founded by Richard King in 1857, is the largest in Texas, and its wealth was vastly augmented by the discovery of oil on its tracts, which made the family a major shareholder of Exxon. The King Ranch is the model for Edna Ferber's novel of Texas aristocracy, *Giant.*

John B. Armstrong, a Texas Ranger and enforcer for the King Ranch, founded his own neighboring ranch in 1882, buying it with the bounty of $4,000 he got for capturing the outlaw John Wesley Hardin. In 1944, almost inevitably, the two fortunes became intertwined through marriage. Tobin Armstrong's brother John married the King Ranch heiress, who was also a Vassar classmate of Tobin's wife, Anne, who came from a wealthy New Orleans family.

The Armstrong Ranch developed far-flung holdings in Australia and South America. Meanwhile, President Ford appointed Anne, a major Republican activist, as U.S. ambassador to the United Kingdom, and President Reagan appointed her a member of the President's Foreign Intelligence Advisory Board. U.S. Senator Kay Bailey Hutchison is reportedly Anne's best friend, and Anne was instrumental in launching her political career. Tobin, for his part, worked as an adviser to the Texas Republican governor William Clements, in which capacity he first encountered the young Karl Rove and decided to give him a helping hand when Rove struck out in the political business on his own.

The Armstrong family's Republican connections have continued and strengthened down to the latest generation of Bushes. Governor George W. Bush appointed Anne a regent of Texas A&M University and Katharine a commission member of the Texas Parks and Wildlife Department, the agency that filed the report on the Cheney shooting. At Tobin's funeral last year, Cheney delivered the eulogy.

While the shooting incident continues to unfold, the Bush administration is pressing a new budget in which oil companies would receive what is called "royalty relief," allowing them to pump about $65 billion of oil and natural gas from federal land over the next five years without paying any royalties to the government, costing the U.S. Treasury about $7 billion. For Texas royalty like the Armstrongs, it would amount to a windfall profit.

The curiosities surrounding the vice president's accident have created a contemporary version of *The Rules of the Game,* with a Texas twist. In Jean Renoir's 1939 film, politicians and aristocrats mingle at a country house in France over a long weekend, during which a merciless hunt ends with a tragic shooting. Appearing on the eve of World War II, *The Rules of the Game* depicted a hypocritical, ruthless, and decadent ruling class that made its own rules and led a society to the edge of catastrophe.

Cheney's Coup

FEBRUARY 23, 2006

AFTER SHOOTING THE AUSTIN LAWYER Harry Whittington, Dick Cheney's immediate impulse was to control the intelligence. Rather than call the president directly, he ordered an aide to inform the White House chief of staff, Andrew Card, that there had been an accident but not that Cheney was responsible. Then a host of surrogates attacked the victim for not steering clear of Cheney when he was firing. Cheney attempted to defuse the subsequent furor by giving an interview to friendly Fox News. His most revealing answer came in response to a question about something other than the hunting accident.

Cheney was asked about court papers filed by his former chief of staff, I. Lewis "Scooter" Libby, indicted for perjury and obstruction of justice in the investigation of the leaking of the identity of an undercover CIA operative, Valerie Plame. (She is the wife of the former ambassador Joseph Wilson, a critic of disinformation used to justify the invasion of Iraq.) In those papers, Libby laid out a line of defense that he had leaked classified material at the behest of "his superiors" (to wit, Cheney). Libby detailed that he was authorized to disclose to members of the press classified sections of the prewar national intelligence estimate on Saddam Hussein's weapons of mass destruction. (The NIE was exposed as wrongly asserting that Saddam possessed WMD and was constructing nuclear weapons.) Indeed, Cheney explained, he has the power to declassify intelligence. "There is an executive order to that effect," he said. Had he ever done that "unilaterally"? "I don't want to get into that."

On March 25, 2003, President Bush signed Executive Order 13292, a hitherto little-known document that grants the greatest expansion of the power of the vice president in American history. The order gives the vice president the same ability to classify intelligence as the president. By controlling classification, the vice president can in effect control intelligence and, through that, foreign policy.

Bush operates on the radical notion of the "unitary executive," the principle that the president has inherent and limitless powers in his role as commander in chief, above the constitutional system of checks and balances. By his extraordinary order, he elevated Cheney to his own level, an acknowledgment that the vice president was already the de facto executive in national security. Never before has any president diminished and divided his power in this manner. Now the unitary executive inherently includes the unitary vice president.

The unprecedented executive order bears the hallmark of Cheney's former counsel and current chief of staff, David Addington. Addington has been Cheney's closest assistant through three decades, since Cheney served in the House of Representatives in the 1980s. Inside the executive branch, Addington acts as Cheney's vicar, bullying and sarcastic, inspiring fear and obedience. Few documents of concern to the vice president, even executive orders, reach the eyes of the president without passing first through Addington's agile hands.

To advance their scenario for the Iraq war, Cheney & Co. either pressured or dismissed the intelligence community when it presented contrary analysis. Paul Pillar, the former CIA national intelligence officer for the Near East and South Asia, writes in the new issue of *Foreign Affairs:* "The administration used intelligence not to inform decision-making, but to justify a decision already made."

On domestic spying conducted without legal approval of the Foreign Intelligence Surveillance Court, Addington and his minions isolated and crushed internal dissent from James Comey, then deputy attorney general, and Jack Goldsmith, then head of the Justice Department's Office of Legal Counsel.

On torture policy, as reported by the *New Yorker* this week, Alberto Mora, recently retired as general counsel to the U.S. Navy, opposed the Bush administration's abrogation of the Geneva Conventions—by holding thousands of detainees in secret camps without due process and using abusive interrogation techniques—based on legal doctrines Mora called "unlawful" and "dangerous." Addington et al. told him the policies were being ended while continuing to pursue them on a separate track. "To preserve flexibility, they were willing to throw away our values," Mora said.

The first vice president, John Adams, called his position "the most insignificant office ever the invention of man contrived or his imagination conceived." John Nance Garner, Franklin D. Roosevelt's first vice president, said it was not worth "a warm bucket of spit." When Dick Cheney was secretary of defense under the first President Bush, he reprimanded Vice President Dan Quayle for asserting power he did not possess by calling a meeting of the National Security Council when the elder Bush was abroad. Cheney well knew the vice president had no authority in the chain of command.

Since the coup d'état of Executive Order 13292, however, the vice presidency has been transformed. Perhaps, for a blinding moment, Cheney imagined he might classify his shooting party top secret.

A Lincoln Portrait

MARCH 2, 2006

REPUBLICANS REPRESENTATIVE of their permanent establishment have recently and quietly sent emissaries to President Bush, like
diplomats to a foreign ruler isolated in his forbidden city, to probe
whether he could be persuaded to become politically flexible. These ambassadors were not connected to the elder Bush or his closest associate, the
former national security adviser Brent Scowcroft, who was purged last
year from the President's Foreign Intelligence Advisory Board and scorned
by the current president. Scowcroft privately tells friends who ask whether
he could somehow help that Bush would never turn to him for advice. So,
in one case, a Republican wise man, a prominent lawyer in Washington
who had served in the Reagan White House, who sought no appointments
or favors and was thought to be unthreatening to Bush, gained an audience with him. In a gentle tone, he explained that many presidents had difficult second terms, but that by adapting their approaches they ended successfully, as President Reagan had done. Bush instantly replied with a
vehement blast. He would not change. He would stay the course. He
would not follow the polls. The Republican wise man tried again. Oh, no,
he didn't mean anything about polls. But Bush fortified his wall of self-
defensiveness and let fly with another heated riposte that he would not
change.

He has been true to his word. On the sale of U.S. port management to a
corporate entity owned by the United Arab Emirates, for example, he has
been adamant. Congressional Republicans, observing Bush's spiraling decline in the polls, down this week to 34 percent in the *New York Times*/CBS
News survey, and facing midterm elections in which they but not the president are on the ballot, are seized with panic. In the House of Representatives, they forced their majority leader, Tom DeLay, under indictment for
illegal campaign funding, to quit his post. Then they bolted from supporting the lobbyist-larded Roy Blunt, DeLay's obvious successor, and selected
John Boehner, less conspicuously tainted instead. At the first news of the

port deal, both the House and Senate leaders hastily threw President Bush overboard. Now he has to apply presidential pressure on his own party's leaders to reel them back. While the Democrats act as a hectoring chorus, the real tension and play are between Bush and the terrified Republican Congress.

Bush's immovability was previously perceived as the determination of a man of simple but clear convictions. But as his policies have unfolded as disastrous, his image has been turned inside out. Instead of being perceived as secure, he is seen as out of touch; instead of being acknowledged as a colossus striding events, he is viewed as driftwood carried away by the flood.

Within the sanctum of the White House, his aides often handle him with flattery. They tell him that he is among the greatest presidents, that his difficulties and refusal to change are testimony to his greatness. The more he is flattered, the more he approves of the flatterer. Secretary of State Condoleezza Rice has risen on a tide of flattery. She is expert at the handwritten little note extolling his historical radiance. Karen Hughes, now undersecretary of state for public diplomacy, was a pioneer of the flatterer's method. The White House legal counsel, Harriet Miers, is also adept.

But it is Vice President Dick Cheney who has sought and gained the most through flattery. While Bush is constantly and lavishly complimented as supreme leader, Cheney runs the show. Through his chief of staff, David Addington, he controls most of the flow of information, especially on national security, that reaches the incurious president. Bush seeks no contrary information or independent sources. He does not delve into the recesses of government himself, as Presidents Kennedy and Clinton did. He never demands worst-case scenarios. Cheney and his team oversee the writing of key decision memos before Bush finally gets to check the box indicating approval.

Addington also dominates much of the bureaucracy through a network of conservative lawyers placed in key departments and agencies. The Justice Department regularly produces memos to justify the latest wrinkle in the doctrine of the "unitary executive," whether on domestic surveillance or torture. At the Defense Department, the counsel's office takes direction from Addington and acts at his behest to suppress dissent from the senior military on matters such as detainees or the "global war on terror."

Tightly regulated by Cheney and Bush's own aides (who live in fear of Cheney), the president hears what he wishes to hear. The aides also know what particular flattery he wants to receive, and they ensure that he receives it.

In *The Prince*, Niccolò Machiavelli highlighted the danger of this practice in a chapter titled "How Flatterers Must Be Shunned." He observed that "courts are full" of "this plague," and that it can be isolated only with difficulty. His solution was that the "prudent prince" must insist that his closest advisers never withhold the unvarnished facts from him. "Because," wrote Machiavelli, "there is no other way of guarding one's self against flattery than by letting men understand that they will not offend you by speaking the truth."

But when disturbing information manages to penetrate the carefully constructed net surrounding Bush, he instinctively rejects and condemns it. In July 2004, on being briefed on the grim analysis of the growing Iraqi insurgency written by the CIA Baghdad station chief, Bush said, according to *U.S. News & World Report*, "What is he, some kind of defeatist?" Bush prefers to soak up the flattery. He responds only to praise of himself as the warrior president at the battlements, fighting the enemies at the gates and the defeatists within.

In the aftermath of the Iraq invasion, Bush was flattered by comparisons to Franklin Roosevelt and Harry Truman that portrayed him winning a world war and present at the creation of a new international order. However, since the election of 2004, a period during which the violence in Iraq has not diminished, Bush has been told he more closely resembles the beleaguered Abraham Lincoln. He is the Great Emancipator who has freed fifty million people in Afghanistan and Iraq but has not yet won the war. "It is courage that liberated more than fifty million people from tyranny," Bush declared on Veterans Day, November 11, 2005. Withstanding setbacks and suffering slings and arrows, he imagines himself enduring before inevitable and ultimate victory.

On May 11, 2005, Rice appeared on CNN's *Larry King Live* to say: "I've often wondered, in the darkest hours of the Civil War, what people were saying to Abraham Lincoln about whether this was going to turn out all right." Just a month earlier, on April 20, Bush had dedicated the Abraham Lincoln Museum and Library in Springfield, Illinois. Segueing seamlessly from the Civil War to the war on terror, from Gettysburg to Iraq, he conflated Lincoln's struggle and his own: "Our deepest values are also served when we take our part in freedom's advance—when the chains of millions are broken and the captives are set free, because we are honored to serve the cause that gave us birth. . . . So we will stick to it; we will stand firmly by it."

This year, on January 23, at Kansas State University, in one of a series of speeches he gave to explain once again his Iraq strategy, Bush digressed into a reverie about Lincoln's troubles. "I believe in what I'm doing," he said. "And I understand politics, and it can get rough. I read a lot of history, by the way, and Abraham Lincoln had it rough. I'm not comparing myself to Abraham Lincoln, nor should you think [so] just because I mentioned his name in the context of my presidency—I would never do that. He was a great president. But, boy, they mistreated him. He did what he thought was right."

The greater Bush's difficulties, the more precipitously he falls in the polls, the more he is beseeched by anxious Republicans to change course, and the harsher the realities, the tighter he clings to his self-image. Cheney and the others encourage his illusions, at least partly because the more intensely Bush embraces the heroic conception of himself, the more he resists change, and the firmer their grip.

"It is an infallible rule," Machiavelli wrote in his chapter on flatterers, "that a prince who is not wise himself cannot be well advised, unless by chance he leaves himself entirely in the hands of one man who rules him in everything, and happens to be a very prudent man. In this case he may doubtless be well governed, but it would not last long, for that governor would in a short time deprive him of the state."

Once More unto the Breach

MARCH 9, 2006

ON THE EVE OF GEORGE W. BUSH's presidential campaign in 2000, the neoconservative Kenneth Adelman cast him as a Prince Hal who "puts the indiscretions of his youth behind him" and "redeem[s] his father's reign." After September 11, 2001, Bush was crowned as Henry V by a clerisy of pundits. None of the celebrants cited, from *Henry IV, Part 2,* the advice the dying king imparts to his son: "Be it thy course to busy giddy minds / With foreign quarrels; that action, hence borne out, / May waste the memory of the former days." (Adelman, appointed by President Bush to the Defense Policy Board, declared in anticipation of the Iraq war that it would be a "cakewalk.") From Ground Zero to the deck of the USS *Abraham Lincoln* ("Mission Accomplished"), the president struck bold poses, but his choreographed gestures have especially illuminated his hollow crown in the darkened breach of New Orleans.

Last week, for the first time, the public saw the spontaneous Bush behind closed doors, in a leaked videotape that recorded one of his briefings the day before Hurricane Katrina struck. Bush in cinéma vérité does not resemble Bush in tableau vivant. In a teleconference at his Crawford, Texas, compound on August 28, Bush listens to disaster officials inform him that the storm will be unprecedented in its severity and consequences. "This is, to put it mildly, the big one," says Michael Brown, then director of the Federal Emergency Management Agency. Max Mayfield, director of the National Hurricane Center, warns, "This hurricane is much larger than Hurricane Andrew ever was," and that he has a "very, very grave concern" that "the levees will be topped." Bush asks not a single question, says, "We are fully prepared," and departs.

This videotape is as defining for Bush's presidency as the audiotapes of President Kennedy's councils of state during the Cuban missile crisis were for his. Kennedy's tapes revealed him as probing, subtle, prudent, and decisive. Bush's tape exposes a deaf man spouting talking points. After the hurricane hit, he stayed on vacation, went to a birthday party, strummed a guitar with a country and western singer and, on September 1, said, "I don't think anybody anticipated the breach of the levees." On his flight back to Washington four days after Katrina's landfall, his aides gave him a DVD of television news reports of the hurricane's impact, about which he had done nothing to learn on his own.

As the catastrophe unfolded, he clapped FEMA's Brown on the back: "Brownie, you're doing a heck of a job." But soon the administration settled on Brownie as the scapegoat, prevented him from defending himself, and forced him to resign. Like a good liegeman, he was expected to fall on his sword.

Suddenly, last week, the sacrificial Brown stormed back onto the stage, the betrayed turning on his betrayers. He proclaimed on every media outlet that he would no longer play the fall guy, detailed the warnings he had given, named malefactors running up the chain of command, and demanded the resignation of Secretary of Homeland Security Michael Chertoff. Brown even pointed out that Bush was the only person ever to call him "Brownie." Rejecting the honorific diminutive, he exchanged vassalage for vengeance.

In New Orleans, a sad Mardi Gras has come and gone, while crews from the morgues continue still to recover bodies in their house-to-house searches. The city has lost more than half of its residents; most of the refugees are African Americans, and their old neighborhoods remain scenes of devastation. Having rejected a plan for rebuilding offered by Republican Louisiana Representative Richard Baker, Bush traveled to New Orleans for another photo opportunity this week to announce a program that would supposedly give money to the homeless but whose restrictions would make it impossible to rebuild homes. Not one federal penny so far has been spent on new housing. Six months after the tempest, New Orleans, one of the glories of American life and culture, lies in ruins, and Bush visits to pose as visionary.

In a recently published hagiography on the theme of Bush as Prince Hal, *Rebel-in-Chief: How George W. Bush Is Redefining the Conservative Movement and Transforming America*, written by the right-wing pundit Fred Barnes, Bush explained to him that his job as president is to "stay out of minutiae, keep the big picture in mind." To illustrate his self-conception, Barnes writes, Bush "called my attention to the rug" in the Oval Office. Bush said that he wanted the rug to express that an "optimistic person comes here." He delegated the task to his wife, Laura, who designed a rug featuring bright yellow rays of the sun. In his Oval Office, Prince Hal imagines himself grown into a Sun King.

Sex Police Chief Arrested

MARCH 14, 2006

PRESIDENT BUSH'S CHIEF domestic policy adviser, Claude Allen, had a scheme. He bought electronic goods and clothing at Target, a mass-market department store chain, and loaded them into the trunk of his car. Then he took his receipt, filled up a cart at Target with the exact same items, and brought them to the returns desk for credit. Last Thursday, Allen was arraigned in district court in Maryland on charges of felony theft. Police have documented twenty-five separate cases in which Allen engaged in his elaborate charade of purchasing products and receiving refunds. Each felony count is punishable by up to fifteen years in prison.

Claude Allen was the most prominent African American on Bush's White House staff, a rare gem, handled carefully, his résumé carved and polished. Risen from obscurity, a child from a poor neighborhood of Washington, D.C., he rose to sit at the president's right hand. When the president nominated him for a federal judgeship on the Fourth Circuit Court, covering the Southeastern states, it seemed he was being groomed even for the Supreme Court. Associate Justice Clarence Thomas, indeed, was one of his mentors. Democrats, however, blocked his nomination after Allen unconvincingly explained that when he had said in 1984 that "the queers" supported the Democratic governor of North Carolina, Jim Hunt, he only meant to suggest "odd, out of the ordinary, unusual," nothing at all to do with gays. With his judicial nomination in limbo, Allen continued in the West Wing.

Allen's career was itself out of the ordinary, but also telling of the price exacted of an ambitious African American in the contemporary Republican Party. He began his ascent as an aide to the far-right Senator Jesse Helms of North Carolina, whose political career from start to finish offered the clearest and longest example of Southern racial demagogy in recent American political history. Having proved his loyalty, Allen was promoted by the Helms machine, becoming a clerk for another Helms protégé, the federal judge David Sentelle.

Then Allen was recruited by the conservative Republican governor of Virginia, Jim Gilmore, as secretary of the state's Health and Human Services Commission. In that job, Allen became the point man for the agenda of the religious right. He opposed health insurance for poor children because the program would cover abortion counseling and services for rape and incest victims under the age of eighteen. He also advocated funding of abstinence promotion rather than programs for reproductive health. Allen vehemently campaigned against condoms, insisting that they did not prevent AIDS and their use only encouraged promiscuity. "It's like telling your child, 'Don't use the car,' but then leaving the keys in the Lamborghini and saying, 'But if you do, buckle up,' " he said.

When Bush gained the presidency, his chief political strategist Karl Rove selected Allen to act as enforcer and informer in the Department of Health and Human Services. The new secretary, Tommy Thompson, the former governor of Wisconsin, had a reputation for streaks of dangerous moderation, so, to guard against potential heresies, Allen was inserted as deputy.

Allen took charge as chief of the administration's sex police. Reproductive health programs were jettisoned and replaced with abstinence-only campaigns. Federal grant recipients were forbidden from discussing contraceptives, except to instruct that they were "ineffective." At Allen's direction, all information about the effectiveness of condoms was deleted from the website of the Centers for Disease Control.

Allen's diligence won him appointment as the White House director of domestic policy, closer than ever to Bush and Rove, present several days a week at Oval Office briefings. Allen carried out orders on sex policy ruthlessly. And he was invaluable as a symbol to combat the impression that Bush was indifferent to African Americans. After Hurricane Katrina hit the Gulf coast, making refugees of more than 1.5 million people, mostly poor African Americans, Allen was trotted out as character witness. "Just the mere fact you have pictures of the president on TV embracing grieving mothers, embracing pastors of churches that have been destroyed," he said, "that speaks about the personal character of our president, who is truly concerned about healing our nation."

Early this year, Allen informed the White House chief of staff, Andrew Card, and legal counsel, Harriet Miers, that he had been charged with a misdemeanor involving a credit card mix-up. Not only did he stay in the White House, but he was also given the honor of sitting in First Lady Laura Bush's box during the president's State of the Union address. In February, however, he resigned, offering the public excuse that he wanted to spend more time with his family. Only last week, when he appeared in court, was the reason for his departure apparent.

Claude Allen must now face the ruin of his glittering career as an orphan of the White House. The "faith-based" sex policies he helped direct remain in place. For African Americans, who were believed gullible enough to be swayed by the tokenism of his presence at the pinnacle of power, the effect is as though he never existed. Last October, even before Bush's latest precipitous fall in public opinion, the NBC–*Wall Street Journal* poll showed his support among African-Americans at two percent. The margin of error in the poll was four points, so it is possible that Bush's rating was six, or perhaps minus two.

Blood and Sand

MARCH 16, 2006

ON THE EVE of the third anniversary—March 20, 2003—of the invasion of Iraq, President Bush began the fourth of his series of speeches attempting to articulate his strategy for the war. None of his previous explanations had succeeded in bolstering public confidence, so he tried again. His speech on March 13 was a reiteration of the theme he had elaborated in his last round. Bush is rigidly adhering to the guidelines suggested by the public-opinion specialist Peter Feaver, a professor at Duke University recently hired to serve on the National Security Council. He has advised the president to insist that the difficulties in Iraq are the price we must pay for victory and that, just as Bush stands for "victory," his critics, by implication, represent defeat. In his peroration, Bush reached for that last point, his high note, sounding the clarion call of certainty that is most familiar and comfortable for him. "The battle lines in Iraq are clearly drawn for the world to see," he said, "and there is no middle ground."

Yet Bush's speech provided a text contradicting his own key officials. On the crucial issues of Iranian involvement in Iraq, the worthiness of Iraqi security forces, the democratic nature of the Iraqi government, the cause of human rights, U.S. intentions about staying or leaving, long-term strategy, and even the origins of the war, the words of the president and his men clash. The president contradicts the U.S. ambassador to Iraq, Zalmay Khalilzad, while the chair of the Joint Chiefs of Staff, General Peter Pace, and the U.S. commander in Iraq, General John Abizaid, contradict the president. At the same time, Secretary of Defense Donald Rumsfeld blithely contradicts the Joint Chiefs on the entire strategy.

The inconsistent story reflects the occasional weakness of White House associates, Khalilzad especially, for acknowledging harsh realities, letting slip the veneer of bravado, and failing to armor with euphemism. Bush and Rumsfeld, of course, remain impregnable fortresses of denial.

It is already hard to remember the heady days when the Iraq adventure began, trumpets blaring and banners unfurled. At the time, Vice President

Dick Cheney and the administration neoconservatives arranged for the airlift of exiled Iraqi leader Ahmed Chalabi and about five hundred of his fighters into the country. He had been a major source of the disinformation about weapons of mass destruction that had provided the justification for the war. Now he was expected to assume power, restore order, and make Iraq into a base for the projection of U.S. influence throughout the Middle East. Instantly, Iraq would become a beacon of democracy. Awestruck, the Palestinians would forswear terrorist groups like Hamas. From the Iraqi bastion, the United States would topple the regimes of Syria and Iran, by military force if need be. The Iraq example would serve for invasions elsewhere. Saudi Arabia and Egypt would have no choice but to democratize, their rulers yielding to secular figures in the inspiring mold of Chalabi. Like Saddam Hussein's regime, the entire region was supposedly a house of cards.

No one more conspicuously displayed the moral glamour and intoxication with absolute power of the moment than the pundit Charles Krauthammer. The month before the war was launched, in February 2003, at a conference sponsored by the *National Interest* journal, and in columns in *Time* magazine and the *Washington Post,* he proclaimed that the Iraq war would recast the entire Middle East in the neoconservative image and that the task would be accomplished first in Iraq during a brief eighteen-month occupation.

At the *National Interest* conference, Krauthammer dismissed concerns about finding WMD, the purported casus belli. "There is one thing that I think everybody has overlooked—we are going to have retroactive evidence. Even though I would like us to be able to have a smoking gun, I don't know how close we are going to come to producing it when the President decides that it is time."

The war, Krauthammer continued, was necessary for "American credibility." It was time to end a "hands-off, offshore policy. . . . Iraq will be the first act in the play of an America coming ashore in Arabia. . . . It's not just about weapons of mass destruction or American credibility. It's about reforming the Arab world."

In a column in *Time* on February 17, 2003, boldly titled "Coming Ashore," Krauthammer proudly embraced the arrogance of power. "Reformation and reconstruction of an alien culture are a daunting task. Risky and, yes, arrogant." Yet 9/11 justified not only invading Iraq but also, he insisted, overthrowing twenty-two other Arab governments. "Before 9/11, no one would have seriously even proposed it. After 9/11, we dare not shrink from it." And then out came his bugle again: "America is coming ashore."

Three years after coming ashore, some neoconservatives are experiencing the torments of disillusionment. Their most cherished dreams are encrusted with the blood and sand of Iraq. There are no second chances. Having proclaimed Iraq as the ultimate test, neoconservatism is being judged according to its own standard. Francis Fukuyama, a neocon philosopher and signer of the original statement of the neocon Project for the New American Century, has produced a succinct synopsis of his disillusionment, *America at the Crossroads: Democracy, Power, and the Neoconservative Legacy.* Like the communists of a previous generation, he rejects a god that failed.

"I did not like the original version of Leninism and was skeptical when the Bush administration turned Leninist," he writes. Fukuyama chastises the neocons for believing that all societies and cultures share universal aspirations and can rapidly undergo the same path of modernization. He describes the administration's "bureaucratic tribalism" as "poisonous," and blames its closed-mindedness for its failures.

But the administration brushes aside the laments of the disillusioned— whether Fukuyama or William F. Buckley Jr. ("One can't doubt that the American objective in Iraq has failed") as coming from mere scriveners. Bush pays no more attention to the criticisms of conservative Republicans than to those of liberal Democrats. He is consistent in his rejection of criticism of any kind from any quarter. But his granitic impassivity does not resolve any actual problem; nor does ignoring critics make his arguments more convincing.

More striking, Bush seems unaware of or unconcerned with the conflict between his recent statements and those of his ambassador and generals in Iraq. Khalilzad, who has been assigned the mission impossible of creating a strong Iraqi state through negotiations with the hostile factions, said last week that the invasion had opened "a Pandora's box" of sectarian violence that might spread across the whole Middle East. With this single remark, he attributed the source of the Iraqi crisis to the invasion. Instead of marking "coming ashore" as the first step in the march of democracy, he depicted it as the beginning of a nightmare.

"Sectarian and ethnic conflict is the fundamental problem in Iraq," Khalilzad said at a news conference last month. He warned the Shiites that the key ministries of the interior and defense must be in the hands of people "who are nonsectarian, broadly acceptable, and who are not tied to militias." This was a direct challenge to the Shiite militias that have burrowed into these ministries and are using them as cover for assassinations and death squads. "American taxpayers expect their money to be spent properly. We are not going to invest the resources of the American people and build forces that are run by people who are sectarian," he said. The "potential is there," he concluded grimly in remarks last week, for full-scale civil war.

By contrast, Bush's latest speech argued confidently that civil war is being averted and that the Iraqis have turned away from "the abyss." The evil, as always, is the "terrorists." He returned to the old slogans as though the power of positive thinking will restore their credibility: "By helping Iraqis build a democracy, we will inspire reformers across the Middle East."

In his speech, Bush tried to cast aspersions on the nefarious machinations of the Iranians in Iraq. "Some of the most powerful IEDs [improvised explosive devices] we're seeing in Iraq today include components that came from Iran," he said. But the next day General Pace, asked if he had any proof of the president's claim, replied, "I do not, sir." Bush's statement raised the larger question of Iranian influence in Iraq, how it occurred, and its extent, but he did not address it.

Bush explained how much progress was being made in training the Iraqi security forces, ignoring Khalilzad's warning about their infiltration by Shiite militias. And Bush repeated his formula: "As Iraqis stand up, America and our coalition will stand down." Yet in testimony on Tuesday before the House, General Abizaid said he would not rule out permanent U.S. military bases. In other words, the United States is likely to remain indefinitely. There will be no final handover, no conclusive standing down.

What, then, is the mission in Iraq? Democracy? Defeating terrorism there so it won't come here, as Bush repeated in his speech? Having opened the Pandora's box, is it to keep the lid on as best we can? Is it to prevent a civil war?

On March 9, Secretary of Defense Rumsfeld testified before the Senate Appropriations Committee that the mission is to stop a civil war. "The plan," he said, "is to prevent a civil war and, to the extent one were to occur, to have the . . . Iraqi security forces deal with it to the extent they're able to."

So this is the plan: The U.S. presence will thwart a civil war. The current communal civil war is not a civil war. If a civil war that is bigger than the ongoing one breaks out, the United States will step aside and not suppress it. Instead, the Iraqi security forces will be deployed. The assumption is that they will be a neutral military force above the fray and able to impose the control of a central state. Once again, Khalilzad's cautionary note about Shiite manipulation of the security forces is silenced.

Rumsfeld's "plan," such as it is, drew the derisive condemnation of Moqtada al-Sadr, the powerful radical Shiite cleric and leader of one of the Shiite militias. In a tone of moral indignation after bomb attacks in Iraq this week, al-Sadr said of Rumsfeld, "May God damn you. You said in the past that civil war would break out if you were to withdraw, and now you say that in case of civil war you won't interfere." No one argued with al-Sadr's logic.

In his opening statement, Rumsfeld explained that the current "war on terror" is just like the Cold War. "We had to steel ourselves against an expansionist enemy, the Soviet Union, that was determined to destroy our way of life," he said. "Though this era is different, and though the enemy today is different, that is our task today." Such is the "perspective of history," he claimed.

Rumsfeld seems to have missed the briefings on the Pentagon's own grand strategy, as elucidated by Rear Admiral Bill Sullivan, vice director for strategic plans and policy for the Joint Chiefs. In his recent presentation "Fighting the Long War—Military Strategy for the War on Terrorism," Sullivan devoted a whole section to why the "long war" is not the Cold War. He pointed out "key differences: Religious basis of violent extremism versus a political ideology. Extremists are predominantly a stateless enemy. We cannot discredit all of Islam as we did with communism, it is a divine religion. We can only discredit the violent extremist." For Rumsfeld, these niggling distinctions are beside the point. If he decrees that the "war on terror" is the modern Cold War, then it must be and will be.

Bush promises to deliver more speeches on Iraq. Rumsfeld will undoubtedly provide more lessons in history. They have condemned themselves to their Sisyphean labors, endlessly pushing the rock up the hill, because they will not or cannot politically explain the actual mission in Iraq today: tamping down sectarian violence sufficiently to begin the withdrawal of U.S. troops on a strict timetable dictated by the convening of the Iraqi assembly and the approach of the American midterm elections. About whether that is possible and what happens next, the administration is clueless. But none of that can be articulated. Time and again, Bush asks for demonstrations of faith and will in place of logic and strategy.

The Love Song of Francis Fukuyama

MARCH 21, 2006

FRANCIS FUKUYAMA was one of the twenty-five original signatories of the Ur-document of the modern neoconservative movement, the Project for a New American Century's 1997 statement of principles calling for a return to "Reaganite military strength and moral clarity." As a historical footnote, not one of the signers supported President Reagan in his détente with the Soviet leader Mikhail Gorbachev that helped end the cold war; many of them were fierce critics of Reagan's rejection of the neoconservative dogma. Indeed, one of the signers, Frank Gaffney, was dismissed from his position as deputy assistant secretary of defense as a prelude to Reagan's embrace of Gorbachev.

In September 2000, PNAC issued a statement calling for a "process of transformation, even if it brings revolutionary change" in U.S. foreign policy, but fretted that domestic political conditions would not permit such a convulsion "absent some catastrophic and catalyzing event—like a new Pearl Harbor." One year later, the "new Pearl Harbor"—the September 11 terrorist attacks—provided the casus belli for the "revolutionary" upheaval of U.S. policy under Bush.

Now, three years after the invasion of Iraq, Fukuyama has published a cri de coeur, describing the Bush administration's blunders and a "poisonous" factionalism that has mangled a once supposedly coherent neoconservative philosophy. Among other revelations of *America at the Crossroads: Democracy, Power and the Neoconservative Legacy*, Fukuyama has discovered that the neocon pundit Charles Krauthammer is a dreamer in his projection of the United States' ability to remake the world in the neocons' ideal image. Attempting to rescue neoconservatism from itself, Fukuyama posits that the Bush administration in Iraq is guilty of heresy, of liberal taint, in its belief in "social engineering." Fukuyama wants to emphasize the conservatism over the *neo*. "I did not like the original version of Leninism and was skeptical when the Bush administration turned Leninist," he writes. But Fukuyama's effort to rescue the reputation of neoconservatism from Bush eerily echoes dissident communists' attempts to separate the idea of communism from Stalin. Fukuyama's disenchantment has not yet progressed to the final god-that-failed stage. He still evades the pragmatic judgment that Bush's consequences are the inescapable results of neoconservatism and not its aberration.

Fukuyama's discussion, in the *Guardian* of March 21, of the incident involving the purchase of U.S. ports operations by Dubai Ports World (a company owned by the United Arab Emirates) as sheer Democratic demagogy unfortunately neglects nuance, complexity, and context. In fact, Frank Gaffney, Fukuyama's fellow PNAC signer, now the director of a neoconservative think tank called the Center for National Security, played Paul Revere on the DPW deal. He was the catalyst of the controversy. "It seems a safe bet that you, like most Americans, would think it a lunatic idea, one that would clear the way for still more terror in this country," Gaffney stated. "If the president will not, Congress must ensure that the United Arab Emirates is not entrusted with the operation of any American ports." Gary Bauer, another PNAC signer, now a leader of the religious right, joined Gaffney's crusade. The DPW issue was a permutation of the national security fear that has been so successfully and consistently pioneered and exploited by the Bush administration since 9/11. But the deal did not become a political fiasco until the Republican congressional leadership abandoned Bush. The Republicans' craven calculation is that separating themselves from the unpopular Bush is becoming essential to their control of the Congress in this year's midterm elections. Fukuyama's simplistic tale of partisanship misses these unexpected realities. Perhaps he is unaware of the actual politics.

Over time, the founding fathers of PNAC have diverged. Only Fukuyama presents himself as disillusioned. Dick Cheney and Donald Rumsfeld, both original signers, head the "cabal" that, according to Lawrence Wilkerson, chief of staff to Colin Powell when he was secretary of state, dominates national security policy. Zalmay Khalilzad, a PNAC signer and now the U.S. ambassador to Iraq, is assigned the overwhelming task of somehow negotiating a settlement that will avert civil war there. And I. Lewis "Scooter" Libby, former chief of staff to Vice President Cheney, has been indicted for perjury and obstruction of justice and will stand trial in January 2007.

Libby was a ringleader inside the White House, encouraged by Cheney, in the smear campaign against Joseph Wilson. Before the Iraq war, Wilson, a former ambassador to two African countries as well as the last acting ambassador to Iraq and former African affairs section chief of the National Security Council, was sent by the CIA to Niger to report on rumors that Saddam Hussein was seeking to purchase yellowcake uranium there for use in producing nuclear weapons. Wilson discovered that the claim was bogus. He was therefore stunned to hear President Bush's 2003 State of the Union address giving credence to the story. Wilson waited until after the invasion to write an op-ed piece in the *New York Times* to set the record straight. That prompted a concerted effort, in which Libby played a central role, to discredit him. The Bush White House leaked to the conservative columnist Robert Novak the identity of Wilson's wife, Valerie Plame, as an undercover CIA operative. At the CIA's request to the justice department, a special prosecutor was appointed. When Libby appeared before the grand jury, he repeatedly testified that he learned about Plame's identity from the journalists Tim Russert of NBC News, Matthew Cooper of *Time* magazine, and Judith Miller of the *New York Times*. All of them testified under oath that Libby's grand jury statements were untrue.

The Libby Legal Defense Trust has raised millions of dollars. This fund not only defrays his lawyers' considerable expenses but also perhaps enables Libby to cover up the full involvement of Cheney. Wealthy Republican donors have flocked to contribute. The trajectory from PNAC to the Libby Legal Defense Trust charts the fall of neoconservatism. Among the members of the trust's advisory committee is one political philosopher: Francis Fukuyama.

Libby's website hails him as "one of the unsung heroes in fighting the war on terror" who has unfairly had "his good name attacked". By his association, Fukuyama must believe this, too. But so far Libby's would-be Zola has declined to write his "J'accuse." Or is E. M. Forster the inspirational model? It was Forster, after all, who wrote: "If I had to choose between betraying my country and betraying my friend, I hope I should have the guts to betray my country."

Apocalypse Now

MARCH 23, 2006

On his latest public-relations offensive, President Bush went to Cleveland on Monday to answer the paramount question he said people have on their minds about the Iraq war: "They wonder what I see that they don't." After mentioning "terror" fifty-four times and "victory" five, dismissing the prospect of "civil war" twice, and asserting that he is "optimistic," he called on a citizen in the audience, who homed in on the invisible meaning of recent events in the light of two books, the Book of Revelation and *American Theocracy* by Kevin Phillips. Phillips, the questioner explained, "makes the point that members of your administration have reached out to prophetic Christians who see the war in Iraq and the rise of terrorism as signs of the Apocalypse. Do you believe this, that the war in Iraq and the rise of terrorism are signs of the Apocalypse? And if not, why not?"

Bush's immediate response, as transcribed by CNN, was, "Hmmm." Then he said, "The answer is I haven't really thought of it that way. Here's how I think of it. First, I've heard of that, by the way." The official White House Web site transcript alters the punctuation, dropping the strategic comma, adding *the*, and thereby changing the meaning: "The first I've heard of that, by the way."

But it is certainly not the first time that Bush has heard of the apocalyptic preoccupation of much of the religious right, having begun his alliance with it as his father's liaison to its leaders in the 1988 presidential campaign. Jerry Falwell told *Newsweek* two years ago that he brought Tim LaHaye, then an influential right-wing leader and the author of the Left Behind book series, to meet Bush at the time: "I'm pretty sure I introduced Tim to George W." LaHaye's Left Behind novels, dramatizing the rapture, the battle of Armageddon, and the Second Coming, and ending with the vanquishing of the secular antichrist, have sold tens of millions of copies.

It is, however, almost certain that his Cleveland Q&A was the first time Bush had heard of Phillips's new book. Phillips was the visionary strategist for the presidential campaign of Richard Nixon in 1968, foreseeing in its lineaments the making of political realignment. His 1969 book, *The Emerging Republican Majority,* spelled out the shift of national power from the Northeast to the South and Southwest, which he was one of the first to call the Sun Belt. He grasped that many Southern Democrats, in reaction to the civil rights revolution, would become Southern Republicans. He also had a sensitive understanding of the resentments of urban ethnic Catholics against blacks on issues like crime, school integration, and jobs. But he never imagined that evangelical religion would compound and transcend these animosities to transmute the coalition he helped fashion into something that now horrifies him.

In *American Theocracy* Phillips describes Bush as the founder of "the first American religious party," in a country that has "never had a national religious party of any kind." The terrorist attacks of September 11 gave Bush the pretext for "seizing the fundamentalist moment." Rather than forging a new realignment, Bush won narrow victories by the manipulation of a "critical religious geography" and the hyping of issues such as gay marriage. This was a politics beyond mere resentment. Phillips writes, "New forces were being interwoven. These included the institutional rise of the religious right, the intensifying biblical focus on the Middle East, and the deepening of insistence on church-government collaboration within the GOP electorate." The rise of the religious right, according to Phillips, portends a potential "American disenlightenment," already apparent in Bush's hostility to science.

Even Bush's failures have become pretexts for advancing his transformation of the American government. On March 7, for example, he issued Executive Order 13397, establishing a Center for Faith-Based and Community Initiatives at the Department of Homeland Security. He has already created such centers in other federal departments. Exploiting his own disastrous emergency management in the wake of Hurricane Katrina, Bush is funneling funds to churches on the Gulf Coast as though they can compensate for governmental breakdown. Last year, the White House deputy director for faith-based initiatives, David Kuo, resigned with a statement that "Republicans were indifferent to the poor" and that the White House had "minimal commitment" to "compassionate conservatism."

As Bush's melding of church and state accelerates, the faith-based turns into the reality-based. The theocratic impulse, which has always been about earthly power, has provoked intense and unexpected opposition. Within hours of its publication, *American Theocracy* skyrocketed to become the number one best-seller on Amazon. At the movie theaters, *V for Vendetta*—a dystopian thriller in which an imaginary Britain is a metaphor for Bush's America, ruled by a totalitarian, faith-based regime, where gays are rounded up and the hero is a Guy Fawkes–like terrorist who blows up Parliament—is a surprise number one box-office hit. Bush has succeeded in getting American audiences to cheer for terrorism.

Card Shuffle

MORE SENIOR WHITE HOUSE aides have left as a result of criminal indictments in Bush's second term—the vice president's chief of staff, the top administrator for federal procurement policy at the Office of Management and Budget, and the director of domestic policy—than through normal attrition. So when the physically depleted chief of staff, Andrew Card, submitted his resignation after five years on the job, it was treated in Washington as a seismic event. In a fit of wishful thinking, the *Washington Post* ran a front-page story on Wednesday headlined "Card's Departure Seen as a Sign President Hears Words of Critics." Lacking earthly evidence, Card's quitting was read like portents in the heavens. Unmentioned was Bush's frantically defiant appearance in the Rose Garden immediately after the Oval Office ceremony accepting Card's resignation. With his entire cabinet arrayed behind him in a phalanx, flanked by Vice President Dick Cheney on one side and Secretary of Defense Donald Rumsfeld and Joint Chiefs of Staff chair General Peter Pace on the other, Bush insisted that he would stay the course in Iraq. "We're not going to lose our nerve," he proclaimed.

For months, Bush has been giving speeches declaring that unwavering support for his approach, whatever it is, will yield "victory." Once again, in the Rose Garden, he pledged he would not "retreat" before "the terrorists." His message remains the same as ever. "I mean," he said in a slightly exasperated tone during an interview with ABC News on February 28, "my policy has not changed."

If anything, the replacement of Andrew Card with Joshua Bolten, his understudy, highlights Bush's steadfast refusal to make substantive changes not only in the personnel of de facto power, dominated by Cheney, but also in any of his ruinous policies. It is the opposite of a changing of the guard; rather, it is equivalent to promoting a younger butler to the presidential suite when the older one retires.

Card's neutered politics was his chief virtue. He was the last of the old Bush family retainers out of the New England tradition. I first met him in the mid-1970s in Boston, when he was a liberal Republican state representative. In 1980, he ran George H. W. Bush's primary campaign for president in Massachusetts against Ronald Reagan, when Bush ridiculed Reagan's "voodoo economics." Two years later, Card campaigned for the Republican nomination for governor but finished third, badly trailing a conservative upstart. Card was anathema to the right in Massachusetts. He then began his ascent in Washington, sponsored by Vice President Bush. First, he headed the intergovernmental affairs office in the Reagan White House. Once the senior Bush was elected president, Card was appointed his deputy chief of staff and then secretary of transportation. After Bush's defeat in 1992, that portfolio enabled Card to become the top lobbyist for the Automobile Manufacturers Association. With the return of another Bush to the White House, Card's family loyalty, Washington experience, and bureaucratic proficiency made him a logical choice for George W. Bush's chief of staff.

His selection itself indicated Bush's view of the office. Some chiefs of staff are the most powerful figures next to the president, like Eisenhower's Sherman Adams and Reagan's James Baker. But in the current Bush White House, the vice president occupies that role. Card had little influence over policy; he walked through the West Wing without leaving footprints. He was the chief of staff as efficient enabler. He survived because he put loyalty—his loyalty to this Bush exemplifying his loyalty to the family—above all. In a pinch, he even waited on tables.

The former secretary of the treasury, Paul O'Neill, in his memoir, *The Price of Loyalty*, recounts an anecdote that begins with President-elect [George W.] Bush interrupting O'Neill's discussion of policy: " 'Where's lunch?' They'd ordered cheeseburgers, but after fifteen minutes, they had not arrived. 'Go get me Andy Card,' Bush said to one of the Secret Service agents. . . . [Card was] stolid and jovial, a man of solid, loyal character. Bush looked impatiently at Card, hard-eyed. 'You're the chief of staff. You think you're up to getting us some cheeseburgers?' Card nodded. No one laughed. He all but raced out of the room.'"

Joshua Bolten, the new chief of staff, is Card's Card. A banker at Goldman Sachs, he served as Card's deputy before his appointment as director of the Office of Management and Budget. In that position, Bolten constantly talked of progress and "improvement" in the deficit, paralleling Bush's proclamations about progress in Iraq. With each new budget, Bolten insisted the federal deficit was being lowered, and two years ago, he predicted it would be cut in half (from more than $500 billion) within five years. Now, Goldman Sachs, Bolten's former firm, projects about $5 trillion in deficits over the next ten years. Bolten's budgets were dead on arrival, received in congressional offices and deposited in the circular file without even being used as doorstops. Proficient at crunching these fantasy numbers, he has proved himself as loyal as Card, and the natural factotum to succeed him. Once again, Bush is staying the course.

No evidence shakes, deters, or changes Bush—no intelligence report, criminal investigation, or calamity. Like all failed presidents, Bush is a captive in an iron cage of his own making. The greater his frustration, the tighter he grips the bars. For any comparable example of ideological and personal inertia and inability to adapt to reality, one must go back to Herbert Hoover's rigidity in the face of the Depression.

It was neither obvious nor foretold that Hoover would respond with blinkers to the crisis that befell him. Hoover was considered the preeminent progressive of his age, the most capable man in the country, and one of the most cosmopolitan Americans of the time. He was well educated as an engineer and scientist, was a self-made millionaire, having become wealthy in international mining and banking, and lived for years in London. After World War I, President Woodrow Wilson summoned him, based on his sterling reputation, to organize relief for Europe and Russia. His organizational skills and the scale of his humanitarian projects were unexcelled. Appointed secretary of commerce by President Warren G. Harding, his integrity was completely untouched by the scandals of that administration. Reappointed by the inactive and reclusive President Calvin Coolidge, Hoover turned his department into a dynamo of policy innovation. In 1928, nominated by virtual acclamation, campaigning for a "New Era" that would "abolish poverty," he was elected president in a landslide. Six months after his inauguration, the stock market crashed. He was "the greatest innocent bystander in American history," according to the newspaper editor William Allen White.

Historians now agree that Hoover did take important steps to deal with the Depression, for example, creating the Home Loan Bank system and the Reconstruction Finance Corporation, among other measures. However, it was all too little, too late. He clung desperately to an ideology of social Darwinism masquerading as laissez-faire individualism. And he came to regard change outside the narrow parameters of his vision as evil, threatening the self-reliant American character as he understood it. In the name of ideology, he vetoed public works and unemployment insurance.

Hoover repeatedly expressed his faith that the Depression was ending as though such faith itself were sufficient to restore the economy. On May 1, 1930, he said his policies had "succeeded to a remarkable degree" and "we have now passed the worst." A month later, he declared there was no need for further measures: "The depression is over." After he left the White House, his illusions persisted. "Many persons left their jobs for the more profitable one of selling apples," he wrote.

Hoover entered office with an overwhelming one-party dominance over Congress. In the 71st Congress, the Republicans had a one-hundred-seat majority over the Democrats in the House of Representatives and a seventeen-seat majority in the Senate. Two years later, in 1930, the Democrats controlled the House by six seats, and the Senate was deadlocked.

In 1932, Hoover campaigned against the promise of the New Deal as something that "would destroy the very foundations of our American system." When he heard Hoover's remark, Franklin D. Roosevelt said: "I simply will not let Hoover question my Americanism."

Like Hoover, Bush builds walls of denial as the facts tumble down on his policies. And, like Hoover, who proclaimed prosperity to be just around the corner, Bush almost daily announces progress in Iraq. Like Hoover, he sustains a Micawber-like optimism that something will turn up in the face of worsening conditions. Hoover's rigid approaches inspired a crisis of confidence. His inviolate integrity fostered greater frustration about him as his honesty turned into sanctimonious armor. He suffered a crisis of credibility because his statements were glaringly at odds with reality. But Hoover was not responsible for creating the Depression. And no one accused him of being a liar. Bush, by contrast, has created his crisis himself.

On the day after Bush made his brave statement in the Rose Garden about "nerve" against "the terrorists," his ambassador to Iraq, Zalmay Khalilzad, is reported to have observed that there have been more assassinations by Shiite militias than killings by the Sunni insurgency. Khalilzad also delivered a message to Shiite leaders that President Bush "doesn't want, doesn't support, doesn't accept" the man they had selected to be prime minister, Ibrahim al-Jaafari, and demanded that they depose him.

Thus regime change enters a new phase, though not in Washington.

I, DeLay

APRIL 4, 2006

THE RESIGNATION OF TOM DELAY marks the crashing conclusion of his garish career but hardly the end of his legal troubles or the demise of the partisan political machine he constructed. The former majority leader of the House of Representatives has been the Republican strongman in the Congress, known as "the Hammer." As the party whip, he hung a bullwhip on his wall as a symbol of intimidation. The style of the former exterminator from Sugar Land, Texas, was bullying and crude. He called the Environmental Protection Agency the "Gestapo," ran a smear operation out of his office that would have won the admiration of Senator Joseph McCarthy, and grabbed whatever he wanted as his right. When a meek restaurateur in a Capitol Hill steakhouse politely asked DeLay to put out his large cigar because of a local no-smoking law, DeLay bellowed, "I am the federal government!" And he was not wrong.

DeLay enforced harsh discipline on the Republicans, bondage they savored as the essence of power. In return, anything a loyal House member wanted, DeLay would provide: "the Hammer" was also known as "the Concierge." Rules, including the House's own, meant nothing to him; they were irritating hindrances to be broken at his will. In order to gain passage of a bill favoring the big drug companies—preventing the Medicare prescription-drug program for the elderly from negotiating lower prices—he extended debate long past the deadline and was accused of offering the bribe of a campaign contribution to a wavering Republican. DeLay stomped on the Ethics Committee, stopping it from meeting to investigate this episode until public outcry forced him to back off. He greeted slaps on his wrist as badges of honor.

DeLay walked over bodies in his own party to reach his pinnacle. He led coups against the previous speaker of the House, Newt Gingrich, tribune of the right, yet too amenable to negotiation with President Clinton as far as DeLay was concerned.

DeLay's most notable achievement was coercing House Republicans to vote for the impeachment of President Clinton. Without his arm-twisting, impeachment would have certainly failed. A sizeable group of relatively moderate Republicans was opposed. They saw no merit in the ridiculous charges and understood that impeachment was being pressed out of crude partisanship. But DeLay threatened their financial supporters (by suggesting that their business interests would be blackballed from receiving congressional relief) and threatened to bankroll right-wing candidates against the moderates in Republican primaries to bleed them white. So, one by one, they caved in. Moderate Republicans were moderate when Tom DeLay told them they could be. Under DeLay's thumb, the House Judiciary Committee voted for impeachment after refusing to establish any constitutional standards for their action. The constitution was swept away in his exercise of power. President Clinton was acquitted by the Senate, but DeLay was unblemished by his abuse. Fear of him never ran higher.

Over more than a decade, DeLay forged a political machine that he called the K Street Project, after the downtown avenue of steel and glass buildings housing the large law and lobbying firms in Washington, DC. DeLay kept a black book in which he noted who gave money to and hired Republicans. When a trade association tried to employ a Democrat, it was issued a warning that it would be punished. From the K Street Project to the Republicans flowed tens of millions of dollars in campaign contributions. Meanwhile, the contracts from corporations for lobbying and legal work went to these Republican firms. It was a perfectly designed system of legal graft.

When President George W. Bush assumed office, one-party rule commenced. DeLay served as Bush's "Hammer." Back in Texas, the two of them had shattered the state's Democratic party. Now DeLay and Bush worked together at the national level to accomplish the same goal. Karl Rove, Bush's chief political adviser, who had been instrumental in the Texas takeover, was the go-between in the relationship. And the go-between in the Rove-DeLay relationship was a lobbyist named Jack Abramoff.

While exercising absolute power in the House, DeLay was determined to augment it further by thoroughly rigging the outcome of congressional elections in Texas. He created a political action committee, raised millions from his K Street allies, and poured the money into the Texas legislature, which in turn redrew the lines of congressional districts to wipe out the remaining Democrats. DeLay's scheme succeeded in giving him an even bigger Republican margin. But the district attorney of Travis County, Texas, investigated and indicted two of his aides and finally DeLay himself for illegally using corporate campaign funds.

As this scandal unfolded, the many-sided corruption of Jack Abramoff came under scrutiny by federal prosecutors. The ring tightened around DeLay, whose dealings with Abramoff were extensive and who called him one of his "closest friends". DeLay's former press secretary, Emily Miller, turned state's evidence. And his former communications director, Michael Scanlon, an Abramoff business partner, pleaded guilty in a deal with the prosecutors. In January, Abramoff himself pleaded guilty to fraud, tax evasion, and conspiracy to bribe public officials, and has been tattling for months. Last week, DeLay's former deputy chief of staff, Tony Rudy, another lobbyist, pleaded, too, his sentence to be decided on the extent of his cooperation. Thus surrounded, DeLay quit. His worst days lie ahead.

The Republican machine and its K Street Project hum along without their conductor. But the Republicans face the most difficult election cycle since they took control of the Congress in 1994. DeLay's further tribulations will illustrate the corruption endemic to the operation he built. The Republicans must hang onto the hope that the campaign funds they raise through the system DeLay devised will enable them to overcome his corrupt taint.

Tethered Goats

APRIL 6, 2006

SINCE THE IRAQI ELECTIONS in January, foreign-service officers at the U.S. Embassy in Baghdad have been writing a steady stream of disturbing cables describing drastically worsening conditions, say State Department officials who have seen them. Violence from incipient communal civil war is rapidly rising. Last month, there were eight times as many assassinations committed by Shiite militias as terrorist murders by Sunni insurgents. The insurgency, according to the cables, also continues to mutate. Meanwhile, President Bush's strategy of training the Iraqi police and army to take over from coalition forces—"When they stand up, we'll stand down"—is perversely and portentously accelerating the strife. State Department officials in the field report that Shiite militias use training as cover to infiltrate key positions. Thus the strategy to create institutions of order and security is fueling civil war.

Rather than being received as invaluable intelligence, the warnings are discarded or, worse, considered signs of disloyalty. Rejecting the facts on the ground apparently requires blaming the messengers. So far two top attachés at the embassy have been reassigned elsewhere for producing factual reports that were too upsetting, according to the State Department officials.

The Bush administration's response to the increasing disintegration in Iraq is to act as if it has a strategy that is succeeding. "More delusion as a solution in the absence of a solution," a senior State Department official told me. Under the pretense that Iraq is being pacified, the U.S. military is partially withdrawing from hostile towns in the countryside and parts of Baghdad. By reducing the numbers of soldiers, the administration can claim its policy is working going into the midterm elections. But the jobs that the military will no longer perform are being sloughed off onto State Department "provincial reconstruction teams" (PRTs) led by foreign-service officers. The stated rationale is that the teams will win Iraqi hearts and minds by organizing civil functions.

385

The Pentagon has informed the State Department that it will not provide security for these officials and that State should hire mercenaries for protection instead. Apparently, the U.S. military and the U.S. Foreign Service do not represent the same country in this exercise in nation-building. Internal State Department documents listing the PRT jobs, dated March 30, reveal that the vast majority of them remain unfilled. So Foreign Service employees are being forced to take the assignments, in which "they can't do what they are being asked to do," as a senior State Department official told me.

Foreign-service officers, as a rule, are self-abnegating in serving any administration. The State Department's Intelligence and Research Bureau was correct in its skepticism before the war about Saddam Hussein's possession of weapons of mass destruction, but it was ignored. The State Department was correct in its assessment, contained in the seventeen-volume *Future of Iraq Project*, of the immense effort required for reconstruction after the war, but it was disregarded. Now the State Department reports from Iraq are correct, but their authors are being punished. Foreign-service officers are to be sent out like tethered goats to the killing fields. When these misbegotten projects inevitably fail, as those inside State expect, the department will be blamed. The passive resistance to these assignments by foreign-service officers reflects informed anticipation of impending disaster, including the likely murders of diplomats.

Amid this internal crisis of credibility, Secretary of State Condoleezza Rice has washed her hands of her department. Her management skills are minimal. She has left the task of coercing people to fill the PRTs to her counselor, Philip Zelikow, who, by doing the dirty work, is trying to keep her reputation clean. Rice's trumpeted "transformational diplomacy" turns out to be a slogan justifying the transfer of U.S. embassy and consular staff principally in Europe to PRT positions in Iraq.

While the State Department was racked by collapsing morale, Rice traveled last week to northern England to visit the childhood home of the British foreign secretary, Jack Straw. After landing at Liverpool's John Lennon Airport, she demonstrated bafflement about some lyrics in "A Day in the Life" ("Four thousand holes in Blackburn, Lancashire"), sang a few bars of "Sgt. Pepper's Lonely Hearts Club Band," and declared that though the Bush administration had committed "tactical errors, thousands of them" in Iraq, it is right in its strategy. Then, after her self-affirming confession, she and Straw took a magic carpet to Baghdad to attempt to overthrow Prime Minister Ibrahim al-Jafaari in favor of a more pliable character. "I heard the news today, oh boy / The English army had just won the war."

"Did you ever imagine in your wildest dreams that after Vietnam we'd be doing this again?" one top State Department official remarked to another last week. Inside the department people wonder about the next "strategy," after the hearts-and-minds gambit of sending diplomats unprotected to help secure victory turns into a squalid, overlooked fiasco. "Helicopters on the roof?" asked one official.

The President of Truth

APRIL 13, 2006

PRESIDENT BUSH has been in search of himself for two and a half years. His voyage of self-discovery began on September 30, 2003. Asked what he knew about senior White House officials anonymously leaking the identity of the covert CIA operative Valerie Plame Wilson, he expressed his earnest desire to help the special prosecutor, Patrick Fitzgerald, ferret out the perpetrators. "I want to know the truth," he said. "If anybody has got any information inside our administration or outside our administration, it would be helpful if they came forward with the information so we can find out whether or not these allegations are true and get on about the business."

Bush didn't stop there. He issued an all-points bulletin requesting help for the prosecutor. "And if people have got solid information, please come forward with it. And that would be people inside the information who are the so-called anonymous sources, or people outside the information—outside the administration. And we can clarify this thing very quickly if people who have got solid evidence would come forward and speak out. And I would hope they would." The day before, the president had sent out his press secretary, Scott McClellan, to announce that involvement in this incident would be a firing offense: "If anyone in this administration was involved in it, they would no longer be in this administration."

Last week, however, Fitzgerald revealed in a filing in his perjury and obstruction of justice case against I. Lewis "Scooter" Libby, former chief of staff to Vice President Dick Cheney, that Libby had been authorized by the president and vice president to leak to reporters parts of the October 2002 national intelligence estimate on Iraq's weapons of mass destruction.

The White House's initial response was for an anonymous "senior administration official" to leak to the *New York Times* that Bush had played "only a peripheral role in the release of the classified material and was uninformed about the specifics," as the *Times* reported. The White House source, trying to remove the president from the glare, fingered Cheney as the instigator.

On Monday, Bush appeared at Johns Hopkins University's Paul H. Nitze School of Advanced International Studies, where a graduate student asked him about his role in the leak of classified information. The president, who had once perplexedly said, "I want to know the truth," replied, "I wanted people to see the truth and thought it made sense for people to see the truth." Was blind but now he sees? Grace (or Patrick Fitzgerald) had led him home.

Bush acted in the beginning as an innocent injured party. He pretended to be utterly baffled by events. His feigned unawareness was intended to deflect attention from himself. His call to find those responsible was an attempt to ensure that the facts would never be known. When he was exposed, he donned a new guise. Instead of the seeker of truth, he became the truth teller.

But the classified information he authorized to be selectively leaked—that Saddam Hussein was seeking to purchase yellowcake uranium in Niger for use in nuclear weapons—was not the truth, and its release was intended to buttress a falsehood. Indeed, last week, the former secretary of state Colin Powell told the journalist Robert Scheer that the notorious sixteen words in Bush's 2003 State of the Union address concerning Iraq's supposed efforts to buy uranium—the claim that the former ambassador Joseph Wilson was sent to Niger to investigate—were bogus. "That was a big mistake," Powell said. "It should never have been in the speech. I didn't need Wilson to tell me that there wasn't a Niger connection. He didn't tell us anything we didn't already know. I never believed it." Thus, three years after the event, Powell finally admitted publicly that the president spoke falsely about the reason for war, that there were interested parties inside the administration determined to put false words in his mouth, and that the secretary of state, knowing this, lacked the power to stop it.

As the man of truth, Bush offered a convoluted explanation of the declassification process. He retreated into technical legalisms that as the man of action he had disdained. "You're not supposed to talk about classified information, and so I declassified the document," he said at Johns Hopkins. "I thought it was important for people to get a better sense for why I was saying what I was saying in my speeches."

Once again, he offered a misleading statement. The completely irregular process of Bush's declassification, so unprecedented that Scooter Libby was unsure it was legal, was a badge of guilt. The declassification reflected a vengeful impulse against a critic and was an inadvertent confession of the fragility and tenuousness of Bush's case for war.

Fitzgerald's filing of April 5, the cue for Bush's latest theater of the absurd, fills in details of the narrative. Through Fitzgerald's further filings before the January 2007 trial of Scooter Libby, other crucial information may yet emerge. In his prosecution of Libby, Fitzgerald is establishing indisputable facts about the history of the Bush presidency and its methods of operation.

Fitzgerald writes that the Office of the Vice President viewed Wilson's revelation of his mission to Niger and what he didn't find there "as a direct attack on the credibility of the vice president (and the president) on a matter of signal importance: the rationale for the war in Iraq." So, Fitzgerald continues, the White House undertook "a plan to discredit, punish or seek revenge against" Wilson that included revealing the covert identity of his wife. The "concerted action" against Wilson was centrally organized and directed. The prosecutor writes that he has gathered "evidence that multiple officials in the White House discussed her employment with reporters prior to (and after) July 14 [2003]"—the date her professional activities, tracking weapons of mass destruction for the CIA, were made public and thus compromised by the conservative columnist Robert Novak.

While one part of the "concerted action" was the attempt to damage Wilson by attacking him through his wife, another was to manipulate the press to undermine Wilson's credibility. Cheney ordered Libby to act as the leaker. The plan, according to Libby's testimony, was to "disclose certain information in the NIE" to the *New York Times* reporter Judith Miller. Libby and Miller had worked this way before, when she had published a series of stories asserting that Saddam Hussein possessed WMD, based on leaks she received that were, in circular fashion, cited by the administration as authoritative reports by the "newspaper of record." Libby testified that he was directed to tell her that the NIE "held that Iraq was 'vigorously trying to procure' uranium."

In the setup for the leak, Fitzgerald writes, Cheney "advised defendant that the President specifically had authorized defendant to disclose certain information in the NIE" and that that approval was a secret. Libby was a team player, but he was also anxious about a declassification that was "unique in his experience."

The formal rules for declassification were amended by Bush's Executive Order 13292 of March 25, 2003, on "Classified National Security Information." Under any circumstances, the president has the authority to unilaterally declassify official secrets and intelligence "in the public interest." But a decision to declassify a document normally passes through the originating agency and then through the Office of the National Security Adviser. Then the document is stamped "declassified," and the declassified order is appended to the document.

None of these procedures was followed in this case, which is why Libby's antenna was gyrating. He sought the advice of Cheney's counsel, David Addington, Libby's close ally. In approaching Addington, Libby must have known what he would hear. Addington is the foremost legal advocate in the White House of the idea that the president should be completely unfettered in his authority, whether in the torture of detainees, domestic surveillance, or any other matter. Unsurprisingly, Addington "opined that presidential authorization to publicly disclose a document amounted to a declassification of the document."

Only four people—Bush, Cheney, Libby, and Addington—were privy to the declassification. It was kept secret from the director of the Central Intelligence Agency, the secretary of state, and the national security adviser, Stephen Hadley, among others. Indeed, Hadley was arguing at the time for declassification of the NIE but was deliberately not told that it was no longer classified. Fitzgerald writes about Libby: "Defendant fails to mention . . . that he consciously decided not to make Mr. Hadley aware of the fact that defendant himself had already been disseminating the NIE by leaking it to reporters while Mr. Hadley sought to get it formally declassified." Casting Hadley as the fool was part of the game.

On July 8, Libby met with Miller. In this dance, Libby misrepresented the contents of the NIE, which Miller apparently accepted at face value, as she had accepted such leaks in the past. With an air of mystery, telling Miller she should identify him in her story as "a former Hill staffer," Libby vouched for a document he knew to be at least partially false, failing to note that the NIE, significantly, did not prove that Saddam was seeking uranium in Niger; on the contrary, the NIE contained a caveat from the State Department's Bureau of Intelligence and Research saying that the rumors "do not, however, add up to a compelling case." For her part, Miller thought she was receiving classified, not declassified, material, as she wrote in the *Times* after her release from jail, where she had been held on contempt of court charges after refusing to reveal her sources to Fitzgerald.

Ten days after their meeting, which did not result in a story, the already declassified NIE was formally declassified as though it had never been declassified in secret. The date of its declassification in the official government record, in fact, reads July 18, 2003, not the date that Bush declassified it for the purpose of Libby's leaking.

After the launch of the federal investigation, Libby became frantic. Fitzgerald writes that "while the President was unaware of the role that the Vice President's Chief of Staff and National Security Adviser had in fact played in disclosing Ms. Wilson's CIA employment, defendant implored White House officials to have a public statement issued exonerating him." But there was no forthcoming statement. Libby begged Cheney for help "in having his name cleared." But Cheney did nothing for his henchman. In a White House that demands impeccable loyalty, loyalty was not being returned.

Libby not only knew that Hadley had leaked Plame's identity; he also knew that Karl Rove, the president's principal political adviser, had leaked her name to Novak. Libby linked himself to Rove in his desperate cover-up. He gave Scott McClellan a handwritten note, almost in the form of a haiku, as a script for his press briefing. It read:

People have made too much of the difference in
How I described Karl and Libby
I've talked to Libby.
I said it was ridiculous about Karl
And it is ridiculous about Libby.
Libby was not the source of the Novak story.
And he did not leak classified information.

On October 4, 2003, McClellan informed the White House press corps that Rove and Libby (and Elliott Abrams, a member of the National Security Council) were innocent of the charges of leaking Plame's name: "Those individuals assured me that they were not involved in this."

Then Libby appeared before the grand jury, where he several times claimed under oath that he learned about Plame's identity from reporters. On October 28, 2005, he was indicted for perjury and obstruction of justice.

Fitzgerald's filing demolishes Libby's projected defense as a busy man with so many important matters of state on his mind that he just can't remember exactly who told him what about Plame. Here, in his own words, Libby recalls precisely his anxiety about the "unique" declassification and the others who leaked Plame's name. Libby may now wonder why he should play the fall guy, unless he hopes for a presidential pardon on the morning of January 20, 2009, the day Bush leaves office.

President Bush, having previously play-acted as unknowing, is now engaged in the make-believe that he is helping people "see the truth." Yet the White House refuses to declassify the one-page summary of the NIE used to brief Bush. Presumably, it contains the caveats from various intelligence sources on Saddam's WMD, showing that the case remained unproved and shaky when Bush presented it as conclusive.

The White House also refuses to release the transcripts of Bush's and Cheney's testimony before the prosecutor. As witnesses, they are not bound by any rule of secrecy and are free to discuss their testimony publicly. During the Watergate investigation, the Supreme Court ruled unanimously that President Nixon had to turn over his secret audiotapes to the prosecutor. Fitzgerald obviously already has the White House transcripts. Only the public is kept ignorant of their contents. Why won't the White House release them now? Indeed, there is a precedent. On June 24, 2000, Vice President Al Gore made public his testimony to the Justice Department investigation into campaign finance. (Although Bush and Cheney insisted on giving testimony without being sworn under oath, thus precluding any later charges of perjury, they remain legally liable. Under Title 18, Section 1001 of the U.S. Code, anyone who testifies falsely in a federal inquiry may be fined and sentenced to five years in prison.)

Bush is entangled in his own past. His explanations compound his troubles and point to the original falsehoods. Through his first term, Bush was able to escape by blaming the Democrats, smearing the motives of his critics and changing the subject. But his methods have become self-defeating. When he utters the word *truth* now, most of the public is mistrustful. His accumulated history overshadows what he might say.

The collapse of trust was cemented into his presidency from the start. A compulsion for secrecy undergirds the Bush White House. Power, as Bush and Cheney see it, thrives by excluding diverse points of view. Bush's presidency operates on the notion that the less prior debate, the better the decision. The State Department has been treated like a foreign country; the closest associates of the elder President Bush, Brent Scowcroft and James Baker, have been excluded; the career professional staff have been bullied and quashed; the Republican-dominated Congress has abdicated oversight; and influential elements of the press have been complicit.

Inside the administration, the breakdown of the national security process has produced a vacuum filled by dogmatic fixations that become more rigid as reality increasingly fails to cooperate. But the conceit that executive fiat can substitute for fact has not sustained the illusion of omnipotence.

The precipitating event of the investigation of the Bush White House—Wilson's disclosure about his Niger mission—was an effort by a lifelong foreign-service officer to set the record straight and force a debate on the reasons for going to war. Wilson stood for the public discussion that had been suppressed. The Bush White House's "concerted action" against him therefore involved an attempt to poison the wellsprings of democracy.

The Decider

APRIL 19, 2006

THE ANALOGY BETWEEN IRAQ and Vietnam has proved to be most compelling to the generals who planned and conducted the invasion of Iraq. They kept to themselves their profound disquiet about the rapid rejection of the original plan for invasion, one that had taken ten years to develop; the inadequate downsized force; the absence of preparation for the occupation; and the disastrous decision to disband the Iraqi military.

Almost all these generals voted for George W. Bush in 2000 as a statement of conservatism; they never expected radicalism. Serving their civilian neoconservative superiors, they endured contempt. Defense Secretary Donald Rumsfeld's closest aide, Undersecretary of Defense for Intelligence Stephen Cambone, joked that the problems of the Army "could be solved by lining up fifty of its generals in the Pentagon and gunning them down," report Michael R. Gordon and General Bernard E. Trainor in their new book on the Iraq invasion, *Cobra II*. It was the sort of joke that Uday Hussein could have made. On September 10, 2001, Rumsfeld held a Pentagon town meeting at which he declared the "bureaucracy"—the career military professionals—to be "a serious threat to the security of the United States."

The generals have been wary of engaging in public debate for fear of being misconstrued as politically motivated. But they are haunted by Vietnam and deeply influenced by H. R. McMaster's 1997 book, *Dereliction of Duty*, which argues that the Joint Chiefs of Staff of the Vietnam era failed in their constitutional responsibility to object strenuously to misguided strategies. (McMaster is currently a colonel serving in Iraq.) As the generals have stepped forward, one by one, to demand the resignation of Secretary Rumsfeld, they have spoken in the language of McMaster's book.

On March 19, retired army Major General Paul Eaton, who was in charge of training the Iraqi army, said Rumsfeld is "incompetent strategically, operationally and tactically, and is far more than anyone responsible for what has happened to our important mission in Iraq."

On April 2, retired marine General Anthony Zinni, former chief of U.S. Central Command, said, "Poor military judgment has been used throughout this mission."

On April 9, retired marine Lieutenant General Gregory Newbold, the former director of operations for the Joint Chiefs of Staff, wrote: "Inside the military family, I made no secret of my view that the zealots' rationale for war made no sense. . . . But I now regret that I did not more openly challenge those who were determined to invade a country whose actions were peripheral to the real threat—al-Qaeda."

On April 12, retired army Major General John Batiste, who commanded the 1st Infantry Division in Iraq and was the military aide to the former deputy secretary of defense, Paul Wolfowitz, said: "Decisions are made without taking into account sound military recommendations." He described Rumsfeld as "abusive" and went on national television to denounce the Bush administration's "axis of arrogance."

The next day, retired army Major General John Riggs and Major General Charles Swannack, the former commander of the 82nd Airborne, went public. "They only need the military advice when it satisfies their agenda," said Riggs. Swannack emphasized that Rumsfeld bore "culpability" for the abuses at Abu Ghraib prison in Iraq.

In response, the Bush administration has mounted a full-scale PR defense. On Monday, Rumsfeld appeared in the guise of King Solomon on the radio talk show of the right-wing Rush Limbaugh: "This, too, will pass," he said. On Tuesday Bush proposed a syllogism: "I'm the decider, and I decide what's best. And what's best is for Don Rumsfeld to remain."

But the revolt of the generals, speaking for much of the serving senior officer corps, is unprecedented in scope and depth. Its roots lie in the military's anguish over Vietnam, but the past has become urgent because of the present.

While the White House press secretary, Scott McClellan, resigns, Rumsfeld stays. Clinging to Rumsfeld as indispensable to his strength, Bush reveals his fragility. The two men prefer not to understand that time and opportunity lost can never be regained. Their denial extends beyond the realities of Iraq and its history to the history of the United States. It is extremely peculiar that they have learned no lessons of nation building from the tragedy of failed political leadership during post–Civil War Reconstruction, whose collapse consigned African Americans to second-class citizenship for a century. Bush & Co. disdain nation building as something soft and weak connected to the Clinton presidency, just as they belittled and neglected terrorism as a Clinton obsession before September 11 and as the president dismissed history itself as weightless.

"History? We don't know. We'll all be dead," Bush remarked in 2003. "We cannot escape history," said Abraham Lincoln. The living president has already sealed his reputation in history.

The Passion of George W. Bush

APRIL 27, 2006

The urgent dispatch of Karl Rove to the business of maintaining one-party rule in the midterm elections is the Bush White House's belated startle reflex to its endangerment. Besieged by crises of his own making, plummeting to ever-lower depths in the polls week after week, Bush has assigned his political general to muster dwindling forces for a heroic offensive to break out of the closing ring. If the Democrats gain control of the House or Senate, they will launch a thousand subpoenas to establish the oversight that has been abdicated by the Republican Congress.

In his acceptance speech before the Republican National Convention in 2004, the "war president" spoke of "greatness" and "resolve" and repeatedly promised "a safer world" and "security," and compared himself "to a resolute president named Truman." Afterward, Bush declared he had had his "accountability moment". Further debate was unnecessary; the future was settled.

But Rove's elaborate design for Republican rule during the second term has collapsed under the strain of his grandiosity. In 2004, Rove galvanized "the base" (ironically, "al Qaeda" in Arabic) through ruthless divide-and-conquer and slash-and-burn tactics. But with Bush winning the election by a bare 50.73 percent, he and Rove failed to forge the unassailable Republican realignment that he sought.

Rove is an amateur historian whose goal was modeled on the apparently unlikely figure of President William McKinley. Bush's radicalism bears little resemblance to McKinley's stalwart conservatism except for his friendly orientation toward big business. Rove zeroed in on McKinley because his election in 1896 created a natural Republican presidential majority that was broken only by the party split of 1912, when Theodore Roosevelt ran as a Progressive, and in 1932, when Franklin D. Roosevelt ushered in a Democratic realignment. Rove and Bush had hoped to use the second term to force radical changes that would alter American government, society, and politics. At last, they planned to undo the New Deal and return to the Republican Eden. But Rove's proposal for the privatization of Social Security, among other schemes, was aborted without even a single congressional hearing.

The Republican cathedral of his dreams in ruins, Rove has now discharged formal control of moribund domestic policy to a protégé, Joel Kaplan (a former law clerk of Justice Antonin Scalia's). The reshuffle of the White House senior staff includes the elevation of another Rove protégé, Josh Bolten, to chief of staff, replacing Andrew Card, a New England factotum of the Bush family left over from the term of the elder Bush, who was not one of Rove's creations. As Bolten has explained privately, Rove remains at the apex of a new iron triangle, just as he stood at the peak of the Texas triangle of Karen Hughes, Joe Allbaugh, and himself that managed George W. Bush's 2000 campaign for president.

Rove's lieutenants have been delegated to hold the fort while he begins the epic defense of the embattled regime. His mission is to salvage the Republican majority in Congress from the blighted corruption of its leadership and rescue the Bush White House from the consequences of its own radical policies on everything from the endless Iraq war to skyrocketing gasoline prices. In 2004, Rove was still able to manage the Bush campaign on the momentum of fear from September 11. No longer perceived by the public as a rock of security, Bush's rigid leadership is seen as the source of turbulence. Security was his promise, but disorder has become his byproduct.

So Rove must depend on the tricks of his trade: arousing the fear of gays and other threats (like Hollywood) to traditional family values, as he did in 2004; spinning national security to cast the Democrats as weak and unpatriotic, as he did in 2002; using well-financed front groups and his regular corps of political consultants to outsource smears and produce them as television and radio commercials, as he did to destroy John McCain in the Republican primaries of 2000 and John Kerry in 2004; and conducting whisper campaigns about the personal lives of those he seeks to annihilate, as he has done since 1994, when his devastating rumors that Texas Governor Ann Richards was a lesbian helped install his patron in the Lone Star Statehouse and pave the way to the White House.

Rove must concentrate his mind, with one gimlet eye fixed on the special prosecutor, Patrick Fitzgerald, who on Wednesday summoned him back to testify before a federal grand jury. As Rove develops strategy for elections to come, he is a subject under investigation for dirty tricks past.

The ferocious defense of Bush's radical presidency is being mounted on other fronts as well. In the face of demands from the generals who commanded the troops in Iraq for the resignation of Secretary of Defense Donald Rumsfeld for blind arrogance and unswerving incompetence, Bush has reaffirmed his support. In the last two weeks, Rumsfeld has appeared on fourteen right-wing radio talk shows, securing "the base" and giving full vent to his splenetic personality. On April 18, Laura Ingraham interviewed him on her syndicated program. From the transcript, as it appears on the official Department of Defense website:

> Ingraham: I saw Charles Krauthammer [the conservative pundit] a couple of nights ago saying there is absolutely no chance that you would step down. Is he right about that?
>
> Secretary Rumsfeld: He is a very smart man. [Laughter.]

The administration's die-hard supporters in the Senate, meanwhile, are fighting to prevent the Armed Services Committee from calling the retired generals to testify about Rumsfeld's fitness. Frustrating congressional oversight is essential to preserving executive power. Checks and balances are the enemy of the Bush White House.

Vice President Dick Cheney, a principal author and defender of this constitutional doctrine, maintains his ever-vigilant grip on the executive branch, even as he was caught napping during a meeting last week with the Chinese president, Hu Jintao. David Addington, his chief of staff, extending his discipline far into the national-security apparatus, never rests.

For Rumsfeld and Cheney, the final days of the Bush administration are the endgame. They cannot expect positions in any future White House. Since the Nixon administration, when counselor Rumsfeld and his deputy Cheney watched the self-destruction of the president, they have plotted to reach the point where they could impose the imperial presidency that evaded Nixon. Both men held ambitions to become president themselves. The Bush years have been their last opportunity to run a presidency. Through the agency of the son of one of their colleagues from the Ford White House, George H. W. Bush (whom President Ford considered but passed over for his vice president and chief of staff, giving the latter job to Cheney), they have enacted their notion of executive power. But the fulfillment of their idea of presidential power is steadily draining the president of strength. Their thirty-year project of autocracy has merely produced monumental incompetence.

Yet Rumsfeld and Cheney do not really care. Bad public opinion polls do not concern them. Their ambition is near its end. They want to use their remaining time accumulating as much power as possible in an unaccountable executive.

Ironically, the more Bush tries to entrench his imperial presidency, the weaker he becomes. Believing that his single-mindedness, stark convictions, and bold indifference to criticism have been the secret of his success, he is confounded and baffled by the inability of his constant redoubling of effort to produce the same results as before. Why should the traits that magnetically pulled him up suddenly have the reverse effect of pulling him down? At his peak, he proudly declared, "In Texas, we don't do nuance." Now he reasserts himself as "the decider."

And yet he feels compelled to explain the nuances of his decisions. On Monday, Bush appeared before the Orange County (California) Business Council to justify the origins of the Iraq war and his foreign policy in general. "I also wanted to let you know that it's before you commit troops that you must do everything you can to solve the problem diplomatically. And I can look you in the eye and tell you I feel I've tried to solve the problem diplomatically to the max," he said.

Just the day before, on CBS's *60 Minutes*, Tyler Drumheller, the former CIA chief in Europe, disclosed that during the run-up to the Iraq war, the Iraqi foreign minister, Naji Sabri, had been bribed to hand over military secrets. "We continued to validate him the whole way through," Drumheller said. Sabri's information was that Iraq had no weapons of mass destruction. But the White House dismissed the intelligence. "The policy was set," Drumheller said. "The war in Iraq was coming. And they were looking for intelligence to fit into the policy, to justify the policy."

Drumheller's account is consistent with the famous Downing Street memo, recording British prime minister Tony Blair's conference with his top national-security and intelligence advisers on July 23, 2002. The memo stated: "Bush wanted to remove Saddam, through military action, justified by the conjunction of terrorism and WMD. But the intelligence and facts were being fixed around the policy."

In his Orange County speech, to illuminate his thinking, Bush again summoned the authority of the "higher Father." "I base a lot of my foreign policy decisions on some things that I think are true. One, I believe there's an Almighty." This is one Bush doctrine that is inarguable. But Bush's profession of faith is precisely the message that incites Islamic terrorists in their jihad against the Christian crusader. For Bush, the culture war and the war on terror are one and the same. Understanding that the latter undermines the former, that his policy and politics are at cross purposes, would involve too much nuance.

The more beleaguered Bush becomes, the more he is flattered by his advisers with comparisons to great men of history whose foresight and courage were not always appreciated in their own times. Abraham Lincoln is one favorite. Another is Harry Truman, who established the framework of Cold War policy but left office during the Korean War deeply unpopular, with poll ratings sunk in the twenties. Lately, Bush sees himself in the reflected light of Winston Churchill, bravely standing against appeasers. "Never give in—never, never, never, never, in nothing great or small, large or petty, never give in," Churchill said in 1941 as Britain stood alone against the Nazis. "Bush tells his out-of-town visitors to think of how history will judge his administration 20 years hence and not to worry about setbacks in Iraq," writes the conservative columnist Arnaud de Borchgrave.

Of course, Bush does care about the outcome of the midterm elections. He knows full well the catastrophe that his already wounded presidency would suffer if the Republicans were to lose one or the other chamber of Congress. Once again, he is depending on Rove's skill to salvage the situation. But insofar as his policies are concerned, the "decider" has decided that public opinion doesn't really matter.

On Tuesday, Bush reached the invisible but fateful milestone of one thousand days left in his term. It is a magical number associated with the thousand days of President Kennedy, a period that served as the title of Arthur Schlesinger Jr.'s memoir of that White House. Bush cannot run again and has no obvious successor to hold his team together. On March 22, he announced that he would leave to the next president the decision about the continued U.S. presence in Iraq. In the final days of his backward Camelot he will never, never, never change his basic policies, the source of his unraveling.

The greater the stress, the more Bush denies its cause. In his end time, he has risen above his policy and is transcending politics. He has decided his scourging is his sanctification. Bush will be a martyr resurrected. The future will unfold properly from all the wisdom of his decisions, based on fervent faith, upheld by his holy devotion. Criticism and unpopularity only confirm to him his bravery and his critics' weakness. Being reviled is proof of his righteousness. Inevitably, decades hence, people will grasp his radiant truth and glory. Such is the passion of George W. Bush.

Index

Abbas, Abu, 107
Abbas, Mahmoud, 347
ABC News, 18, 315, 322, 378
Abdel-Rahman, Omar, 319
Abdullah, king of Jordan, 51, 138
Abizaid, John, 367, 370
Abraham Lincoln Museum and Library, 360
Abramoff, Jack, 20, 154–58, 207, 208, 278, 281, 282–85, 334–37, 341, 342, 343, 383–84
Abrams, Elliott, 31–32, 51, 54, 392
Abu Ghraib prison, 8, 19, 60–62, 63–64, 66, 69, 72–73, 78, 195–96, 200, 205, 239, 255, 256, 396
Accidental American, The: Tony Blair and the Presidency (Naughtie), 113–14
Acheson, Dean, 151
Achille Lauro (liner), 107
Adams, John, 172, 356
Adams, John Quincy, 3
Adams, Sherman, 379
Addington, David, 320, 356, 359, 391, 401
Adeli, Seyed Mohammad-Hossein, 141
Adelman, Kenneth, 271, 362
Afghanistan, 6–7, 9, 45, 60, 61, 71, 98–99, 129, 192, 198, 199, 201, 202, 231–33, 234, 349–50
African Americans, 2, 108, 187, 261, 264, 269, 341, 363, 364–66, 376, 396
Against All Enemies (Clarke), 12, 46–47, 48–49
Agnew, Spiro, 164
Agriculture Department, U.S., 13
Ahmadinejad, Mahmoud, 346, 347
Air War College, 103
Alabama Christian Coalition, 284
Alabama National Guard, 88

Albany Times Union, 204
Alcoa, 11, 39
Alhaddad, Sawsan, 329
Alito, Samuel, 13, 19, 293, 326, 331–33
Allawi, Iyad, 137, 214
Allbaugh, Diane, 267
Allbaugh, Joe, 263, 266–67, 273, 400
Allbaugh Company, 266
Allen, Claude, 364–66
Alsop, Joseph, 308
Alterman, Eric, 247
Altria, 341
America at the Crossroads: Democracy, Power, and the Neoconservative Legacy (Fukuyama), 369, 372
American Association of Automobile Manufacturers, 279, 379
American Association of Retired Persons (AARP), 146
American Bar Association, 197
American Civil Liberties Union (ACLU), 200, 203
American Enterprise Institute, 80
American Israel Public Affairs Committee, 32
American Legion, 95
Americans for Tax Reform, 157, 283
American Theocracy (Phillips), 375–77
Amnesty International, 197, 199–203, 313
Annan, Kofi, 124, 151
Anti-Ballistic Missile Treaty, 151
Applebaum, Anne, 45
Aqaba summit, 51
Arafat, Yasir, 32
Arctic National Wildlife Refuge, 255
Armey, Richard, 156, 340
Armitage, Richard, 127–28, 178, 181, 182

Buchanan, Pat, 245
Buckham, Edwin A., 155–56, 336
Buckley, William F., Jr., 369
Bureau of Justice Statistics, U.S., 261
Burger, Warren, 220
Bush, Barbara, 264
Bush, George H. W., 3, 4, 6, 8, 9, 12, 22,
   34, 45, 46, 55, 57, 75, 79, 80, 86, 95,
   100–101, 107, 127, 128, 177, 220–21,
   226, 246, 278, 281, 282, 289, 303, 304,
   305, 306, 310, 353, 357, 379, 400, 401
Bush, Jeb, 2, 159–60
Bush, Laura, 77, 363, 365
Bush, Neil, 267
Bush at War (Woodward), 40, 47, 48, 308
Bush doctrine, 9, 28, 45
Bush v. Gore, 6, 293
Business Roundtable, 156
Bybee, Jay, 8, 196, 319

California, 95–96, 167
Cambone, Stephen, 67, 395
Camp X-Ray, 66
Capital Gang, The (TV show), 246
Card, Andrew, 203, 279, 352, 355, 365,
   378–80, 400
Carlos the Jackal (terrorist), 314
Carter, Jimmy, 21, 130, 250, 304
Carville, James, 244
Casey, William, 74
Cassel, Douglass, 331
Catholic Church/Catholics, 108–9, 110,
   111, 162, 164–65, 166–68, 169–71, 173,
   185, 246–47, 376
CBS News, 60–61
Center for Constitutional Rights, 197
Center for Faith-Based and Community
   Initiatives, 376
Center for National Security, 373
Center for Public Integrity, 279
Centers for Disease Control, 13, 365
Centers for Medicare and Medicaid
   Services, 49
Central Intelligence Agency (CIA), 6, 7, 9,
   27–30, 42–43, 54, 55, 67, 68, 74, 80, 82,
   83, 93, 106, 113, 143–44, 177, 194, 205,
   215–16, 223–30, 231, 238, 241–45, 302,
   303, 306, 308, 310–11, 313, 314, 325,
   328–30, 360, 374, 391

Century Strategies, 157, 283
Chafee, Lincoln, 176–77, 180
Chalabi, Ahmed, 28, 63, 68–70, 71, 80, 83,
   216, 286, 328, 329, 330, 368
Chamberlain, Neville, 57
Cheney, Dick, 4, 7, 8, 9, 10, 12, 17, 20, 27,
   28, 32, 39, 40, 42, 43, 47, 53, 54, 55, 56,
   57, 58, 63, 79–81, 87, 88, 93, 95, 98, 99,
   109, 112, 113, 127, 133, 138, 150, 178,
   179, 182, 186, 189–90, 200, 201, 205,
   211, 214, 215, 219, 226, 236, 238, 239,
   242, 261, 267, 271, 286, 292, 293,
   295–97, 300–306, 310, 315, 316, 320,
   323, 326, 328, 329, 337, 350, 351–54,
   355–57, 359, 361, 368, 373, 374, 378,
   388, 389, 390, 391, 392, 393, 401–2
Cheney, Lynne, 80
Chertoff, Michael, 265, 272, 319, 332, 363
Chicago Sun-Times, 247, 248
Child Interstate Notification Act, 209
China, 217
Chirac, Jacques, 58
Choctaw Indian tribe, 284
Choosing Your Battles (Feaver), 323
Christian Coalition, 154, 282–83, 335
Churchill, Winston, 57, 93, 190, 403
"Church in a Time of Peril" (common-
   ground initiative), 167
Citigroup, 133
Citizens for America, 156, 334–35
Clarke, Richard, 12, 46–47, 48–49, 51, 86,
   267, 312
Cleland, Max, 10–11, 345
Clements, William, 354
Clemons, Steve, 178, 179
Clinton, Bill, 1, 2, 4, 5, 14, 21, 34–35, 40,
   46–47, 50, 52, 77–78, 98, 107, 115–16,
   173, 226, 247, 260, 264, 266, 282, 305,
   339, 340, 359, 382–83, 396–97
Clinton, Hillary, 77–78, 93
Club for Growth, 246
CNN, 16, 17, 227, 241–48, 320, 375
CNN/Gallup poll, 274
CNN/*USA Today*/Gallup poll, 184
Coalition Provisional Authority (CPA),
   72, 89, 125, 130, 214, 272, 343, 344
Coast Guard, U.S., 86
Cobra II (Gordon and Trainor), 395
Colby, William, 303

Novak, Viveca, 194
Novak Zone (TV show), 246

O'Connor, Archbishop John, 166
O'Connor, Sandra Day, 220, 221, 318, 333
Odom, William, 64, 103, 104, 105
Office of Counter-Terrorism, 46–47, 344
Office of Federal Procurement Policy, 284
Office of Legal Counsel, 7–8, 202, 325, 326, 356
Office of Management and Budget, 379
Office of Public Liaison, 279
Office of Reconstruction, 219
Office of Special Plans (OSP), 9, 28, 41, 43, 68–69, 83, 178, 306
Office of the White House Counsel, 202
Ohio, 110, 164, 169
O'Keefe, Georgia, 77
Oklahoma City bombing, 271
O'Neill, John, 16
O'Neill, Paul, 11, 12, 39–40, 47, 49, 93, 379
Operation Enduring Freedom, 134
Operation Iraqi Freedom, 129, 134
Operation Matador, 211
Operation Scorpion, 304–5
Operation Spear, 211
Opus Dei, 247
Organization for the Prohibition of Chemical Weapons, 151
"Origins of the American Military Coup of 2012, The" (Dunlap), 64–65
Orwell, George, 150
Oslo Accords, 32

Pace, Peter, 367, 370, 378
Paine, Tom, 321
Palestine, 4, 32, 34, 71, 140, 346, 347
Panorama (Italian magazine), 223
Pape, Robert, 276–77, 347
Parsons (construction firm), 353
Pashtun, 231, 233
PATRIOT Act, 208–9, 328
Patton (film), 282
Paul H. Nitze School of Advanced International Studies (Johns Hopkins University), 389
Paxon, Bill, 339–40

Pelosi, Nancy, 265
Pentagon, 53, 54, 71, 89, 129, 134, 135, 192, 193, 195, 199, 202–3, 205, 211, 239, 256, 371, 386
Pentagon Papers, 218
Peres, Shimon, 116
Perle, Richard, 54, 246
Pew Research Centre for the People and the Press, 296
Pew Trust, 255
Philip Morris, 98, 341
Phillips, David L., 219
Phillips, Kevin, 164, 375–77
Phillips, Tom, 247
Pillar, Paul, 356
Plame, Valerie, 12, 29, 143–44, 224–30, 241–45, 248, 281, 285, 286–87, 292–93, 296–97, 300, 308, 317, 327, 355, 374, 388–92
Plan of Attack (Woodward), 54–55, 308
Poland, 311
Polsby, Nelson, 337
Popular party (Spain), 44
Powell, Colin, 4, 7, 9, 10, 36–38, 43, 44, 50, 54–56, 64, 68–70, 80, 83, 93, 95, 112–14, 127, 151, 176, 178, 179, 181–83, 189–90, 193, 202, 239, 300, 301, 302, 304, 306, 310, 312, 314, 315, 329–30, 373, 389
Presidential Medal of Freedom, 125
Presidential Studies Quarterly, 326
President's Commission on Intelligence Capabilities Regarding Weapons of Mass Destruction, 176, 180
President's Council on Bioethics, 13
President's Council on Physical Fitness and Sports, 95
Preston Gates & Ellis (law firm), 335, 337
Price of Loyalty, The (O'Neill), 11, 39, 379
Primedia Inc., 156
Prince, The (Machiavelli), 360
Pritchard, Charles, 37, 178, 179
Producers, The (film), 81
Progress and Freedom Foundation, 339
Progress for America, 146
Project for the New American Century (PNAC), 369, 372, 373, 374
Project Relief, 338

Southern Baptist Convention (SBC), 164

South Korea, 155, 178–79

Soviet Union, 74–75, 247, 302, 303–4, 371

Spain, 44–45

Spamalot, 265

Specter, Arlen, 111, 290, 316, 349

St. Petersburg Times, 265–66

Stanford University, 89

Starr, Ken, 230

Star Wars (defense program), 75, 83

State Department, U.S., 67, 89, 113, 127–28, 176, 177, 178, 179, 181–82, 183, 190, 219, 385–86, 387

State of the Union address(es), 29, 39, 42, 137, 141, 146, 178, 218, 223, 227, 238, 241, 345, 347, 374, 389

State of War: The Secret History of the CIA and the Bush Administration (Risen), 328–30

Stevens, John Paul, 222

Stone, I. F., 247

Strategic Arms Limitation Treaty (SALT), 303, 304

Strategic Studies Institute (Army War College), 53, 73, 103, 129

Strauss, Leo, 135

Straw, Jack, 114, 182, 311, 386

Sullivan, Amy, 246

Sullivan, Andrew, 246–47

Sullivan, Bill, 371

Sulzberger, Arthur, 316

SunCruz (casino boat company), 284

Sunni Islam groups, 130, 137, 140, 214, 216–17, 235–36, 256, 346, 381, 385

Supreme Council of Islamic Revolution (SCIRI), Iraq, 217

Supreme Court, U.S., 13, 109, 111, 165, 185, 197, 199, 220–22, 287, 290, 293, 317, 318, 322, 323, 326, 331–33, 364

Suskind, Ron, 15–16

Swannack, Charles, 396

Swift Boat Veterans for Truth, 16, 146, 247

Syria, 151, 182, 256

Taft, Robert, 148

Taft, William H., IV, 202

Taguba, Antonio, 60, 63, 196, 203

Taliban, 9, 86, 141, 231, 347

Talleyrand, Charles Maurice de, 274

Talon News Service, 143, 228

Tauscher, Ellen, 134, 135–36

Tawfiq, Saad, 329–30

Taylor, Zachary, 21

Team B, 303–4, 306

Tenet, George, 6, 43, 52, 68, 83, 125, 177, 178, 224, 328–29, 330

Ten Minutes from Normal (Hughes), 275

Terrill, W. Andrew, 103–5

Tet offensive, 212

Texas, 186

Texas Air National Guard, 16, 88

Texas A&M University, 354

Thatcher, Margaret, 35

Thielman, Greg, 42, 43

Third Way, 2

This Is the Army (film), 77

Thomas, Bill, 133

Thomas, Clarence, 220–22, 290, 364

Thompson, Tommy, 365

Thucydides, 237

Tigua Indian tribe, 157, 284

Time magazine, 49, 194, 224–25, 242, 244, 268, 286, 292, 296, 368, 374

Times-Picayune, 259, 265

Tipton Three, 197

Today Show (TV program), 95

Tomlison, Kenneth, 18

Toppling Saddam: Iraq and American Military Transformation (report), 129

Tora Bora, Afghanistan, 125, 308

Train, Russell, 13

Trainor, Bernard, 236–37, 395

Transatlantic Institute, 255

Transplant (Frist), 163

Treaty of Fifth Avenue, 92

Truman, Harry, 21, 36, 132, 151, 318, 360, 399, 403

Turkey, 140

Twain, Mark, 275–76, 277

Tyler, John, 21

Tyndale, William, 34

Uganda, 261

Unfit for Command (Swift Boat Veterans), 247